Television Antiheroines

Television Antiheroines
Women behaving badly in crime and prison drama

Milly Buonanno, editor

intellect Bristol, UK / Chicago, USA

First published in the UK in 2017 by
Intellect, The Mill, Parnall Road, Fishponds, Bristol, BS16 3JG, UK

First published in the USA in 2017 by
Intellect, The University of Chicago Press, 1427 E. 60th Street,
Chicago, IL 60637, USA

Copyright © 2017 Intellect Ltd

All rights reserved. No part of this publication may be reproduced, stored in a retrieval system, or transmitted, in any form or by any means, electronic, mechanical, photocopying, recording, or otherwise, without written permission.

A catalogue record for this book is available from the
British Library.

Cover designer: Emily Dann
Copy-editor: MPS Technologies
Production manager: Tim Mitchell and Mareike Wehner
Typesetting: Contentra Technologies

ISBN: 978-1-78320-760-2
ePDF ISBN: 978-1-78320-761-9
ePUB ISBN: 978-1-78320-762-6

This is a peer-reviewed publication.

Contents

Acknowledgements	vii
Foreword Diane Negra and Jorie Lagerwey	ix
Editor's Introduction Milly Buonanno	1
Part I: Mafia Women	**25**
Chapter 1: Godmothers in Italian Mafia Story: Or 'Something Else Besides a Mother' Milly Buonanno	27
Chapter 2: *Mafiosa*, Monstruous Beauty: Power and Loneliness of a Female Mob Leader Barbara Villez	49
Chapter 3: *Adieu* Carmela Soprano! Lessons from the HBO Mobster Wife on TV Female Agency and Neo-liberal (Narrative) Power Kim Akass and Janet McCabe	65
Part II: Drug Dealers and Aberrant Mothers	**83**
Chapter 4: Paying the Price: *Penoza* – Combining Motherhood and a Career (in Crime) Joke Hermes	85
Chapter 5: 'Really Good At It': The Viral Charge of Nancy Botwin in *Weeds* (and Popular Culture's Anticorps) Elisa Giomi	105
Chapter 6: Really Bad Mothers: Manipulative Matriarchs in *Sons of Anarchy* and *Justified* Amanda D. Lotz	125
Chapter 7: *La reina del sur*: Teresa Mendoza, a New *Telenovela* Protagonist Yeidy M. Rivero	141

Part III: Women in Prison 159

Chapter 8: Blurred Lines: The Queer World of *Bad Girls* 161
Vicky Ball

Chapter 9: Top Dogs and Other Freaks: *Wentworth* and the Re-imaging of *Prisoner Cell Block H* 181
Sue Turnbull

Chapter 10: Lesbian Request Approved: Sex, Power and Desire in *Orange is the New Black* 199
Suzanna Danuta Walters

Part IV: Villainesses and Anti-antiheroines 217

Chapter 11: Women and Criminality in Brazilian *Telenovelas: Salve Jorge* and Human Trafficking 219
Samantha Joyce and Antonio La Pastina

Chapter 12: 'Your Turn, Girl': The (Im)Possibility of African American Antiheroines in *The Wire* 237
Bruce A. Williams and Andrea L. Press

Chapter 13: Taming Pussytown: How Post-feminism Domesticated *Underbelly: Razor* 255
Leigh Redhead

Contributors 279

Index 283

Acknowledgements

Although, as I say in the introduction, the idea of this book began to dwell in my mind in the early 2010s, the seeds of my interest in real and fictional characters of 'women behaving badly' were planted many decades ago, during my childhood. A southern Italian on my mother's side, during infancy I used to spend summer holidays at my grandparents' house in a coastal town of Calabria. The days were hot, and in the evening children were allowed to linger in the courtyard to enjoy the sea breeze, while listening to the stories steeped in local folklore that made up the narrative repertoire of my grandmother. Ghosts and fairytales were seldom narrated, as she had a special preference for stories about female brigands: those women who, challenging patriarchal gender norms, had embraced the outlaw life in the context of the historical phenomenon of the brigandage in nineteenth-century southern Italy. Some of them, who had achieved equality and even pre-eminence in bravery and leadership vis-à-vis their male companions, had made a name for themselves as intimidating, merciless, yet admirable and respected brigandesses. Folktales had built and disseminated the legend of those female icons of the brigantage, whose transgressive lives and murderous deeds my grandmother – in adamant disregard of grandfather's disapproval over bloody stories, unsuitable for children – was fond of narrating. I owe her the first seminal encounter with the character of the antiheroine.

It may sound clichéd to say that a book is always a collective endeavor, but it is the pure truth when the book is a collection. I'm grateful to all the wonderful contributors for their generosity in joining the project to claim attention to television antiheroines, at a time in which television antiheroes seemed to monopolize consideration and appreciation. I would also like to thank Tim Mitchell and Mareike Wehner for providing excellent editorial assistance along all the steps of the publishing process.

Finally, my life partner Giovanni has been unconditionally supportive of my work, no matter how much time this stole away from more shareable activities and conversations. My interest may well be captivated by fictional antiheroines: He remains my real life all-time hero.

Foreword

Diane Negra and Jorie Lagerwey

As this book goes to print, it is clear that the subject of women's relation to the television medium is having a bit of a moment. In 2015 and 2016, the gender pay gap in Hollywood filmmaking had come under intense criticism from white celebrity feminists like actresses Jennifer Lawrence, who wrote about being paid less than her male co-stars, and Patricia Arquette, who used her Oscar acceptance speech in 2015 to call out gender-biased unequal pay (Lawrence, n.d., Arquette 2015). Recent years have also seen the film industry harshly criticized for a lack of roles for people of colour in front of and behind the camera. The #OscarsSoWhite protest hashtag, African American actress Jada Pinkett-Smith's (unsuccessful) boycott of the 2016 Oscars and black female producer Effie Brown's on-screen conflict with Matt Damon in the HBO documentary series *Project Greenlight* (2001–2005, 2015) are just a few prominent examples of the incidents through which the controversy has coalesced ('Do You Want to Direct This Movie?' 2006).[1]

In the face of an apparently hostile film industry, television is increasingly held up as a welcoming sanctuary for women – and not just the dominant norm of young, white, straight and beautiful women, but also for actresses, writers and producers of colour, older women, lesbian and trans women in front of and behind the camera. Numerous articles in print and digital form, blog posts and various other modes of commentary attest to a dramatic discursive shift that might be roughly plotted as moving from consternation to celebration in regard to women's television roles (e.g. Lyons 2013; Stewart 2015). Seeking to track 'the changing representational politics of femininity in contemporary international television', this volume is part of the environment of acclaim for TV's women, collecting critical analyses of these notably complex, diverse women from around the globe as they appear in the medium across Europe, Latin America, Australia and the United States.

This current celebration of multifaceted women making and performing television was far from inevitable, though. Historically, the medium was understood by marketers and theorists alike as a feminized, domestic one (Spigel 1992). The patterns of women's unpaid household work were embedded in the very structures of prominent genres like soap operas (Modleski 1982). Similarly, women solely as mothers, caretakers and voices of reason were encoded in the blueprints for traditional family sitcoms (Butsch 2005). Indeed even outside those limited roles in certain traditional genres, and despite an enormous increase in recent decades in programming targeted at female viewers (see for example Lotz 2006), contemporary TV women were still all too often understood as wives, mothers, assistants, crime victims, sexual objects or plot devices rather than fully developed characters. (Even celebrated millennial era series such as *Sex and the City* (HBO 1998–2004) and *Gilmore Girls* (WB, CW 2000–2007; Netflix 2016) that seemed to devise ways to push past such limited typologies preserved, for some viewers, an unhelpful emphasis on 'quirky femininity' and aspirational and luxury lifestyling.) Thus, until quite recently, media coverage of the restricted number and nature of female roles on television predominated popular discourse. Typical in this regard is the opening of a 2012 *Huffington Post* piece entitled 'Women in the media: Female TV and film characters still sidelined and sexualized, study finds': 'For every Carrie Mathison, the brilliant, complicated spy played by Claire Danes on *Homeland*, there are six "Real Housewives" – in other words, the way women are represented on television and in film is pretty dismal'. But lately, heightened attention to the under-representation of women in media has been succeeded by favourable notice of an emergent cluster of female showrunners, writers, producers and performers like Shonda Rhimes, Jenji Kohan, Mindy Kaling, Michelle King and Lena Dunham behind the camera, and all of the women discussed in this book in front of the camera.

As the sheer number of complex, narratively central female characters on television has increased, there would seem to be an accompanying emerging cultural consensus that female-centred television is achieving an exceptional verisimilitude. The February 2016 issue of *Elle* magazine, for example, prefaces its lengthy set of features devoted to 'Women in TV' with the following characterization 'With TV more women-rich, women-run and women-relatable than ever before, we don't just watch television anymore, we live it' (129). The essays collected in *Television Antiheroines* valuably expand that lived experience far beyond Hollywood's white celebrity feminists noted earlier. Authors here explore multiple female subjectivities across lines of race (as in Bruce Williams and Andrea Press's analysis of *The Wire*'s [HBO 2002–2008] female characters) and sexuality (as in Williams and Press's essay as well as Vicky Ball and Suzanna Danuta Walters' analyses of ITV's *Bad Girls* [1999–2006] and Netflix's *Orange is the New Black* [2013–ongoing]). In the book, consistent attention is paid to global genres with a history of foregrounding female psychological concerns (such as the *telenovela* analysed in Brazilian form here by Samantha Joyce and Antonio La Pastina and in Colombian/Spanish/Mexican co-production form by Yeidy Rivero), while a number of the pieces draw notice to the rich female characterizations available in conventionally male-centred series such as *The Sopranos* (HBO 1999–2007) and *Sons of Anarchy* (FX 2008–2014). Several of the essays centralize new takes or inversions of old forms like 'bad' women who are still good mothers, calling attention to how this spate of women's TV challenges old social, economic and generic norms.

We, along with Julia Leyda, have written about this new prominence of female-centred Anglo-American television in the years since 2008 (forthcoming), arguing that new series 'are generating frequent and often important dispatches about women's relation to new capitalist subjectivities' (Lagerwey et al. forthcoming). This volume broadens that scope to a global investigation of female-centred forms with a particular focus on the liminality of women associated with criminality. Perhaps mimicking newly vociferous emerging feminisms that reclaim anger as a legitimate female response to patriarchy, recession, racism and heteronormativity, this collection assembles analyses focusing on powerful antiheroines. In it, women in crime TV genres ranging from gangster to prison drama, and storytelling modes from comedy to melodrama offer a counterpoint to the prominence of the white male antiheroes of the last 15 or so years of prestige television like *The Sopranos'* Tony Soprano (James Gandolfini), *Mad Men*'s (2007–2015) Don Draper (Jon Hamm) and *Breaking Bad*'s (2008–2013) Walter White (Brian Cranston).

As Milly Buonanno discusses in her Introduction, this collection's emphasis on 'misbehaving women' is an important intervention into the dominant masculinity of the prominent antihero trope and acknowledges the ways female characters have evolved beyond the often one-dimensional 'strong female character' or 'ass-kicking babe' stereotypes, and equally past the necessity for women on-screen to be 'good'. Here, mothers appear not as the sacrificial matriarchs of melodrama, but in the form of the criminal matriarch of Dutch series *Penoza* ([2010–ongoing] in Joke Hermes's chapter). These 'bad' women are not mild daughters, but mafia scions in series like the French *Mafiosa* ([2006–2014] see Barbara Villez's chapter). And they are not crime fighting superheroes, but prisoners with complex backstories and complicated relationships as in Netflix's jailhouse series *Orange is the New Black* (in Suzanne Danuta Walters's chapter) and Australian drama *Wentworth* ([2013–ongoing] in Sue Turnbull's chapter).

Samantha Joyce and Antonio La Pastina rightly observe in their contribution that 'the trend of more nuanced representations of women varying in race, sexuality, profession and their choices between illicit/licit activities is a global one' (p. 222). The production of television antiheroines may entail striking manifestations of genre hybridity as with Rosy Abate's positioning at the intersection of maternal melodrama and gangster narrative in *Antimafia Squad* discussed here by Buonanno. It can involve the production of female antagonists who engage with the particular ideological intensity of maternal 'misconduct' as Amanda Lotz's contribution to the volume illustrates, or the violation of cultural maternal norms as discussed in Joke Hermes's chapter (a development that seems all the more important, given representations of ambivalent mothering that have lately appeared in series such as *Homeland* [Showtime 2011–ongoing] and *The Good Wife* [CBS 2009–2016]). It may also very well lead to the depiction of resourceful female accommodations to/negotiations of the existing order of male-centred free market neo-liberalism, an argument advanced in this book by Kim Akass and Janet McCabe in regard to Carmela Soprano and by Elisa Giomi in regard to the 'social deviance' of Nancy Botwin in *Weeds* (Showtime 2005–2012).

At their best, such depictions work to document and analyse the structuring influence of new economic systems that serve the few rather than the many, reinforcing norms of competitive individualism even in national contexts that have more collective ideological histories. At their most disappointing, these criminal entrepreneurs eschew collaboration or critique of existing power structures in favour of postfeminist emphases on fashion, hypersexualization and women in competition as in Leigh Redhead's essay about Australian Prohibition period piece *Underbelly: Razor* (2011).

Part of the turn towards celebrating the abundance of complex female characterizations on television, this book maps a new gendered televisual ecology that must be factored for in any attempt to fully understand the early twenty-first-century medium. Individually engaging with culturally specific production and reception contexts, taken together these essays coalesce to tease out representational and cultural-historical themes that transcend national borders. Ultimately, *Television Antiheroines* offers rich evidence of the newly expanded analytic possibilities for studying global television in fruitfully comparative up-to-the-minute ways.

References

Arquette, Patricia (2015), 'Patricia Arquette winning best supporting actress', YouTube, 9 March, https://www.youtube.com/watch?v=6wx-Qh4Vczc. Accessed 5 June 2016.

Bahadur, Nina (2012), 'Women in the media: Female TV and film characters still sidelined and sexualized, study finds', *Huffington Post*, 13 November.

Butsch, Richard (2005), 'Five decades and three hundred sitcoms about class and gender', in Gary R. Edgerton and Brian Rose (eds), *Thinking Outside the Box: A Contemporary Television Genre Reader*, Lexington: University of Kentucky Press.

'Do You Want to Direct This Movie?' (2015), Ben Affleck and Matt Damon (exec. prod.), *Project Greenlight*, Season 4, Episode 1, New York: HBO.

Elle (2016), 'Women in TV', 16: 366, February, pp. 129–145, 197–215.

Grzywacz, Daniel (2015), 'Producer Effie Brown talks *Project Greenlight*, Matt Damon and Peter Farrelly', *Variety*, 18 October, http://variety.com/2015/tv/news/effie-brown-matt-damon-project-greenlight-peter-farrelly-1201620760/. Accessed 5 June 2016.

Lagerwey, Jorie, Leyda, Julia and Negra, Diane (forthcoming), 'Female-centered television in an age of precarity', *Genders*.

Lawrence, Jennifer (n.d.), 'Jennifer Lawrence: "Why do I make less than my male co-stars?"', *Lenny Letter*, http://www.lennyletter.com/work/a147/jennifer-lawrence-why-do-i-make-less-than-my-male-costars/. Accessed 5 June 2016.

Lotz, Amanda (2006), *Redesigning Women: Television After the Network Era*, Urbana: University of Illinois Press.

Lyons, Margaret (2013), 'It was a good year for women on TV', *Vulture*, 17 December, http://www.vulture.com/2013/12/women-on-tv-orange-is-new-black.html. Accessed 5 June 2016.

Modleski, Tania (1982), 'The search for tomorrow in today's soap operas', in Tania Modleski (ed.), *Loving with a Vengeance*, New York: Routledge.

Spigel, Lynn (1992), *Make Room for TV: Television and the Family Ideal in Postwar America*, Chicago: University of Chicago Press.

Stewart, Sara (2015), 'The 10 best feminist shows of 2015', *Indiewire*, 17 December, http://blogs.indiewire.com/womenandhollywood/the-10-best-feminist-tv-shows-of-2015-20151217. Accessed 5 June 2016.

Note

1. *Project Greenlight* follows the behind the scenes process of the movie industry from pitching a script, hiring cast and crew, shooting and releasing a picture. Matt Damon and Ben Affleck star as the leaders of the producing team overseeing and funding the project in which unknowns compete to win the chance to direct the film. In the premiere episode of the series' re-boot, Brown, who pointed out that she was the only woman and the only person of colour in the room, challenged Damon when he defended the group's decision to select only white men as finalists (Grzywacz 2015).

Editor's Introduction

Milly Buonanno

Antiheroine Television

The idea for this collection began to dwell in my mind at the beginning of the 2010s, and was originally occasioned by my surprise while noticing that truly uncommon and unconventional depictions of womanhood being offered by the twenty-first-century television across a broad spectrum of countries were not receiving enough scholarly consideration: an inattention somewhat at odds with the intense scrutiny of female portrayals and how they evolve in time, that has typically been a central concern for gender and media studies, and has largely overshadowed the exploration of masculinity as rightly indicated by Amanda Lotz (2014).

Beyond feeling surprised, 'an undervalued feminist attribute', according to Cynthia Enloe (2004: 13), I was struck and intrigued by some key features of the phenomenon concerned. First of all, far from consisting of just an array of so-called 'strong female leads' – a label that in fact perpetuates clichéd notions of one-dimensional female identity (Truitt 2013; Arnold 2014) – the emerging trend seemed epitomized by the advent of daring women characters that embodied to an unprecedented extent the dark sides of human personality and behaviour. In other words, they proved 'capable of being bad' (Willmore 2013) or they were – as the subtitle of this book reads – 'women behaving badly' in a range of different ways and situations. Although it cannot be denied that in some cases we were offered only just cosmetic updates of villainess figures, which have never been in short supply in popular imagination and fictional storytelling, quite a few female characters created for television in the 2000s were actually endowed with moral ambiguity, damaging flaws, enduring strength, unapologetic wickedness and the relatable qualities that work together to shape a conflicted and nuanced, despicable and admirable antiheroic figure. The antiheroine, a novel version of femininity, was making inroads into television politics of gender representation – I have chosen the moniker 'antiheroine' rather than female antihero, following in the footsteps of Christine Geraghty (2013).

A further peculiarity that drew my attention to the advent of the antiheroine was the international scope of the phenomenon, encompassing a wide range of territories well beyond the United States, from Italy to France to Scandinavia to Australia to Brazil and more besides. As for the United States, the long-overlooked presence (to be followed by full visibility) of the antiheroine lead in television storytelling seemed to be related, in good likelihood, to the antiheroic creative turn that inspired a host of (mostly male-centred) outstanding and acclaimed shows since the late 1990s. I will return to this topic in more detail in the next section. Admittedly, a similar claim could not be made to account for a number of antiheroine characters that I happened to encounter while exploring local programming in geo-cultural contexts that hardly ever witnessed any resounding 'creative revolution' (Martin 2013) in TV drama – although, of course, the capacity of the American television industry and culture to subtly, yet influentially, reverberate its trends around the world cannot be underestimated. Without achieving the status of cultural phenomena and enjoying the worldwide visibility and the critical accolades that graced US dramas, those local shows were, in turn, successful and acclaimed in their respective home markets and often proved good for export and format trade, thus helping to expand the area of dissemination of seeds and fruits of the antiheroine phenomenon.

Furthermore, the trend transcended the 'usual suspects', i.e. the niche subscription-based TV channels and on-demand platforms whose advent and spread is conventionally seen as the major driving force for change in contemporary television storytelling, as regards both aesthetics and politics of representation; actually, the broadcast networks played a part in bringing 'antiheroine television' to life and to a wider audience.

'Antiheroine television' purposely re-echoes 'heroine television' coined two decades ago by Charlotte Brunsdon to designate female-centred shows whose protagonists negotiate femininity 'trying to cope' with contradictory demands made on women. As Brunsdon put it, '[t]hese shows are all in some fundamental way addressing feminism' (1997: 34). Trying to cope with inner contradictions and conflicting external demands is a truly distinctive feature of the antiheroine as well (or the antihero, for that matter). This is not to minimize dissimilarities between the two types of female protagonists, all the more so as what is crucially at stake is the different moral compass of the heroine and the antiheroine; it is, rather, to suggest that 'antiheroine television', in turn, addresses a feminist agenda in a fundamental and uncommon way.

I have to admit that it was not my primary intent to endeavour speculation or investigation on the range of cultural, institutional, even contingent factors that might have prompted the emergence of antiheroic female figures, sometimes a whole line-up of them, sometimes a sole or first experimental prototype, in diverse television landscapes – although the question 'why?' would soon prove inescapable, and I'm committed to address the issue later in this introduction. Instead, I was moved by 'feminist curiosity' to explore atypical portrayals of femininity and wished to seize the somewhat unique opportunity to have international 'variations on a theme' of antiheroine television under scrutiny by analysing particular texts. The feminist thinker Cynthia Enloe – whom I'm evidently indebted to – has astutely reconverted curiosity, a common stereotype of femininity, into a resource for the production of knowledge; she coined the expression 'the curious feminist' (2004) to designate an epistemological stance aimed at unveiling and unpacking gendered structures, discourses and representations that are hidden or unseen, and exhorted to always ask questions. As recalled by Katharine Sarikakis (2013: 110), 'where are the women?' is the central question raised since the 1970s by many curious feminist media scholars. Accordingly, my curiosity was centrally concerned with searching for and looking into the uncharted narrative territories where antiheroine television was flourishing.

Antihero: The Sense of an Ending

Although not firstly occasioned, the project for this collection was largely furthered and shaped by the heated conversation that bloomed in 2013 across the blogosphere – almost exclusively in the United States, with some transatlantic reverberation – about the irresistible rise, and the signs of incipient fall, of the predominantly male antihero lead in American 'quality TV' of the twenty-first century. The debate was destined to intensify in the wake of two different events, both directly pertinent to the issues at stake here, that took place very close to one another in time.

The first was the premature death of James Gandolfini (on 19 June 2013), whose iconic performance in the role of the New Jersey mobster Tony Soprano had successfully endeavoured to create from scratch, as *Salon*'s Willa Paskin put it, a dark yet captivating character 'simultaneously charismatic and menacing, threatening and charming, winning and terrifying' (2013a), thus paving the way for an entire lineage of cable (and some networks') male antiheroes that were to follow in the footsteps of the prototype.

The second was the release (on 27 June 2013) of the soon-to-be widely reviewed and talked about book written by Brett Martin: *Difficult Men*. The 'creative revolution' that, from *The Sopranos* (HBO, 1999–2007) onwards, had brought to life a new generation of groundbreaking cable dramas was told in the book from the perspective of the writers' room, where a group of highly talented 'difficult men' had been working to produce the 'third golden age' of US television. Martin's book joined Alan Sepinwall's *The Revolution Was Televised* (2012) in offering a passionate as much as unapologetically mythologizing take on the (allegedly only men's) revolution that had changed forever the old vast television wasteland; in actual fact, the two books were often reviewed or quoted together (Beck 2013; Maciak 2013).

The eulogies for James Gandolfini were pervaded by a poignant sense of loss that not surprisingly, given the deep interpenetration between the actor and the fictional character he had so compellingly inhabited, extended to Tony Soprano as well (Killoran 2013). It appeared as if Gandolfini's death put a definitive end to the speculations (and the illusions) that the enigmatic season finale of the series had instigated about whether Tony was still alive or dead. And the sense of loss in a short space of time began to make room for the sense of an ending: the feeling that an exhilarating era of male-run and male-centred TV drama, triggered by *The Sopranos* on the eve of the twenty-first century, was approaching its twilight. 'The best is over': again, it seemed as the words uttered by Tony Soprano in his first therapy session with Dr Melfi resonated with feelings that were spreading almost 15 years after it all began.

The lines of argument that were put forward to substantiate this sense of an ending proved somewhat more inflected by desire for novelty than by longing for a gone past of recognized creative greatness. Writing for *ThinkProgress* the same day that Gandolfini's memorial service took place in New York, Alyssa Rosenberg, for instance, made the claim that

> [i]f the purpose of *The Sopranos* was to ask how far we could sympathize with a man like Tony Soprano who was a criminal and the head of a family, a serial cheater who also loved his children, and a man whose closest friendships could end in blood and be bound up by murder, maybe in the intervening years we've found our answers, *and it's time to move on to other questions.*
>
> (Rosenberg 2013a, emphasis added)

Just a few days after, in an article whose title proclaimed 'Enough with the TV antiheroes already', June Thomas from *Slate* voiced the dissatisfaction with the languishing originality of the later epigones of *The Sopranos* – Showtime's *Ray Donovan* (2013–ongoing) offered a case in point – and concluded 'it may be time to find a new model' (2013).

Other television analysts and commentators observed that cable dramas like *Dexter* (Showtime, 2006–2013) and especially *Breaking Bad* (AMC, 2008–2013), which was much acclaimed by critics and audience alike, had pushed the boundaries of the antihero trend so far that it reached a point of no return and of no further progress. In this regard, Margaret Lyons wrote in *Vulture*: 'I started to realize, as the Walter White saga wound down, that television was coming to the end of an era [...] The end of *Breaking Bad* also marks the end of the antihero' (Lyon 2013; see also Jones 2013; VanDerWerff 2013). The very term 'antihero' was deemed obsolete, so worn out as to become meaningless: 'It's time to retire television's most overused buzzword', Laura Bennett exhorted in *New Republic* (2013).

Some others, while refraining from venturing into epochal predictions and maintaining that quality television was still alive and well, nonetheless agreed that the best TV dramas of the 2000s were over or were close to finishing their run; hence the questions raised by Douglas Howard on the British forum for TV studies *CSTonline*:

> How will the networks fill in the void left by the loss of these shows? Do these endings mean that we are on the verge of something else, some turn, some cultural response, some backlash to all that came before, or should we prepare ourselves for the second or third generation of *The Sopranos*[...]?
>
> (Howard 2013)

Ultimately, there was large although not generalized consensus (for a different view, see Franich 2013) that television was at a crossroads where a choice should be made between continuity and change, replication and re-invention. Most importantly in relation to the present book: the conversation, in which appraisals of the just-gone-by television (or perceived as such) joined demands and expectations of a new twist, soon came to encompass an intense discussion that revolved around gender bias in the acclaimed antihero storytelling.

Where Are Complex Women on TV? Everywhere

Recent television scholarship has indicated and addressed the preponderance of masculine protagonists in prime-time drama of the 2000s (Lotz 2014; Albrecht 2015; Mittell 2015): hardly an unheard of phenomenon, it might be said, as decades of feminist research and concerns on gender representation in the media have emphasized. However, some key differences with previous times can be identified in the contemporary situation. The male barycentre in television storytelling had been challenged in the 1990s, when depictions of femininity witnessed significant expansion, following an unprecedented increase in female-centred dramas (Lotz 2006); workplace series, in particular, managed to incorporate female leads into traditionally masculine spaces. The rise of the 'new generation' of male-centred dramas in the twenty-first century seemed to re-masculinize the trend, at the same time undertaking a notable shift in the representation of unconventional versions of masculinities that were explored on both the personal and professional side of the characters' life, at depths never achieved before. Furthermore, to the extent they were heralded as the epitome of quality TV, dramatic narratives featuring men in central roles were acknowledged the status of art forms and fully participated in processes of cultural legitimization of television (Newman and Levine 2012) that implied exclusionary practices and discourses along gender lines, amongst others.

As already mentioned, concerns have been expressed by scholars. Amanda Lotz, in the conclusions of her masterful take on depictions of masculinities in cable drama, raised the question 'why female-centered shows fail to feature the narrative and character depth of the male-centered serials' (2014: 192). 'The distinctive lack of female characters [...] who approach antiheroic status' has been pointed out by Jason Mittell (2015: 143). Both Lotz and Mittell have also voiced hopes that the range of female antiheroes will expand within television's narratives.

The perceived lack of female characters endowed with antiheroic traits like their male counterparts was precisely what triggered the discussion that took place in 2013. It must be acknowledged that Amanda Marcotte had already raised the issue in 2011 when she wrote in *The Good Men Project*:

> But for all the feminism on TV, high quality dramas about *women* haven't taken off. Women get plenty of meaty, complex roles in these top tier shows, but only as supporting characters in shows centered around men's gender drama. [...] I blame the nation's inability to deal directly with women engaged in complex, dramatic struggles that call gender roles into question.
>
> (Marcotte 2011, original emphasis)

However, it was the coalescence in mid-2013 of the specific circumstances I have recalled that helped to create the appropriate conversational context for the issue to be addressed and debated.

'Where is the female Tony Soprano?', asked Akash Nikolas in *The Atlantic* the day James Gandolfini was buried. Paying tribute to the crucial role of *The Sopranos* and Gandolfini alike in pioneering the rise in TV drama of the antihero lead – a flawed, morally ambiguous, even despicable yet likeable character – the piece went on to complain that such a momentous television change did not fully include women. Interestingly enough, Nikolas mentioned a good number of potential candidates with female antihero status, from *Damages* Patty Hewes (FX, 2007–2012) to *Justified*'s Mags Bennett (FX, 2010–2015) to *Scandal*'s Olivia Pope (ABC, 2012–ongoing) to *Homeland*'s Carrie Mathison (Showtime 2011–ongoing), only to conclude that they 'were not the same class as Tony Soprano and his TV descendants' (Nikolas 2013). Other central characters like *Weeds*' Nancy Botwin (Showtime, 2005–2012), *Nurse Jackie*'s Jackie Peyton (Showtime, 2009–2015) and Tara Gregson in *United States of Tara* (Showtime, 2009–2011) were excluded on the grounds of their 'largely comedic roles'; Elizabeth Jennings in *The Americans* (FX, 2013–ongoing) and Claire Underwood in *House of Cards* (Netflix, 2013–ongoing) were dismissed by labelling them as 'co-leading antihero wives'. As Alyssa Rosenberg in *Slate* first (2013b) and then Alison Herman in *Flavorwire* (2013) pointed out, 'Where is the female Tony Soprano?' – to be re-echoed later by 'Where are the complex women on premium cable?' in the *Globe and Mail* (Doyle 2013) and 'Where is the female Walter White?' in *Salon* (Rowles 2013) – was the wrong way to raise the issue; in actual fact, such a question was premised on a narrow understanding of the antihero complex nature, along with the hegemonic pretension that masculine templates should mould female characters, and implied inattention and dismissal for worthy antiheroines that did not measure up to the antiheroic standard of Tony Soprano or Walter White, or Don Draper for that matter.

The dearth of female leads in TV drama was indisputable. Although women were hardly yet 'denied characters' (D'Acci 1994: 111) they had long been, especially inside narrative genres, coded as masculine. But the strong point of the ongoing discussion – which I totally agreed with – was that it considerably helped to bring another more insidious form of gender denial into the open and find a place in public discourse: the unquestioned proclivity to disregard and obscure the worthiness of female protagonists (and the narratives they inhabited) that were flawed and complex and reprehensible yet enthralling in their own terms, whatever the similarities or differences vis-à-vis male prototypes.

This form of denial was never so directly addressed as in the article 'Difficult women' written by *The New Yorker* TV critic Emily Nussbaum (2013) in reaction to Brett Martin's book *Difficult Men*. Nussbaum took issue with Martin's dismissive attitude in referring to *Sex and the City* (HBO 1998–2004), with the palpable condescension usually reserved for anything deemed inferior. It is worth recalling that, in the introduction to their edited collection *Reading Sex and the City* (2004), Kim Akass and Janet McCabe had likewise remarked the condescending or vitriolic tone taken by critics towards the series.

Martin's account of the advent of a new generation of great shows that would feature complicated, ruthless and morally compromised protagonists gave all credit, Nussbaum contended, to *The Sopranos* and its 'blood brothers', failing to acknowledge the groundbreaking role played by *Sex and the City* in featuring iconic single girl characters never seen on television before:

> High-feminine instead of fetishistically masculine, glittery rather than gritty, and daring in its conception of character, 'Sex and the City' was a brilliant and, in certain ways, radical show. It also originated the unacknowledged *first female anti-hero on television*: ladies and gentlemen, Carrie Bradshaw.
>
> (Nussbaum 2013, emphasis added)

Regardless of whether or not the claim that Carry Bradshaw was the first antiheroine on TV could be taken for granted, the article made the very telling point that worthiness assessment and canon-building within the frame of quality TV and/or antihero storytelling were premised on heavily gendered criteria. This brought under the lens that, in addition to being in smaller number, female-centred shows and female characters were further penalized by denying the recognition that many of them should deserve in any fair recollection of innovative television dramas in the 2000s. On this subject, taking the cue from Nussbaum's piece, British television scholar Lisa Kelly expressed in *CSTonline* the wish for 'an alternative history of quality TV' (2013) that would discern the significant contribution of 'difficult women' and female-centred programming in helping the television revolution to happen.

There certainly was not a lack of material for anyone interested in writing such a history (not the ambition of this book, though). Since the early 2000s, a number of difficult, flawed, damaged and, in some measure, reprehensible women hardly in the lineage of female role models have appeared in lead or prominent and compelling roles in mostly US cable dramas. Gemma Teller in *Sons of Anarchy* (FX, 2008–2014), Ava Crowder in *Justified* (FX, 2010–2015), Amy Jellicoe in *Enlightened* (HBO, 2011–2013), Sarah Linden in *The Killing* (AMC, 2011–2014), Sister Jude in *American Horror Story. Asylum* (FX, 2012–2013), Olivia Pope in *Scandal* (ABC, 2012–ongoing): all of them might be added to the previously mentioned characters (see pag 8) without completing the list. More to the point, television programming over 2013 was witnessing an unusual burgeoning of complicated, awkward female characters – regardless of whether they were protagonists in dramatic woman-centred narratives or not. Namely, and again without completing the list: Elizabeth Jennings in *The Americans* (FX, 2013–ongoing), Claire Underwood in *House of Cards* (Netflix, 2013–ongoing), Piper Chatman in *Orange is the New Black* (Netflix, 2013–ongoing), Virginia Johnson in *Masters of Sex* (Showtime, 2013–ongoing), Sarah Manning in *Orphan Black* (BBC America, 2013–2016), Juliette Barnes in *Nashville* (ABC, 2012–ongoing), Robin Griffin in *Top of the Lake* (Sundance TV, 2013), Irene Adler as the criminal mastermind Moriarty in *Elementary* (CBS, 2012–ongoing). Most of them disproved McNamara's assertion in the *Los Angeles Times* that 'women in television still cannot get away with murder' (2013) and rather fitted the concise description provided by Allison Willmore in *Indiewire*: 'They're good at what they do, and *they're also, thank god, capable of being bad*' (2013, emphasis added).

Therefore, a conversation thread emerged and thickened about 'the rise of TV's antiheroine' (Armstrong 2013; see also Adams 2013; Paskin 2013b; Ryan 2013a). In *Entertainment Fuse*, Jean Henegan raised the question in an interrogative mode:

> Is a new age of television dawning, bringing with it the end of the male anti-hero and sweeping in the age of the complex female protagonist? It certainly seems that way, if the influx of new shows anchored by complicated and interesting female leads is anything to go by.
>
> (Henegan 2013)

But Alyssa Rosenberg was adamantly affirmative when, in reply to *The Globe and Mail*'s television critic, she asserted in *ThinkProgress* that 'the answer to Doyle's question "Where are the complex women on premium cable?" is, *especially in 2013, everywhere*' (2013c, emphasis added).

At the time of writing this introduction in late summer 2015, further female characters embodying the antiheroic status had made their way into television programming – Annalise Keating in *How to Get Away with Murder* (ABC, 2014–ongoing), Cookie Lyon in *Empire* (FOX, 2015–ongoing) and Rachel Goldberg in *UnREAL* (Lifetime, 2015–ongoing), amongst others – thus adding quantity and quality to shows with compelling female leads that, according to Zeba Blay in *The Huffington Post*, have now become 'the new normal' (2015). However, it is worth highlighting that this exciting phase of television storytelling featuring different types of difficult women had begun, unnoticed and overlooked, years before and gained momentum and incipient acknowledgement throughout the year 2013 in the wake of circumstances that aroused feelings of loss about the perceived twilight of the antihero golden age, along with a strand of criticism about the predominantly male-centred rendition of the 'creative revolution' of the 2000s.

The lively online discussion taking place that year among television critics proved instrumental in turning my design, just sketched until then, of a book on the changing representational politics of femininity in contemporary international television into the viable project of this anthology.

Women in the Business of Crime

I make the claim that the antiheroine is an interesting subject to be regarded through the feminist lens for the fundamental reason that she challenges, along a spectrum of embodiments, the patriarchal symbolic order: i.e. using Pierre Bourdieu's words, 'an immense symbolic machine tending to ratify the masculine domination on which it is founded'

(Bourdieu 2001: 9), at the same time as it helps to naturalize and de-historicize the socially constructed differences between genders by inscribing them 'in *the order of things*, as people sometimes say to refer to what is normal, natural, to the point of being inevitable' (Bourdieu 2001: 8, emphasis added). To comply with the order of things, women have traditionally been expected to act and behave according to norms of femininity that enforced ideals of female innocence, goodness, nurturance and social conformity, just as men have traditionally been expected to be strong, dominant, combative and even rule-breaking. Admittedly, the binarism of gender roles, capacities and codes of conduct has been consistently debunked and weakened over time, in real life as in popular imagination and media representations, under the impact of feminist waves. However, moral codes and standards of moral evaluation still remain gendered in good measure; the 'venemous rage' (Gunn 2013; Ryan 2013b) directed at Skyler, Walter White's wife in *Breaking Bad*, by devoted fans of the heinous male protagonist, provided symptomatic evidence that a double standard can affect television reception, too.

This double standard implies and ensures that disruption of the order of things by badly behaving women is particularly disquieting because female transgressive agency – all the more so when it comes to illegal or criminal moves – does not just break social norms but violates and subverts the natural properties of true womanhood. On this point, in their groundbreaking work on women's political violence, Caron E. Gentry and Laura Sjoberg contend that, since normal women are understood not to fall from grace, female misbehaviour comes to be regarded as an indicator of womanhood gone wrong and 'is often specially accounted for and explained as a flaw in women's femininity and a flaw in their humanity' (2015: 9).

It is precisely because she embodies the potentiality of turning constructed notions of femininity upside down by eluding or defying gender norms about how women should behave, that the antiheroine character calls for feminist attention and consideration. I am at pains here to point out that, although sharing similarities with the villainess and especially the action heroine – warriors, spies, tough and violent women whose rise in film and television has for some time now sparked considerable scholarly attention (Coulthard 2007; Early and Kennedy 2003; Inness 1999, 2004; McCaughey and King 2001; Mizejewski 2004; Neroni 2005; Tasker 1993; White 2007) – the antiheroine is characterized by the distinctive quality of *liminality*, a peculiar feature of the fictional (and real-life, for that matter) antiheroic figure. In this connection it is time to briefly engage in exploring the notion of antihero.

Amanda Lotz and Jason Mittell have remarked that the literary definition of antihero 'as one who lacks the attributes of the traditional protagonist or hero, such as courage, honesty or grace' (Lotz 2014: 63) fits uneasily with the range of variants of this character type in contemporary TV drama. According to Lotz, the 'flawed protagonist' is a more appropriate albeit concise term; Mittell describes the antihero as 'a character who is our primary point of ongoing narrative alignment but whose behavior and beliefs provoke ambiguous, conflicted or negative moral allegiance' (2015: 142–143). Margrethe Bruun Vaage further clarifies that the antihero notion refers to a 'morally flawed main character whom the spectator is nonetheless encouraged to feel with, like and root for' (2015: XVI).

While these statements look insightfully at key aspects concerning the character flaws and the ambivalent reactions they elicit from the viewing public, returning to the literary theory may prove fruitful in deepening our understanding of the antihero character. In his enlightening book, whose title significantly reads *In Praise of Antiheroes* (1999), Victor Bombert argues – in line with the mentioned scholars – that not the lack of heroic attributes but rather the questionable, ambiguous morality oscillating between good and evil, admirable and despicable behaviour, is the antihero's distinctive feature. This in-betweenness, which I referred to above as liminality, allows for closer proximity of antiheroic characters to the human dimension and experience and can win viewers' allegiance. More importantly here, liminal spaces and figures resist traditionally held dichotomies; in doing so, they cooperate to problematize and call into question dichotomous thinking and binary assumptions, thus displaying a potential for change that is worth considering especially when female characters are concerned.

Bombert interestingly elaborates on the subversive nature of the antihero figure. 'Often a perturber and a disturber' (1999: 2), the antiheroic character is implicitly or explicitly the bearer of criticism and mistrust towards exemplary 'images of ourselves' that are informed by more conventional visions of human morality. Standing against and helping to deflate and challenge those ideal images 'may indeed be the principal significance of such antimodel' (Bombert 1999: 2), whose resistance and opposition to conformity achieve to capture our imagination and even admiration.

Whether or not we are willing to take the compelling hypothesis of the antihero subversive nature as general truth, we have to acknowledge that Bombert's argument deeply and fruitfully resonates with previous claims about the potential of the antiheroine to question the gendered order of things and undermine more normative representations of womanhood in popular culture.

On such premises, this collection intends to explore female portrayals in international antiheroine television, focusing on the ambit of storytelling conventionally coded as most masculine: the crime story, more specifically the tales of organized crime. Being a narrative whose subject is the criminal woman, the women-in-prison (WIP) genre is also mined, albeit to a lesser extent, to counterpoint the male-dominated underworld with the mostly all-female world of the prison institution in which heteronormative ideology of gender can be transgressed and overturned.

The antiheroine figure is certainly multifaceted, and perusing the variants it encompasses might be a worthwhile endeavour for another book; the present one focuses on the narratives that revolve around or comprise characters of 'women in the business of crime', i.e. women who actively participate in, and even lead, criminal organizations. Female leadership in illegal activities is a crucial point. Questionable as any other, this selective choice is driven by the curiosity – meant as motivated desire for knowledge and understanding – to look into the untested phenomenon of female characters crossing the threshold and often taking command of the masculine preserve of criminal underworlds. Granted, the rise of female figures to central roles within fictional genres and subgenres long dominated by male leads is hardly new. However, stories of organized crime have resisted feminization a great deal longer than other kinds of narratives and have until very recently maintained an exclusionary stance, a narrative hostility of sorts towards women (Akass and McCabe 2002; O'Rawe 2011), relegating female characters to the marginal roles of gangster's moll or compliant mob's wife or victims of male violence. Not until the noughties had the rule of male prominence and power been challenged by a wave of antiheroines who have made inroads into the criminal underworlds and have provided evidence of women's capacity to be 'good at being bad' against the myth of female innocence.

> Society still denies women's capabilities to do things it recognizes men as having the capacity to do. The spectrum of women's perceived capacity has expanded, but a spectrum still exists and it is narrower than the spectrum used to comprehend men's capacities.
> (Gentry and Sjoberg 2015: 7)

It is absolutely not the intention of this book to uncritically celebrate characters of women in the business of crime as feminist achievements – nor the authors refrain from expressing criticism and disappointment towards reiteration of stereotypes and missed opportunities to push the representational envelope. It is rather to acknowledge that these types of antiheroines deserve privileged attention. They help to expand 'the spectrum of women's perceived capacity' so as to encompass arenas of agency – first and foremost crime and power – that women have long been deemed unsuitable for, and have been mostly denied the chance to access even in the realm of fictional storytelling. Not less important, antiheroines further challenge normative femininity by deviating (not all of them, though) from the canons of the 'good mother', the romanticized epitome of the true womanhood. Bad mother tropes, informed by deep disapproval of women gone wrong, have long been around in popular culture (Kaplan 1992); but non-normative maternal behaviours, which are performed in the context of narratives that upend true or ideal womanhood, tell the different story of a hegemonic vision of motherhood being undermined.

In actual fact, we are dealing with almost unique portrayals of daring female characters who embody more than any other the disturbing, subversive nature of the antihero; they perform triple transgressions against social norms (as law breakers), gender norms (as women behaving badly) and against the norms of the underworld subculture as well (as women in power within the masculinist crime organization).

A Disturbing Structure of Feeling

These transgressive antiheroines may arouse criticism and concern on the grounds that by stepping into arenas of male agency, all the more so when it comes to wrongdoing, women embrace maleness and are turned into masculinized subjects. I unapologetically admit not sharing similar concerns that in turn stem from theoretical models of gender binarism, as Kerry Fine has persuasively argued in an article whose title tellingly reads 'She hits like a man, but she kisses like a girl' (2012). Perspectives that do not encompass conceptions of recombinant genders cannot 'satisfactorily explain the effectiveness and popularity of women who successfully undermine gender dualism' (Fine 2012: 165). Jason Mittell makes the point clearly when he affirms: 'While some critics suggest that such mixtures "masculinize" feminine forms […] I contend that these recombinations complicate gender dichotomies in ultimately more progressive ways […]' (2015: 259).

A further strand of criticism might more plausibly be levelled against the 'double entanglement' (McRobbie 2009: 12), the post-feminist dialectic of empowerment and containment, celebration and punishment (Gill 2007) that informs the construction of (some) antiheroine characters. Are those portrayals of daring women eventually saying that the gendered order of things can be challenged but not changed? Or are competing readings possible, equally wary of embracing 'the paradigm of misogynist media' (Byerly 1999: 386) and a teleological narrative of progress? In this regard, it may be worth recalling the topos of the woman-on-top that was very common and popular in pre-industrial Europe, as Natalie Zemon Davis has documented in a masterful essay (1975). The woman-on-top was a symbolic form of gender inversion – to be found in art, literature, folklore and ritual practices – that entailed representing women 'out of their place', disguised as men, performing male roles and in command. Like other cultural forms of status reversal, typically encountered during carnivals and festivities, this fantasy of the gender order turned upside down was not meant to disrupt the basic structure of a hierarchical society; quite the reverse (or so it is argued), it helped to stabilize the social order, working as 'a safety valve for conflicts within the system' (Zemon Davis 1975: 130). This is not Zemon Davis's thinking, though. She takes the 'inclusive distinction' approach (the 'both … and' form: Beck 2015) to offer a competing, more complex reading that seems to apply here too.

> I want to argue that the image of the disorderly woman did not always function to keep women in their place. On the contrary, it was a multivalent image that could operate […] to broaden behavioural options for women […] it is also part of the conflict over efforts to change the basic distribution of power within society.
>
> (Zemon Davis 1975: 131)

I wish to conclude this line of discussion in a similar vein. Whether or not the TV antiheroine is here to stay or will prove a temporary trend, we are allowed to think that narratives and multivalent images of transgressive womanhood will help to sow 'the seed of subversion' (Bruner 2002: 94) of long-held ways of conceiving gender behavioural norms and the distribution of power within society.

And again, whether or not this is a transient or lasting phenomenon, we are faced with questions of what antiheroine television can possibly mean and why it has emerged and spread in these early years of the twenty-first century. The greater creative freedom, experienced by writers and producers of TV shows aiming to cater to the niche audiences of narrowcast channels, provides a credible and credited, yet only partial explanation; mass-audience-oriented broadcast networks have, in fact, embraced (pioneered in some cases) antiheroine storytelling, too, as testified by a number of examples included in this collection. This is certainly not to deny that the multichannel expansion of the television environment has helped to create the conditions of possibility for more varied, unconventional and challenging depictions of femininities (and masculinities) to appear. It is, rather, to point out that, regardless of the geo-cultural location and the institutional context, the rise of antiheroine television is to be largely related to an emergent 'structure of feeling' – I use Raymond Williams' concept (1961, 1977) in its somewhat loose meaning of shared moods, perceptions and sensibilities, emerging within a culture in a given time – that the new politics of gender representation in international TV drama has captured and expressed.

The constituents of this structure of feeling are to be found in the nexus between an intensified fascination of the twenty-first century with imaginative exploration of the puzzling interweave of good and evil in human behaviour, *and* the 'taking into account-ness' of feminism (McRobbie 2009) in contemporary popular culture, replete with emphasis on female strength, agency and empowerment. The antiheroine characters we encounter on television nowadays – especially (although not exclusively) when it comes to women in the business of crime – are informed by the interconnected strands of an ongoing longing for moral ambiguity and feminist-inspired ideas of female self-determination and achievement that make up the historically specific structure of feeling strictly associated with antiheroine television.

Williams argued that the emergence of a new structure of feeling, usually the sign of a cultural shift, may remain unnoticed and be overlooked until it is apprehended, articulated and displayed to our awareness in cultural forms and productions. Granted, the prominence gained by the antiheroic ethos in TV storytelling around the turn of the millennium has in no way gone unnoticed, much like the incorporation (and re-adjustment) of feminist principles into mainstream culture has not remained unaddressed – quite the opposite – in feminist scholarship (Budgeon 2011; Genz and Brabon 2009; Gill 2007; Hollows and Moseley 2006; McRobbie 2009; Tasker and Negra 2007). Nonetheless, we have been somewhat slow to perceive the incipient coalescence of the two different cultural strains into an emergent structure of feeling that foregrounded the imagination of women 'good at being bad' in a range of behaviours and domains. Indeed, as indicated by Williams, a new structure of feeling in its embryonic phase very often predates substantiation and articulation in finished cultural products; hence, its elusive formation can possibly escape our awareness or, rather, it can be taken as an idiosyncratic, isolated phenomenon. This is no longer true for what concerns the formation that is considered here, since the rise of antiheroine television with its large body of stories of women behaving badly has conveyed and made all too explicit the presence of related moods and sensibilities in contemporary popular culture.

As they stand against normative visions of femininities, these new moods and sensibilities alongside the associated patterns of gender representation in television storytelling may also be felt as 'a certain kind of disturbance or unease, a particular type of tension' (Williams 1979: 168) – a comment reminiscent of Bombert's take on the antihero. In actual fact, the potential for disturbance, uneasiness and trouble of the antiheroine television can hardly be denied; it goes hand in hand with intriguing appeal and fascination.

This Book

The book is divided into four sections, each including contributions (13 altogether) that focus on different – mostly just one, sometimes two – television dramas of the twenty-first century featuring female involvement in the business of crime in either leading or supporting roles. In keeping with the international scope of antiheroine television as indicated elsewhere in this introduction, the chosen texts cover a broader geographical spectrum than the US-centric stance of most contemporary television scholarship usually allows. Besides a number of US series and serials (*The Sopranos, Boardwalk Empire, Weeds, The Wire, Sons of Anarchy, Justified, Orange is the New Black*), TV shows from Italy (*Squadra Antimafia/Antimafia Squad, Gomorrah*), France (*Mafiosa*), the United Kingdom (*Bad Girls*), the Netherlands (*Penoza*), Latin America (*La Reina del Sur, Salve Jorge*) and Australia (*Wentworth, Underbelly:Razor*) are the majority here. On the institutional side, although ten out of 16 selected shows are meant to address specific audience segments in the narrowcasting environment, the inclusion of non-US originated TV dramas also serves to provide evidence that antiheroine television has taken roots in mass-oriented broadcast networks as well. At any rate, whether they were made to please a narrow or a broad audience, the TV dramas under analysis in this anthology have been selected mainly because they meet the requirement of offering worth considering and discussing variations on the theme of the antiheroine. They are also quite good and generally well-received shows; but it may be worth clarifying at this point that it was never the intention of this book to single out instances of so-called quality television – not, at least, if such semantically ambivalent definition (Buonanno 2013) is meant to apply to a minority of great texts standing in exemplary relation to all the rest. Without this implying that aesthetic concerns are altogether discarded, representational approaches hinging on critical exploration of characters and narratives clearly inform the entire set of chapters.

The opening section of the book – *Mafia Women* – deals with women's involvement in the illegal activities of the criminal organization par excellence, the Mafia. Milly Buonanno's chapter focuses on two lead characters of female bosses running Mafia and Camorra clans in the Italian series *Squadra antimafia/Antimafia Squad* and *Gomorrah*, pointing out the mix of strong taste for power, unapologetic use of violence and ambiguous performances of motherhood that make the protagonists all too distinctive in their bold transgression of normative gender scripts in Mediterranean societies. The analysis explores the narrative strategies through which admiration and sympathy are conveyed towards those controversial yet captivating figures of antiheroines, and moral perspectives are introduced or cast aside, and embraces a dual hermeneutics aimed at assessing the disposition of the texts to allow plural interpretations. Again, a Mediterranean location provides the arena of performance for a woman in command of a Corsican Mafia clan in the French series *Mafiosa*, which is the subject of the second chapter provided by Barbara Villez. We are confronted here with the almost unique character of a tragic antiheroine, a sombre and solitary young woman who has learnt how to wield power and violence to comply with the rules of the criminal underworld and to prove her worthiness for leadership; a deadly and vengeful persona, and yet a tormented soul yearning for a different life, the protagonist eventually succumbs to the tragic fate of her criminal family. Unlike the protagonists above, the Mafia women encountered in the HBO mob series *The Sopranos* and *Bordwalk Empire* do not hold power over the crime organizations, whose bosses they have married. Nonetheless, those characters of mobsters' wives prove able to carve out spaces and roles for themselves in ways that are individually empowering as much as compromising. In this connection, in the third chapter, Kim Akass and Janet McCabe discuss compelling figures of Mafia wives as instances of the relationship between women and power in present-day society, arguing that a character like Carmela Soprano is the epitome of the antiheroine in the neo-liberal era.

Motherhood rather than power becomes the lens through which characters of women in the business of crime are scrutinized in the second section – *Drug Dealers and Aberrant Mothers*. The fourth chapter, by Joke Hermes, is concerned with the female lead in the Dutch series *Penoza*: an initially stay-at-home mom who, following the murder of her mobster husband, is unwillingly thrown into the illegal career of drug dealer in order to provide for her children and keep them safe. Based on newspaper and magazine reviews of the show, the chapter offers a critical reading of such an ambivalent character of mother turned gangster; the claim is made that the novelty associated to a female figure embracing a criminal life barely disguises the adhesion of the narrative to the precept, inherent to the traditional motherhood ideology that a mother should do anything for her children. At the same time, the precept is questioned by the inability of the protagonist to fully perform protective motherhood. Another mom turned drug dealer is featured in Showtime's comedy-drama series *Weeds*, the subject of the fifth chapter by Elisa Giomi. Maternal feelings and duties are not a major motivation for the series' lead character – a neglectful and careless mother – to eagerly undertake a criminal career, which she clearly embraces without apologies as a fitting way to make a living and to enjoy an affluent life-style. As elucidated in the chapter, the character's depiction is predicated on a complex intertwining of social and gender transgressions, and textual strategies aimed at softening the subversive potential of the antiheroine are displayed throughout the narrative; however, neither the professional criminal nor the aberrant mother experience punishment. Matriarchal figures of bad women and bad mothers to be found in the FX drama series *Justified* and *Sons of Anarchy* are explored by Amanda Lotz in the sixth chapter. The professional involvement in crime of the two female characters under analysis is passed over here in favour of a closer scrutiny of their manipulative and abusive behaviour against their family and, in particular, their children. One is a self-interested, insensitive and physically intimidating mother, the other one a complex instance of possessive, destructive motherhood contradictorily performed in the name of family good and maternal love: although such uncommon embodiments of monstrous mothers do not invite identification, they make a compelling presence in the narrative. The text discussed in the seventh chapter acts as a bridge to the next section, since it incorporates themes of sexual transgression within the story of a Latino narco queen. Yeidy Rivero explores the construction of gender and sexuality in the transnational *telenovela La Reina del Sur*, pointing out the uniqueness of the female lead: a woman in power in the male-dominated world of drug trafficking, and also a sensitive, loyal and supportive friend of other women. Although the protagonist's sexual relationships meet normative expectations, the admiration and strong affective bond she develops with her lesbian business partner insinuates that she may possibly be bisexual, in defiance of the strict heteronormativity that reigns in the *telenovela* world.

The contributions included in the third section – *Women in Prison* – address yet another dimension of female transgression: sexuality. The criminal behaviours that brought the women to incarceration remain in the background, as critical attention here is cast on challenges to heteronormativity; likewise, in keeping with the ensemble cast that is peculiar to narratives of women in prison (WIP), textual analyses do not primarily focus on single lead characters. Opening the section with Chapter 8, Vicky Ball offers a queer feminist reading of the British series *Bad Girls*, bringing into discussion other filmic and televisual examples of the WIP genre. At odds with the familiar tropes of an exploitation genre, wherein depictions of lesbian characters are usually pathologized and othered, the concerned narrative allows for homonormative constructions of gender and sexuality; equally relevant, criminal femininities in the series appear to be shaped and re-shaped by an ongoing dialectic of heroism and villainy. Chapter 9 deals with the Australian prison drama *Wentworth*, a revisitation of the soap opera *Prisoner* that ran for eight years in the 1980s. In reconstructing the cultural and social contexts in which the two series emerged, Sue Turnbull highlights a number of significant differences between the original and the re-imagined show, particularly with regard to now explicit lesbian sexuality and more rewarding narrative arcs of characters. Despite the violence, abuse and power struggles, the series depicts female inmates as endowed with their own moral codes and, most of the time, having to face circumstances that lead them to behave badly – and the audience to root for them. In the tenth chapter, Suzanna Danuta Walters analyses the Netflix series *Orange is the New Black (OITNB)* in the broader context of other criminal women in prison in film and television, and locates its representations of queer sexuality in the longer history of lesbian visibility and invisibility in popular culture. The chapter observes that while sexuality in *OITNB* is depicted with a frankness rarely seen in popular culture, it is refracted in and through racialized identities and tropes. More central to the argument, however, is the acknowledgement that the series adopts narrative strategies aimed at humanizing characters of female offenders, thus rendering the bad women in prison (some of them) as antiheroines worthy of empathy.

The fourth and last section of the book – *Villainesses and Anti-antiheroines* – is concerned with female figures that do not fit into the antiheroine category, although their involvement in the business of crime undoubtedly turns them into women behaving badly. Apparently at odds with the central thrust of the book, the inclusion of such characters is meant to explore some of what might be called 'the condition of impossibility' of being an antiheroine. Co-authored by Samantha Joyce and Antonio La Pastina, Chapter 11 introduces an unprecedented villainess figure to be found in the Brazilian *telenovela Salve Jorge*: a successful businesswoman who, behind a mask of respectability, hides her powerful position as the boss of an international organization of human trafficking in women for prostitution and slavery. The awful nature of the guilt – a heinous crime perpetrated by a woman against other women – prevents the narrative from gracing the character with the moral oscillation that is a distinctive feature of the antiheroine. The villainess only inhabits the space of evil, regardless of the appeal that her elegance and membership of a social elite may have for a fraction of the audience. In such a way the *telenovela* performs a mission of conveying educational messages and sparking ethical discussions, while at the same time broadening the range of female representations. In Chapter 12, Bruce Williams and Andrea Press address depictions of African American female criminals in the HBO series *The Wire*. Without denying the high worthiness of the show and its realistic rendering of the murky underworld of drug trafficking in Baltimore, the chapter makes the claim that characters of underclass women of colour are denied the nuanced and sympathetic portrayals more often afforded to their male counterparts. The unattractive features of criminal personalities and blameworthy black mothers, offering very little room for empathic identification, are rather stressed and detailed when it comes to these female characters. Thus, the refraction of gender in and through marginalized race and underclass turns the show into an inhospitable narrative terrain for the African American antiheroines to emerge. The 13th and last chapter by Leigh Readhead engages with the analysis of the Australian series *Underbelly: Razor*, based on two real-life female bosses who trafficked in illegal alcohol, cocaine and prostitution in the 1920s and 1930s. As argued in this chapter, the series puts in place devices that reinforce representational archetypes and a binary characterization of gender; furthermore, the narrative focus on the domestic and maternal rather than public space and criminal action, thereby dilutes the transgressive potential of the story of two powerful, ruthless and feared female criminals. This undermining of women in positions of power both reflects and upholds the politics of gender representation in the Australian mainstream media: hardly a propitious context for the burgeoning antiheroine characters in television storytelling.

On the whole, the 13 contributions offer a first in-depth and wide-ranging look at a cultural shift in gender representation that challenges normative femininities in ways worthy of discussion and open to refreshing dispute in the field of feminist media scholarship.

References

Adams, S. (2013), 'Scandal and the year of the female TV antihero', *Criticwire*, 27 December, http://blogs.indiewire.com/criticwire/year-in-tv-2013-scandal-antihero. Accessed 8 January 2014.

Akass, K. and McCabe, J. (2002), 'Beyond Bada Bing! Negotiating female narrative authority in *The Sopranos*', in D. Lavery (ed.), *This Thing of Ours*, New York: Columbia University Press, pp. 146–161.

—— (eds) (2004), *Reading Sex and the City*, London: I.B. Tauris.

Albrecht, M. M. (2015), *Masculinities in Contemporary Quality Television*, Burlington and London: Ashgate.

Armstrong, J. K. (2013), 'The rise of TV's Anti-Heroine', *Damemagazine*, 18 October, http://www.damemagazine.com/2013/10/18/rise-tv-anti-heroine. Accessed 22 October 2013.

Arnold, S. (2014), 'Ghettoising the "Strong Female Lead": Netflix, demographics and gendered categorisation', *CSTonline*, 4 July, http://www.cstonline.tv/ghettoising-the-strong-female-lead. Accessed 10 July 2013.

Beck, R. (2013), 'Myths of the golden age', *Prospect*, 26 September, http://www.prospectmagazine.co.uk/arts-and-books/myths-of-the-golden-age-richard-beck-prestige-tv. Accessed 10 October 2013.

Beck, U. (2015), *What is Globalization*, Cambridge: Polity Press.

Bennett, L. (2013), 'Against antiheroes', *New Republic,* 17 August, http://www.newrepublic.com/article/114346/anti-antihero-against-cultural-buzzwords. Accessed 22 August 2013.

Blay, Z. (2015), 'How feminist TV became the new normal', *The Huffington Post*, 18 June, http://www.huffingtonpost.com/2015/06/18/how-feminist-tv-became-the-new-normal_n_7567898.html. Accessed 20 June 2015.

Bombert, V. (1999), *In Praise of Antiheroes*, Chicago and London: The University of Chicago Press.

Bourdieu, P. (2011), *The Masculine Domination*, Stanford: Stanford University Press.

Bruner, J. (2002), *Making Stories*, New York: Farra, Straus and Giroux.

Brunsdon, C. (1997), *Screen Tastes: Soap Opera to Satellite Dishes*, London: Routledge.

Budgeon, S. (2011), *Third Wave Feminism and the Politics of Gender in Late Modernity*, London: Palgrave Macmillan.

Buonanno, M. (2013), 'The transatlantic romance of television studies and the "tradition of quality" in Italian TV drama', *Journal of Popular Television*, 1: 2, pp. 175–189.

Byerly, C. M. (1999), 'New, feminism and the dialectic of gender relations', in M. Myers (ed.), *Mediated Women: Representations in Popular Culture*, Cresskill: Hampton Press, pp. 383–403.

Coulthard, L. (2007), 'Killing Bill: Rethinking feminism and film violence', in Y. Tasker and D. Negra (eds), *Interrogating Postfeminism: Gender and the Politics of Popular Culture*, Durham and London: Duke University Press, pp. 153–175.

D'Acci, J. (1994), *Defining Women: Television and the Case of Cagney & Lacey*, Chapell Hill: North Carolina University Press.

Doyle, J. (2013), 'Where are the complex women on premium cable?', *The Globe and Mail*, 2 July, http://www.theglobeandmail.com/arts/summer-entertainment/where-are-the-complex-women-on-premium-cable/article12937880/. Accessed 11 July 2013.

Early, F. and Kennedy, K. (eds) (2003), *Athena's Daughters: Television's New Woman Warriors*, Syracuse and New York: Syracuse University Press.

Enloe, C. (2004), *The Curious Feminist: Searching for Women in the New Age of Empire*, London: University of California Press.

Fine, K. (2012), 'She hits like a man, but she kisses like a girl: TV heroines, femininity, violence, and intimacy', *Western American Literature*, 47: 2, pp. 152–173.

Franich, D. (2013), 'The myth of antihero fatigue and the revisionist/reductionist history of TV's golden age', *Entertainment Weekly*, 3 October, http://www.ew.com/article/2013/10/03/breaking-bad-sopranos-antihero. Accessed 15 October 2013.

Gentry, C. E. and Sjoberg, L. (2015), *Beyond Mothers, Monsters, Whores: Thinking About Womens' Violence in Global Politics*, London: Zed Books.

Genz, S. and Brabon, B. (2009), *Postfeminism: Cultural Texts and Theories*, Edinburgh: Edinburgh University Press.

Geraghty, C. (2013), 'Re-appraising the television heroine', *CSTonline*, 6 September, http://cstonline.tv/re-appraising-the-television-heroine. Accessed 7 September 2013.

Gill, R. (2007), *Gender and the Media*, Cambridge: Polity Press.

Gunn, A. (2013), 'I have a character issue', *The New York Times*, 23 August, http://www.nytimes.com/2013/08/24/opinion/i-have-a-character-issue.html?_r=0. Accessed 25 August 2013.

Henegan, J. (2013), 'Is the era of the female protagonist dawning?', *Entertainment Fuse*, 24 August, http://www.entertainmentfuse.com/is-the-era-of-the-female-protagonist-dawning/. Accessed 5 September 2013.

Herman, A. (2013), 'Just because there is no female Tony Soprano doesn't mean TV can't have great female antiheroes', *Flavorwire*, 1 July, http://flavorwire.com/401219/just-because-theres-no-female-tony-soprano-doesnt-mean-tv-cant-have-great-female-antiheroes. Accessed 7 July 2013.

Hollows, J. and Moseley, R. (eds) (2006), *Feminism in Popular Culture*, Oxford and New York: Berg.

Howard, D. (2013), 'Quality television: The next generation', *CSTonline*, 20 September, http://cstonline.tv/quality-television-the-next-generation. Accessed 21 September 2013.

Inness, S. A. (1999), *Tough Girls: Women Warriors and Wonder Women in Popular Culture*, Philadelphia: University of Pennsylvania Press.

—— (ed.) (2004), *Action Chicks: New Images of Tough Women in Popular Culture*, New York: Palgrave Macmillan.

Jones, M. (2013), 'Antihero era of television proves exhausting, wearisome', *Washington Square News*, 18 September, http://www.nyunews.com/2013/09/18/antihero/. Accessed 4 October 2013.

Kaplan, A. (1992), *Motherhood and Representations: The Mother in Popular Culture and Melodrama*, New York: Routledge.

Kelly, L. (2013), 'Television's difficult women', *CSTonline*, 31 October, http://cstonline.tv/televisions-difficult-women. Accessed 2 November 2013.

Killoran, E. (2013), 'James Gandolfini is dead: Can Tony Soprano rest in peace?', *International Business Times*, 21 June, www.ibtimes.com/james-gandolfini-dead-can-tony-soprano-rest-peace-1318595. Accessed 22 June 2013.

Lotz, A. (2006), *Redisigning Women. Television after the Network Era*, Urbana and Chicago: University of Illinois Press.

—— (2014), *Cable Guys: Television and Masculinities in the 21st Century*, New York: New York University Press.

Lyon, M. (2013), 'Can we make Walter White our last antihero, please?', *Vulture*, 1 October, http://www.vulture.com/2013/10/let-antiheroes-end-with-walter-white.html. Accessed 29 October 2013.

Maciak, P. (2013), 'Kill the leading man: Two histories of 21st century television', *Los Angeles Review of Books*, 14 August, https://lareviewofbooks.org/review/kill-the-leading-man-two-histories-of-21st-century-television. Accessed 17 August 2013.

Marcotte, A. (2011), 'How to make a critically acclaimed TV show about masculinity', *The Good Men Project*, 11 September, http://goodmenproject.com/arts/how-to-make-a-critically-acclaimed-tv-show-about-masculinity/#sthash.pp61Enso.dpuf. Accessed 14 November 2012.

Martin, B. (2013), *Difficult Men: From the Sopranos and The Wire to Mad Men and Breaking bad: Behind the Scenes of a Creative Revolution*, New York: Penguin Books.

McCaughey, M. and King, N. (eds) (2001), *Reel Knockouts: Violent Women in the Movies*, Austin: University of Texas Press.

McNamara, M. (2013), 'Can women break the antihero's hold on TV?', *Los Angeles Times*, 16 August, http://articles.latimes.com/2013/aug/16/entertainment/la-et-st-critics-notebook-drama-women-break-antihero-hold/2. Accessed 17 August 2013.

McRobbie, A. (2009), *The Aftermath of Feminism*, London: Sage.

Mittell, J. (2015), *Complex TV: The Poetics of Contemporary Television Storytelling*, New York and London: New York University Press.

Mizejewski, L. (2004), *Hardboiled & High Heeled: The Woman Detective in Popular Culture*, New York and London: Routledge.

Neroni, H. (2005), *The Violent Woman: Femininity, Narrative and Violence in Contemporary American Cinema*, Albany: State University of New York Press.

Newman, M. Z. and Levine, E. (2012), *Legitimating Television: Media Convergence and Cultural Status*, New York: Routledge.

Nikolas, A. (2013), 'Where is the female Tony Soprano?', *The Atlantic*, 27 June, http://www.theatlantic.com/entertainment/archive/2013/06/where-is-the-female-tonysoprano/277270/. Accessed 29 June 2013.

Nussbaum, E. (2013), 'Difficult women: How "Sex and the City" lost its good name', *The New Yorker*, 29 July, http://www.newyorker.com/magazine/2013/07/29/difficult-women. Accessed 1 August 2013.

O'Rawe, C. (2011), 'Roberta Torre's Angela: The mafia and the "Woman's Film"', in D. Renga (ed.), *Mafia Movies: A Reader*, Toronto: University of Toronto Press, pp. 329–337.

Paskin, W. (2013a), 'James Gandolfini, gone too soon', *Salon*, 20 June, http://www.salon.com/2013/06/20/james_gandolfini_gone_too_soon/. Accessed 24 June 2013.

—— (2013b), 'The TV Club, 2013: Entry 1', *Slate*, 25 December, http://www.slate.com/articles/arts/tv_club/features/2013/the_year_in_tv/the_year_in_tv_was_2013_the_year_the_antihero_died.html. Accessed 2 January 2014.

Ryan, M. (2013a), 'Best TV of 2013: Weirdos, oddballs, veterans and left-field gems', *The Huffington Post*, 12 October, http://www.huffingtonpost.com/maureen-ryan/best-tv-2013_b_4419561.html. Accessed 15 October 2013.

—— (2013b), 'Anna Gunn and "Breaking Bad's" Skyler White: Just the tip of a very big iceberg', *The Huffington Post*, 25 August, http://www.huffingtonpost.com/maureen-ryan/anna-gunn-breaking-bad-skyler-white_b_3810989.html. Accessed 2 September 2013.

Rosenberg, A. (2013a), 'The death of James Gandolfini and the twilight of television's antihero era', THINKPROGRESS, 27 June, http://thinkprogress.org/alyssa/2013/06/27/2227271/the-death-of-james-gandolfini-and-the-twilight-of-televisions-antihero-era/. Accessed 27 June 2013.

—— (2013b), 'Why we'll never have a female Tony Soprano', *Slate*, 27 June, http://www.slate.com/blogs/xx_factor/2013/06/27/james_gandolfini_and_the_male_anti_hero_why_we_ll_never_have_a_female_tony.html. Accessed 27 June 2013.

—— (2013c), 'Why "The Bridge" star Diane Kruger picked television over movies, and the state of roles for women', THINKPROGRESS, 3 July, http://thinkprogress.org/alyssa/2013/07/03/2251921/the-bridge-diane-kruger/. Accessed 20 July 2013.

Rowless, D. (2013), 'Where is the female Walter White?', *Salon*, 8 September, http://www.salon.com/2013/09/08/stop_imposing_a_double_standard_on_skyler_white_partner/. Accessed 23 September 2013.

Sarikakis, K. (2013), 'Arriving at a crossroads: Political priorities for a socially relevant feminist media scholarship', in L. McLaughlin and C. Carter (eds), *Current Perspectives in Feminist Media Studies*, London: Routledge, pp. 105–111.

Sepinwall, A. (2012), *The Revolution was Televised: The Cops, Crooks, Slingers and Slayers Who Changed TV Drama Forever*, New York: Touchstone.

Tasker, Y. (1993), *Spectacular Bodies: Gender, Genre and the Action Cinema*, London and New York: Routledge.

Tasker, Y. and Negra, D. (eds) (2007), *Interrogating Postfeminism: Gender and the Politics of Popular Culture*, Durham and London: Duke University Press.

Thomas, J. (2013), 'Enough with the TV antiheroes already', *Slate*, 1 July, http://www.slate.com/blogs/browbeat/2013/07/01/the_tv_anti_hero_from_tony_soprano_to_ray_donovan_why_so_many_and_when_will.html. Accessed 8 July 2013.

Truitt, J. (2013), 'The Skyler White Problem: Can we accept complex female characters?', *Feministing*, 20 August, http://feministing.com/2013/08/20/the-skyler-white-problem-can-we-accept-complex-female-characters/. Accessed 10 September 2013.

Vaage, M. B. (2015), *The Antihero in American Televison*, Routledge: London.

VanDerWerff, T. (2013), 'Breaking Bad ended the antihero genre by introducing good and evil', *A.V.Club*, 30 September, http://www.avclub.com/article/ibreaking-badi-ended-the-anti-hero-genre-by-introd-103483. Accessed 21 October 2013.

White, R. (2007), *Violent Femmes: Women as Spies in Popular Culture*, London and New York: Routledge.

Williams, R. (1961), *The Long Revolution*, Harmondsworth: Penguin.

—— (1977), *Marxism and Literature*, Oxford University Press: Oxford.

―――― (1979), *Politics and Letters: Interview with New Left Review*, New Left Books: London.
Willmore, A. (2013), 'The good wives: Isn't it time to give a rest to the character of the TV antihero's disapproving spouse?', *Indiewire*, 13 August, http://www.indiewire.com/article/television/the-good-wives. Accessed 30 August 2013.
Zemon, Davis N. (1975), *Society and Culture in Early Modern France*, Stanford: Stanford University Press.

Part I

Mafia Women

Chapter 1

Godmothers in Italian Mafia Story: Or 'Something Else Besides a Mother'

Milly Buonanno

'Never Happen in the States': It Happens in Italy

In season 2, episode 4 of *The Sopranos* ('Commendatori' 2000), Tony Soprano (James Gandolfini) travels to Naples to make a deal with a clan of the Camorra, the powerful crime organization that reigns in Campania. Tony's attitude to the trip is informed by his nostalgia-inducing imagination and expectation of a southern Italian world (or underworld) where the patriarchal power structure remains intact. Hence, his disconcerted reaction and sneering remark when he discovers that the Camorra boss with whom business must be conducted is a woman, the voluptuous Annalisa Zucca (Sofia Milos), who has replaced her senile father and her husband, jailed for life, as the head of the family. 'A fucking woman boss? Never happen in the States. Never' ('Commendatori' 2000).

An inconceivable violation of the gendered hierarchies of Mafia power, as perceived by Tony Soprano, the access of women to leadership positions within criminal organizations actually happens in Italy: both in real life (Fiandaca 2007; Ingrascì 2007; Gribaudi and Marmo 2010) and, more recently, in fictional representations of Mafia and Mafia-like groups in a number of media.

Although contemporary Italian cinema has tentatively explored the phenomenon of women involved in the business of crime – for instance, in Roberta Torre's *Angela* (2002) (O'Rawe 2011) and Edoardo Winspeare's *Galantuomini/Brave men* (2008) – deeply captivating stories and iconic figures are more to be found in television narratives. This chapter revolves around the fictional characters of two female bosses, Rosy Abate (Giulia Michelini) and Imma Savastano (Maria Pia Calzone), whose rise to power in the quintessential masculine domain of illegal trafficking and bloodthirsty violence has developed into a major storyline of the successful prime-time serial dramas *Squadra antimafia/Antimafia Squad* (Canale 5, 2009–) and *Gomorra. La serie/Gomorrah: The Series* (Sky Atlantic, 2014–), respectively.

Owing to the diverse mix of shaping factors, as will be seen in the following pages, Rosy and Imma emerge as quite different personae of female mob bosses. Each manages in her own way to gain control of criminal markets and families, either by challenging or taking advantage of the gender allocation of roles in crime organizations that preclude (Mafia) or allow (Camorra) women's rise to top positions. Moreover, the dialectic principle of the 'unity of opposites', which seems to inspire the identity construction of the two characters, implies that a criminal career – the pinnacle of female transgression of womanhood boundaries – goes hand in hand with the pinnacle of ideal womanhood: motherhood (Rich 1995).

Motherhood matters and makes a significant impact on Rosy and Imma's lives, although neither can be considered a truly good or bad mother: they perform ambivalent motherhood in different and even opposing ways. The title of this chapter quotes Linda Williams' famous essay 'Something else besides a mother' to indicate that Rosy and Imma's 'desire for fulfilment as a woman' (Williams 1984: 16) rises above motherhood.

These portrayals of powerful women criminals and reprehensible mothers (to say the least) are totally unprecedented in the whole history of Italian TV drama and, more specifically, in the long tradition of the Mafia story that has been a staple of TV drama production and consumption in Italy since the 1980s (Buonanno 2012). This is hardly surprising and transcends the Italian case. Action heroines, armed women and violent and criminal women have emerged in different periods of cinema history, and television drama has recently witnessed a similar trend internationally. Current scholarship (Tasker 1993; D'Acci 1994; Brunsdon 1998 and 2013; Inness 1999 and 2004; Creeber 2001; McCaughey and King 2001; Mizejewski 2004; Lotz 2006; White 2007; Jermyn 2008 and 2010) has especially focused on police and action dramas, exploring the different ways in which television storytelling has engaged, not without limits and contradictions, in transgressing norms of traditional femininity.

> For a female character to become the heroine of such a series, she must appropriate agency, action, command, the occupation of public space, discursive authority and the control of the investigative gaze. All of these, of course, run counter to the norms of femininity.
> (Thornham 2007: 69)

Yet, in television and cinema alike, the genre that has mostly preserved the deep masculine connotations of its diegetic world (Larke-Walsh 2010), thus remaining largely impermeable to the rise of female protagonism, has been precisely the Mafia story. The Mafia story is by generic conventions 'male', by reason not so much of socio-anthropological faithfulness to the macho centrality and culture of *Cosa nostra* and Mafia-like organizations as of the deep symbolic connections between violence, power and money – the dominant themes in the Mafia story – and the social construction of maleness. The genre 'traditionally foregrounds phallic masculinity' (O'Rawe 2011: 329) and manifests 'hostility towards women' (Akass and McCabe 2002: 147) by reducing female representation to the dichotomy of usually powerless or ancillary mothers/wives and mistresses/femmes fatales (Livia and Carmela Soprano being evidently an exception, or rather a vanguard).[1]

In the Italian context, a further determining factor comes into play. In keeping with the cultural policy adopted by public service broadcasting (RAI), which is the main producer of domestic TV dramas and boasts a track record of acclaimed Mafia stories, the characters of 'bad guys' and negative heroes are hardly, if ever, accorded the narrative prominence granted to them by the classic gangster movie and, more recently, by so many US cable series (Lotz 2014). As conceived and realized by public television drama departments, stories of macro-criminality very often turn out to be biopics of anti-Mafia fallen heroes, or, at any rate, the narrative emphasis is put on characters of law enforcement crime-fighters.

Public television has doubtlessly set the standard for a hero-centred version of the Mafia story, but the deep-seated fascination of the Italian public with this genre of drama has prompted free commercial and subscription-based television to make inroads into such a lucrative narrative territory. Crime storytelling has thus witnessed a re-configuration and has been, to a greater or lesser extent, re-imagined according to the 'logics of distinction' and identity strategies adopted by the competing players, differently positioned within the television system. Canale 5, the flagship channel of commercial broadcasting, has shifted the narrative barycentre closer to the criminal front (*Il capo dei capi*/*The Boss of Bosses*, 2007) without undermining the key role of positive albeit flawed heroes. It has also lessened the gender gap, in keeping with the trend already established in police series (*Distretto di polizia*/*Police District* [Canale 5, 2000–2012]) to represent women in command. As for Sky, in its ambitious pursuit of the HBO model, the satellite television that addresses niche audiences has chosen to focus on the dark side of Italian society, since its first move into the field of original production (*Romanzo criminale*/*Crime Novel: The Series*, 2008–2010), and is committed to narrating, in tones of gritty realism, the stories of criminal antiheroes who inhabit a violent and merciless world without heroes or redemption.

The increased visibility of female bosses on the national media and judicial scene may well have made an impact on, and provided inspiration for, writers[2] and producers. Retracing the genesis of the antiheroines Rosy Abate and Imma Savastano nonetheless entail acknowledgement that policies of differentiation, in the context of changing television system, helped to create the conditions for challenging the traditional standards of the Mafia story and exploring unprecedented profiles of femininities.

Blood and Tears: The Queen of Palermo

Antimafia Squad was premièred on Canale 5 in spring 2009 and immediately gained both popularity and critical acclaim. It was still in production when writing this chapter after running for six seasons during which the serial – merging crime drama with melodrama – has unfolded what would be old stories of conflicts between state forces and the Sicilian Mafia, and of deadly wars between competing Mafia families, had not the conventional crime storytelling been refreshed by the unconventional allocation of leadership roles to female characters. As Charlotte Brunsdon puts it, 'old stories can be told in new ways once the central generic actor is female' (2013: 379). In *Antimafia Squad*, both the police unit and the criminal organization are led by women; Rosy's counterpart, a friend turned antagonist, is the deputy superintendent Claudia Mares[3] (Simona Cavallari).

Mafia drama and melodrama might at first glance appear to be polar opposites, as crime is associated with the male realm of action and violence, whereas 'melodrama has frequently been identified as a woman's genre' (Gledhill 1987: 33) owing to the rush and clash of emotions, sentiments and passions (Brooks 1976). The reductive identification with the female realm of affects and emotionalism has turned melodrama into a long disparaged genre; and its spread into male territories is still liable to be regarded, from a commonsensical perspective, as an improper intrusion, a form of contamination in the true sense. In fact, the Mafia story and melodrama are much less incompatible than a simplifying dichotomous approach seems to take for granted. When it comes to the rush and clash of emotions, the Mafia story can be as good as melodrama; betrayal, revenge and suffering are central motives of both types of storytelling, whose merging has made the subgenre of gangster melodrama 'a staple in film since the earliest days of silent movie' (Messenger 2002: 8), well before exploding in popularity with *The Godfather* trilogy (Coppola 1972, 1974, 1990). Melodrama in turn resists exclusive identification as a 'woman's genre', since the melodramatic mode is embedded in most of the male action stories, as Linda Williams (1998) has persuasively argued, calling into question the identification of melodrama as a gendered genre. Following Williams, Jason Mittell has recently recognized 'the ubiquity of melodrama' (2015: 245) throughout television. Furthermore, even assuming that melodrama is in the main 'a heroine's text' (LaPlace 1987: 151), melodramatic heroines are not just suffering victims or damsels in distress; it is worth recalling in this connection that as early as in the first two decades of the twentieth century, the 'serial-queen melodrama' genre flourishing in American cinema created the first modern figures of action women. Admittedly, those heroines were virtuous and not inclined to commit crimes, but they dared feminine norms by appropriating traditional masculine behaviours, including the ability to fight and use weapons, and they personified fantasies of female empowerment (Singer 1996; Neroni 2005).

A gangster (*cum* police) melodrama re-focused on a female lead character, *Antimafia Squad* adopts a stylistic signature to both visually and symbolically recognize the double ascendency of a narrative of crime and affects and how this shapes feelings, drives agency and helps to build the protagonist's identity. I refer here to the flood of tears pouring down Rosy's face and to her own or others' blood displayed on Rosy's body and clothes in many scenes of the serial drama: a flurry of blood and tears intended to give high visibility to the intense suffering and the murderous way of life of the protagonist. The metaphor 'to have blood on one's hands' is visualized whenever she throws herself onto the mortally wounded bodies of family members (in the double meaning of the word family), or persons she cares a great deal about (like Claudia Mares), and gets up with the blood-stained hands that are a prelude for her deadly vengeance. All this works as the reiterated reminder that (conventionally feminine) deep emotional suffering and (conventionally masculine) murderous criminal violence can be harboured in the same female persona. Thus, what I have defined as a double ascendency of the storytelling, the coming together of the Mafia story and melodramatic pathos, allows for dualistic definitions and representations of femininity and masculinity to be challenged and transgressed.

But there is no transgression at the beginning of Rosy's journey. Rosy Abate is in her twenties when she comes back to Sicily from New York, where she has grown up with her three brothers,[4] to marry her Italian-American fiancé in her family's homeland. Educated and brought up as a princess by her older brother who treasures her, the future Mafia boss makes her entrance in the shape of a pretty young woman who does not refrain from somewhat childish manifestations of affective exuberance and who nurtures – as a yesterday's girl rather than an emancipated New Yorker of the 2000s – the simple dream of marrying the man she loves, raising children and cooking great Sicilian food. The capricious despotism that she inflicts on her fiancé, who is mildly disposed to let her tyrannize him ('I have no right to speak, she's the boss': [*Squadra antimafia/Antimafia Squad* 2009]), nevertheless gives us a glimpse of the commanding temperament of a potential 'woman on top' and the reversal, in the couple's relationship, of traditional gender roles.

The shrewd concealment strategy put in train by her brother has allowed Rosy Abate to be unaware of the criminal nature of the family's lucrative activities. This unawareness stands for guarantee and protection of her innocence – even according to the police, who keep the Abate family under constant surveillance: 'she is clean' (*Squadra antimafia/Antimafia Squad* 2009), The camera shots of her arrival at Palermo airport that linger over her fashionable shoes, her visible cleavage in the plunging neckline of her short and close-fitting dress, her glossy red lips and, in addition, the mischievous performance of a mock quarrel with her fiancé followed by a passionate reconciliation, emphasize the young woman's sexualized corporeality (if only in a soft mode) and her impulsive and romantic temperament. Her lively and seductive femininity, while it equates Rosy to other women of her generation, helps to substantiate her extraneousness to the norms of female containment enforced by the patriarchal Mafia culture. Hence, her identity 'is initially represented by difference' (Larke-Walsh 2010: 182), as in the case of Michael Corleone in *The Godfather*[5] (Coppola 1972): a prelude to the radical redefinition of identity following Rosy Abate's later integration into the Mafia's culture and organization.

Rosy Abate's process of identification with *Cosa nostra* goes through a sequence of traumatizing experiences: her brothers arrested, in flight, in hiding, then put to death by killers from rival families or during police operations, her own life exposed to ambushes and attacks, her husband becoming a victim of one of these. The excessive weeping and gestures to which Rosy succumbs in her reaction to trauma and mourning are peculiar of a melodrama character. But here, in particular, the uncontrolled display of her emotions exteriorizes not only the grief of separations and losses, her rage against those responsible, her desire for revenge and her sense of being overwhelmed by the outbreak of hostilities and threats, but also the huge emotional pressure generated by the radical rupture with her innocent past and her growing awareness that she is going through the process of becoming a Mafia woman ('I look in the mirror and can hardly grasp who I am' ['L'incontro/The Meeting' 2009]). When Rosy's younger and most loved brother dies riddled with blows from the police, she first flings herself on his body in despair but then gets up dry-eyed with a posture and expression of someone who is ready for a challenge, a veil of deceitfulness in her stare. She would say later that at that moment she finally felt certain that she was a Mafia woman, 'I finally grasped who I was' ('Scontro finale/Final Clash' 2011). Accordingly, as the only surviving Abate, she would later decide to stay in Sicily to gather up and manage the family's inheritance.

It is worth insisting on this point: Rosy Abate's 'Mafiosity' in the narrative of *Antimafia Squad* has the almost ineluctable compulsion of a destiny and is presented in a deterministic framework that is entirely consistent with the framework applying in the past to gender belonging: that is to say, 'one is born a Mafiosa' (or, in the words of the character, 'I was born a Mafia woman and I shall die a Mafia woman' ['Scontro finale/Final clash' 2011]). In fact, by identifying herself with Mafia culture and criminality, Rosy is expressing her (proud) acceptance of a sort of heredity that is both genetic and cultural: on her part, a manifestation of *amor fati* or 'love of her fate'. Or to quote Bourdieu: 'the choice of destiny, but a forced choice, produced by conditions of existence which rule out all alternatives as mere daydreams' (1984: 178).

When the embrace of a foreordained female destiny entails, as in this case, entry into a criminal career and organization, there is room for the exercise of 'dual hermeneutics' (Johnson 2007: 16). You can, in fact, put forward a critical interpretation and denounce the narrative's adhesion to a patriarchal ideology that, in denying the character's capability of and right to self-determination, assimilates her, subjugates her and effectively makes her complicit in a male and masculinist culture. But it is equally possible to propose a different hermeneutics, acknowledging in Rosy's manifestation of *amor fati*, the reversal of a cultural stereotype of femininity that does not cease to be premised on determinist and sexist assumptions just because it reinstates an allegedly positive image of women. I am referring to the symbolic nexus, strongly enmeshed in cultural tradition, between the feminine gender and a deeply rooted habitus of softness and morality, based on a conception of the woman as alien by nature from violence and a criminal disposition, especially by virtue of her maternal and nurturing attitude. The violent and criminal woman is probably the most threatening of female figures, since in adopting 'unnatural' behaviours, she is attacking a fundamental principle of opposition between the genders: violence as a form of male domination (Bourdieu 2001), not infrequently exercised on the women themselves, 'as well as a defining characteristic of masculinity' (Neroni 2005: 45). As she goes forward to meet her fate as a Mafia woman, fully aware of what that means in terms of ruthlessness and illegality, Rosy Abate is questioning a stereotype that in effect sanctions the man's exclusive right to acquire and exercise power by means of crime and violence.

The story's development proves Rosy's determination as she becomes known as 'The Queen of Palermo', pursuing goals of self-affirmation and leadership in the traditionally male-dominated organization of Mafia criminality. It is important in this connection to note that Rosy Abate's metamorphosis into a Mafia woman – or rather, if you adopt the character's point of view, the emerging of her true Mafia identity – does not involve the loss or discarding of personal agency and individuality, to be subordinated to the collective identity of *Cosa nostra* and the gender norms of the criminal underworld. For Rosy, the painful process of becoming a Mafia woman does not merely constitute a passing from innocence to guilt, but a formative stage during which she develops a sense of individuality and will to empowerment, along with cynicism, astuteness and deceitfulness. The young girl who used to identify her self-realization in being a good wife, a good mother and a good cook metamorphoses into an ambitious, assertive, entrepreneurial woman who is not content to be part of a powerful and illegal organization in the submissive and ancillary role reserved for females. She wants to be the boss, and she knows a woman can do it. Hence, a character like Rosy does not only infringe the gender precepts and prescriptions of conventional society; she also, perhaps more importantly, challenges and subverts from within the gendered rules of Mafia masculinist power.

Explicitly and repeatedly, the serial gives an account of the resistance and opposition encountered by Rosy Abate in her ascent to the heights of Palermo's Mafia: scornful and vulgar comments; rejections in the style of Tony Soprano ('I do not make deals with women' ['La talpa è Alfiere?/Alfiere is the Mole?' 2009]); indignation at the subversion of the 'natural' principles of male dominance ('Is the world turning upside down? Now this female wants me to answer to her?' ['La talpa è Alfiere?/Alfiere is the Mole?' 2009]). In parallel, the narrative is at pains to credit her astuteness and mistrust, her gritty ability to impose and assert herself, her skill in forming alliances, the broad scope of her expansion strategies ('she studied in America, she thinks big' ['Il ritorno di Ivan/Ivan Returns' 2010]), and other gifts of mind and character that eventually earn Rosy acceptance and respect in the Mafia environment. Nevertheless, the statements of appreciation towards her are deeply imbued with masculinist culture, for which there are no values outside masculinity. 'My sister is a man, she has a woman's body but she is a man' ('Il ritorno di Ivan/Ivan Returns' 2010), her older brother states, as he would be unable to surrender the command of the family to a woman; whereas even a rival boss is compelled to admit 'it must be said you have the balls' ('Braccata/Hunted' 2010).

Rosy Abate aims to be the incarnation of the modern face of the entrepreneurial Mafia that is fully integrated in the market logics of the neo-liberalist world economy; she wins over her allies with the promise of the huge profits that the organization could derive from the reconversion into an economic and financial holding company ('we make money and others will make crime' ['Braccata/Hunted' 2010]). Nonetheless, she is not afraid of resorting to the abusive and violent forms of Mafia power: threats, blackmail, torture, attacks and murders, commissioned or executed with her own hands. She does not hesitate to kill the man she loves so as to avenge betrayal and humiliation; having heard that the Colombian drug dealer whose lover she became while in hiding wants to get rid of her, she lures him into a honey trap and gets him strangled by a killer while he is still lying in her arms. She also displays Machiavellian astuteness in eliminating her most powerful enemies and orders massacres. The serial derives new inspiration from *The Godfather* (Coppola, 1972) to show, in cross-cutting, a deadly attack launched by Rosy on a rival clan, while her son ('Rifiuti tossici/Toxic Waste' 2011) is being baptized in a church; the ritual promise 'I renounce Satan for ever', spoken by the mother and the spiritual godmother of the little boy, echoes around the baptismal font while the menfolk of the Mafia 'godmother' are massacring their rivals.

The toxic image of Rosy Abate with blood-stained hands would certainly be unbearable in its dogged emphasis on a female incarnation of human ruthlessness, were it not also a marker of the fullness of the power acquired and exercised by the character – the power of life and death – and had the narrative not offered other ways of being Rosy (other possible objects of identification or dis-identification): namely the defeated and suffering subject. The narrative structure of the classic gangster story is a rise-and-fall trajectory: therefore, Rosy Abate's criminal career is told in *Antimafia Squad* as a repeated sequence of rises and falls. Time and again she engages in pursuing ambitious plans – the gaining or regaining of a position of power in the Mafia organization, the appropriation of huge sums of money extracted from other criminal groups, the monopoly of a new and lucrative illegal market – that she manages to achieve with clear determination and variable degrees of force. But even when she wins, her achievements do not last long; there is always a police operation or the opening of a new front on the war between the clans that provoke a (temporary) defeat, so that much of Rosy's life is spent in fleeing, hiding, running abroad, and in criminal trials, imprisonment, escapes, psychiatric hospitals and finally convents. Interestingly enough, the defeats end up by constituting a further indicator of the strength and endurance of an indomitable character who never surrenders and is not afraid to start again and keep fighting to regain leadership and accomplish revenge. Rosy is a fighter and, in this respect, she doubtlessly inspires admiration.

The Suffering Mother

Nevertheless, with a good dose of sadism (not unfamiliar in the melodramatic mode), the narrative inflicts on the protagonist the most tragic and irreversible defeat on her identity's most vulnerable front: her motherhood. The adoring mother of a little boy, born from her relationship with the man who she had loved and then killed before she knew she was pregnant, Rosy Abate has to face the motherhood dilemma of every career woman (admittedly, an anomalous one): how to be a good mother and a Mafia boss. Maternity does not make Rosy give up being a Mafia woman, but it impels her to reshape her business strategies: for example, by exporting toxic waste to the Third World so as not to poison Sicilian soil 'because our children must grow up healthy' ('Minacce/ Threats' 2011). Above all, having experienced the harshness and risks as well as the heady resources of power and money conferred by a Mafia career, she is determined that her son shall have a different life. Here, there is no reappraisal or repentance on the part of the protagonist ('the Abate family does not repent' ['La lista/The List' 2011]), only a strong maternal desire to create the conditions of a clean and safe life for her son. Rosy is narratively positioned on a slippery ridge that makes it difficult for her motherhood performance to be labelled in unequivocal terms. On one hand, the love of her child and her wish to remove him from the family's criminal heritage, recreating for him the conditions of innocence of her own infancy and youth, make Rosy a good mother according to the canons of mainstream culture – although from the perspective of that mainstream culture she could be regarded as an aberrant mother simply by reason of being a Mafia woman, a woman who caresses her child with blood-stained hands. On the other hand, Rosy turns out to be a deviant mother when measured against the yardstick of the criminal subculture that sanctions the mother's primary duty of inculcating the codes of honour, *omertà* and vengeance into their children and ensuring the handing down of Mafia rules from one generation to the next. Once more, Rosy's choice indicates that her individuality prevails over adhesion to the collective identity of the Mafia community. Driven by her maternal desire to keep her son safe, she goes so far as to renounce her parental responsibility and entrust the care of the child to the loved and hated policewoman Claudia Mares.

The complex and intense relationship between the policewoman and the Mafia woman – a mixture of attraction and hostility, trust and jealousy, tenderness and rage, and, from a certain moment onwards, a shared maternal concern – is one of the underlying themes of *Antimafia Squad*. Rosy owes her life to Claudia, who saved her from an attack in which her parents died, and the two women were friends during Rosy's 'age of innocence'. When they find themselves fighting on opposing sides of the law, each of them becomes for the other an implacable enemy, the antagonist in a fight with no quarter that almost assumes the traits of an obsession and sometimes expresses itself in the form of reciprocal violence, both physical and symbolic. Yet, the antagonism between the policewoman and the Mafia woman does not sever the bind of intense affection between Claudia and Rosy; the link between the two strong and unconventional but conflicting female personalities is confirmed at each moment to be as problematic and painful as it is deep and irrevocable.[6] Claudia remains the only person in the world that Rosy can trust, the only one to whom she feels she can entrust her son.

Giving up one's own children to ensure that they have a better life is a sacrificial gesture that is typical of the heroines of the maternal melodrama (Kaplan 1987; Viviani 1987; Williams 1984). The genre has been obsolete for quite some time, having largely lost the capacity to resonate with the present-day conceptions of motherhood. Nevertheless, the maternal melodrama is a two-faced genre in its portrayal of women: motherhood is celebrated in its altruistic and sacrificial attitude, but, at the same time, the woman-mother is punished for some sin of hers: 'she pay[s] for her sin' (Viviani 1987: 94) through the punishment (self-inflicted) of separation from her children.

Through the maternal theme, *Antimafia Squad* introduces a punitive moral perspective from which Rosy Abate's criminal ascent is regarded not so much, or not only, in terms of a sequence of crimes to be expiated in accordance with the law, but also as an ambitious life project whose achievement entails and demands the price of renouncing any other claim. The guilt rests in wanting too much – Mafia power and the joys of motherhood – and Rosy has to atone for this. Rosy herself is aware of the ineluctable nemesis which her *hubris* has to confront; when the little boy falls ill with leukaemia (and Claudia fights for the mother, who is in prison, to be allowed to donate bone marrow to save his life), she sombrely asserts, '[d]ivine nemesis hits the person who has sinned to punish her for her wrongdoing' ('Il rapimento di Rosy/Rosy kidnapping' 2012).

A logic of counterpoint comes into play, as the appropriation of roles and action modalities historically associated with masculinity entails that the woman will be expropriated of the quintessential prerogative of femininity. In this connection, it has been pointed out that narratives where feminine empowerment is thematized and enhanced often betray a punitive tendency towards female characters, thus deploying forms of containment aimed at warning women that 'they can't have it all'. 'In appropriating the male gaze the female "hero" has stepped into the "masculine" position and for this she will be punished both narratively and by the loss of "feminine" characteristics' (Thornham 2007: 69).

In *Antimafia Squad*, the punishment, if this is the case, goes well beyond the painful separation of the mother from her child. Rosy will be deprived of her child forever: he will be abducted and then killed in cold blood by a heinous criminal figure.[7] In these circumstances, the distressing ordeal to which Rosy is subjected is made particularly harsh; in fact, not only does the infanticide happen almost under her eyes, but the mother is denied the comfort of giving the boy a last kiss because his body is carried away by the murderer to be buried in an unknown location. If only she had arrived earlier – here the script has recourse to the powerful emotional device of 'too late' (Neale 1986) – she could perhaps have saved her son. In the despairing reaction of the mother, given over entirely to primal unrestrained savage body language, the narrative achieves the apex of melodramatic pathos.

Such merciless cruelty towards the protagonist transcends the limits of a punitive nemesis and introduces a different perspective that the narrative itself is at pains to explain a bit later. In a state of shock, in which she will remain for a long time and run the risk of insanity, Rosy is taken to hospital; male and female detectives standing in the corridor and watching through a glass partition see the convulsions that are still shaking her body, although she is under sedation. To stay with the theme of maternal melodrama, the two characters looking at the inside of a room through a glass partition recall the final scene of *Stella Dallas* (Vidor 1937) – although the role of the mother is reversed here: she is not a spectator, but an object to be looked at – and they can be seen as the figures of spectators embodying specific subject positions. Watching the signs of suffering emanating from Rosy Abate's body, the woman becomes the interpreter of the punitive sight: 'She is a murderer, it's right that she should suffer the consequences' ('Alleanze/Alliances' 2013); but her male companion is upset and retorts 'This is too much, even for someone like her'. The overwhelming excess of grief, even with regard to the enormity of the guilt of 'someone like her', thus suggests that a competing subject position is possible, and that Rosy's multifaceted identity – the career Mafia woman, the indomitable fighter, the forever friend/enemy, the sacrificial mother – now allows for a further classification: the victim of destiny's cruel persecution, a true melodramatic heroine with whom, as viewers, we cannot but empathize.

The last episode of the sixth season ends with a close-up shot of Rosy who, taken from behind, turns round slowly and gives an oblique and enigmatic gaze to the camera: maybe she will come back in a new shape.

'Donna Imma': The First Lady of the Neapolitan Underworld

The nuclear Savastano family, small in size – husband and wife, and a post-adolescent son – but great on power, lives on the outskirts of Naples in a luxurious villa,[8] whose vast interiors are decorated and furnished in a heavy baroque taste, in an exorbitant display of the wealth and prominence of the household. A high wall surrounds the entire building, concealing it from the gaze of the outside world. This walled spatiality, which serves to assure the family's protection and secrecy, and favours the invisibility that helps to create an aura of power, also stands for a metaphorical allusion to the narrative's choice to preserve the story from the intrusion of a viewpoint that is external and alien to the criminal underworld. Inspired by Roberto Saviano's best-selling novel *Gomorra* (2006), already adapted for the big screen by the award-winning director Matteo Garrone[9] (2008), *Gomorrah: The Series* tells 'a grimly authentic tale of Naples gangsters' (Collins 2014) from a perspective that is completely internal to the sub-culture of the illegal Camorra system.[10] The violent, merciless world inhabited by the community of characters in *Gomorrah* does not contemplate alternatives or antagonisms that are not ingrained in the conflict-ridden logic of the very system; and it is portrayed and experienced as if it were the only possible world, estranged from and uncaring towards anything beyond the walled horizon of a crime-centred, profit-driven and power-oriented way of life. In this crudely realistic, black- and blue-toned tale – without precedent in Italian storytelling as for the total absence of confrontation or clashes between the forces of good and evil, between heroes and antiheroes[11] – there are no paradises of lost innocence or any mainstream society in the background to provide the yardstick of normalcy and morality against which to measure deviant behaviour; and the punishing paradigm governing the final fate of 'guilty' women, found in melodrama, is substantially deconstructed, while punishments, losses and deaths are an everyday reality of a permanent war.

The character Imma Savastano takes shape in this context. It is worth noting that the role of women in Naples' illegal economy has always been of great importance (as the episode of *The Sopranos* cited at the beginning of this chapter acknowledges in its own way). The urban, rather than rural, origins of the Camorra and its roots in the Neapolitan working class, characterized by a low level of gender segregation, allow for a more egalitarian allocation of male and female roles. Unlike other criminal organizations, women within the Camorra system can hold senior positions of leadership up to the point of becoming the feared and respected *capesse* (female bosses) of the clans, endowed with the same privileges and the opportunity to wield the power and violence attributed to men (Zaccaria 2009). *Gomorrah* recognizes this sort of 'breaking of the glass ceiling' in Neapolitan crime syndicates.

As the wife of the revered and obeyed 'don' of a clan that is dominant in drug trafficking, and the mother of a young boy who is expected to be his father's successor, Imma Savastano – 'Donna Imma' according to the honorific title conferred on a respected woman in Southern Italy – holds the position of first lady in the clan's social hierarchy. She performs this role with the modulated imperious attitude of a person who is accustomed to enjoying the privileges of her rank, sometimes standing beside her husband in meetings of the close circle of his faithful – who pay her homage and abstain from using vulgar language in her presence – and observing in all circumstances an apparent impassivity that makes her face resemble an enigmatic mask, disquieting and subtly intimidating. As is expected from the wife of a boss, and also from one blessed with the physical attractions of a mature lady, Imma displays a flashy and expensive elegance: a tangible testimony, like the residence and furnishings, to the high standing of the family to which she belongs.

The narrative of *Gomorrah* is not concerned with the female identity in transition. Imma Savastano is narratively constructed from the start as a figure who is fully integrated in the society and culture of the criminal underworld: the discreet but unequivocal signs of a sentimental and erotic relationship with her husband, evident in many scenes, also suggest that she has fulfilled female aspirations of happiness in married life. But she is less happy as a mother. Far from embodying an archetypal model of nurturing and fiercely protective Mediterranean motherhood, Imma is strict with, and lacking in affection for, her son Genny; clearly disappointed and irritated by her clumsy and immature boy, spoilt by his father's indulgence, she thinks that he is inadequate and unprepared to inherit family power. Imma's main concern is of a 'dynastic' nature; the fragility of her son, who is emotionally and physically vulnerable by reason of his lack of experience and his spinelessness, worries her in particular because it could mean the end of the Savastano hegemony. 'You must toughen up, you are a Savastano' ('Sangue africano/African Blood' 2014), she reminds him in icy tones when she finds him retching after having participated for the first time in a bloodthirsty 'punitive expedition'. A little later on in the story, Imma will behave like an authentic phallic and manipulative mother (Kaplan 1992), sending Genny to Honduras to negotiate an agreement with a drug cartel, but actually to stand unknowingly for a hostage to guarantee the contract. We have here the reversal of the paradigm of the self-sacrificing mother, since Imma knows that she is exposing her son to mortal danger and yet she is willing to sacrifice him: she has taken this possibility into account and reacts with her habitual impassivity when the news reaches her that a dismembered body has been found in the area where Genny is held hostage by the Honduras drug lords. Months later she will be glad to welcome the return of her son, a survivor of the ordeal that has transformed him into an arrogant and violent individual, hungry for power, the worthy Savastano heir she has always wanted. An aberrant mother? Doubtless, from a mainstream culture perspective and without implying adhesion to a patriarchal vision of idealized motherhood; from her personal yet culturally inflected perspective, Imma is instead certain that she is acting like a good mother for the good of her son, and proudly claims responsibility for sending him to Honduras 'to learn, and it seems to me that it has worked' ('Scheda bianca/Unmarked Ballot Paper' 2014).

In this case, as in others, Imma is acting without her husband's knowledge in her position of regent of the clan, a role that she assumes after the arrest and detention in solitary confinement of the Savastano boss. The Camorra criminal organization, as I have indicated earlier, allows women to fill leadership positions and, in particular, to take the place of males in the family, should compelling (and in truth frequent) circumstances such as arrest, hiding or death open up a power vacuum. Unlike Rosy Abate, Imma does not encounter gender-related obstacles when it comes to taking her husband's place at the head of the clan.

The status shift from first lady to acting boss brings into the open the main trait of Imma Savastano's personality: her taste for power. Although she formally acts on behalf of her husband, who still rules his territory from prison, and paves the way for her son, her prompt seizing of the opportunity to set and enforce her own strategic agenda inclines our imagination to go back to her life as first lady: a cherished and respected, even heard boss's spouse, yet an intelligent ambitious woman who for years has had to content herself with an ancillary position in relation to her husband, basking in his reflected glory. It is all too evident that Imma is seizing the chance to satisfy a long-repressed will for power, the long-held desire to be something else besides a wife and a mother, to be a leader in her own right. If a large part of Imma's behaviour makes sense only in the context of crime-inflected gender norms, her achieved aspiration to gain freedom of decision and action strikes a chord and resonates with women's (feminist?) expectations well beyond the walled spatiality of the Camorra world. One does not need to be a criminal woman to understand and to wish to make the difference between marrying power and exercising it oneself. It is not by chance that Imma's first decisions made in her new capacity of acting boss are diametrically opposed to those that her husband would have made. She exposes their son to a harsh learning experience in order to rectify the damage caused by his father's indulgence; and she undermines the status of the young up-and-coming gangster, whom her husband has earmarked to be second in line of succession, by relegating him to low-level duties.

But Imma can also be compassionate and use her power for good and to do justice, taking the law into her own hands. She offers a (illegal) job to a disabled young woman – 'if you want, you can', the girl's mother says confidently – and takes under her wing a lesbian girl who is threatened and in the end killed by a merciless usurer. The man will be executed on Imma's order.

Like Rosy Abate, Imma Savastano does not hesitate to resort to homicidal violence (though never with her own hands). This is to be expected of a female Camorra leader, but here the narrative is at pains to take an explicit position against the discursive construction of femininity and violence as polar opposites and to let Imma address the following statement in a business meeting with male representatives of various clans:

I know what you are thinking. You divide the world between those who do not kill and those who do. And since I am a woman, you believe that I belong to the first category. You are wrong'.

('Roulette spagnola/Spanish Roulette' 2014)

Nobody could doubt this after witnessing the meeting between Imma and the business consultant who is guilty of having squandered the clan's money in bad investments. Seated at a restaurant table, Imma orders the desperate weeping man to commit suicide (so as to avert the suspicions of the police) and at the same time continues to calmly enjoy her plate of *spaghetti e vongole*. The graceful care with which she extracts the clams one by one from their shells with the points of her fingers, while pronouncing the death sentence in a conversational tone, makes the scene an iconic marker of this impressive character of assertive, intimidating and power-oriented antiheroine.

The young gangster who she demoted will get his vengeance by having her killed. To consider this as a punishment would probably be a moralistic interpretation, alien to the purposes of a narrative that refrains from suggesting the moral criteria for administering rewards and punishments.

Conclusion

The unusual importance accorded to leading female characters who are endowed with outstanding personality and unprecedented power to wield command within male criminal worlds allows us to identify in *Antimafia Squad* and *Gomorrah*, if not a watershed in the history of Italian TV drama, an essential reference point for discussions on new and varied portrayals of femininity that challenge persistent male domination in the very terrain of the most testosterone-driven genres.

Nonetheless, *Antimafia Squad* and *Gomorrah* cannot be defined as narratives of declared feminist inspiration. The increasing media visibility of women taking control of Mafia and Camorra clans; the greater freedom of creative experimentation – compared to the restraints placed by cultural policies and by the family audience of public television – which can benefit mainstream commercial networks and, still more, niche satellite channels; the influence of the kind of banal feminism or 'gender mainstreaming', in Angela McRobbie's definition (2009), by now entered into common sense; the awareness that young and young-adult mixed-gender viewers (an elective target of the two programmes) are by now thoroughly familiar with American television programmes, which are full of female characters more daring and diversified than those in Italian programmes: all these factors, taken together, have most probably encouraged the construction of the unusual and controversial portrayals of women offered by *Antimafia Squad* and *Gomorrah*. Furthermore, part of what has made Rosy and Imma so compelling must be ascribed to the actresses Giulia Michelini and Maria Pia Calzone, who inhabited their characters deeply: thus confirming that 'actresses have real power over their characters' (Skirrow 1987: 168). Indeed, even texts that emanate from concepts unconcerned with or unrelated to the cultural and political issue of gender representation 'may nonetheless be part of a feminist project' (D'Acci 1994: 9).

Obviously, we have to be cautious in uncritically embracing a teleological 'narrative of progress' (Harris 2006: 1; Nelson 2000; Ball 2012) to account for the phenomena of feminization that run through present-day televisual storytelling, and still more in making an unreflective conflation between feminization and feminism. However, it is less a matter of charting the indicators of feminism in a given text or programme than of enacting a 'reading strategy' (Sheridan 1988) aimed at exploring the disposition of the text to allow plural interpretations: some of which may perhaps discern meanings that are consonant with feminist ideas and positions. With regard to the reading strategy, I have already mentioned the 'dual hermeneutics' above. *Antimafia Squad*, in particular, offers a range of opportunities to practise this. The narrative, for example, undoubtedly supports a critical reading of the misogynist and sexist ideology that demands women to atone for the 'guilt' of their ambition and success. Yet, it equally allows an alternative interpretation which, in the dramaturgical practice of putting characters under as much stress as they can bear, identifies the possible conditions for an appraisal of women's untiring and indomitable capacity to resist, as against the stereotype of women's fragility and need for protection. And still, as regards the point that is most exposed to controversy and dispute, we can criticize the masculinization of the criminal characters Rosy Abate and Imma Savastano, arguing that female agency and empowerment are somehow constructed by appropriating masculine codes of behaviour. This does not preclude acknowledging the potential for resistance, if not indeed for subversion towards male power (Mäntymäki 2013) inherent in female agency that diverges from the script of feminine norms – and this is certainly the case with the powerful Mafia women.

Rosy Abate and Imma Savastano are complex and recombinant female figures. They are each a 'different combination of masculine and feminine attributes' (Inness 1999: 88) and their appropriation of socially constructed male traits and behaviour 'broadens the range of feminine gender markers' (Fine 2012: 156), thus calling into question and subverting the binary structure of gender identifications. Each of them has to encounter irreparable losses – the loss of a child (Rosy) or of her own life (Imma) – but both of them achieve the fulfilment of their desire to be 'something else besides a mother'.

References

Akass, K. and McCabe, J. (2002), 'Beyond Bada Bing! Negotiating female narrative authority in The Sopranos', in D. Lavery (ed.), *This Thing of Ours*, New York: Columbia University Press, pp. 146–161.

'Alleanze/Alliance' (2013), Beniamino Catena, dir., *Squadra antimafia/Antimafia Squad*, Season 5, Episode 5, 14 October, Milano: Mediaset.

Ball, V. (2012), 'The "feminization" of British television and the re-traditionalization of gender', *Feminist Media Studies*, 12: 2, pp. 248–264.

Bourdieu, P. (1984), *Distinction: A Social Critique of Judgement and Taste*, Harvard: Harvard University Press.

—— (2001), *Masculine Domination*, Stanford: Stanford University Press.

'Braccata/Hunted' (2010), Beniamino Catena, dir., *Squadra antimafia/Antimafia Squad*, Season 2, Episode 8, 10 June, Milano: Mediaset.

Brooks, P. (1976), *The Melodramatic Imagination*, Yale: Yale University Press.
Brunsdon, C. (1998), 'Structures of anxiety: Recent british television crime fiction', *Screen*, 39: 3, pp. 223–243.
—— (2013), 'Crime series, women police, and fuddy-duddy feminism', *Feminist Media Studies*, 13: 3, pp. 375–394.
Buonanno, M. (2012), *Italian TV Drama and Beyond: Stories from the Soil, Stories from the Sea*, Bristol and Chicago: Intellect.
—— (2014), 'Donne al comando fra action e melodramma. Il caso di *Squadra antimafia*', in M. Buonanno, *Il prisma dei generi. Immagini di donne in TV*, Milano: FrancoAngeli, pp. 49–77.
Collins, A. (2014), 'Gomorrah box-set review-a grimly authentic tale of Naples gangsters', *The Guardian*, https://www.google.it/search?num=100&site=&source=hp&q=gomorra+premiato+a+cannes&oq=gomorra%2Bcannes&gs_l=hp.1.2.0i30l2j0i8i30l3.1625.5062.0.8753.15.15.0.0.0.0.181.1627.0j13.13.0....0...1c.1.64.hp..3.12.1460.0.BY1WzKdyIDQ. Accessed June 2015.
Coppola, F. F. (1972, 1974, 1990), *The Godfather I, II, III*, Paramount Pictures, The Coppola Company, Zoetrope Studios.
Creeber, G. (2001), 'Cigarettes and alcohol: Investigating gender, genre, and gratification in prime suspect', *Television & New Media*, 2: 2, pp. 149–166.
D'Acci, J. (1994), *Defining Women: Television and The Case of 'Cagney and Lacey'*, Chapel Hill: University of North Carolina Press.
Distretto di polizia/Police District (2000–2010, Italy: Canale 5).
Fiandaca, G. (ed.) (2007), *Women and the Mafia: Female Roles in Organized Crime Structures*, New York: Springer.
Fine, K. (2012), 'She hits like a man, but she kisses like a girl: TV heroines, femininity, violence, and intimacy', *Western American Literature*, 47: 2, pp. 152–173.
Garrone, M. (2008), *Gomorra*, Fandango, Rai Cinema.
Gledhill, C. (1987), 'The melodramatic field: An investigation', in C. Gledhill (ed.), *Home Is Where the Heart Is*, London: BFI Publishing, pp. 5–39.
Gomorra: La serie/Gomorrah: The Series (2014–ongoing, Italy: Sky Atlantic).
Gribaudi, G. and Marmo, M. (eds) (2010), *Meridiana. Rivista di storia e scienze sociali – Donne di mafia*, 67, special issue, Roma: Viella.
Harris, G. (2006), *Beyond Representation*, Manchester: Manchester University Press.
'Il rapimento di Rosy/Rosy Kidnapping' (2012), Beniamino Catena, dir., *Squadra antimafia/Antimafia Squad*, Season 4, Episode 1, 10 September, Milano: Mediaset.
'Il ritorno di Ivan/Ivan Returns' (2010), Beniamino Catena, dir., *Squadra antimafia/Antimafia Squad*, Season 2, Episode 1, 27 April, Milano: Mediaset.
Ingrascì, O. (2007), *Donne d'onore. Storie di mafia al femminile*, Milano: Bruno Mondadori.
Inness, S. A. (1999), *Tough Girls*, Philadelphia: University of Pennsylvania Press.
—— (ed.) (2004), *Action Chicks: New Images of Tough Women in Popular Culture*, New York: Palgrave Macmillan.
Jermyn, D. (2008), 'Women with a mission: Lynda La Plante, DCI Jane Tennison and the reconfiguration of TV crime drama', in C. Brunsdon and L. Spigel (eds), *Feminist Television Criticism: A Reader*, 2nd ed, Maidenhead: Mcgraw-Hill Open University Press, pp. 57–71.
—— (2010), *Prime Suspects*, London: BFI.

Johnson, M. L. (ed.) (2007), *Third Wave Feminism and Television*, London: I.B. Tauris.

Kaplan, E. A. (1987), 'Mothering, feminism and representation: The maternal melodrama in the woman's film 1910-1940', in C. Gledhill (ed.), *Home Is Where the Heart Is*, London: BFI Publishing, pp. 113–137.

Kaplan, E. A. (1992), *Motherhood and Representation: The Mother in Popular Culture and Melodrama*, London: Routledge.

'La lista/The List' (2011), Beniamino Catena, dir., *Squadra antimafia/Antimafia Squad*, Season 3, Episode 8, 27 May, Milano: Mediaset.

LaPlace, M. (1987), 'Producing and consuming the woman's film', in C. Gledhill (ed.), *Home Is Where the Heart Is*, London: BFI Publishing, pp. 131–167.

'La talpa è Alfiere?/Is Alfiere the Mole?' (2009), Pier Belloni, dir., *Squadra antimafia/Antimafia Squad*, Season 1, Episode 4, 21 April, Milano: Mediaset.

Larke-Walsh, G. S. (2010), *Screening the Mafia*, Jefferson and London: McFarland and Co.

'L'incontro/The Meeting' (2009), Pier Belloni, dir., *Squadra antimafia/Antimafia Squad*, Season 1, Episode 3, 14 April, Milano: Mediaset.

Lotz, A. (2006), *Redesigning Women: Television After the Network Era*, Urbana and Chicago: University of Illinois Press.

—— (2014), *Cable Guys: Television and Masculinities in the 21st Century*, New York and London: New York University Press.

Mäntymäki, T. (2013), 'Women who kill men: Gender, agency and subversion in Swedish crime novels', *European Journal of Women's Studies*, 20: 4, pp. 441–454.

McCaughey, M. and King, N. (eds) (2001), *Reel Knockouts: Violent Women in the Movies*, Austin: University of Texas Press.

McRobbie, A. (2009), *The Aftermath of Feminism*, London: Sage.

Messenger, C. (2002), *The Godfather and American Culture: How the Corleonese Became 'Our Gang'*, Albany: State University of New York Press.

'Minacce/Threats' (2011), Beniamino Catena, dir., *Squadra antimafia/Antimafia Squad*, Season 3, Episode 3, 22 April, Milano: Mediaset.

Mittell, J. (2015), *Complex TV: The Poetics of Contemporary Television Storytelling*, New York: New York University Press.

Mizejewski, L. (2004), *Hardboiled & High Heeled: The Woman Detective in Popular Culture*, London: Routledge.

Neale, S. (1986), 'Melodrama and tears', *Screen*, 27: 6, pp. 6–23.

Nelson, R. (2000), 'Performing (Wo)manoeuvres: The progress of gendering in TV drama', in B. Carson and M. Llewellyn-Jones (eds), *Frames and Fictions on Television*, Exeter: Intellect Books, pp. 62–74.

Neroni, H. (2005), *The Violent Woman*, Albany: State University of New York Press.

O'Rawe, C. (2011), 'Roberta Torre's Angela: The mafia and the "woman's film"', in D. Renga (ed.), *Mafia Movies: A Reader*, Toronto: University of Toronto Press, pp. 329–337.

Rich, A. (1995), *Of Woman Born: Motherhood as Experience and Institution*, New York and London: W.W. Norton & Company.

'Roulette spagnola/Spanish Roulette' (2014), Stefano Sollima, dir., *Gomorrah: The Series*, Season 1, Episode 6, 20 May, Milano: Sky.

'Rifiuti tossici/Toxic Waste' (2011), Beniamino Catena, dir., *Squadra antimafia/Antimafia Squad*, Season 3, Episode 2, 15 April, Milano: Mediaset.

Romanzo criminale/Crime Novel: The Series (2008–2010, Italy: Sky).

'Sangue africano/African Blood' (2014), Stefano Sollima, dir., *Gomorrah: The Series*, Season 1, Episode 4, 17 January, Milano: Sky.

'Scheda bianca/Unmarked Ballot Paper' (2014), Claudio Cupellini, dir., *Gomorrah: The Series*, Season 1, Episode 6, 27 May, Milano: Sky.

'Scontro finale/Final Clash' (2011), Beniamino Catena, dir., *Squadra antimafia/Antimafia Squad*, Season 3, Episode 10, 10 June, Milano: Mediaset.

Sheridan, S. (1988), *Grafts: Feminist Cultural Criticism*, London: Verso.

Singer, B. (1996), 'Female power in the serial-queen melodrama: The etiology of an anomaly', in R. Abel (ed.), *Silent Film*, New Brunswick: Rutgers University Press, pp. 163–193.

Skirrow, G. (1987), 'Women/acting/power', in H. Baeher and G. Dyer (eds), *Boxed In: Women and Television*, New York and London: Pandora, pp. 164–183.

Squadra antimafia/Antimafia Squad (2009–ongoing, Italy: Canale 5).

'Squadra antimafia/Antimafia Squad' (2009), Pier Belloni, dir., *Squadra antimafia/Antimafia Squad*, Season 1, Episode 1, 31 March, Milano: Mediaset.

Tasker, Y. (1993), *Spectacular Bodies: Gender Genre and the Action Cinema*, London: Routledge.

The Sopranos (1999–2007, New York: HBO).

Thornham, S. (2007), *Women, Feminism and Media*, Edinburgh: Edinburgh University Press.

Torre, R. (2002), *Angela*, Movieweb S.p.A., Rita Rusic Co.

Vidor K. (1937), *Stella Dallas*, Samuel Goldwyn Productions.

Viviani, C. (1987), 'Who is without sin? The maternal melodrama in American film, 1930–39', in C. Gledhill (ed.), *Home Is Where the Heart Is*, London: BFI Publishing, pp. 83–99.

White, R (2007), *Violent Femmes: Women as Spies in Popular Culture*, London: Routledge.

Williams, L. (1984), 'Something else besides a mother', *Cinema Journal*, 24: 1, pp. 2–27.

—— (1998), 'Melodrama revised', in N. Browne (ed.), *Refiguring American Film Genres: History and Theory*, Berkeley and Los Angeles: University of California Press, pp. 42–88.

Winspeare, E. (2008), *Galantuomini/Brave men*, Italy: Acaba Produzioni, Rai Cinema.

Zaccaria, A. M. (2009), 'Donne di camorra', in G. Gribaudi, *Traffici criminali. Camorra, mafie e reti internazionali dell'illegalità*, Torino: Bollati Boringhieri.

Notes

1 See Chapter 3 in this collection.

2 The scriptwriter Stefano Bises, who is recognized as the creator of the two characters, said he was intrigued by news about a female regent of a Mafia clan turned state witness, so some elements of her biography were incorporated into the portrait of Rosy Abate. However, regardless of real-life examples, Bises makes the claim that characters of women behaving badly create unique and inspiring opportunities to push the boundaries of the writer's imagination (personal conversation, June 2015. I take the opportunity to thank him for his courteous availability).

3 I am forced to shift this character of flawed heroine, whom I have analyzed at length elsewhere (Buonanno 2014), to the margins of my discourse here, but it is important to note that the complex relationship between the two female friends/enemies is an essential component of the story.
4 Here is the background to the story: Rosy and her three brothers, the children of a Mafia boss who has been defeated and assassinated together with his wife during a war between clans, are forced to flee to the United States. Many years later, the brothers go back to Sicily and regain their position on the Mafia power map. Rosy joins them on the occasion of her marriage, after which she intends to settle in New York for good.
5 The authors of *Antimafia Squad* acknowledge that they drew inspiration, here and elsewhere in the development of the story, from the character of Michael Corleone in *The Godfather*.
6 Nowhere does the narrative make explicit suggestion about an undeclared lesbian love between the two women. But it is perhaps significant that Rosy has sentimental and sexual relationships with the same men that Claudia has loved, one of whom is the father of her son. Furthermore, Rosy pays her last tribute to the mortally wounded Claudia by kissing her on the mouth.
7 This happens after a succession of dramatic events. Claudia dies while once again saving the life of Rosy, who will avenge her by pursuing and killing the assassin (another Mafia woman) before going back to her life in hiding. Some time later, Rosy, at the head of an armed command group, attacks the secret hiding place where the police are guarding her son and takes him with her. But her maternal dream of reinstating the mother-son relationship in a distant land, with new identities, is not destined to come true: the child is abducted and, although Rosy does not hesitate to meet the request for an enormous ransom, murdered.
8 The villa that was rented during the filming had actually belonged to a Camorra boss.
9 Garrone's *Gomorra* was awarded the Grand Prix of the Jury at Cannes film festival in 2008.
10 Note that the Camorra's organization is described by its members as a 'system'.
11 The critical acclaim that accompanied the far-flung international distribution of *Gomorrah: The Series*, sold in more than 50 territories, is almost without precedent for Italian television drama.

Chapter 2

Mafiosa, Monstrous Beauty: Power and Loneliness of a Female Mob Leader

Barbara Villez

Introduction

The main character of the French television series, *Mafiosa*, exemplifies the antiheroine as described in the introduction to this work. In the first episode, she is plunged into the role of the leader of an organized crime clan on the island of Corsica. She assumes the role unapologetically and her life can be seen as the tragic waste of a beautiful young woman whose family, money and studies could have led her to success and happiness. Instead she is the centre of violence and corruption that she accepts unhesitatingly, but she also hates her life.

This chapter seeks to draw a parallel between la Mafiosa and the island on which she lives. Called the island of beauty, Corsica is a favourite vacation spot in France. The landscape is wild, the people colourful yet suspicious. Organized crime cohabits with a separatist movement, both condemning the island to regular violence, so regular that it has become banal. Violence and treachery are constants in Sandra's life as well. Sandra and Corsica reflect and contrast each other. The ambiguous nature of sunny Corsica is echoed in dark Sandra Paoli, seductive but dangerous, complex yet merciless, beautiful but lonely. Sandra possesses all the characteristics of the antiheroine, and Corsica, the perfect backdrop for her, reinforces this image.

From the start, Sandra Paoli (Hélène Fillières) is full of contradictions. Pleading in court, supposedly to save her client from prison, she manages to annoy the judges to the extent that they apply an even stricter sentence. Has she failed? Not really, since the plan was to get an enemy of the clan out of the way. A quick telephone call and a wide grin confirm this and suggest that she can organize her arguments to obtain twisted results in court. At least this is the first impression viewers have of her.

Sandra Paoli is the central character of the Canal Plus series *Mafiosa* (2006–2014). She is an attractive, young lawyer who dresses with subtle feminine elegance. Her pretty long hair, tailored suits and heeled pumps or boots correspond to the model set by fashionable women working in law firms in the American television law series of the last 20 years. After her successful ruse in court in the first scene of the pilot, she drives to meet her uncle François Paoli (Daniel Duval) for lunch in a nearby Corsican village. François Paoli is a clan boss and arrives at the restaurant escorted by nervous bodyguards. As Sandra leaves her car, she hears shots fired and her expression informs viewers that she fears her uncle was the target. She runs to where she was supposed to meet him, only to discover that François has indeed been shot. He will die in her arms. The title of the series and the first scenes of François arriving at the restaurant in the company of muscular unsmiling men on the lookout inform viewers that they are about to embark on a series set in the bed of Mafia crime in Corsica. François Paoli was head of the clan and his niece, Sandra, who adored him, will spend little narrative time on the 'right' side of the law.

Sandra's brother, Jean-Michel Paoli (Thierry Neuvic), worked closely with François and because of his relatively high position in the clan, legitimately expects to succeed his uncle as boss. Jean-Michel is married to a greedy and jealous Marie-Luce (Caroline Baehr). They have one feisty teenage daughter, Carmen (Phareelle Onoyan) at the beginning of the series, and before the end of season 1, a new baby boy, Matteo. Marie-Luce will never be a major antiheroine because she will only last into season 2 and also because – typical of fictional Mafia wives – she spends most of her time complaining and gambling. She is totally powerless and will do anything to protect Jean-Michel and keep him with her. This makes it easy for the police to manipulate her, which leads nervous clansmen in the second season to keep her quiet for good.

At the lawyer's office, in a scene that brings a first major twist to the story, François' will is read, and this scene sets up the context for the rest of the series. In his last testament, François has designated Sandra as his successor to run the clan. Sandra is as surprised as everyone else and takes several sequences following this scene to decide whether or not to accept the enormous responsibility François has placed on her, as well as the sacrifices that will go with it. Marie-Luce lets out all her jealous anger that serves to give a context to one of the important themes of the show: family. Sandra tells Jean-Michel that he is the natural leader of the clan and that she feels ill equipped to run the business. Of course, were she to refuse, there would be no series. Thus, as expected, she takes on the challenge to lead a gang of mobsters on an island notoriously suffering from violence, crime and separatist terrorism.

The producers and writers of the show[1] took their inspiration from the situation of this 'Ile of Beauty' where vendettas among criminal clans or between the police and nationalist groups abound. Real events are the source of fictional incidents in the series and even the name Paoli goes back to a famous local family. Filippo Antonio Pasquale Paoli was a political leader of the independent Corsican state in the eighteenth century. He was a principal contributor to the constitution of the 'Republic of Corsica'. The independence of Corsica from Genoa had long been a disputed subject and seeing that they were losing control over the island, Genoa secretly sold it to the French who announced the annexation of the island in 1768. Paoli led, and lost, a guerrilla war against France. Some descendants of his family have remained members of active separatist factions to this day. Pierre Paoli, for example, the national secretary of the Corsica Libera Party, was held in preventive detention for many months in 2012 during an investigation of his implication in a series of bombings all over Corsica on the eve of a local holiday, celebrating the Immaculate Conception, particularly observed by the nationalists.

Sandra is a woman struggling to assert her authority in a macho environment. Her loyalty and determination are often questioned, leading her to betray family in order to gain the confidence of the clan. Violent crimes motivated by power takeovers or misjudged treachery serve as a backdrop of each episode, which is a parallel to the reality of the island of Corsica, constantly plagued by both political and criminal violence. The show, which ended in 2014, was sold to 61 countries including Russia and Italy where Mafia stories are quite familiar. The BBC brought the series to the UK where it shared audience popularity with *Spiral* (French title, *Engrenages*, 2005–ongoing), another Canal Plus success. Contrary to what viewers could expect from the first scenes of the pilot, Sandra Paoli is almost never torn between the two sides of the law she straddles at the beginning of the series. However, her struggle to command an army of men unable to understand why she does not simply remain in the kitchen, or in bed, both echo and contradict the realities of the world of organized crime as well as the drama of Corsica.

Through the Window

In reality, women have been gang bosses for years. Often they have become stern clan leaders in order to stand in for a husband or brother, incarcerated or in flight. In some cases, they took the reins when their men were assassinated. A 2009 article in the French news magazine, *Express* (Broussard et al. 2009: 28–29), documented the history of some of these *mafiose* in Italy, Mexico, Nigeria and Australia who fill in during the absence of their men and then are reluctant to give up their leadership again.

In frequent cases, young women are married off to seal alliances between two families or end a feud. Young women, and even older women, capable of rousing less suspicion and crossing borders more easily unnoticed, have been assigned to transport drugs, pass messages or receive instructions to transmit to their husbands' or fathers' collaborators. Italian judges have long been reluctant to convict women associated with the Mafia. Reproducing stereotypical opinions, they have considered it impossible for these women to be active and willing gang members. Many judges have refused to believe that women count for anything in the organization of these clans and therefore could not be responsible for crimes they committed (Padovani 2009: 47). Actually, the majority of these 'mamas' are the real source of family values: loyalty, respect and obedience to the elders. The *Express* article further reveals that because the younger generation has obtained higher education degrees, daughters are more often invited to participate in business decisions than their mothers were.

One could expect for Sandra Paoli's legal training to have prepared her for the family's business activities, but strangely she does not make very wise decisions. Numerous wrong moves bring more trouble than money. For example, she enters into an alliance with a rival drug dealer to import Asian products that bring down both the police and the family on her back. She runs for political office in Corsica and gets involved in corrupt elections where even ballots of the dead are counted. This is one of several examples of how Corsican reality is intertwined with the fictional narrative, since such votes have been known to contribute to political successes in the past. At another moment, Sandra negotiates with an important member of the separatist movement, but her promise is false and this makes her a target for the nationalists on the island.

Sandra's biggest challenge, however, is imposing her authority on the macho universe she must take over: the Paoli clan. The men think it is crazy for a woman to be their boss and they are extremely wary of her ability to be their leader or to measure up to the standard of her uncle François. What does she know about the business? Does she have the money to carry out the operations? Does she understand the rules? They express their doubts about her in numerous scenes, sometimes confronting her, sometimes talking among themselves behind her back. 'Does Miss Paoli have the means to satisfy her ambitions?' 'I have the means, she answers. In 24 hours this cargo will be in my hands' ('Episode 1.8' 2007). As of season 3, secondary characters who work with Sandra, especially Tony (Eric Fraticelli) and Manu (Frédéric Graziani)[2] zigzag between collaborating with her, following orders and then refusing to obey her, considering that she has totally gone mad. They even plan to kill her in season 4, but this fails in what, by this point, has become unsurprising chaos. The police, who had been tracking all this and savouring the idea of the gang taking each other out, are suddenly ordered by their superior to intervene. They join the chase on a typically sinuous Corsican road, arrest Sandra and actually save her life. In addition, Manu has just had a heart attack, thus putting an end to the plan to kill Sandra. Chaos seems to be run of the mill in the clan: spontaneous shootings follow unfounded suspicions of members of rival gangs. In season 4, a policeman who has several accounts to settle burns Tony's car and murders one of his friends, making Tony speculate on who is responsible and then retaliate. This leads to further retaliations. In the midst of what often become scenes of comic discussions, Sandra's men, and the police watching them, all seem amateur bad boys. Sandra, in comparison, is the darkest figure, humourless, changing and the most complex.

Quite early into season 1, Sandra shows herself capable of dishonesty, cruelty and extreme violence, which, as Yvonne Jewkes notes, is not actually unusual among women criminals, despite media portrayals of female perpetrators (Jewkes 2004: 128). Sandra's spontaneous violence and ill-advised alliances lead her to make very bad mistakes. The elders of the clan criticize her constantly. When she asks for help in season 1, she is told: 'Half your men are in jail, you keep making dumb mistakes, prove to me that you can get out of this mess and we'll do business together' ('Edpisode 1.1' 2006). In season 3 (3.5) one of the elders, a loyal family friend and collaborator, chides her for playing at being boss. He compares her to her father[3] who did prison time for being a real boss, killing men to protect operations and make enemies pay for the wrongs they caused the clan. All she is good for, he concludes, is going after money. 'No one has confidence in you, no one is afraid of you'. A building belonging to the family is burned down and Sandra's grandfather warns her that she must retaliate: 'The one who did this must pay with his head. I am counting on you Sandra' (1.1). Chaos reigns again when Jean-Michel is arrested and the men feel Sandra cannot meet the challenges of their ongoing activities. At Jean-Michel's return, Sandra holds a meeting and walks around, inspecting the men as a general would review his troops: 'OK I am starting all over. Those of you who want to, can come back into the family. I have new projects. Those who want to leave, go right now. Later will be too late' ('Episode 2.3' 2008).

Sandra does not only do things, she wants to show that she is doing things.[4] Indeed, what really matters is that the others notice her actions. As Goffman (1959) would explain, Sandra is playing a role; this behaviour seems unnatural for her at the outset. She wears the mask of a mob leader and puts on a tough exterior, just as she donned her lawyer's robe when she pleaded in court. With time, through the seasons, violence becomes routine for her. Following Butler's idea (1988) that repetitive behaviours construct an identity, here that of a dark, brutal criminal, we see Sandra constantly repeat threats, shout reprimands and get involved in crimes that contribute to her acquired role as mobster. Each challenge to her authority, or to the clan's hold on operations, is seen as a crisis that she surprisingly reacts to by losing the distance for which her legal training should have prepared her. Instead, from somewhere deep inside her, an unexpected capacity for violence emerges as her answer to the crisis. Like a molecule, she reacts rather than responds to problems with wisdom and she turns anyone presenting an obstacle into an enemy. Sandra will threaten a local official who stands up to her or sneer at a would-be playboy trying to pick her up in a bar. 'Lower your eyes when you speak to me', she says to a future collaborator in a casino ('Episode 4.2' 2012). Her actions and attitudes are meant to be symbolic and carry messages; they are 'performed' to be read and understood by the men in her universe, mostly those who distrust her, some who desire her and especially those who want her out of the way. Her language, facial expressions and dress, as will be discussed further on, serve as signs that construct a reality. It is never clear whether she had all this within her from the start, but most likely these performative elements arouse to allow her to face the challenges regularly bombarding her from the men of her universe. She is constantly aware that whatever she does is watched and judged. She does not deal with women in the same way. Most of the women surrounding her are blood ties and are rarely seen in professional situations. Even in the very few professional encounters she has with women, her manner is less aggressive, her tone firm but milder. For the women in her family, she always manifests tenderness and kindness, but at the same time, shows herself to be a master of straight-faced dishonesty.

Sandra's ability to lie is an intricate example of a performance within a performance. One of the most interesting instances of this occurs when Sandra assures her niece, Carmen, that she had absolutely nothing to do with killing her brother, Carmen's father, and vows to find the person who did commit the murder and make him pay for it. Since the viewers saw Sandra shoot Jean-Michel ('Episode 4.1' 2012), they know she is lying, but she is totally expressionless, does not bat an eyelash and is so convincing that for a minute the audience will doubt what they know. There is no sign in her performance that she herself does not believe what she is saying. She is a rock, giving no indication of any guilt or discomfort in the presence of her niece. The actress, here, inhabits a person masterly performing a lie. Sandra's performance is incredibly believable because she has decided that it makes no difference whether she did shoot Jean-Michel or not, they would get someone for it in any case. Both Sandra and the actress, Hélène Fillières, are challenged by the performances they must deliver.

Upon committing the murder, however, Sandra gives herself away. She trembles and is clearly on the brink of hysteria. Crying as she shoots Jean-Michel, she hears him commend her for her guts – she has accomplished something he could never do. When he says he is in pain, she finishes him off, not as a further act of violence but out of love and suffering for him. They were very close and yet there was not enough room on the island for both of them. Theirs is both a story of family and a story of Corsica. By the end of season 3, Jean-Michel and Sandra had become business rivals. They tried to get each other out of the way. She took advantage of his absence while he was in prison. They arranged to have each other assassinated, but neither of them could go through with it. Season 3 ends with Jean-Michel tricking Sandra into thinking he is protecting her from death threats made against her by the militant nationalists. He arranges for her exile, sells her hotel to local officials, gives her nightclub, the Bellagio, to a long-time collaborator and methodically kills off her closest business partners. Season 4 begins with Sandra, back from exile, living in Paris, under an alias. She is in a relationship with an honest man who does not know her real identity. She has finally understood that Jean-Michel had set her up and in order to get back both the material gains and the power that he took away from her, she has to get him out of the way. Again, she coldly mounts a plan, persuading one of his close collaborators to help her. She leaves Paris in the middle of the night and takes a boat from Marseille to Corsica. There, she surprises Jean-Michel who was expecting to have a business meeting with new partners. However, her act is more than a mob vendetta, it is a paroxysm of family treachery and a metaphor for the tragedy of Corsica.

Sandra conducts her battles on several fronts. There is the family, the men of the Paoli clan and competing businessmen. She must also deal with local officials who do not trust her although they seem to have no difficulty tolerating the mob. The nationalists are another challenging force against her. At one point, she tries to negotiate with Grimaldi (Pierre Leccia), an unpleasant militant who considers Sandra's acquisitions to belong to Corsica and Sandra herself as Corsica's worst enemy. Negotiations with him fail and she kills Grimaldi before he is able to eliminate her. Even though there was no love lost between them, here again she trembles as she shoots him; she is on the verge of hysteria ('Episode 3.7' 2010). She pulls his big body up to her car while Manu and Tony look on, silently impressed. Tony helps her load the body into the trunk of her car. It is very clear that when she takes the type of action they would take, actions unexpected for a woman, they gain confidence in her and respect for her.

When the nationalists have understood that Grimaldi has been killed, they declare Sandra Paoli Corsica's greatest enemy and they vote on a course of action to take against her. As expected they all vote to eliminate her and in the following episode ('Episode 3.8' 2010) they inform Jean-Michel that they suspect Sandra of having killed Grimaldi and warn him to get her out of the area. It is at this point that he sees an opportunity to set up her exile. The season ends with her thanking him on the phone for taking good care of her, while the conversation is punctuated with scenes of Jean-Michel and his men killing off her collaborators and celebrating his take over in the family's bars. The tug of war that marked most of season 2 and all of three ends with Sandra duped and isolated, but season 4 zigzags back to Sandra, in Paris, planning her revenge against her brother and her repossession of power.

After her arrest that ends season 4, Sandra is soon released from prison for lack of evidence to prove she shot her brother. Her (male) lawyer (who becomes a recurrent character in this season) comes to pick her up and she informs him that she knows she is in danger with her own men: 'I have to arrange for them to need me' ('Episode 5.4' 2014). Her repetitive performance of toughness is in proportion to the dangers she faces, which are repetitive as well. She believes that she is doing what is necessary and that her aggressive manner is the only way to handle the challenges she faces. At the end of the series, it is not actually Sandra who commits the final acts of violence, but by condoning them, she shows, at least from the outside, that she has learned the rules. She even helps to organize certain vendettas, some of these senseless because provoked by corrupt police detectives in order for the gang to obliterate itself.

In the Mirror

On the inside, Sandra remains a complex and contradictory figure. From the start, she has been independent yet fragile. Having to prove her ability to be the leader, she plays at showing a strong side and constantly demands to be obeyed. However, she is lucid about her need to appear fierce and that loneliness is the price she will have to pay for her power. Assuming the role her uncle/father bestowed on her, she puts on the costume of a ferocious criminal and she has come to believe this of herself, but in the last two seasons she has become numb, insensitive to her transformation. Despite the presence of cousins or her niece Carmen and a few brief flings, she is alone – alone in a room or alone among men who distrust her. She is a dark, sad character not daring to turn her back to anyone and secretly nostalgic for warmth and protection. Her nostalgia for family happiness is clearly expressed in the credits of season 2: a super 8 film of Sandra and Jean-Michel when they were children, playing cowboys in the vast green garden of a Corsican house. They are running around holding toy pistols and playing to the music of 'Somewhere over the Rainbow'.[5] In season 5, Sandra is eager to renew ties with Orso Paoli (Carlo Brandt), another uncle who was not on speaking terms with Sandra's father. He quit the clan and moved to the mountains, not necessarily undertaking strictly legal activities, but only dealing in petty crimes. She invites him to participate in her project to buy into the failing ferry business, which will allow her to get out of the clan's illegal activities.

The project to renew ties with Orso is also a way for Sandra to come back to family. She speaks of family all the time. She tells Manu and Tony that they are more like family to her than her blood ties. She is very close to her cousin Chrystelle (Emmanuelle Hauck), Orso's daughter, who lives with her for a while. Sandra also repeatedly tries to re-establish a close relationship with Carmen, who seems to desire that just as much, despite her suspicions that Sandra might be her father's murderer. In season 1 (episode 6), Sandra pouts as Jean-Michel and Marie-Luce celebrate the news of a second baby on the way. The few scenes where Sandra smiles are those where she is in the garden of her big house surrounded by Matteo (Jean-Michel's baby), Carmen or Chrystelle's daughter. On the other hand, Sandra's relationships with men are all ill-fated and she knows they will never bring her children, happiness or fulfilment of any kind.

From the start, Sandra's intimate relations are mainly with 'bad boys'. She has relatively few love interests during the five seasons of the series and they all start out as sexual rather than romantic attractions. An insignificant surfer is killed before her eyes in season 1. Rémi Andréani (Fabrizio Rongione) is a pathetic little gangster; it is not clear at first to which gang he belongs. He shows his interest in her but is brushed off by Sandra for quite a while until she warms up to him in season 2 when his role in her clan has become clear. Be it the result of Sandra spending too long a time without a man or because Rémi manages to grow on her, they enter into a secret relationship that both amuses and pleases her. Just before that affair ends with his violent death, Andréani and Sandra are sharing a tender moment when he suddenly asks her how she sees her life. Does she imagine herself with children? 'Stop, she kids him, we are monsters' ('Episode 2.7' 2008). He continues the conversation declaring: 'I could kill for you ... and die for you' to which she answers, 'I don't deserve you'. This exchange is abruptly interrupted by Jean-Michel, bursting into the room and shooting Andréani (who had been falsely denounced by the police as betraying the family). Sandra refuses to accuse her brother when questioned by the police ('I saw nothing – I was in the bathroom'), but to Jean-Michel she screams that he killed the man she loved before her eyes.

Her next relationship is with Nader (Reda Kateb), who tries to make a pass at her in a bar. She brushes him off at first, but later, feeling lonely, calls him and has him brought to her house. Nader is Moktar's nephew and a loser, an insignificant, petty thief. Moktar, played by the controversial rap singer turned popular actor Joey Starr, is a drug dealer who enters into a lucrative import business with Sandra. Moktar kills Nader who, when interrogated by the police, had ended up giving them information on Moktar's and Sandra's drug trade. Nadar has time to say goodbye to Sandra because he knows that he will have to pay for this denouncement and she knows what will happen to him. At the end of season 3, Jean-Michel eliminates Moktar and other collaborators of Sandra's when he sends her into exile and takes over her activities.

At the start of season 4, Sandra is back from exile in South America. She is alive and well and living in Paris under a new name, Julie Tassone. She has a nice new boyfriend, Enzo (Stefano Accorsi). Enzo runs a legitimate and successful nightclub in Paris and he seems very smitten with her. For a short moment, this might appear as a chance for her to change her life. However, Sandra has plans to get back at Jean-Michel, and Enzo slowly discovers the truth about her. She reveals some details to him directly, like her real name and the fact that she is 'in business' in Corsica. He does not really understand what kind of business she is talking about until his lawyer tells him what he has learned about Sandra Paoli. Enzo begins to worry and finally tries to break up with her. By then, she has killed her brother and is back in Corsica. To win him over again, she has a new sports car delivered to him, which he refuses. He calls her and she retorts by having some of her men nearly run him off the road one evening to frighten him. He goes to Corsica to tell her in person that all is over between them and that she must leave him alone. She admits that when he refused her gift, she lost control and 'acted stupidly, violently' but then she becomes angry again and yells 'Get lost … do you know who I am?' ('Episode 4.7' 2012). Sandra will slip deeper and deeper into depression. All the following scenes are dark; most of them take place at night or in ill-lit rooms, the shutters closed. Everything is so dark, her facial expressions are difficult to decipher.

Sandra's appearance echoes this darkness. Her black clothes and make-up make her look older, thinner, nearly unhealthy. It seems as though the years, the violence, the worries and betrayals have worn her down and transformed her physical appearance. She has taken on the look, as well as the personality, of a bitter, isolated gang leader. As her character becomes sombre and taciturn, she replaces her tailored feminine elegant clothes with monotonous black pants and leather jacket. Her different tops are usually black, sometimes white but styleless and overly simple. She wears flat boots and her hunched over stance manifests depression and reduces her thin feminine silhouette to an androgynous figure. Before stealing to Corsica in the night to kill her brother, she cuts her hair and spends the rest of season 4 and most of season 5 boyish, drawn and numbed from the substances she consumes. She spends a lot of time alone or with Tony and Manu. During the day she often sleeps on a couch in her living room. Performance, Schechner explains, affects reality (1988) and Sandra's performance to be accepted as a clan leader led to a transformation of her personality. Her reactions became increasingly violent and uncontrolled and at the same time she ended up secluding herself from the others. Her confused state, when awake, suggests that besides chain smoking and drinking alcohol, she has also plunged into drug abuse.

The scenario could not insist more on her being alone, sad and silent. She seems to have lost much more than she ever gained from business ventures. Her reactions no longer make sense to Tony and Manu: she sends them to kill Enzo but they see no reason to do this since he has done nothing to the gang. There is no reason to kill him just because he walked out on a woman. Her behaviour and judgement contribute to her isolation and worry her men: 'Since the beginning this has been ridiculous, a woman running things' ('Episode 4.8' 2012). She has destroyed her ties with her family; she has lost the men she loved; the clan repeatedly loses confidence in her. Season 4 ends with the last lie exposed. As seen above, Sandra is arrested for the murder of Jean-Michel. Carmen, who is in the car with her, hears the police announce the motive for this arrest. When Sandra answers her stare by lowering her eyes, Carmen understands that it is true.

Sandra now needs to be nurtured, having lost most of the close family members she had at the start. She seems to understand that her way of life has ruined her life and the way out she finds is through investment in a failing business. This is again a reference to reality, as the ferries in Corsica were failing, leading to layoffs and strikes that caused more chaos and violence once again. Sandra wants to take over the ferries, not so much through a magnanimous intention to save jobs, but as a way to save herself and leave behind the activities of the clan. She tells her lawyer 'Sometimes I just wish my life would stop – just for a day – that my life can be restful and nothing happens' ('Episode 5.4' 2014).

Tony and Manu want to finish up the ferry project so they intimidate a potential buyer who abandons the project, leaving the way free for Sandra. In order to block her from acquiring them, Livia, the owner of the ferries, and Jean-Michel's last girlfriend, transfers ownership to Carmen by contract. Carmen then challenges Sandra to know how far she would go to get control, including fighting against 'your niece that you love and whose father you should not have killed' ('Episode 5.3' 2014). Carmen also negotiates the ferries with the nationalists, pledging to hand over control to them if they kill Sandra, thus avenging her father, but she fears she will end up like her aunt and be responsible for people getting hurt. People do indeed get hurt and Bonafedi (Jean-Marc Michelangeli), a nationalist leader, is tortured and killed. Manu and Tony plan to eliminate Livia and Carmen, but in the end Manu cannot go through with it and only Livia is killed as her car explodes before Carmen reaches it. Sandra knew about this and did nothing to stop them.

Another manifestation of Sandra's needing to be taken care of occurs when she asks her lawyer to leave his other clients and devote his time solely to her business. Once she has acquired the ferries, she appoints him general director and asks him to take care of everything (legally). Sandra is now slowly entering into an important new romantic adventure. At first when she meets Charly, a Sicilian call girl she picks up in a Parisian bar, it is merely a sexual attraction. Later, feeling alone, similar to when she summoned Nader, she calls Charly and has her brought to Corsica. However, it is not for sex, Sandra just wants to be held in her arms. She seeks the warmth Charly is capable of offering her – their relationship has nothing to do with protection, violence or obedience; there is no power struggle involved. Charly tells Sandra what she knows all too well: 'You had me come because you are alone. You are rich, you are powerful, but you are alone … you are empty Sandra. You kill people as if they are shit and you pay a whore for a little human warmth'. For the first time, Sandra acknowledges that she has taken on a role: 'Before I was not like this' ('Episode 5.5' 2014). The series and Sandra's life now waver between a promising future and inescapable violence. When the ferry deal is sealed, Charly dances at a celebration party and Sandra tells her 'My world is going to change' ('Episode 5.7' 2014). But a series of vendettas suggest that things might not change after all: Tony kills Orso, then he shoots Manu, his best friend, and the clan is obliged to retaliate so Tony dies as well. Sandra comments on these murders to Charly: 'You see that is what my life is like'. Charly argues, 'You have chosen this life, you can change it', but Sandra just says, 'No' ('Episode 5.8' 2014).

Five months later, Sandra is going to sell her house and is seen sitting in the garden with Charly, surrounded by people eating and laughing, like old times. Children run around the table, which is covered with traditional dishes. Charly says she is sorry to see the house go because of the good memories there. Sandra responds that they will create new memories.

In a subsequent sequence, the two are walking together, in the water at the beach. Sandra is dressed in white pants and a silky, simple but more feminine, shirt. She smiles as they continue to make plans for a new future. It is not that Sandra has become more feminine because she never became masculine, but she seems freer of the attitudes and actions that she had to carry out in order to measure up to what the clan expected of her. Perhaps she no longer has to play that role that is a source of contentment and serenity.

As far as television codes go, viewers understand that Sandra will not so easily become free of all her violence. She goes back to the house to retrieve something before the sale and finds the single 8 film of when she and Jean-Michel were children, the film used in the credits of season 2. As Sandra moves to embrace the image of her brother projected on the wall, Carmen suddenly appears at the door of the attic, pointing a gun at her. The season finale and the series, as a whole, end there: will Carmen kill Sandra and make her pay for Jean-Michel's murder? Will Sandra be punished for her violent acts? Will Carmen become the next Sandra and perpetuate the family tragedy? An answer would offer a prediction for Corsica that no one is able to make.

Sandra/Corsica – Two Islands of Beauty

Sandra is an interesting character to watch since her behaviour, and her evolution, is not always predictable. However, the real critical value of the show lies in the metaphoric relationship between Sandra and the island of Corsica. Sandra is a metaphor for Corsica. She begins as a strikingly beautiful young woman, a lawyer with a promising career ahead of her. Her clothes attest to her success since she dresses in unostentatious elegance. Nevertheless, from the start, she is isolated and her life is ruined by crime and violence. Corsica is an island of natural beauty where many French people from the mainland have come over the years to build luxurious summer homes. The French cherish Corsica for its beautiful beaches, its untamed landscape and its glorious weather. It is the favourite vacation spot of many, even those who do not have immense family homes.

However, like Sandra, Corsica is not easily accessible and often suffers from its status as an island. What is worse, for centuries Corsica has been battered and ruined by crime and violence. The Mafia has run organized crime on the island and vendettas are frequently reported in the news. The island has suffered from petty crimes as well; breaking into uninhabited homes during the off seasons has become a plague. Corruption is another well-known problem for Corsica: pay-offs, votes cast by the dead in local elections, deals for individual profit to the detriment of the island. Developing companies have constructed too many hotels, which disfigure the beachfront. The Mafia has brought gambling and drugs to the island. Corrupt policemen, like those in the series, provoke vendettas or are accused of burning down unlicensed snackbars along the coast. Separatist militants commit terrorist acts (bombings, or assassinations like the famous murder of the French prefect Claude Erignac in 1998).

The island, like Sandra, is thus locked into a system of ongoing violence. Corsica has its own way of doing things, loyalty among Corsicans make changes difficult; outsiders have trouble setting up businesses or households. Traditional values are very important and local culture is in competition with French culture. There is a local dialect, a mixture of French and Italian, and the actors in the series often codeswitch, slipping into this dialect. Viewers are then offered subtitles. Scenes often make reference to local dishes and the way to make a good coffee. The music used in the credits and multiple scenes is always local. The scenery used in the credits of seasons 3 to 5 pans the mountains of this island of beauty. Corsica is sadly doomed to its history.

Sandra is tied to the island to the point of becoming identified with it and like the island is doomed to her story. Her life has been devastated by violence and crime, but this has been mostly of her own doing. The end of the series mirrors the ambiguity of her life. She has brief hope for a new life with Charly and a chance to leave her illegal activities behind. She is dressed in white, smilingly relaxing in the garden. She has just taken legal measures to change her story, to leave behind the monster she saw herself to be and start a new peaceful life with Charly. She wants to be happy, but she cannot walk away from her contradictions that easily. This antiheroine will again be forced to face the consequences of her treachery and her misjudgements. In line with her life, the last scene does not offer any clear answer. It is suggested that the family tragedy will perpetuate itself: her niece is armed and comes to Sandra's house to make her pay for all the horrible things she has done to the family. But this scene ends abruptly, offering no closure, which reinforces the ambiguity of Sandra's story. She may die or manage to start over. A happy ending is hardly the final note for an antiheroine. It is more interesting not to know.

References

Broussard, Ph. (2009), 'Mafia: Quand les femmes prennent le pouvoir', *Express*, 13–19 August, pp. 28–39.

Butler, J. (1988), 'Performative acts and gender constitution: An essay in phenomenology and feminist theory', *Theatre Journal*, 40: 4, pp. 519–531.

'Episode 1.1' (2006), Louis Choquette, dir., *Mafiosa*, Season 1, Episode 1 (12 December, France: Canal+).

'Episode 1.8' (2007), Louis Choquette, dir., *Mafiosa*, Season 1, Episode 8 (2 January, France: Canal+).

'Episode 2.3' (2008), Eric Rochant, dir., *Mafiosa*, Season 2, Episode 3 (24 November, France: Canal+).

'Episode 2.7' (2008), Eric Rochant, dir., *Mafiosa*, Season 2, Episode 7 (8 December, France: Canal+).

'Episode 3.7' (2010), Eric Rochant, dir., *Mafiosa*, Season 3, Episode 7 (13 December, France: Canal+).

'Episode 3.8' (2010), Eric Rochant, dir. *Mafiosa*, Season 3, Episode 8 (13 December, France: Canal+).
'Episode 4.1' (2012), Pierre Leccia, dir., *Mafiosa*, Season 4, Episode 1 (19 March, France: Canal+).
'Episode 4.2' (2012), Pierre Leccia, dir., *Mafiosa*, Season 4, Episode 2 (19 March, France: Canal+).
'Episode 4.7' (2012), Pierre Leccia, dir., *Mafiosa*, Season 4, Episode 7 (9 April, France: Canal+).
'Episode 4.8' (2012), Pierre Leccia, dir., *Mafiosa*, Season 4, Episode 8 (9 April, France: Canal+).
'Episode 5.3' (2014), Pierre Leccia, dir., *Mafiosa*, Season 5, Episode 3 (21 April, France: Canal+).
'Episode 5.4' (2014), Pierre Leccia, dir., *Mafiosa*, Season 5, Episode 4 (21 April, France: Canal+).
'Episode 5.5' (2014), Pierre Leccia, dir., *Mafiosa*, Season 5, Episode 5 (28 April, France: Canal+).
'Episode 5.7' (2014), Pierre Leccia, dir., *Mafiosa*, Season 5, Episode 7 (5 May, France: Canal+).
'Episode 5.8' (2014), Pierre Leccia, dir., *Mafiosa*, Season 5, Episode 8 (5 May, France: Canal+).
Goffman, E. (1959), *The Presentation of Self in Everyday Life*, London: Penguin Books.
Jewkes, Y. (2004), *Media & Crime*, London: Sage Publications, p. 128.
Padovani, M. (2009), *Mafia, mafias*, Paris: Gallimard.
Schechner, R. (1988), *Performance Theory*, London: Routledge, pp. 157–163.

Notes

1 Created by Hugues Pagen and produced by Nicole Collet, Canal+.
2 In season 5, Philippe Corticchiato played the role of Manu following the sudden death of Frédéric Graziani.
3 By now, viewers have learned that François Paoli was Sandra's father, having slept with his brother's wife. This is why he was so specially fond of her.
4 Written for the film *The Wizard of Oz* (Fleming, 1939), music Harold Arlen, lyrics Edgar Yipsel Harburg.

Chapter 3

Adieu Carmela Soprano! Lessons from the HBO Mobster Wife on TV Female Agency and Neo-liberal (Narrative) Power

Kim Akass and Janet McCabe

Given that questions of morality and individualism, gender, sexual politics and power are never as straightforward as they first appear in any HBO original TV series, there is, as this chapter will contend, more to the social-climbing mobster wife, Carmela Soprano (Edie Falco), than her self-centred, apolitical affluent lifestyle would initially suggest. Of such a character, Regina Barreca writes, 'the women play roles that are difficult to categorize but impossible to overlook' (2002: 36). No one would ever claim Carmela as a role model for contemporary feminism, but neither should anyone dismiss her ability to navigate androcentric hierarchies and highly coded patriarchal worlds to emerge as a formidable figure in her own right. As we shall see, the socially ambitious consort and cuckolded Mafia wife from New Jersey offers us uneasy, if not uncomfortable gendered lessons in the art of working from *inside* dominant structures of power, at once centred on a ruthless individualism and simultaneously integral to culturally engrained social hierarchies and socio-sexual norms. One is impossible without the other. Emily Nussbaum put it best when she described Carmela as, 'At once a spiritual seeker and a spoiled parasite, she's the woman who chose to walk back into the darkness and try to negotiate a better deal' (2007).

Understanding women like Carmela is made additionally difficult because this unsettling vignette of female agency exposes the more disquieting aspects of being female and feminine in the *fin de siècle* context of an ascendant neo-liberal capitalism. 'Even if we ultimately decide that shows like *The Sopranos* [...] are *not* feminist', observes Lisa Johnson, 'the narrative arcs and visual rhetoric of these texts provoke rich, energetic conversations *about* feminism' (2004, original emphasis). Carmela is a *product* of our complex post-feminist age of troubled emancipation, *produced* by a premium cable subscription company trading in a dynamic global TV marketplace and committed, as Christopher Anderson describes, 'to pursue innovations in a way that the broadcast networks are not' (2007: 31). In so many ways, Carmela inculcates how the free market ideologies of neo-liberalism have been assimilated and made useful particular traits of liberal feminism: personal autonomy, identity politics, self-determinism and the rhetoric of free choice. Of neo-liberalism, Charlotte Rottenberg concludes, 'Despite the power and influence of neoliberal rationality, it is also constantly generating internal contradictions and incoherencies' (2014: 433). Taking such a definition of ambivalence and disconnect, we seek to explore how Carmela makes visible the deeply gendered divides structuring the neo-liberal economic paradigm. We suggest that she performs a *particular* cultural purpose, translating the criminal underbelly of the gangster genre into the hidden and troubling contradictions that constitute a form of subjectivity for women under capitalism. Fabricated through social hierarchies of family and community, tightly woven into a network of dependencies, the subjectivity of the mobster's wife reveals entrenched gender norms where success remains highly circumscribed by androcentric institutions and ways of thinking that function to limit the role of women within the public sphere.

The mobster's wife is ceaselessly driven by a compulsion to prosper in modern America. Carmela, in so many ways, translates the liberal feminist self-interest and self-styled individualism into being a neo-liberal, self-made woman, where everything she does is defined in entrepreneurial terms. Her calculated risk to give up studying business at Montclair State University to marry Tony Soprano (James Gandolfini) and 'retreat from the public world of work' (Negra and Tasker 2007: 2) may, on the surface at least, speak to the rhetoric of choice and an empowered self-determinism. Yet structured deep in the narrative and generic forms of television (family drama, soap opera), shaped by the political legacy of the gangster genre (power, money) and the mobster defined as 'a creature of the imagination' (Warshow 2008: 584), our contemporary Mafia wife emerges as a compelling antiheroine of the neo-liberal era: she is, in fact, a gangster of neo-liberalism anchored in free-market ideologies and the scripted ideals of American womanhood, only to reveal the gendered structures of the neo-liberal market rationality that continue to condition women's participation in the public realm in specific, often discriminating ways. Disclosed in her autonomous choices is that sense of how, as Rottenberg claims, 'neoliberal rationality individuates subjects, eliding structural inequalities while instating market rationality' (2014: 431). It is in how Carmela reveals structural inequalities and institutional chauvinism in her will to empowerment that intrigues us most and is the subject of this chapter.

Previous studies by us have dissected how a woman like Carmela is not necessarily accounted for by an ideological feminism, and often dismissed as an irrelevance as a consequence (Widdess 2007), possesses enormous agency and narrative authority nonetheless. Her character is formed directly out of learning from generic histories and working from within multiple institutions with varied and shifting bases of oppression. No longer simply another casual fatality of male (generic) violence, Carmela Soprano proves proficient at carving power from that which seeks to disenfranchise, and even oppress, her the most. Knowledge *is* power; the more she understands her husband's life and infidelities, the more leverage she acquires over him (Akass and McCabe 2002; 2006). Stony silences and censorious stares are key weapons in her armoury and always more affective than anything she could possibly do or say.

Narrative pre-eminence promises representational transcendence. Carmela as a woman may recognize that the world is masculine and governed by men, as Simone de Beauvoir described: '[T]hose who fashioned it, ruled it and still dominate it' (1997: 609). Carmela may revel 'in immanence' (1997: 608), constituted in the closed, closeted and interdependent world of Church, family and Mafia (Akass and McCabe 2006), but she still believes that she can somehow beat the rap and 'have it all' if only she can manage herself better. No longer prepared to tolerate Tony's philandering ways, her fifth season attempt to dissolve the marriage puts pay to that illusion (Akass and McCabe 2007). Her decision to leave her husband appears to undermine her entire narrative existence, with a slow, steady and measured four-season (five years) upward progress destined to take a precipitous plunge in one single episode. Brutality comes from the recognition that there is no *outside* of the Soprano marriage, only penury, social ostracism and non-recognition (McCabe and Akass 2007). In coming in at the end, and where this chapter intervenes as we explore the sixth and final season, Carmela arrives at acceptance and makes peace with the androcentric world in which she is so deeply complicit and morally entangled. She may disavow the social, cultural and economic forces structuring her inequality, but she simultaneously takes responsibility for her well-being premised on carving a social positioning for herself, predicated on a careful cost-benefit calculation. She gives up striving for transcendence in her acceptance of the knowledge that she can recoup her sovereignty: if only she plays by the strict and compromised generic rules and optimizing her resources through incessant self-management and entrepreneurial initiatives.

It is our aim in this chapter to add to our lengthy dialogue about Carmela and the insights her character offers us for contemporary feminism and feminist thought within a context of neo-liberal capitalism. What we argue here is that the Mafia wife is a menace to feminism; as a character gendering the new political economy, and so allowing the androcentric nature of the cultural order to come into view, she articulates feminism's central paradox within neo-liberalism. For Nancy Fraser (2013a), owing to the current state of western late-capitalism, feminism should now be poised to regroup and consolidate. But this time, she warns, we ignore the unfolding economic and political crises at our peril. If Fraser's accusation that feminism has traded 'one truncated paradigm for another – a truncated economism for a truncated culturalism' (2013a: 5), then it is urgent that we study the cultural work of a gendered character like Carmela and how she functions as a contemporary 'creature of our [neoliberal] cultural imagination' (Warshow 2008: 584). We argue that this recognition, or mis-recognition, of such a female character and her narrative function in the world of *The Sopranos* can be used politically to give us insight into the dilemmas for current feminist thinking. Nancy Fraser said it best when she wrote:

> No serious social movement, least of all feminism, can ignore the evisceration of democracy and the assault on social reproduction now being waged by finance capital. Under these conditions, a feminist theory worth its salt must revive the 'economic' concerns of Act One – without, however, neglecting the 'cultural' insights of Act Two.
> (2013a: 5)

With an eye on Fraser's warning that we must 'be sensitive to the historical context in which we operate' (2013a: 5), and 'probe the fateful coincidence of the rise of identity politics with the revival of free-market fundamentalism' (2013a: 9), a fictional character like Carmela Soprano emerges as an uneasy paradox representing a new neo-liberal feminine subjectivity. She makes visible the deep economic fissures and gendered inequalities structuring our modern capitalist economy. She inhabits that very structure informed by market rationality as she at the same time personifies it. In short, she gives us invaluable insight into the way women are positioned within the current political, sociocultural and economic climate.

To speculate is to accumulate has never been so true as Carmela seeks to redistribute illicit wealth, making it legitimate, to secure a substantial financial future. She has imbibed the rules of exploitation and economic risk, but in so doing bolsters the very system that oppresses women like her. No wonder her path is fraught. The more we struggle to find appropriate ways to think and talk about the compromised, corrupted, complex life of the Mafia wife from New Jersey, the deeper our understanding is of a new set of political concerns structuring the relationship between women and power in the contemporary financial age; and it is in this context of Carmela as modern gangster par excellence that this chapter seeks to address. Tony once said to his spiteful and vengeful mother, Livia Soprano (Nancy Marchand): 'Everyone thought Dad was the ruthless one but I got to hand it to you, Ma. If you'd been born after these feminists, you would've been the real gangster' ('Down Neck' 1999). Carmela is, of course, no Livia, but she does nonetheless represent the new order of economic brutality and financial exploitation. Her mother-in-law may epitomize the old world order of ruthless individualism and irrational violence, but Carmela exposes the new with its merciless contradictions for women working *inside* dominant discourses that preserve the pre-eminence of free market ideologies. Cultivating the scripted ideals of American womanhood as a form of Foucauldian self-governance, where women take individual responsibility for their own sense of well-being beyond the collective, has always been part of Carmela's modus operandi. Her 'success' has long been predicated on a steely disavowal of social, cultural and economic forces that produce gendered inequalities, whereby she almost takes advantage of those very structures that seek to disenfranchise and limit opportunities for women.

Remembrances of Things Past: Appropriating Gangster Mythology for Neo-liberalism

To further understand why Carmela as a model of female neo-liberal power catches our attention, it helps considerably to remind ourselves of *what had come before*. Orthodox studies of the gangster genre, from the classic Warner Bros. studio films of the 1930s to the *Godfather* trilogy and into new Hollywood, observe a central narrative ambivalence where women are concerned (Sacks 1971; Schatz 1981). Power is largely seen as something held by men, with women defined as hardly anything other than archetypes: virgin (mother, sister) and whore (seductress, mistress). Viewed through these gendered codes and pervasive generic forms brings into focus women's subservience and male dominance. Gender appears as a categorical axis against which the male gangster can 'assert himself as an individual, [and] draw himself out the crowd' (Warshow 2008: 585), and further serves to construct woman – the whore, the Madonna – as narratively subordinate and vulnerable to male humiliation and violence, sexism and patriarchal restraint.

To all intents and purposes Tony continues in this generic tradition. But he is now subject to the laws of the new political economy. In a neo-liberal world of free market ideologies, economic power for Tony profoundly shapes gendered relations and defines strict hierarchal social and familial roles. It structures the sexual politics of the domestic sphere and *flows through relationships*, or tight networks of relationships and dependencies. Androcentric patterns dominate the social hierarchy, organizing who matters and who is socially recognized as mattering most within the network – and determining who will be looked after and who will not. The structural privileging of men and masculinity order the public and private spheres, in which women are primarily located in the enclave of the home.

In the patriarchal world par excellence of the Mafia where women have traditionally mattered little, Carmela operates inside meticulous codes – of marriage sanctified by the Catholic Church, of motherhood extolled by popular media rhetoric, of family valorized by the Mafia and its generic laws. It is a lesson in formidable unseen power whereby the legitimate wife and mother quite literally lay down the law; she is privileged, she *is* privilege in her dependency on patriarchal patronage. This is what gives her definition. Working *inside* power structures – of heterosexual marriage and motherhood sanctified by the Catholic Church, the State and the Mafia – a character like Carmela emerges directly out of assimilating those hard lessons from the generic histories and working within these traditions and structures of institutional and narrative power.

Her authority comes from ways of thinking that have reconciled with the various and continuously shifting bases of oppression and what oppresses her. Participating in what oppresses others, and at times even dangerously entangles her, Carmela, in making her own way, reveals what Fraser calls, 'a dangerous liaison with neo-liberal efforts to build a free market society' (2013b). If, as Robert Warshow argues, '[t]he real city, one might say, produces only criminals; the imaginary city produces the gangster: he is what we want to be and what we are afraid we may become' (2008: 584), Carmela genders this imaginary sense of being in the neo-liberal world. Her will to succeed harnesses the narrative of female empowerment and turns it into capital accumulation. Never losing sight of the economics and aggressively pursuing financial security, as she de-politicizes 'the personal' reified in her role as Christian wife and devoted homemaker, her representation uneasily fuses identity politics with a neo-liberal market logic. Carmela genders the political economy of the post-capitalist, post 9/11 America: a gangster of neo-liberalism. Economic gains may entwine with personal humiliations and compromise, but this is the contract for securing economic success and upward social mobility.

Well provided for and socially legitimatized, her role as bourgeois wife-mother-homemaker defines her exchange value; but with no real economic clout beyond symbolizing the law of alliance, Carmela can offer no true resistance to the structures of male dominance, power and privilege that condition her pre-eminence within networks of dependency. Her mistake is to believe that her ability to procreate, raise children and shoulder the domestic responsibilities is on an economic par with Tony's paid labour outside the home. Her support of family is not equivalent to her husband's wage and her hard work as a full-time mother and homemaker is not compensated for at all, as she suffers from what Fraser calls, '"hidden poverty" due to unequal [income] distribution within families' (2013a: 119). Carmela finds this out to her cost when she invites Tony for lunch at Vesuvio to tell him she intends to file for divorce ('Unidentified Black Males' 2004). In declaring that she will 'aggressively pursue [...] equitable distribution of our assets', she is told in no uncertain terms that she is 'entitled to shit'. Tony tells Carmela that she has lived off his sweat, in full knowledge of how his money is made and how it circulates as a consequence, adding that she 'wanders around the fucking mansion in $500 shoes and diamond rings'. Her husband may in the past have spoken endlessly of his respect for his wife, but his complete undervaluing of Carmela's labour and abilities speaks directly to how this narrative world is structured principally around the heterosexual, male-headed nuclear family, which exists at all because of the man's wages. Supporting children and the wife-and-mother entitles Tony to impose his 'will to power' over the marriage. Of this 'family wage' ideal, Fraser contends, it 'serves to define gender norms and to discipline those who would contravene them, reinforcing men's authority in households and channelling aspirations into privatised domestic consumption' (2013a: 213). Profoundly gendered, the economic rules of the Sopranos' marital arrangement may legitimize the couple, enforcing it as a social ideal and insulating Carmela from the vagaries of the labour market; but conversely, institutionalized androcentric definitions of work (paid) and family (unpaid) naturalize gender inequalities, which, in turn, trivialize and deprecate those dependent on the breadwinner.

With such knowledge, marital reconciliation is unavoidable. Carmela may resist, and she may attempt to get rid of her adulterous husband, but there is no escaping the entrenched politics of this economic contract. Tony may be unseen, but his 'omnipotent armature' (Foucault 1991: 301) is nonetheless felt. With his far-reaching networks, he is able to set a whole process in motion that will quite literally turn Carmela into an outlaw if she leaves the marriage. On hearing the news that her divorce lawyer has recused himself from the case, she returns home to find Tony's car parked in the drive ('Unidentified Black Males' 2004). She silently moves around her domestic realm; the phone rings. It is Meadow (Jamie-Lynn Sigler). Finn DeTrolio (Will Janowitz) has proposed and she has accepted. 'Wonderful news. I'm surprised'. Forever the pragmatist, Carmela asks if Finn will finish dental school. There is a party to plan. Parents to meet. 'I'm going to cry', she says. But are these tears of joy? Looking out the window watching Tony floating on his inflatable in the pool, she silently sobs.

Carmela is down, but she is not out.

Season 6 ('Members Only' 2006) opens with a montage of establishing shots, concluding with Carmela surveying her investment – the bare shell of her new spec house bought with the $600,000 extorted from her husband to compensate her for his philandering. Exposed timbers, window frames wrapped in plastic and protective coverings blowing like laundry in the wind is a fitting metaphor for the way Carmela is laundering dirty money to secure a legitimate financial future. Built for pure investment and to maximize profit, the structural skeleton represents the 'something else in her life' ('Long Term Parking' 2004) and stands as an apt metaphor for this final season of *The Sopranos*. Carmela may be taking a risk on an, as yet, unconsolidated ultra-luxury real estate market, but she knows the script and has researched the financial markets. Rising like a ghost, a spectre of the neo-liberal imagination, the house is haunted by Adriana La Cerva (Drea de Matteo), an apparition of where it can go so terribly wrong for the gangster's moll who thinks she can contravene the strict generic rules. For not playing it smart with the FBI and keeping *stumm*, Adriana ended up in the secluded backwoods of New Jersey with two bullets in the back of her head ('Long Term Parking' 2004). No wonder Carmela is worried.

Tony's near-fatal shooting by a confused Uncle Junior (Dominic Chianese), who is suffering from early dementia, precipitates a truce in the Soprano marriage. But, as her husband lies unconscious in his hospital bed, the shifting sands of neo-liberal privilege prove as capricious as the fragile structure of Carmela's spec house. Behind the scenes, the men begin to plot. Paulie 'Walnuts' Gualtieri (Tony Sirico) and Vito Spatafore (Joseph R. Gannascoli) decide to withhold Tony's share of their latest haul in case of his demise. Silvio Dante (Steven Van Zandt) may have made it clear that Carmela's share will pay for Tony's medical bills, but, in true Mafia style, the men are already manoeuvring to recalibrate the economic power base. This final outing for *The Sopranos* reveals much about the threat to Mafia income in this new age of neo-liberalism, as the men discuss business without their patriarch to guide them. With money and power always the focus of Mafia life, the erosion of their income brings new challenges: it is not only the widows' drain on coffers that give cause for concern, but the competition from rival criminal organizations. Even the Mafia are not immune from the capricious politics of neo-liberal economics and the new global financial markets, as they find their old world business model being eroded by the norms and practices of a new fiscal rationale. Carmela's spec house becomes ever more vital as the mobsters make it clear that even the boss's wife cannot depend on the kindness of the clan during a time of global recession.

Adriana is not the only spectre haunting Carmela. One only needs to think of Angie Bonpensiero's (played by Toni Kalem) fall from affluent grace to become a low-waged worker ('For all Debts Private and Public' 2002). Following the murder of husband Salvatore 'Big Pussy' (Vincent Pastore), Angie finds herself handing out polish sausage samples for the Pathmark supermarket chain ('Fun House' 2000). The old gender order collapses with the loss of the family wage. Her sense of self, previously constructed and interpolated through the heterosexual, male-headed nuclear family where she lived principally on her husband's earnings, has gone. With the literal demise of the male-breadwinner, female-homemaker economic paradigm that defined her subjectivity, Angie has become subject to a new phase of capitalism, where she is struggling to support herself in a female-headed household. Once economically dependent on her husband's ability to earn more money than her, she is now dependent on an unstable labour market and shift work. In the immoral and bloodthirsty Mafia world, the welfare paternalism of the illegitimate gangster family gives way to that of 'legitimate flexible capitalism' (Fraser 2013b), which, in turn, leads to another form of impoverishment: decreased wage levels, job insecurity and a decline in living standards.

Carmela's economic dependence on older Mafia patronage is underscored by Tony's repeated failure to fix the building inspection on her spec house. With only soft pine for support, the structure is an apt metaphor for the end of *The Sopranos* as, like the shifting sands of capitalism, even the most glossy façade and overpriced finish is undermined by an insubstantial foundation. As the main breadwinner, Tony assumes that his wage is the principal, if not only, source of economic support for the family, while anything made by his wife is purely supplemental. To a large extent Tony indulges Carmela, but when her obsession with the spec house interferes with domestic duties, he, fearing for his future home comforts, tells Silvio to drop his request to get the structure passed. If, in the past, Carmela's narrative and generic power has depended on those long silences and steely stares, this season sees her abandoning this modus operandi as she repeatedly asks Tony if he has sorted out the building inspector. Thinking that he has been clever, he tells his wife that the stop work order cannot be lifted. Once more his ability to regulate the economic life of the family has the potential to derail his wife's ambitions.

But the Mafia don should know better than to try and outsmart Carmela. Without the house to keep her occupied, Carmela turns her attention to Adriana's disappearance. A chance meeting with a dishevelled and unkempt, Liz LaCerva (Patty McCormack), casts suspicion on Adriana's whereabouts, as her mother confesses to Carmela that she suspects Christopher Moltisani (Michael Imperioli) of murdering her daughter ('The Ride' 2006). Following this encounter, Carmela dreams of Adriana while holidaying in Paris with Rosalie Aprile (Sharon Angela), another 'gift' to distract her from the building project: in her dream a gendarme tells Carmela that Adriana is dead ('Cold Stones' 2006). Learning that Liz LaCerva tried to commit suicide, and haunted by her Parisian dream and the impending failure of the spec house, Carmela tells Tony that she is thinking of hiring a private investigator to uncover the truth behind Adriana's disappearance. After all, she has been missing for two years without a word and no one knows anything. Within days Carmela has the inspection report and all thoughts of Adriana are banished. Carmela turns her attention back to financial planning and her nascent career as a property developer ('Kaisha' 2006). Inequality between men and women are disavowed, as the issues of social justice and belonging are abandoned in favour of professional ambition. Revealed here is the erasure of any gendered solidarity and collective action for women like Adriana, abused and forgotten, and finding social justice is simply traded in the pursuit of individual entrepreneurialism.

In this rapidly changing free market economy, the neo-liberal gangster woman reliant on herself is fast displacing the traditional male alliances and ways of gendered being. With new market opportunities and businesses moving into the neighbourhood, the Capo Don finds that his collective forms of governance and managing family welfare eroding as new regimes of economic morality come into being. Neo-liberal market forces rationalize and undermine his traditional ways of doing business. Particular forms of exchange and extortion are made redundant. When Patsy Parisi (Dan Grimaldi) and Burt Gervasi (Artie Pasquale) go to collect from a recently opened coffee shop belonging to a corporate chain, the new manager tells them that he cannot lay his hands on that kind of money and besides, 'corporate won't care about any vandalism' ('Johnny Cakes' 2006). In the virtual fiscal world of credit cards and centralized stockkeeping, there is absolutely no hard cash to exchange and damages are covered by insurance. With Tony selling his factory to the conglomerate, Jamba Juice, another source of 'protection' money, has vanished. Reflecting on the changing market and shifting demographic profile of the old neighbourhood, Patsy and Burt comment that it is 'over for the little guy'. As it is not only rival families that are a drain on the Soprano family fortune, but the encroachment of large corporations will not yield to the old rules of extortion. Managers can be replaced, and two little guys from the hood cannot access cash from the new economic flows of corporate neo-liberalism.

What Carmela reveals through her business acumen is not simply about a new economic order, but rather about creating a new sense of the self, which, as Wendy Larner describes, 'encourages people to see themselves as individualized and active subjects responsible for enhancing their own well-being' (2000: 13). Carmela has always proved more adept at understanding the political and economic vicissitudes of a rising neo-liberalism than Tony. As subject she has always known inequality and exclusion and, as a result, her new selfhood is individualized without any recourse to the feminine collective. Nowhere is this more apparent than with the Mafia widow who without male patronage is cast adrift and left to navigate the neo-liberal public sphere alone. When Carmela, Rosalie and Gabriella Dante (Maureen Van Zandt) meet up with Angie to organize their annual charity silent auction ('Live Free Or Die' 2006), the friends realize that the ex-sausage sampler has come a long way since her days as a poorly paid worker in the local supermarket. Constantly on her cell phone, Angie arrives late, takes charge and then leaves abruptly. Later, Carmela discovers that Angie has secretly diversified her business. To boost the meagre income from her legitimate company, given to her by Tony as widow's compensation, she has branched out into loan sharking and trading in stolen car parts. In response to the news, Rosalie remarks: 'She's one of us: now it's like she's one of them [*read: mobster*]. Neo-liberalism has recalibrated the public sphere for women like Angie. No longer defined by charity work and leisurely lunches, her new selfhood is defined by self-reliance and personal initiative as well as an ability to set her own career objectives and make autonomous choices. Discretely building her illegal business empire, Angie has worked alone and away from female solidarity. As a high-powered businesswoman, she is now positioned to personally donate a much-larger-than-anticipated sum of money for the silent auction, but her career paradoxically is antithetical to working with the other women towards a common goal, beyond funding it. Any collective action by women in *The Sopranos* is confined to volunteering and charity work, but never extends into the public world of waged labour. Economic success is defined as a private affair with meritocratic advancement based on personal achievement rather than collective action.

Neo-liberalism has transformed not only how the workplace operates, but also the governance of the home with family alliances and power relations spatially mapped out in and through the flow of domestic spaces. Home is currency, and the ideal of the male-breadwinner/female-homemaker family has long served as the central organizing principle to Mafia-organized capitalism. It has structured the vicissitudes of patriarchal power as well as proved a potent symbol of professional success, social mobility and the pursuit of personal happiness. Building a home is the gamble Carmela takes with her spec house. She invests in the value of home, not only as real estate investment, but also her ability to turn that scripted ideal into material spatial arrangement that can be sold to the highest bidder.

Neo-liberalism has thus recalibrated the domestic sphere into an economic commodity to be traded on the open market. No better example of the ruthlessness of this ambition can be seen than when Ginny Sacrimoni (Denise Borino-Quinn) loses her palatial house to Janice Soprano (Aida Turturro), who greedily covets her home ('Moe n' Joe' 2006). With Johnny now dead, the men's promises to look after the widow come to nothing when it is time to promote Bobby 'Bacala' Baccalieri (Steve Schirripa), who needs a domestic stage befitting his new status as made-man. This spatial *mise-en-scène* of domestic accomplishment leads to Ginny being pushed out of her home and receiving only half of what the property is worth. Not only are we reminded that a female-led household is more often than not an impoverished one, but also that a beautiful home reifies professional ambition and individual success.

To make good on this goal, then, it seems that the progressive neo-liberal gangster wife is compelled to pursue success through making good financial deals. The sale of Carmela's spec house comes at the midway point of the long narrative arc of the sixth and final season ('Chasing It' 2007). Months of hard work and negotiation have returned only a meagre one per cent profit. She has made $6000 from her initial $600,000 investment, proving how hard it is to make a legitimate living in the current economic climate. When Carmela shares her good news with Tony, he urges his wife to gamble his half of the profit on a pro-football game. A row ensues in which Tony reminds his wife just how much of the family money she is entitled. 'I thought this was my money', is her reply. Later, Tony wastes no time in telling Carmela that if she had gambled her legitimate profit she would have turned it 'into a fucking million dollars'. Compared with the rewards of organized crime, gambling and extortion, the profit from the ultra-luxury spec house appears inconsequential. Still, finding a new role as her children grow older and identifying creative solutions to secure her financial future, she is intent on this career path, which will inscribe her as an entrepreneurial subject. She will need to be because without Tony the burden of the family will fall squarely on the shoulders of this lone widow.

Happily Ever After: Legacy …

In the end, and as we have argued, it is not whether Carmela is feminist or not that intrigues us, but the way her character has performed important cultural work within the HBO television ecology and beyond. A character like hers functions to reveal the very power structures that continue to condition and circumscribe women's lives in the contemporary era. So what are we to make of her legacy at HBO, when her immediate successor offers us a return to history in our contemporary age of economic downturn and austerity? After a decade of economic excess, where the Soprano family prospered, a new era ushered in by the near-collapse of the global financial system in 2007–2008 finds a new antiheroine of recessionary America, namely: Margaret Thompson (née Schroeder) (Kelly Macdonald) from *Boardwalk Empire* (2010–2014). Battered wife, pregnant with few material assets and young children to support, Margaret, through enterprising self-fashioning, transforms herself from impoverished Irish immigrant into the respectable wife of an influential politician and proto-gangster, Nucky Thompson (Steve Buscemi), with a lucrative property portfolio in Atlantic City.

Set on the eve of Prohibition in 1919, *Boardwalk Empire* reveals a society on the brink of profound social, political and economic change. Few women have any legal rights, let alone suffrage. Margaret may start the series as a victim of domestic violence, but it soon becomes apparent that she is a survivor who will bend the rules to ensure her upward social mobility. Before long, she has made a string of decisions that will secure her children's future financial security, even if she has to go against her own deeply held convictions. 'Nights in Ballygran' (2010) sees her reporting illegal alcohol distribution in her neighbourhood to Nucky. When the trade continues, and ignorant of Prohibition Agent Nelson Van Alden's (played by Michael Shannon) sexual obsession with her, a frustrated Margaret reports the activity to him. This exchange of information leads to Nucky's arrest, and the steamy sexual exchange between the couple on his release means that Margaret can no longer hide her attraction for a gangster who goes against every moral principle that she appears to hold true.

Later, armed with a steely resolve but a conflicted conscience, Margaret visits Mrs McGarry (Dana Ivey), President of the Atlantic City Women's Temperance League, a woman whose opinion Margaret holds in high esteem ('Family Limitation' 2010). The exchange between the women reveals much about the limited power structures that inhibited women's movement at the time. When Margaret tells Mrs McGarry that she has had an offer from a man that 'runs things' and an association with him would 'provide for me and my children', the older woman asks whether it is of a financial, domestic or sexual nature. She confesses that it is all three and marriage is not part of the deal; Mrs McGarry replies that there are various unflattering words for 'that sort of woman'. Margaret is defiantly insistent: 'He would provide ma'am'. As Mrs McGarry fixes her with a stony glare, we expect the worst. How can a proto-feminist like her ever have sympathy for the stark and conflicted choice that Margaret will have to make? The older woman's answer is instructive, as she reveals that her lifestyle is funded by the sale of a quarter share in an oil field and the subsequent death of her husband. It is only through the transfer of capital and felicitous marriage that she can fund her lifestyle and devote herself to causes that she considers important like the temperance movement. Telling Margaret that the movement is to protect women but the ballot box will free them, she adds: 'You must do what you see fit. You owe no-one an explanation'. Reaching into a drawer she gives a surprised Margaret a leaflet entitled 'Family Limitation', telling her: 'This contains useful knowledge – I highly recommend you read it'.

If the first season of *Boardwalk Empire* is a study of how women are forced to use sex and sexuality to get on in the world, season 2 shows us that those decisions are never easy. Attempts to appease her conscience see Margaret, who is by now living a life of respectability with Nucky, grappling with decisions over her support for his illegal activities and her knowledge that she is complicit. Despite her misgivings, Margaret and Nucky marry in the season finale ('To the Lost' 2011), but it is a marriage that will last only until her new husband discovers that she has deeded his land to the Church and, throughout season 3, it is a marriage in name only. Being married to the mob was never easy but the mobster wife soon realizes that it is not only life with Nucky that is restrictive. The cancellation of the prenatal care classes by order of the Bishop of the Catholic Church and the discovery that Nucky has a mistress sees Margaret unable to reconcile her life lived under patriarchal dictum, whether inside the law or outside; and rather than being reunited with her gangster husband while mourning the death of her lover, Margaret moves to Brooklyn. Her journey shows that there is no escape from patriarchal law but, unlike Carmela, she chooses poverty rather than complicity and a certain freedom.

We have argued in the past that Tony's journey from the 'fringes of New York City up to his front door in the leafy New Jersey suburbs' (Akass And McCabe 2002: 147) is a generic journey from cinema to television; but by way of conclusion what we have argued here is that this journey also speaks of the changing political economy of a contemporary America. Colonizing one domain with another – the city with the home – involves a trajectory from a Fordist industrial capitalist system to a neo-liberal one shaped by global forces and free market ideologies. But over the course of six seasons that journey evolved further from a pre-9/11 prosperous neo-liberal America to one defined by national trauma, economic recession and the war on terror. We would do well to remember that Carmela may have only made one per cent on her investment, but she got out before the market collapsed.

Within a society defined by neo-liberalism, its economic principles and market rationale, Carmela plays the very system that disenfranchises many other women, often pushing them into low-paid work and depressed living conditions. Returning to the 1920s with a character like Margaret Thompson, on the other hand, we learn how Carmela has reached the zenith of women's power within patriarchy. Mrs McGarry's prediction that women will only find freedom through political emancipation has shown that the right to vote has given women only limited freedom in a world where men still hold the means of production and economic privilege. In the words of Charlotte Rottenberg, women are forced to 'identify and work within the potential fault lines of [neoliberalist] logic and conceits' (2013: 433), but, moreover, they do so as individuals and with very little recourse to a feminist sisterhood.

In the end, these characters from HBO have gendered the economic journey of contemporary America, from the suburban housewife of the boom years to the impoverished immigrant of the past that speaks so eloquently of austerity following the collapse of global markets. These women may be separated by decades, but the rules remain the same, as women continue to personify the socio-political collateral of collapsing economic markets.

Carmela Soprano, like her generic foremother Margaret Thompson, metaphorically shows the price to be paid for living a life of untold luxury and being dependent upon the spoils of organized mafia crime. Men may pay with their lives, but women suffer an economic death with the loss of social position and impecuniousness: they *are* the gangsters of neo-liberalism.

References

Akass, K. and McCabe, J. (2002), 'Beyond the Bada Bing!: Negotiating female narrative authority in *The Sopranos*', in D. Lavery (ed.), *This Thing of Ours: Investigating The Sopranos*, New York: Columbia University Press, pp. 146–161.

────── (2006), 'What has Carmela ever done for feminism?: Carmela Soprano and the post-feminist dilemma', in D. Lavery (ed.), *Reading The Sopranos: Hit TV from HBO*, London: I.B. Tauris, pp. 39–55.

────── (2007), 'Married to the mob: Separation and divorce in *The Sopranos*', in K. Leydecker and N. White (eds), *After Intimacy: The Culture of Divorce in the West Since 1789*, Bern: Peter Lang, pp. 257–276.

────── (2008), 'What has HBO ever done for women?', in G. R. Edgerton and J. P. Jones (eds), *The Essential HBO Reader*, Lexington: The University Press of Kentucky, pp. 303–314.

────── (2011), '"Blabbermouth Cunts"; or, Speaking in Tongues: Narrative Crises for Women in *The Sopranos* and Feminist Dilemma', in D. Lavery, D. L. Howard and P. Levinson (eds), *The Essential Sopranos Reader*, Lexington: The University Press of Kentucky, pp. 93–104.

Anderson, C. (2008), 'Overview: Producing an Aristocracy of culture in American Television', in G. Edgerton and J. P. Jones (eds), *The Essential HBO Reader*, Lexington: The University Press of Kentucky, pp. 23–41.

Barreca, R. (2002), 'Why I like the women in *The Sopranos* even though i'm not supposed to', in R. Barreca (ed.), *A Sitdown with The Sopranos: Watching Italian American Culture on TV's Most Talked-About Series*, New York: Palgrave Macmillan, pp. 27–46.

Beauvoir, S. de ([1949] 1997), *The Second Sex*, London: Vintage.

Boardwalk Empire (2010–2014, USA: HBO).

'Chasing It' (2007), Tim Van Patten, dir., *The Sopranos*, Season 6, Episode 16, 29 April, New York: HBO.

'Cold Stones' (2006), Tim Van Patten, dir., *The Sopranos*, Season 6, Episode 11, 21 May 2006, New York: HBO.

'Down Neck' (1999), Lorraine Senna Ferrara, dir., *The Sopranos*, Season 1, Episode 7, 21 February, New York: HBO.

'Family Limitation' (2010), Tim Van Patten, dir., *Boardwalk Empire*, Season 1, Episode 6, 24 October, New York: HBO.

'For All Debts Public and Private' (2002), Allen Coulter, dir., *The Sopranos*, Season 4, Episode 1, 15 September, New York: HBO.

Foucault, M. (1991), *Discipline and Punish: The Birth of the Prison* (trans. Alan Sheridan), London: Penguin.

Fraser, N. (2013a), *Fortunes of Feminism: From State-Managed Capitalism to Neoliberal Crisis*, London: Verso.

—— (2013b), 'How feminism became capitalism's handmaid—and how to reclaim it', *The Guardian*, 14 October, http://www.theguardian.com/commentisfree/2013/oct/14/feminism-capitalist-handmaiden-neoliberal. Accessed 12 July 2015.

'Fun House' (2000), John Patterson, dir., *The Sopranos*, Season 2, Episode 13, 9 April, New York: HBO.

'Johnny Cakes' (2006), Tim Van Patten, dir., *The Sopranos*, Season 6, Episode 8, 30 April, New York: HBO.

Johnson, L. (2004), 'Way more than a tag line: HBO, feminism, and the question of difference in pop culture', *The Scholar and Feminist Online*, 3: 1 (Fall), http://sfonline.barnard.edu/hbo/printint.htm. Accessed 12 July 2015.

'Kaisha' (2006), Alan Taylor, dir., *The Sopranos*, Season 6, Episode 12, 4 June, New York: HBO.

Larner, W. (2000), 'Neo-liberalism: Policy, ideology, governmentality', *Studies in Political Economy*, 63, pp. 5–25.

'Live Free Or Die' (2006), Tim Van Patten, dir., *The Sopranos*, Season 6, Episode 6, 16 April, New York: HBO.

'Long Term Parking' (2004), Tim Van Patten, dir., *The Sopranos*, Season 5, Episode 12, 23 May, New York: HBO.

'Members Only' (2006), Tim Van Patten, dir., *The Sopranos*, Season 6, Episode 1, 12 March, New York: HBO.

'Moe n' Joe' (2006), Steve Shill, dir., *The Sopranos*, Season 6, Episode 10, 14 May, New York: HBO.

Negra, D. and Tasker, Y. (eds) (2007), *Gendering the Recession: Media and Culture in An Age of Austerity*, Durham and London: Duke University Press.

'Nights in Ballygran' (2010), Alan Taylor, dir., *Boardwalk Empire*, Season 1, Episode 5, 17 October, New York: HBO.

Nussbaum, E. (2007), 'The loneliest Soprano', *New York*, 25 November, http://nymag.com/arts/tv/profiles/29992/. Accessed 9 July 2015.

Rottenberg, C. (2014), 'The rise of neoliberal feminism', *Cultural Studies*, 23: 3, pp. 418–437.

Sacks, A. (1971), 'An analysis of the gangster movies of the early thirties', *The Velvet Light Trap*, 1, pp. 5–11.

Sandberg, S. (2013), *Lean In: Women, Work, and the Will to Lead*, New York: Alfred A. Knopf.

Slaughter, A. M. (2012), 'Why women still can't have it all', *The Atlantic*, July/August, http://www.theatlantic.com/magazine/archive/2012/07/why-women-still-cant-have-it-all/309020/. Accessed 20 July 2015.

Schatz, T. (1981), *Hollywood Genres: Formulas, Filmmaking and the Studio System*, New York: Random House.

Tasker, Y. and Negra, D. (eds), (2007), *Interrogating Postfeminism: Gender and the Politics of Popular Culture*, Durham and London: Duke University Press.

'The Ride', (2006), Alan Taylor, dir., *The Sopranos*, Season 6, Episode 9, 7 May, New York: HBO.

The Sopranos (1999–2007, USA: HBO).

'To the Lost' (2011), Tim Van Patten, dir., *Boardwalk Empire*, Season 2, Episode 12, 11 December, New York: HBO.

'Unidentified Black Males' (2004), Tim Van Patten, dir., *The Sopranos*, Season 5, Episode 9, 2 May, New York: HBO.

Warshow, R. ([1948] 2008), 'The gangster as tragic hero', in J. Gross (ed.), *The Oxford Book of Essays*, Oxford: Oxford University Press, pp. 581–586.

Widdess, J. (2007), 'Review of *Reading The Sopranos*', *Feminist Media Studies*, 7: 1, p. 155.

'To the Lost' (2011), Tim Van Patten, dir., *Boardwalk Empire*, Season 2, Episode 12, 11 December, New York: HBO.

Part II

Drug Dealers and Aberrant Mothers

Chapter 4

Paying the Price: *Penoza* - Combining Motherhood and a Career (in Crime)

Joke Hermes

'A lead character can make or break television drama. This actress makes it and turns it into more than what it would seem to be on paper. Powerful and raw, elegant and emotionally pure.' The jury of the film- and television award parade De Gouden Kalveren (the Golden Calves) could hardly have put it more astutely when they lauded Monic Hendrickx and crowned her – quite rightly – 'best actress in television drama.' Because if there is one reason to follow *Penoza* since 2010, it is Hendrickx playing Carmen van Walraven.

(Maas 2013)

This long quotation from a regional Dutch newspaper does what all Dutch newspapers did: it lauds *Penoza* (NPO 3, 2010–2015), acclaimed Dutch television crime drama series featuring a strong female lead character. Interestingly, the heroine is an antiheroine. She makes a career in crime, not the first thing one thinks of when reading 'elegant and emotionally pure'. This chapter inquires into what it is that makes *Penoza* attractive beyond its lead character. The question is a poignant one, given that, contrary to its good press, *Penoza*'s strong woman lead character can be read as a throwback to earlier times rather than a reversal of traditional notions of gender.

From a feminist perspective, women behaving badly invite us to revisit stereotypes and to recombine gender notions. As Buonanno suggests in her Introduction: antiheroines help expand the spectrum of women's perceived capacity to encompass areas of agency that they have long been deemed unsuitable for. At first glance, this is exactly what *Penoza* does. However, while *Penoza*'s lead actress Monic Hendrickx does an excellent job, her character, Carmen van Walraven, is a woman who seems to live a life that could be set in the 1950s untouched by second-wave feminism. Veiled by the greater audacity of featuring crime from the perspective of a successful criminal family business, the series offers a second layer of rewriting morality that appears to erase feminism in favour of a mythical notion of what makes women strong. *Penoza* offers an old myth of motherhood as its solution to how to understand the working woman after over a century of struggle over women's rights.

Penoza's core ideological work hardly touches on the rights and wrongs of criminal dealings; the series offers a different type of 'usable story' (Mepham 1990: 59). *Penoza* is a story that helps come to terms with how to think about being a woman and a mother in neo-liberal times that favour individualism and ambition. Stories, Mepham argues, are a form of enquiry that helps us as individuals to come to forms of social self-understanding (1990: 60). Television in such cases functions as 'transmodern teacher' (Hartley 1999: 41).

As television's pedagogy is shaped in the trial and error of using and renewing generic conventions, its lessons can be deeply ambiguous. These do justice to the deep insecurities and ideological strife that build societies, a prominent one of which, today, has to do with how to understand and define gender. Television's lessons deserve careful critical attention to untie some of the knots it so brilliantly presents as solutions – which they may not be. Of course such undoing of knots is not without risk. Pitching *Penoza*'s version of how women can be strong against the feminist discussion of motherhood is not a confrontation with a guaranteed outcome.

This chapter discusses *Penoza* based on an analysis of its reception in newspaper and news magazine reviews, published over its three seasons aired to date (September 2010 – July 2015) and the announcement of a fourth season (to start in September 2015).[1] All major Dutch newspapers, newsweeklies, monthly and a fair number of the regional papers wrote about *Penoza*, using the array of possibilities print news media have: announcing the new series on its television pages; critical reviews in the media, culture and weekend sections; bylines reviewing television programming and interviews with the actors playing main characters and with the makers of the series. Recurring themes are the quality of the cast and the comparison of *Penoza* with *The Sopranos*. The novelty of a mother who becomes a gangster and the featuring of a 'strong woman' are major themes, followed by the commercial success of the series (it has been sold to a number of other countries), the series' explicit violence and how 'real' it feels. Morality is hardly a topic at all. The fact that a mother is allowed to employ whatever means she has to provide for her children and to keep them safe apparently is both morally self-evident and self-explanatory.

The Facebook page and Twitter feed initiated by *Penoza*'s broadcaster KRO add fairly little to the newspaper coverage. They do include more criticism, almost absent in the newspapers. There are those who feel *Penoza* gets to be too violent and that its plotlines become too convoluted and artificial. Overall audience reactions are as positive as those of the reviewers and journalists in the press. Summarizing the reviews and news items, it can be said that 'motherhood' is clearly the most central of the recurring themes that intrigues across different media. This provides the focus in this chapter for the reading of what makes *Penoza* such lauded and well-watched television.

Penoza has been screened on public television from 2010 onwards by public broadcaster KRO. Like other locally made crime series, it has had reasonable to increasingly good ratings. It is different from almost all other crime fiction produced by the Dutch public and commercial broadcasters. Its main character is a woman and she is a criminal. Without ever intending to become a career criminal, Carmen van Walraven-de Rue, daughter of an Amsterdam mobster, finds herself drawn into the world of crime when her husband is murdered on their driveway in front of their youngest son. Carmen has just asked him to withdraw from the crime empire he has built with two associates who are boyhood friends.

In three seasons shot over five years (a fourth season is to start in September 2015), Carmen changes from a concerned mother who feels it is not safe to become a police informant into a career criminal who, together with two associates of her own, controls her drug supply lines. While the figure of a woman heading a crime syndicate is not entirely novel, in the Dutch context there is quite a discord between a woman as mother who fights to make sure her loved ones are safe and a criminal mastermind who is implicated in the death of a series of men as well as her own sister. In Carmen as mother and criminal who wants to get out, the series has found its golden dilemma. Likened by Dutch director Johan Nijenkamp to the eternal love triangle in a soap opera (*The Bold and the Beautiful* springs to mind), a crime series around a character who has learnt to ignore the dubious morality of a criminal life from childhood onwards but has little other qualifications to earn a living and protect her loved ones could go on forever, especially in a family-focused culture such as the Dutch one. Television critic Beerekamp explains at the beginning of the second season:

> Just as *The Godfather II* was better than its original, to everyone's surprise, director Diederik van Rooijen and scenarists Pieter Bart Korthuis and Franky Ribbens outdid themselves with the comeback of crime tsarina Carmen van Walraven (Monic Hendrickx). The premise is that organized crime and a fulfilling family life are hard to combine. This is not so much illustrated by serious abuse, as it is by the way in which family members – wives, children and grandchildren – are involved in abductions and pay-offs. All of that in apparent disregard for how important family relations are to those who love traditional Dutch 'stamppot' (stew).
>
> (Beerekamp 2013)

In an interview, Monic Hendrickx underscores how important Carmen being a mother is:

> Her motherhood is what holds the series together. If not, it would be an ordinary bang-bang-you're-dead series. She needs her children to have a safe future; that is what drives her. Her children grow up though, she gets to have empty nest syndrome. How to protect your children when they leave home?
>
> (Takken 2012)

Apparently the fact that Carmen van Walraven never chose to lead a life of crime is important, the television critics agree. Van Gelder characterizes *Penoza* as '(a) series about a woman who has to save her children' (2010). Actress Hendrickx explains again and again what she feels is Carmen's predicament:

> (Carmen) does not like the world of the mob, but she does love him (her husband who is a major weed dealer). When he is murdered, she takes control. Of necessity, to protect her children, and perhaps because something in her genes makes her susceptible to an adrenalin high.
>
> (Nauta 2010)

While the death toll mostly consists of men and grows to a considerable number, and children are abducted to be held hostage, Monic Hendrickx's Carmen van Walraven presents the mother as unwitting and initially unwilling career woman. In a sleight of hand move, feminist notions of women's rights and the construction of gender difference as a power and social control mechanism are dismissed. By offering what should be the abject figure of a mother who becomes a wholesale drugs seller as a kind of hero instead, *Penoza* suggests we never needed feminism to define women's strength. Why would it do so? Is this an easy way out of having to think about where Dutch society stands in regard to gender relations, a return to a fantasized period of unproblematic and clear-cut gender distinctions? Or, does the series mark a historical moment for the Dutch rewriting of motherhood ideology from a romantic to a more feminist or perhaps a neo-liberal one? Is it a coming to terms with the deep Dutch conservatism regarding how children ideally should be taken care of by charting the transition of a stay-at-home mum who after two seasons as unwilling victim decides to embrace the only career perspective she sees?

Penoza: Quality 'Polder' Crime Drama

Before turning to discussion of the tradition of Dutch crime drama and the continuing strong Dutch allegiance to a conservative notion of motherhood, it is useful to follow the critics in how they offer a frame to understand and value *Penoza*. The long quotations provide background to the analysis presented here and 'couleur locale' to understand discussion about *Penoza* and itself. As said, the television critics like *Penoza*. What they call the 'polder' version of *The Sopranos* (van Rhee 2013b) satisfies all the major requirements for quality drama: 'a stable, intelligent scenario, elegant acting including the smaller parts. And of course, in the demanding lead role Carmen who keeps taking on new colours and emotions: Monic Hendrickx' (Rijghard 2013). In true Dutch egalitarian fashion that values normality and ordinariness above any form of eccentricity or putting oneself above or apart from others, all the praise for the series needs counterbalancing. The title of the series offers a useful handle to do so rather than consideration of mothers-as-drug-dealers. *NRC* critic Limburg is unhappy with the series' 'silly' name:

> The title is a real pity. If you are going to copy *The Sopranos* – the mix of crime and family life – why not also steal the name? Why borrow the first name of lead character Carmen van Walraven (an often amazing Monic Hendrickx) from Carmela Soprano, but give the series a silly [...] comedy name. Why not name the series after the family like the Americans did [...]?
>
> (Limburg 2010)

Likening *Penoza* to *The Sopranos* is something of a heresy, given that it was made on a budget likely less than a tenth of the HBO production. Still, *Penoza*, although home-grown television drama, is so good, it deserves to be mentioned in the same breath as international top drama that is in a league all of its own, argues van der Kooi:

> Unfair to compare *Penoza* (to *The Sopranos* and *The Wire*) but the first episode vindicated the fact that I tipped the series here unseen, arguing that a top cast (Monic Hendrickx, Fedja van Huêt, Marcel Hensema, Olga Zuiderhoek) does not appear in a crap series. The casting of Hendrickx as mob woman Carmen van Walraven [...] may be surprising, she is grandiose in the first episode in which she is, as is Carmela (!) Soprano, the 'wife of' and not the spider in the web that she will become according to the series synopsis.
>
> (van der Kooi 2010)

Other early reviews follow a similar carefully enthusiastic approach to evaluating *Penoza*. Interestingly, Dutch Carmen van Walraven, who in the narrative holds Tony Soprano's position, is likened to Carmela. Critic Beerekamp's exposé makes clear how Carmen as antiheroine holds a non-position. Easier to understand her as a wife and mother than as the career criminal she will become.

> Imagine that Tony Soprano is shot in front of his family at the end of the very first episode of the very first season. And that his wife Carmela is asked by a crime partner to mind the shop because she has 'the brains'. That is exactly what has happened in the first two of eight episodes of the Dutch crime series *Penoza* (KRO). Even if writer Pieter Bart Korthuis and director Diederik van Rooijen were to maintain that the Monic Hendrickx character is called Carmen by chance and that the narrative and décor of Amsterdam and the Vinkeveen lakes are really very different from *The Sopranos*' New Jersey, there are still a number of significant resemblances.
>
> Both series are set against a background of the economies of scale and the hardening of organised crime. Carmen's father [...] was also a criminal but he is a 'chip from the old block' who would never cross certain boundaries. Husband Frans [...] smuggles hash but gets involved in rip deals with hundreds of kilos of coke much against his wish.
>
> *Penoza* also plays of the tensions between the upper- and the underworld. Children of criminals attend ordinary schools that do not much appreciate when they bring a gun. Carmen and Carmela both would like to live a decent life while knowing that the villas they live in cannot be kept on an ordinary salary.
>
> (Beerekamp 2010)

Later reviews are comfortable in continuing the international comparison and understanding Carmen in a traditional gender frame, while *Penoza* stands the test of being well-made entertainment and possibly more. Longer articles in news weeklies *Vrij Nederland* (van der Jagt 2012) and *Elsevier* (van der List 2013) open with the by now commonplace reference to

The Sopranos. *Penoza* producer Alain de Levita, veteran Dutch television maker of earlier groundbreaking successful crime series, is not afraid to even bring *Breaking Bad* into the *Penoza* equation with blatant disregard for *Penoza*'s gender intervention.

> It is a format of a kind. *Breaking Bad* is an example, and *Dexter* and *The Sopranos*. We see anti-heroes, people who end up in situations they cannot get out of and who try to make the best of it. Audience finds it easy to identify. It makes you want to forgive the main characters for their crimes. When someone gets shot, it is in a good cause, to protect the children, or the family.
>
> (Onkenhout 2013)

Mostly though, *Penoza* is complimented for its realism. As the new man in Carmen's life, played by Eric Corton, in an interview says: '*Penoza* is about real problems' (van der Heuvel 2014). In an earlier article, series writer Korthuis is quoted as saying that *Penoza* has 'couleur locale': 'To make it realistic I set store by detailed Dutch scenery. There is a coke transport that has the coke in the fish. Or the coke is stored in a shed that warehouses flower bulbs. There is a bit of a joke when Carmen has to do duty inspecting for head lice in school' (Takken 2012). *De Volkrant* (Onkenhout 2013) offers a similar quotation from Korthuis: 'This is not a fake American series. You can feel it is the Netherlands'.

Recognizing scenery, musical references, jokes and turns of phrase is something audiences appreciate. Throughout television's history, this approach has assured the success of local drama produced relatively cheaply (compared to international drama). *Penoza*'s production crew and actors underline that *Penoza* does more than most and is careful and spot-on in its referencing. At least as important a factor in *Penoza*'s increasing success in the ratings seems to be the series' 'emotional realism'. The term was coined by Ien Ang (1985) in her study of prime-time glamour soap opera *Dallas*. While as far from realism as *Penoza* (the Netherlands does not boast a huge number of female top criminals), the oil millionaires in *Dallas* presented human dilemmas and problems that felt real according to those who wrote to Ang about what they felt made watching *Dallas* worthwhile.

Ang (1985: 42) is critical of reflective notions of realism and suggests we need to understand 'emotional realism' following the work of Barthes (1984) at the level of connotation.

> It is striking; the same things, people, relations and situations which are regarded at the denotative level as unrealistic, and unreal, are at connotative level apparently not seen at all as unreal but in fact as 'recognizable'. Clearly, in the connotative reading process the denotative level of the text is put in brackets.
>
> (Ang 1985: 42)

Going back to her *Dallas* letter writers, Ang finds that in order for them to experience *Dallas* as 'taken from life', they abstract from the denotative level of the text. While concrete situations and complications are regarded as symbolic representations of more general living experiences – all of which clearly are in the realm of the emotional rather than the cognitive – *Dallas*, Ang goes on to argue, becomes meaningful in a tragic structure of feeling. It is its psychological realism that viewers find convincing rather than its scenery or settings (Ang 1985: 43–50). It is one thing to suggest that a soap opera appeals to the 'melodramatic imagination' (Ang 1985: 61) and quite another to suggest that the popularity of a crime series depends precisely on such a structure of meaning. When *Penoza* is cited as being real, the critics mostly applaud its cinematography and scenic choices. Actors Corton and Hendrickx however appeal precisely to the emotional realism of *Penoza* as that which draws in and hooks viewers: *Penoza* presents 'real' people with real problems, no matter that the circumstances of their lives may be somewhat far-fetched.

Understanding the becoming meaningful of a television series via Barthes' (1984) notion of myth, which follows up from the levels of denotation and connotation, is useful in explaining how and why Carmen being a mother is given such airplay. Before coming to a short discussion of motherhood mythology and feminism's historically uneasy relation to it, it is useful to situate *Penoza* in the (relatively short) Dutch tradition of television drama production. It is meant to argue two points. The first is the Dutch preference for dark and tragic drama; the second is how femininity and feminism especially in the crime series – and perhaps partly as a result of this predilection – are fraught with uneasy tension.

Dutch Crime Drama

The Netherlands belongs to a small language community. Its history of television production is limited when it comes to drama and of global importance when it comes to format trade. Both these characteristics are directly linked to the advent of commercial broadcasting in the Netherlands in 1989. Half a century of a highly mixed television diet, consisting of home-made productions and a vast number of international series and shows, has apparently made the Dutch a very good – because impatient – test audience. To succeed in the Netherlands has become a mark of quality (Benjamin 2012). Relevant here is that expertise gained in soap production (one of the innovations the new commercial stations brought to the screen) was used half a decade later to make the first of a range of successful Dutch crime series, delivered by both the commercial and the public broadcasters. Alain de Levita, producer of *Penoza*, started his career making the first of these series called *Baantjer* (RTL 1995–2006).

Making soaps is mostly about budget control while hooking a loyal audience. The first Dutch soap series to be made was *Goede Tijden, Slechte Tijden/Good Times, Bad Times* based on an Australian script and Australian production expertise. Compared to the German version (they started producing their own *Gute Zeiten, Schlechte Zeiten* based on the same original script), O'Donnell (1999) is amazed to find a great preference for tragedy and very little humour in the Dutch one, which is a lot jollier. As if its reformed protestant tradition informs Dutch television production rather than the equally important but less uniquely Dutch catholic tradition the country also boasts, *Penoza* is both dark and relatively cheap in as far as its production cost is concerned. In interviews, De Levita, *Penoza*'s producer, and Korthuis, its writer, underline the dexterity with which budgets are controlled.

> What does it cost?
>
> Alain de Levita: 'In the Netherlands we are not very good at making film, but we are in television. We belong with the best television countries in the world. Budgets are low, we spend our money adroitly. A *Penoza* episode will cost two tot two-and-a-half hundred K. [read: thousand Euros]'
>
> Pieter Bart Korthuis: 'In Denmark they spend an enormous amount of money on series. That is why they make only one a year. For one episode they spend a million.'
>
> Alain de Levita: 'With *Penoza* we come really close to the Danes. The Americans felt the quality was really high [note: the *Penoza* remake rights have just been sold to ABC in the United States]. When they heard what we spend on making the series, they would not believe it. They use our total budget to make one episode.'
>
> (Onkenhout 2013)

Other newspapers also underline international success and low production cost (Groenier 2013; Valk 2013). The regional newspaper *De Gelderlander* adds that director Van Rooijen has his cast improvise more than is usual. Given the quality of the actors, this may also be a clever way of cutting cost while boosting quality (Flier 2013). By summer 2015, the series had been sold to seven other countries (van der Jagt 2015).

There is one other element beyond being cheap and relatively dark that may have contributed to *Penoza*'s success. The series has an interesting pedigree. It was initially commissioned by Talpa for a commercial broadcaster and became collateral damage when Talpa begged out (eventually the John de Mol production house was sold to ITV). Public broadcaster KRO eventually expressed an interest in *Penoza*. From the 1990s onwards, KRO had been branding itself via signature crime series (mostly imported) and a number of locally made series that never managed to get the ratings the commercial series realized in the same period. With *Penoza*, they appear to have managed to combine popular appeal of the commercial crime series with the kind of quality KRO likes to see in its drama series, ensured by high profile stage actors and an undercurrent of tragedy.

> Korthuis developed and wrote *Penoza* initially for Talpa who were looking for a longer running series. That he eventually ended up with KRO, he saw as an advantage. 'I never wanted to make a bam-bam-you're-dead series, and public broadcasting allows for far more emphasis on characters and less on action.'
>
> (van der Jagt 2012)

The long and the short of it is that *Penoza* more and more became serious drama and steers away from comedic interludes. In the early days, the references to Carmen's father's criminal activities allowed for some levity. Director Van Rooijen answers the observation of the *NRC* interviewer by suggesting that initially a little humour was felt to be in order:

> The series is not without humour. Witness the young man who at his wedding is introduced to his new in-laws and mentions to his bride: 'Harm S., Johan M., there are seriously little people with last names in your family.'
>
> Van Rooijen nods: 'You need to be able to laugh from time to time. The criminal milieu has its own amicable codes, and that opened the backdoor to a little comedy. As viewer you will have to deal with a lot of misery the coming weeks. But the humour had to come from those people themselves. We did not want to make the Amsterdam mob ridiculous. We have tried to make it as credible as possible.'
>
> (Van Gelder 2010)

The host of Dutch crime series that preceded *Penoza*, produced in the late 1990s and early 2000s, screens a remarkable number of women, including station chiefs and senior detectives. Women's emancipation is implied to be a good thing – something of a surprise, given that motherhood ideology remains strong in the Netherlands, as shall be discussed in the section below. The best explanation for the high number of women in these series seems to be in the extraordinary emphasis on the group of policemen and women as a work family. This is underlined by the high number of sibling relationships in police teams, the occasional (divorced) couple and by the meal served by the senior detective's wife in their big live-in kitchen in *Baantjer* at the end of each episode. After the team has enjoyed a good dinner, the senior detective, in true father figure style, explains how he broke the case. In less flagrant examples, too, the police teams in the Dutch series underline Ella Taylor's (1989) assertion that families (whether real or work families) are a key element in television fiction (see also Hermes 2005: 45–46). While vastly different from these police series, *Penoza* offers an even stronger emphasis on family ties, now elevated to storyline level and couched in terms of loyalty and betrayal and a mother's obligations to her children.

The Housewife Legacy: Motherhood in Dutch Culture

According to Korthuis, *Penoza*'s main writer for season 1 to 3, the secret of *Penoza*'s success might well be that it has found a way to portray a female criminal who is neither too hard nor too soft and is therefore convincing: 'She is hard and soft. In her criminal activities and in her relationships, she is a vulnerable woman' – something American series have never managed to achieve, nor was handled well in the American *Penoza* remake *Red Widow* (ABC, 2013), which was not a success (Onkenhout 2013). The Dutch television reviewers like Carmen for being 'strong and independent, a power woman but also vulnerable' (Maas 2014). The feminist monthly *Opzij* describes Carmen as 'fragile and hard' (van Wiggen 2012). Actress Monic Hendrickx perceives her character as an interesting set of contradictions.

> 'Carmen is not a strong woman. For instance, she does not find a balance between her temper and her emotions, she has no overview. She enjoys the good life provided for by the shady dealings of her husband. Her children, in the end, make her vulnerable'.
> (Nauta 2010)

In a later interview, Hendrickx adds that Carmen has become addicted to adrenalin and excitement (Onkenhout 2013). She is a lead character with a negative goal (she wants to escape from the life of crime that also draws her in). Korthuis therefore quits after three seasons: 'How long can you go on with a main character who is negatively motivated?' (Onkenhout 2013). In another interview Hendrickx remarks that Carmen becomes more extreme in the third season and more vulnerable. She turns into a hardened criminal and her children start to revolt (Groenier 2013). Others also remark on how Carmen in season 3 decides to no longer be a victim, but head for a position of power and influence. She will start doing business with a Colombian cartel on her own. As *Algemeen Dagblad* points out: 'Carmen is no longer innocent, she becomes immoral' (van Rhee 2013a). *De Volkskrant* too now calls her an amoral choice (Onkenhout 2013) – an epithet not given earlier. Despite Carmen now pursuing a criminal career, her motivation never changes. As *De Gelderlander* has it: She is a mother who has no choice but to keep going in the criminal world to protect her children (Flier 2013). As in the earlier seasons, her very choices will consequently endanger her children. This is proof not of the faulty logic of her choice, but of the strength of her feelings as a mother even when she starts to sense the strength of very different feelings to do with wielding power in a dangerous world, of being a career woman par excellence. A perfect mix according to series writer Korthuis in a long spread in *De Volkskrant*:

> Pieter Bart Korthuis: 'One of the people involved in the American remake said that countless attempts have been made to narrate a crime series from a woman's perspective. It never worked, he said, because these women were always too masculine. They were a mafia mum, a butch, or the equivalent of a soccer wife. A main character that has motherly feelings and penetrates into the world of crime (and secretly likes the high that gives her) is a combination they had not seen before.'
> (Onkenhout 2013)

While Carmen gets addicted to being in charge, the series fares well by steadfastly presenting Carmen as a mother. Doing so muddies any attempt to present the life of crime (or crime fighting for that matter) as clean or clear-cut, as 'professional' activities that do not touch the core of the characters involved. It makes for strong (crime) drama. As a feminist invested in the gender trouble, an antiheroine might raise *Penoza* is most of all a piece of popular fiction that tells a story of what it might be like to be a woman today: to be a mother, to become a worker and, by season 3, a professional. The telling of that story involves querying and rewriting dominant ideology regarding motherhood and professionalism. It is what makes popular fiction such a fascinating domain; it is ultimately a mirror, be it a somewhat distorting one, that helps understand contemporary culture and society, including the options open to individuals, whether women or men, young or old to rewrite what is expected of them conventionally. Writer Korthuis feels he is playing with fire here. He loves how the series transcends conventions and dislikes it at the same time. As noted earlier, he quits the series because of Carmen's negative motivation. In the long extract below, he tries to explain 'the beauty' of *Penoza*:

> Writer Pieter Bart Korthuis wonders whether viewers will remain committed to Carmen now that she is wittingly making wrong choices. 'The idea is that she feels safer on top of the ape rock. She transforms from a semi-innocent woman into a criminal. She has become her husband. She doesn't do what she does for the fun of it or for the money but simply because it has become her world.'
>
> 'Penoza 1 and 2 were really flight stories with Carmen as victim. Now she becomes a leader, it is dancing on a tightrope. I mean: the audience does not necessarily have to sympathize with her. As long as they understand why she makes her choices and oversteps the boundaries. That is the challenge for season 3. What is new also is that problems are increasingly created by her own environment rather than by outsiders, for instance her lover John [Eric Corton] who starts sticking his nose into her business. And the way she has raised her children will come back to her like a boomerang. While she was involved in dirty business, she always held on to the illusion that she could keep all this from her children. But of course she did do damage to them by exposing them to the mores of the underworld. And when they follow their mother's example and run of the rails, we see that she has failed. That is *Penoza*'s extra layer. All parents will recognise that phase of trouble in raising one's children. The beauty of it is that you see Natalie, Lucien and Stijn grow up in front of the cameras because we had considerable time lag between the series. That is really rare in Dutch series.'
>
> (van Rhee 2013a)

It is interesting that Korthuis moves away from motherhood and motherhood ideology by framing *Penoza*'s narrative as about parenting rather than as being about motherhood. *Penoza* will remain ambiguous on whether women should try to become professionals. At first (and second) sight, *Penoza* argues the opposite case. Not many of the women characters are portrayed primarily other than in their relation to family members while most of the men are portrayed in their professional capacity (a police inspector, other career criminals). When Carmen does decide to become a professional in season 3, she will get shot at the end of the season, by the look of it lethally. Being a professional comes at a price.

It is fascinating that Carmen as a character is an unapologetic reference to the archetypal mother: She does anything for the children – and she makes a mess of it. Her daughter

Natalie is a disturbed girl suffering from some kind of depression. Because of her, mother and children return from their exile after having given evidence against the family (the murder of Carmen's husband was an inside job) and land in a new series of dangerous complications in season 2. Boris, the youngest, brings a gun to school to defend himself against bullying, which is not appreciated by the school. The older brother experiments with drugs and will get his girlfriend killed. And this is not counting her children rebelling against Carmen and Carmen's views on life and how to live it. While wholly unrealistic at a denotative level, Carmen invites our sympathies at the connotative level, at the level of emotional recognition. The emotional realism *Penoza* achieves depends, so it seems, on the deep contradiction at the heart of the myth of motherhood wrought by feminism. Lodged painfully as a result of half a century of second-wave feminist debate around motherhood that may well have produced one of the deepest divides in the movement and may be part of how feminism never came to fully convince so many women and men. The 'problem' of motherhood is central to the next (and last) section of this chapter.

To understand the appeal of *Penoza*, one needs to understand Carmen as a mother struggling to make a living and, from season 3 onwards, struggling to be a professional and to build a career. Carmen becomes such a recognizable figure because she so utterly fails in what she feels that she must do and yet keeps on doing it: try and protect her children by crossing any number of boundaries to do with danger, violence and loyalty. Carmen's children are not her Achilles' heel, they are who she is but they cannot define her to the point of containing her when she has to decide on how to survive. This might well be a result of the unique Dutch historical background to the series. Not in reference to what may at some point may have been the tolerance of the Dutch for diversity but its more poignant dark and repressed side: its dogmatic insistence that normality is good and that to stand out is wrong. For women, this translates into strong motherhood ideology. Children need their mothers to take care of them. To send them to day care was long seen as a selfish act of abuse. This changed towards the end of the twentieth century but, as *Penoza* shows, has remained a sore point: what are mothers obliged to do for their children? How far does their responsibility go?

Fraught Feminist Heritage and Two Myths of Motherhood

The Netherlands has traditionally had unparalleled low labour market participation of women. In 1985, 40 per cent of women between 15 and 64 worked, which changed somewhat in the 1990s, but the higher percentage directly relates to a vast increase in part-time workers, the majority of whom are women (Van Nimwegen et al. 2002: 21). 'Champions of late motherhood' in Europe, one out of three mothers stops working after the first child while a majority of the other two-thirds change to working part-time (Van Nimwegen et al. 2002: 22). Researching career success of Dutch fathers and mothers, Van Engen et al. (2009) point to the importance of motherhood ideology in the Netherlands. While the authors distinguish between traditional and modern motherhood ideology (the latter allowing for the possibility that parents of either sex are able to 'mother'), the overall picture is that the Dutch feel children need to be cared for by their parents rather than in institutional arrangements. The antiheroine has her work cut out for her. She needs to challenge not one but two mythical notions that together tie women firmly to their homes and children rather than allow them careers and that have taken root across centuries: children need to be raised at home and women are best equipped to do so.

In his study of the Dutch Golden Age (the seventeenth century), Simon Schama (1988) points to the then unique notion of childrearing in the Netherlands, which was based on love. While more can be said about the particularities of this notion, the Dutch apparently have long set excessive store on good parenting (Dekker 2008; Dekker and Groenendijk 1991). Now that government policy favours higher labour market participation of women and stimulates childcare arrangements, individual couples tend to hesitate before starting a family. It is felt to be serious business, an enormous responsibility that will demand that at the very least one of the parents give up on their personal ambitions and devote themselves to the child or children. Traditional motherhood ideology, which prescribes that women should preferably be mothers and fathers should pursue a successful career to provide for the entire family, remains strong, even though from the 1970s onwards it is accepted that mothers will also work (Van Engen et al. 2009).

While international examples have served the Dutch well in making emancipated crime drama featuring an unusual number of interesting women characters (Hermes 2005: 45), other media have set decidedly less favourable examples. In a study of motherhood myths in magazines, Johnston and Swanson have concluded that the messages in them are contradictory (2003: 23). At least in the United States the most popular magazines for women in the childbearing age appear to be solely populated by white and non-employed mothers. The magazines suggest moreover that mothers would be happier if they were more competent across their three major roles of providers, protectors and playmates (2003: 30). Clearly a self-serving message (why else buy the magazines?) but also a reminder that feminism has not offered much of an alternative for (neo-)traditionalist notions of motherhood.

An antiheroine worth her salt thus needs to take on the idea that women are 'naturally' best suited to caring for children and feminism's less than heroic history in understanding and possibly changing motherhood as well. Given the fraught discussion of motherhood in twentieth century feminism, this is easier to say than to do. To wit: according to Elizabeth Fox-Genovese (1996), feminism essentially ignored women's roles as mothers for a long time. Noteworthy exceptions are Adrienne Rich's (1977) *Of Woman Born*, in which she distinguishes between the oppressive institution of motherhood and its sometimes enriching experience, or Roiphe's (1997) *A Mother's Eye* that likewise pleads the case of motherhood. Feminism's theoretical impasse regarding motherhood dates to the 1960s and 1970s when to have children was taken by some as a sign of a lack of commitment to the feminist cause (Simons 1984: 350). This line of argumentation can be traced back to Beauvoir's (1989) rationalist assessment of what motherhood did to a woman's life. Betty Friedan's (1982) *The Second Stage* is the first to take issue with feminism's 'egoistic individualism' and the predominant anti-family, anti-male and anti-life attitude she observes (quoted in Simons 1984: 355). The book (i.e. Ruddick 1980) is part of the early 1980s massive offensive to stop separating women and mothering. While an important moment, given the division second-wave feminism had created between white women and women of colour exactly over motherhood and mothering, motherhood will remain deeply problematic.

Feminism after all set out to break both the taboo surrounding those who mother in a patriarchy and those who are not mothers, argues Ann Snitow (1992). In order to do so, early second-wave feminism produced a number of 'demon texts' (that understood motherhood as betrayal to the cause) for which feminists have been apologizing ever since (1992: 34). Shulamith Firestone's (1970) position that pregnancy is barbaric is just one of them. Such overly strong statements were part of what Snitow calls the harsh feminist self-questioning in the 1970s to do with taking motherhood for granted (1992: 37). To illustrate: 'family', according to Barbara Ehrenreich and others, was a grave in which the more autonomous word 'women' got buried (reported in Snitow 1992: 40). These strong sentiments run into a major backlash by the end of the 1980s. They leave Snitow wondering in 1992 how feminism might stand to gain by privileging motherhood. After all if the first wave of feminism from the end of the nineteenth century onwards is about the vote, the second wave was about the right to abortion (1992: 43).

Although 20 years later, and a continent apart, Snitow's reconstruction remains elucidating. Clearly, neither feminism nor for that matter what was then called 'patriarchy' managed to wholly contain motherhood in one single myth. As Snitow reminds us, after the 'demon' texts, feminism did break the taboo of discussing the experiences of mothers: the joy and fascination in mothering (even in a patriarchy) as well as the pain, isolation, boredom and murderousness (1992: 34). These seem a more relevant frame than the later romanticization of supermom to understanding why *Penoza*'s Carmen offers an emotionally realist reflection on motherhood. While disconcerting in her unwavering allegiance to her own idea of what a mother should do (rather than actually wondering whether her particular type of mothering is doing much for her daughter and sons), Carmen's fight with criminals is a fitting projection of the struggle that motherhood is.

There is an alternative interpretation for Carmen's motherhood to be the most referenced quality of the character in the press reviews of the series that is equally based on the simple facts that a mother entering a life of crime as a lead character is unusual in popular television drama and that the Netherlands have quite an unusually strong adherence to the idea of motherhood. The alternative interpretation would stress not only the traditional stay-at-home-mum version but also the I-am-a-better-mother-when-I-can-also-work version. This newer construct is part of government initiatives to get more women (including mothers) to work. Given Dutch seriousness about the moral duty of mothering, this will necessitate debate and rumination and careful consideration of all possible consequences. Popular culture is good at doing just that. It helps reflect on mothering from any and all ideological angles. Whether the angle is that of a life of crime as a test of fire of one's stamina as a mum, or whether it is a careful exploration of what might go wrong when a mother takes up a career. Carmen's life of crime allows for both: at any given moment, a viewer can fault the series, realism on denotational grounds. Its narrative is far-fetched and over the top and gets to be more and more 'Hollywood' style as the series becomes be darker and darker (Meerman 2015). So far, this is not what viewers do. They let the actors know they love them (van Rhee 2013b). Telling is what people call out to Monic Hendrickx who plays Carmen Walraven. In an interview for *De Limburger*, announcing the fourth season, she says: 'People call out to me [...]: Hey, Carmen: You are a good mother! You are really great man!' (Meerman 2015). Which neatly sums up how *Penoza* not only references but apparently temporarily solves all confusion about mothering and gender: a mum can be a great guy.

> The great thing about Carmen [...] is that she is both mafia and a mother. A working mum with balls. When she gives her children a hug after having endangered their lives for the umpteenth time, it has as much impact as when she roundly curses a Yugo and puts him in his place. You follow Carmen's ups and downs with beating heart, as if it is your own family fighting for her life. Sometimes it is as if you are the one getting hit in a fight, or who takes up a gun while setting up another illegal drugs deal. *Penoza* comes close, that is its power.
> (Maas 2013)

As an antiheroine, Carmen is not easily appropriated for the feminist cause. Given that feminism's own ambiguous track record in discussing and understanding motherhood is itself a major obstacle to do so, it would probably be best to cherish Carmen as a working women who is loved despite being less than successful in her attempts to care for her children. As an antiheroine, she mostly urges feminist self-reflection. It is a slight deception for the 'curious feminist' who would prefer popular culture to do the work of changing the world for her. Then again, *Penoza* may well help shift deeply lodged Dutch convictions regarding how mothering can and should be done. The series producers might well try and go for a government subsidy to promote women's emancipation. The series' double take on political correctness could of course confuse policy-makers, but what extraordinary campaign material it would provide.

References

Ang, I. (1985), *Watching Dallas: Soap Opera and the Melodramatic Imagination*, London: Methuen.
Barthes, R. (1984), *Mythologies* (trans. A. Lavers), New York: Noonday Press.
Beauvoir, S. de (1989), *The Second Sex*, New York: Vintage Books.
Beerekamp, H. (2010), 'De polderversies van Italiaans New Jersey'/'The polder versions of Italian New Jersey', *NRC*, 20 September.

—— (2013), 'Doodeerlijk geweld'/'Honest violence', *NRC*, 14 January.
Benjamin, J. (2012), 'Buitenland houdt van Hollandse tv-ideeën'/'Abroad they like Dutch ideas for television', *NRC*, 23 June.
Dekker, J. (2008), 'Moral literacy: The pleasure of learning how to become decent adults and good parents in the Dutch Republic in the seventeenth century', *Paedagogica Historica*, 44: 1–2, pp. 137–151.
Dekker, J. and Groenendijk, L. (1991), 'The Republic of God or the Republic of Children? Childhood and child-rearing after the reformation: An appraisal of Simon Schama's thesis about the uniqueness of the Dutch case', *Oxford Review of Education*, 17: 3, pp. 317–335.
Firestone, S. (1970), *The Dialectic of Sex: The Case for Feminist Revolution*, New York: Morrow.
Flier, M. (2013), 'De grote belofte van *Penoza*'/'*Penoza*'s promise', *Gelderlander*, 13 September.
Fox-Genovese, E. (1996), *Feminism is not the Story of My Life: How Feminism's Elite Has Lost with the Real Concerns of Women*, New York: N. Talese.
Friedan, B. (1982), *The Second Stage*, London: Michael Joseph.
Groenier, R. (2013), '*Penoza* is rock 'n roll', *BN/De Stem*, 28 September.
Hartley, J. (1999), *Uses of Television*, London: Routledge.
Hermes, J. (2005), *Re-reading Popular Culture*, Oxford: Blackwell.
Johnston, D. and Swanson, D. (2003), 'Invisible mothers: A content analysis of motherhood ideologies and myths in magazines', *Sex Roles*, 49: 1–2, pp. 21–33.
Limburg, D. (2010), '*Penoza* stoppen is zonde van het creatief kapitaal'/'Stopping *Penoza* is a waste of creative capital', *NRC*, 5 November.
Maas, R. (2013), '*Penoza*. Carmen bezorgt je misdadig spannende zondagen'/'*Penoza*. Carmen ensures criminally exciting Sundays', *Limburgs Dagblad*, 12 October.
—— (2014), 'De stoere littekens van kenau Monic'/'The scars of kenau Monic', *Limburgs Dagblad*, 6 March.
Meerman, G. (2015), 'Donkere reeks *Penoza* op komst'/'Expect dark series of *Penoza*', *De Limburger*, 2 July.
Mepham, J. (1990), 'The ethics of quality in television', in G. Mulgan (ed.), *The Question of Quality*, London: BFI, pp. 56–72.
Nauta, H. (2010), 'Tja, wat is dat, deugen?'/'What does it mean to be morally unflawed?', *Trouw*, 10 September.
O'Donnell, H. (1999), *Good Times, Bad Times: Soap Operas and Society in Western Europe*, London: Leicester University Press.
Onkenhout, P. (2013), 'De juist mix van gansterbaas en luizenmoeder'/'The right mix of a gangster boss and a headlice mother', *De Volkskrant*, 28 September.
Penoza (2010–2015, Netherlands: NPO 3).
Rich, A. (1977), *Of Woman Born: Motherhood as Experience and Institution*, New York: Norton.
Rijghard, H. (2013), 'Coke tussen de kinderschoenen'/'Coke in the children's shoes', *NRC*, 16 March.
Roiphe, A. (1997), *A Mother's Eye: Motherhood and Feminism*, London: Virago.
Ruddick, S. (1980), *Maternal Thinking: Toward a Politics of Peace*, Boston: Beacon Press.
Schama, S. (1988), *The Embarrassment of Riches: An Interpretation of Dutch Culture in the Golden Age*, New York: Random House.

Simons, M. (1984), 'Motherhood, feminism and identity', *Women's Studies International Forum*, 7: 5, pp. 349–359.

Snitow, A. (1992), 'Feminism and motherhood: An American reading', *Feminist Review*, 40, pp. 32–51.

Takken, W. (2012), 'De luizenmoeder blijft maffiamama'/'Head lice mother remains maffiamama', *NRC*, 23 November.

—— (2013), 'Interview TV producent Alain de Levita', *NRC*, 16 March.

Taylor, E. (1989), *Prime Time Families: Television Culture in Postwar America*, Berkeley: University of California Press.

Van Engen, M., Dikkers, J., Vinkenburg, C. and de Rooy, E. (2009), 'Carrièresucces van vaders en moeders'/'Career success of fathers and mothers', *Gedrag en Organisatie*, 22: 2, pp. 146–171.

Van Gelder, H. (2010), 'Dat criminele milieu heeft ook iets amicaals'/'There is something friendly about that criminal milieu', *NRC*, 18 September.

van der Heuvel, J. (2014), 'Van keiharde Penoza naar zoete "Taart"'/'Tough Penoza to sweet "Cake"', *Telegraaf*, 13 July.

van der Jagt, M. (2012), 'Op de set bij Penoza'/'On the Penoza set', *Vrij Nederland*, 2 June.

van der Kooi, W. (2010), 'Henk en Ingrid', *De Groene Amsterdammer*, 25 August.

van der List, G. (2013), 'De gangster als held'/'The gangster as hero', *Elsevier*, 13 September.

Van Nimwegen, N., Blommesteijn, M., Noors, H. and Beets, G. (2002), 'Late motherhood in the Netherlands: Current trends, attitudes and policies', *Genus*, 58: 2, pp. 9–34.

van Rhee, A. (2013a), 'Penoza 3', *Algemeen Dagblad*, 27 September.

—— (2013b), 'Interview Eric Corton', *Algemeen Dagblad*, 12 December.

van Wiggen, F. (2012), 'Hendrickx is de onderwereld de baas'/'Hendrickx lords it over underworld', *Opzij*, 1 December.

Valk, E. de (2013), 'Drie afleveringen *Penoza* gaan in één aflevering Red Widow'/'Three episodes of *Penoza* fit into one episode of Red Widow', *NRC*, 18 March.

Note

1 In total 45 unique articles referencing *Penoza* in the Dutch press from a length of 250 words upwards (the longest articles are over 2000 words, most are under a 1000) in the period August 2010–July 2015 were collected and analysed. Articles in syndicated newspapers (the regional press) are only counted once. All quotations are translated by the author.

Chapter 5

'Really Good At It': The Viral Charge of Nancy Botwin in *Weeds* (and Popular Culture's Anticorps)

Elisa Giomi

Introduction

This chapter focuses on Nancy Botwin (Mary-Louise Parker), the lead female character in the award-winning series *Weeds*, a black comedy created by Jenji Kohan that aired on the cable network Showtime from 2005 to 2012. Nancy is a widow and suburban mother-of-two, who, after her husband dies from a heart attack, earns a living selling marijuana. The series covers seven years, during which Nancy raises two sons, Silas and Shane, gives birth to a third, Stevie, and eventually becomes a grandmother; she gets re-married three times (each husband dies) and collects a plethora of lovers, both male and female. Additionally, her business dealings cause her to move home a number of times, spending a nomadic period in an RV as well as three years in jail. Nancy passes from selling pot under the protection of/on behalf of others, to growing it herself and starting her own business and then creating a fruitful chain of marijuana shops that she eventually sells to Starbucks. Starring alongside Nancy, in addition to her three sons, is a family acquaintance (Doug Wilson) and her brother-in-law Andy Botwin.

On a general level, this character belongs to a female lineage that, over the last 40 years, has seen an increasing number of heroines driving popular culture narratives: police officers and lawbreakers, prisoners and warriors, astronauts, Amazons, Samurais, cowgirls, superwomen and spies… women have gradually occupied genres and roles that have traditionally been male and have started to display skills, behaviours and psychological traits that were once culturally coded as masculine.

Since the early 1990s, an increasing number of studies have focused on such figures (Clover 1992; Roberts 1993; Tasker 1993, 1998; Inness 1999; McCaughey and King 2001; Early and Kennedy 2003; Inness 2004; Neroni 2005; Schubart 2007; Owen, Stein and Vande Berg 2007; Brown 2011; Jones, Bajac-Carter and Batchelor 2014; Brown 2015; Gjelsvik and Schubart 2016). Over the years, the terms of the debate have changed slightly, though, with most critiques being concerned with assessing whether tough/strong women subvert or merely re-enforce gender expectations.

(Hyper-)sexualization and 'availability in traditional feminine terms' have been underlined as problematic since Tasker's groundbreaking work (1993: 19). More recently, scholars have registered the ambivalent nature of female leads as 'rooted in stereotyped female roles' and at the same time likely to disrupt them (Inness 2004: 5); some have overtly claimed that these characters are revolutionary: the co-presence of toughness/violence and feminine, even hyper-sexualized, traits is seen as challenging traditional constructions of womanhood (McCaughey and King 2001) and the gender binary system as a whole (Brown 2011: 9).

All the aspects discussed in the literature – sexualization, violence, fluidity of gender identity – are also particularly relevant to the design of the Nancy character; yet, she possesses a more radical quality compared to many past and present heroines: as a woman in the business of crime, the nature of her transgression is twofold, involving both gender norms and the law. Interestingly, whereas gender issues are widely covered in studies on *Weeds*, the topic of crime/criminality is marginal. Contributions address aspects related to Nancy's sexuality, motherhood, gender identity (Beck 2012; Bradshaw 2013; Walters and Harrison 2014; Snyder 2014), as well as racial and ethnic stereotypes (Gillota 2012; Forster 2013). Drug dealing only becomes a key aspect in the analysis of the drama's portrayal of Mexican narco-culture (Jaramillo 2013; Mercille 2014).

In order to compensate for this absence, I will start by analysing Nancy's construction as a pot dealer, and compare the narrative trajectory, through which her social deviance is established, to that of other transgressive women who have populated TV and films since the 1980s. I will draw a similar comparison when examining Nancy's gender deviance: in both cases, my aim is to show how this mother-of-three breaks down many of the themes/rhetorical devices commonly deployed to contain the subversive potential of non-normative female leads, thus embodying a particularly destabilizing antiheroine figure.

Her impact on the symbolic order needs to be mitigated somehow: I therefore examine the strategies put into action in order to normalize/compensate for Nancy's transgression of social and gender norms. I will also highlight how the series, in its most 'conservative' drives, mobilizes narrative tropes and forms of representing feminine subjectivity that are typical of post-feminist sensibility (Gill 2007).

Finally, I claim that Nancy's social and gender deviances are made to interact in ways that represent one of the most interesting, albeit controversial, traits of *Weeds*. The intertwining of Nancy's identity as both lawbreaker and woman is firmly placed at the heart of the drama's representation politics, and produces precise ideological implications.

The theoretical framework I will adopt is represented by the analysis developed within Feminist Culturalist Television Criticism and Feminist Film Theory. From a methodological point of view, I watched all the 102 episodes constituting the eight seasons and analysed them using N-Vivo software, coding references at 'nodes' (categories) that were in part suggested to me by previous studies on (anti)heroines in popular culture, and in part were developed throughout the viewing process.

The 'Biggest Game in Agrestic': And Beyond

We first meet Nancy Botwin while she is giving a speech in front of the local School Parents Council. Her constitutive traits are set up at once: she is assertive and capable of personal initiative, and she is a caring and responsible mother, who argues for the importance of introducing healthy food in the school cafeteria. Her goodness is even increased by the sharp contrast with the other mothers' meanness: instead of paying attention to Nancy's words, they chatter about her look and maliciously wonder 'how she is going to make it with children and no husband'.

Yet in the following scenes we are confronted with a different, almost opposite face of Nancy. During a fight between her second born Shane and another boy, Nancy is seen to act more childishly and vengefully than the kids: instead of favouring a 'peace process' and teaching the two the morality of forgiveness, the woman trips Shane's rival (who has his arm put in plaster cast!) and provokes him to fall. The juxtaposition of these scenes is paradigmatic of the construction of Nancy as a multifaceted character; more specifically, Nancy is endowed since the very beginning with a quality of antiheroism understood as 'liminality', that is, being in between good and evil (Introduction, p. X). Nancy's moral ambiguity is effectively developed throughout the series, but obviously, what contributes first and foremost to it is her activity of pot dealer. This is the subject of the current section. Nancy's status as – according to her own definition – 'the biggest game [drug-dealer] in the private community of Agrestic' ('You Can't Miss the Bear' 2005) is presented to us as a given. Nevertheless, throughout the series, Nancy undergoes a radical transformation as a criminal, which is on both a practical and 'spiritual' level. At the beginning, Nancy appears to be naïve and helpless, and she ignores even the most basic 'rules of conduct' of the underworld. Throughout the series, she becomes increasingly smart, learning how to avoid traps, blackmailers and police checks, and how to find new business partners as well as 'exit strategies' allowing her to turn dangerous situations to her own advantage. As she becomes acquainted with the world of crime, her body language undergoes a change as well. In the episode 'Last Tango in Agrestic' (2006), we see her engaging in a goofy physical confrontation with Heylia (the matriarch of the African American family with whom Nancy partners in the first three seasons); two seasons later, she subjugates her friend-enemy Celia Hodes by hitting her with the gun, causing her to lose a tooth and a considerable amount of blood ('No Man is Pudding' 2008). A true gangster is born, endowed with self-control and physical agility, capable to exercise power and calculated violence.

Nancy's 'spiritual' transformation as a criminal is more complex and includes the motivational aspect. Initially, she perceives her illegal activity as the product of a need, and she strongly refuses to be labelled as a drug dealer ('I'm not a drug-dealer, I'm a mother who distributes illegal products through a sham bakery!' ['Dead in the Nethers' 2005]). By the end of season 1, Nancy seems to have changed approach: for the first time, she refers to her business as a 'choice', claims her right to it ('I don't have to apologize for being a weed-dealer') and even displays satisfaction with herself: 'turns out I'm really good at it'. What remains immutable is her reasoning that she is doing this 'for [her] family' ('The Godmother' 2005).

This interpretation of her parental obligations does, however, seem to expose Nancy to difficulties, risks and all kinds of humiliation… to the point that a question arises in the viewer's mind which is perfectly expressed by local drug cartel boss U-Turn (under whose 'protection' Nancy works in season 3): '[W]hy don't you get a fucking job!?' ('The Brick

Dance' 2007). Actually, Nancy periodically does try to get one and start the 'normal life' that she declares to long for intensely ('Glue' 2009), but she invariably ends up returning to this illicit business. In season 3, she leaves her job as the executive assistant for Sullivan, a developer from the affluent neighbouring community of Majestic, because she senses the opportunity to expand her drug business into that district; in season 4, she moves to the fictional town of Ren Mar and starts working at a maternity store, but soon begs Guillermo – her former business partner/protector in Agrestic – to enrol her as a drug carrier through the US-Mexico border. Likewise, in season 6, the Botwins leave Ren Mar and change their identity to the Newmans in order to avoid both legal problems and revenge after Shane killed Pilar, a political advisor to the Mexican drug lord and Nancy's husband Esteban Reyes. They settle in Seattle and take menial jobs as strike-breaking labour at a local hotel, until the moment when Nancy jumps at an opportunity to gain extra income by making a deal with the hotel concierge to supply hash to guests.

In these three situations, Nancy's motivation for returning to criminal activities are: low wages ('My son earns far more than me!', she complains about her job at Random House ['Bill Sussman' 2007]); the need for more money to be able to build 'a fucking personal bathroom!' ('No Man is Pudding' 2008); the inability to cope with menial nature of a hotel maid's routine ('A Yippity Sippity' 2010). In short, Nancy refuses to undergo a proletarianization process, and what she is really struggling for is not simply 'providing for her family', but the less noble goal of keeping her middle-class lifestyle. This adds to her profile as a bad girl.

Nevertheless, the most interesting reason for Nancy's involvement in the business of crime is disclosed to us in season 6. After leaving Seattle, the Botwins start an off-the-grid life aboard an RV. When circumstances force them to escape from the last place they have settled, Nancy, who is carrying her newborn with her, is not upset by this umpteenth, abrupt change and looks excited instead: 'this family is going to make hash… lots of it… it's fantastic!' ('Gentle Puppies' 2011). Although her business activity has not failed to reward Nancy with numerous personal benefits, including material ones, so far she has kept justifying herself exclusively on the grounds of refusing low-income jobs and, most of all, parental duties. This is the first time Nancy explicitly expresses enthusiasm about her activity per se.

This radical change in Nancy's attitude is consolidated in the following season, 7, when Nancy definitively develops a taste for crime and comes to terms with her identity as a drug dealer: 'I'm fine with what I've done… I know myself', she tells the officer at the half-way house in which she is staying after being released from jail ('Synthetics' 2011).

Nancy's development of self-awareness is paralleled by another transformation, which also begins in season 6. Until then, she has always been the leader of a male team made up of relatives and friends; yet at the same time, Nancy has always benefited from the protection/guidance of experienced drug dealers and/or veteran criminals: Conrad, Heylia's nephew and Nancy's occasional lover, in seasons 1, 2 and 3; DEA officer and husband Peter Scottson in season 2; Guillermo in seasons 3 and 4; and Esteban, Nancy's husband and boss, in 4 and 5. After leaving the last, Nancy still relies on her family members and acquaintances, but she has definitively freed herself from male protection. This configures a reworking of gender power relations and completes the profile of a criminal in her own right.

She Doesn't 'Need to Apologize': And the Narrative Does Not Either...

One particularly interesting aspect of the narrative's trajectory throughout which Nancy's social deviance is established concerns what I propose to call, in rhetorical terms, the *Excusatio*. This is a common denominator in many popular culture products and encompasses different textual strategies intended to provide justification for the female (anti)hero featuring in typically male genres/roles/contexts. As this heroine represents an anomaly, 'the narrative takes a lot of trouble to explain why she is in a man's world, what she is doing there' (Schubart 2007: 533).

The most common forms of *Excusatio* are indirect and stem from precise narrative configurations. For instance, the first studies on popular culture's portrayal of female criminality individuated in the 'rape-revenge motive', the most extreme and recurring articulation of a heroine's double transgression of law and gender norms (Clover 1992: 6). The rape-revenge first emerged in the 1970s and 1980s and is still used to motivate contemporary heroines' missions (hacker Lisbeth Salander from Stig Larsson's *Millennium Trilogy*, 2005; the teenage private detective Veronica Mars, 2004) or it is used to explain their toughness more generally (narco-trafficker Teresa Mendoza from Telemundo's *telenovela La Reina del Sur/The Queen of the South*, 2011). Fortunately, Nancy does not have to bear such a trauma, and the only rape she endures, by her husband Esteban ('Machetes Up Top' 2009), is portrayed ambivalently as a source of pleasure to her.

Female heroism can be legitimized in relation to a father loved and lost – as in *The Silence of the Lambs* (Demme, 1991), to name but one – and often female transgression is also justified in these terms, with the heroine identifying with her father and searching for 'reconciliation with authority' (Tasker 1998: 69). This is the case with Luc Besson's Nikita (1990), the cinematic version of the Lara Croft character (Giomi, 2007), Beatrix Kiddo from *Kill Bill vol. 1* and *vol. 2* (Tarantino, 2003 and 2004) and many others. Alternative explanations for the alleged 'unnaturalness' of the way these women act may lie with a missing mother, or an entirely dysfunctional family, as in the 'Daughter Archetype' analysed by Schubart (2007: 3995).

Nancy had a conflicted relationship with her father, yet she is completely uninterested in reconciling with him (and least of all with authority). The nicest thing she is able to say to her father when visiting her parents' grave in her hometown (Dearborn, Michigan), is: 'I'm really liking this new side of you. Less judgemental, more accepting, willing to listen' ('Dearborn-Again' 2010). She appears to be emotionally detached from her mother as well, who is described as alcohol-addicted by Nancy's sister, Jill ('To Moscow, and Quickly' 2010), and by Nancy herself as incapable of affection ('A Beam of Sunshine' 2012). A clearly dysfunctional family then, yet references to it amount to only four out of 102 episodes: too few to locate Nancy within the Daughter Archetype or to claim that her transgression is justified on these grounds.

The only rationale provided regarding Nancy's status as a drug dealer, as we have seen, is based on her responsibilities as a widowed mother. Nancy is obviously not the first woman in the business of crime to be a mother at the same time. Gangster stories offer a vast array of such characters who have acquired increasingly strong roles since Connie Corleone (*The Godfather*, Coppola, 1972) to Karen Hill (*GoodFellas*, Scorsese, 1990) and, recently, the Sopranos women. Carmela Soprano, in particular, represents the most emancipated version of mob wife, combining traditional family roles with the fearlessness of a gangster's moll. Nancy is far more radical, though: like Carmela, she inhabits a realm identified by a patriarchal structure, challenges male authority and pursues her own goals (whereas other mob wives only act to protect their family and never follow a personal agenda); yet, whereas Carmela is 'forceful without having to use a gun or resort to physical violence' (Yaquinto 2004: 224), Nancy is completely familiar with both of these approaches.

Neroni observes that the trauma caused by female violence is revealed by the 'extraordinary length to which the narrative must go to explain or situate' those who deploy it (Neroni 2005: 11) or display transgressive behaviours more generally. This could not be clearer than in the case of *Weeds*: references linking Nancy's activity and her obligations/problems as a mother, either directly or indirectly, run throughout the series, reiterated with significant regularity and appear in 68 out of 102 episodes. Also, Nancy's physical aggression is most apparent when her children are in danger: we see her slapping the father of Meghan, Silas' former girlfriend, after realizing the man hit Silas ('Mrs. Botwin's Neighborhood' 2006); shooting in a particularly calm way one of Esteban's henchmen, who accidentally shot Shane in the arm; and heroically rescuing Shane when he gets kidnapped by Esteban's men ('A Shoe for a Shoe' 2010): 'You can't defeat a mother lion when you threaten her cubs', she tells her former husband while escaping.

Maternity as a motivating factor, with the 'female hero acting to protect her children, either biological or adoptive' (Tasker 1998: 69) is another well-established trope since Sergeant Ripley from *Aliens* (Cameron, 1986) and Sarah O'Connor from *Terminator 2* (Mattei, 1990). It carries a precise ideological implication: as with all forms of *Excusatio*, it is an attempt to mitigate these characters' destabilizing effect, and it does so on the grounds of a particularly essentialist position. This is perfectly expressed by the highly stereotyped image of the mother lion: women are allowed to be aggressive, violent, transgressive only in the name (and within the limits!) of their biological functions.

However, such implications do not completely apply to Nancy, whose involvement in the business of crime is presented not only as a means to provide for her children, but as a source of self-realization and, most of all, something highly enjoyable too. Having expected to find forms of *Excusatio* that were in proportion to the level of Nancy's transgressions, on the contrary, I found no real justifications for her social deviance provided by the narrative, and indeed her 'behaving badly' is amplified by a truly 'hedonistic' approach.

Nancy's Gender Deviance and Other Transgressions

Nancy's deviation from gender norms is constantly reflected in the nicknames she is given, all of them referring to her possession of spiritual attributes that are culturally coded as 'masculine': Nancy is 'a warrior [...] armoured and ready for battle' ('All About My Mom' 2009), a 'girl who's got balls' ('Risk' 2007), a '*marimacha*' ('I Am the Table' 2008). The latter – a 'denigrative way to call a lesbian', as *Weeds*' character Guillermo explains – epitomizes at best the threat posed by Nancy to the gender binary system.

Ironically, unlike Guillermo, the viewer knows that Nancy really does not have a normative sexuality: she admits having had a relationship with a woman in the past ('Good Shit Lollipop' 2005) and entertains a love affair with her female cell mate of three years, Zoya; she is inclined to experimentation, she uses vibrators ('Fashion of the Christ' 2005), frequently changes partners and shows a 'consumerist' attitude towards sex. Throughout the series, her sexuality becomes almost extreme, and she is seen to take increasing pleasure in rough intercourses, which becomes violent when she meets Esteban.

Nancy also disrupts gender expectations because she is egocentric and careless. In 'Su-Su-Sucio' (2009), Jill blames her for leaving her to take care of their dying parents while Nancy 'was off playing ballerina and then getting laid' when they were both young girls. As an adult, Nancy has not changed much. While heroines – unlike heroes – are normally centred on both family and community 'privileging relationships and the collective over the individual' (d'Enbeau and Buzzanell 2014: 157), Nancy discards her original community Agrestic (she even plays a part in setting it on fire); she is unable to make friends anywhere she goes, and practically all of her interpersonal relations are instrumental. Most of all, heroines are oriented towards social change, whereas Nancy's priority is clearly that of wealth accumulation, and her horizons – though enlightened by occasional philanthropic gestures – remain entirely private, even idiosyncratic, limited to herself and her nuclear family.

Nancy's indifference to the moral universe of 'regular' heroines increases the list of charges against her: she transgresses legality, gender norms and rules of heroism for her gender. More: rules of *antiheroism* for her gender are infracted, too. Nancy is seen to lack those forms of *Excusatio* commonly found in the representation of criminal/transgressive women, but she deviates from their 'standard' narrative trajectory for other reasons as well. Despite her self-perception as 'mother lion', despite some (isolated) self-abnegation moments, clearly Nancy is 'not the mother of the year', as Silas often remarks. Her neglectful parenting jeopardizes her three sons' lives on several occasions and turns two of them into dysfunctional individuals: Silas refuses to go to college and follows in Nancy's footsteps and Shane, who was emotionally unstable and violent as a child, becomes an alcoholic (and a sociopathic) adult. Nothing new: Hollywood storylines have always had plenty of deviant mothers, but those mothers 'have precisely been deviant in order to be punished, to serve as reminders of the power of normative familialism and rigid gender ideologies'. On the contrary, Nancy – like other contemporary TV aberrant mothers – does not incur any form of punishment, thus departing from what has constituted 'the norm in Hollywood for eons' (Walters and Harrison 2014: 48).

And not only in Hollywood, of course: Rosy Abate, probably the most powerful figure of a Mafia woman ever seen in an Italian TV drama (*Squadra antimafia/Antimafia Squad*, Various Directors, 2009–ongoing) shares a common interest for the business of crime with Nancy as she mostly embodies 'the modern face of the entrepreneurial Mafia' (Chapter 1, p. 9). Yet she wants too much: the Mafia power and motherhood pleasures and is punished by having her child kidnapped. Nancy, too, is vehemently accused by Jill of 'wanting it all' ('tote-full of marijuana, fuck strangers upside down [...] and toddler wanders in at 3am wet with pee!' ['Do Her/Don't Do Her' 2011]), but her sons will always stand by her side.

There is no alibi for Nancy's multiple transgressions, and no punishment either: she is an unconventional, groundbreaking female figure under all profiles.

Normalization Strategies

Despite – or may be because of – the lack of either an alibi or a punishment, the narrative still needs to domesticate Nancy Botwin somehow. In terms of her social deviance, the main means through which Nancy's activity is made more acceptable is a 'values reversal', which underpins the whole series and is effectively suggested in the teasers for seasons 1, 2 and 3: what looks like a wealthy and nice North-American suburban context, on closer examination, appears conformist and alienating, populated by people, houses and cars that – as the theme song ('Little Boxes' by Malvina Reynolds, 1962) reminds us – 'look all the same'. In the teaser's final scene, the shadow cast by a growing marijuana leaf suggests that pot is something hidden, and despite being invisible, present in Agrestic. The 'suburban dystopia' (Forster 2013) of this suffocating community filled with automatons, not only makes marijuana, by contrast, the only living and authentic element there, but also turns it into something 'redeeming'. Similarly, the façade of 'respectability' that Nancy's friends and acquaintances exhibit, which hides their corruption, psychosis, racism, class-ism and sexism, has the effect of making Nancy appear to be the 'good one, not a hypocrite', as Celia's daughter declares in 'You Can't Miss the Bear' (2005).

Social legitimization also works by depicting pot smoking as a normal activity, in which practically everybody engages: Shane's karate coach and college students ('Dead in the Nethers' 2005), the elderly at the hospice ('Grasshopper' 2007), members of the Christian church ('Release the Hounds' 2007), rich ladies who buy pot packaged with the cosmetics sold by Celia ('Suck 'n' Spit' 2009); Shane's schoolmates and professors in Ren Mar ('Wonderful Wonderful' 2009); Doug's posh colleague at his office ('A Hole in Her Niqab' 2011). Nancy is the only one who does not smoke, which adds to her positive portrayal, along with the ethical limits she sets herself: the scope of her criminal activities is limited to pot, she refuses to sell heroin ('Mother Thinks the Birds Are After Her' 2008), and when she discovers that the tunnel excavated under her maternity store is used for the USA/Mexico traffic of guns and women, she suffers terribly and decides to report Guillermo to police ('If You Work for a Living, Then Why Do You Kill Yourself Working?' 2008).

As to Nancy's gender deviance, many factors combine to rehabilitate her in terms of her emotional and sexual conduct. After her husband's death, it takes a long time before Nancy returns to sexual activity, and for more than half of season 1, she is represented as a still-in-love wife, crying in front of a home video of her and her husband making love ('Dead in the Nethers' 2005). Her inner faith to Judah remains intact throughout the series, despite Nancy's intense and pleasurable sex life and three husbands: this clearly serves to relocate her within a traditional, even 'virginal', construction of femininity.

As an aside, the strongest drivers of normative femininity are felt at the level of Nancy's appearance. She adheres to class and race stereotypes – white, middle class, well-educated – and to gender ones as well: she is beautiful and attractive, though lacking any hyper-sexualized physical attributes (apart from her dress sense that frequently attracts the label of 'whore'). Nancy's look is also characterized as fashionable, but, most of all, it conveys the idea of a Lolita-like femininity: sparkly mini-dresses, flowers and little pigtails in her hair (combined with her habit of dreamily sipping coffee) make her erotic yet at the same time childish, which in a different age would have been inappropriate to her (undefined) age and role as mother.

Yet in contemporary popular culture, the MILF stereotype has become one of the most common representations of middle-aged women. Nancy actively and ironically engages with this stereotype (the special strain of cannabis from which she makes her fortune is called 'MILF Weed'), but its ideological implications are quite controversial for women. Negra looks at the diffusion of MILFs since the early 2000s onwards as proof of the ability of post-feminist culture to define various female life stages within the parameter of 'time panic' (Negra 2009: 1045): '[W]omen's lives are simultaneously ever governed by notions of temporal propriety and conformity, but also assessed in relation to *women's perceived abilities to defy time pressure and impacts*' (emphasis added). Underneath the apparent widening of women's freedom (the permission to be sexually desiring even as you age), new forms of discipline for female subjects are concealed.

The MILF trope expresses the ambivalence of female empowerment also because it connects to another post-feminist theme, that of partially failed mother: this is the key ingredient of Showtime's distinctive 'female problem' genre, a term that reflects the network's 'branding around the anti-hero mother figure' (Bradshaw 2013: 161), also found in *The United States of Tara* (Showtime, 2009–2011), *Nurse Jackie* (Showtime, 2009–2015) and *The Big C* (Showtime, 2010–2013). It is true that Nancy is not punished for her transgression of maternal norms: she does not lose her children or their love, and in the final episode she is even rehabilitated by her youngest child Stevie, who thanks her 'for always being there' ('It's Time [Part 2]' 2012); yet her own relation to motherhood is a very tormented one: Nancy constantly doubts/complains about her parenting choices, very frequently depicts herself as 'the worst mother in the world' ('Yeah. Like Tomatoes' 2006) and goes as far as admitting she wishes she had no children ('From Trauma Cometh Something' 2011).

What is more, this is only a part of the pathologizing process she undergoes. The feeling is that the 'pay-off' for her gender deviance is a lack of self-confidence and even frustration: practically every episode ends with Nancy feeling inadequate or helpless; despite her autonomy and initiative in her 'professional' life, she frequently depends on Andy's advice in the emotional/affective realm, which is where she is often made to appear dysfunctional.

References like this abound, but one is particularly explicative: in 'Saplings' (2012), Rabbi Dave Bloom (who later will marry Nancy) wonders if she's able to 'truly love someone'; Andy – the man who knows Nancy better – answers he has no idea, and claims Nancy probably does not know either, or 'she has an idea, but what she really needs is the exact opposite of her idea: someone smart, warm, stable, romantic' ('It's Time [Part 2]' 2012). The image emerges of a woman who, underneath the surface of assertiveness and sexual agency, is a victim of her self-deception process, incapable of recognizing her own good and pursuing it and, in the end, is in need of a Prince Charming to rescue her. This is in line with the post-feminist representation of feminine subjectivity as uncertain, and permanently at risk of failure, that is often found in popular culture texts and provides another powerful domestication strategy.

Social and Gender Deviance, Sexuality and Crime: The Ultimate Normalization Strategy

Social and gender deviances interact in quite interesting ways in *Weeds* and their interaction can be seen as a manifestation of a 'deeper' and more general intertwining: that of sexuality and crime, which lays at the heart of the series' representation politics.

The first and most emblematic example is found at the end of season 1. Nancy confronts local drug dealer Alejandro who has started to persecute her and her family as a revenge for invading 'his' market. Both of them refuse to give up their business and in the middle of a violent discussion in an alley, they suddenly have sex on Alejandro's truck, out of the blue and in a quite animalistic way. Afterwards, Nancy goes back to her car, takes a BB gun and aims it to Alejandro's penis: 'this dick does nice work. I'd hate to see it full of holes. This was unexpected, but it's never going to happen again. Stay away from my house!' ('The Punishment Light' 2005). Scared, Alejandro runs to his car and vanishes. These shocking ten seconds immediately destroy the virginal image of Nancy as devoted spouse still in love with her husband and that of innocuous, naive newcomer on the drug-dealing scene: for the first time, she actively engages with the underworld's distinctive practices and language – violence included – and offers a very convincing performance.

Also, this scene sets a precedent: from this moment onwards, Nancy will regularly use sex for both her pleasure and as a means to secure her business: simply an enjoyable 'side dish' to her transactions or a means of persuasion and even control over both partners and rivals. Examples of this kind are countless, to the point that Snyder notes: 'If Nancy were a superhero, her superpower would be sex' (Snyder 2014: 488). According to her, this scene is precisely the moment when Nancy discovers such a superpower.

Behind the galvanizing, even empowering surface, though, a precise and more problematic intersection of gender, power and sex lurks. This scene has the flavour of a double initiation ritual, where the transformation of Nancy from beginner to Criminal with capital C is paralleled by the transition from the chaste role of widow to that of sexual predator. A similar parallel is found on many other occasions. For instance, when Nancy decides to reprise her activity after serving a three-year jail sentence (another 'baptism', therefore): 'it is so good to be back in the game, dealing, catching balls' ('Vehement v. Vigorous' 2011), she says thrilled while seductively sitting on the lap of her new lover and accomplice, Zoya's brother (who later will watch Nancy and Zoya having sex).

In short, the construction and staging of Nancy's social deviance is deeply intertwined with, even pivoting on, the construction and staging of her gender/sexual deviance. This is no news: femme fatales and dark ladies have a long-entrenched reputation for combining criminal and non-normative sexual behaviour (and quite significantly Cesare Lombroso even claimed that the Prostitute and the Criminal Woman possessed similar physical 'degenerative' features!); to be peculiar is not the intertwining of social and gender deviance per se, but the mere connotation of Nancy as a sexed subject – no matter if transgressive or not – in the aforementioned situations: why does the narrative choose to show its heroine having sex for the first time precisely when she starts to 'gets serious' as a criminal? The history of film and television is not full of male characters whose initiation as criminals is performed throughout such a strict parallelism with sex. But in a patriarchal world, women have forever signified – or have been made to signify – (sexual) difference, and it is clearly even more so in the male-dominated realm of criminality. This needs to be reaffirmed, Nancy's gender needs to be made visible and the viewer reassured that she is an exception within this realm.

Nancy's construction as a sexual object – apparently a strategy opposed to displaying her sexual agency – definitively serves the same purpose. Although the camera never fetishizes Nancy's body, practically none of her business interlocutors refrains from (vulgar) allusions to her sexual attractiveness or even attempts to sexually degrade her. Such behaviours are in line with the realistic portrayal of the patriarchal and 'macho' world of drug-dealing; at the same time, they have the effect of marking Nancy as an unusual player in the field: just like the continuous references to Nancy's race – she is called 'Snowflake', 'Blanca', 'white ass' – are a signal that the norm is non-whiteness, so turning Nancy into object of (hetero)sexual desire is a means to foreground her gender, reminding us that the norm is maleness (and hegemonic masculinity, of course).

Such operation does not only involve sexuality, but also other biological functions of Nancy, and it intensifies in key moments such as when Nancy's career takes off or, on the other hand, is at risk, or when it jeopardizes Nancy's own life. This is what happens at the end of season 4: while Nancy is in Esteban's office, he receives confirmation of her involvement in the police's discovery of the tunnel under the maternity store and the related human trafficking. In order to prevent Esteban from killing her, Nancy hands him an ultrasound and reveals that she is pregnant with his child. The two dimensions of Nancy's discursive construction – as a criminal and as a sexed subject – that have thus far run parallel, gradually 'thickening' and often overlapping, here reach a climax and a chiastic asset: the higher the risk Nancy's business exposes her to, the stronger the sexual connotation she undergoes, which here consists of displaying Nancy's reproductive power.

The visual composition of this thrilling scene is a chiastic one, too. Two images are exchanged on the table, with no words to accompany them: a picture of Nancy together with Captain Roy, showed by Esteban to prove to her that he knows she was the mole, and the ultrasound depicting Nancy's uterus that she hands him in return. This exchange of images faithfully reflects the 'values' exchange that is taking place: the reproductive power of her female body, able to generate (and generate 'a boy', as Esteban wished) is the currency of exchange Nancy skilfully uses to have her life spared.

Despite this particular scene possessing an empowering quality, the overall relationship between sexuality and crime played out in *Weeds* provides the ultimate normalization strategy: the unceasing highlighting of (different aspects of) Nancy's sexuality while she attends to her 'duties' as criminal, alongside indissolubly connecting her to her biology, serves to discursively represent her as a female subject within a male-dominated turf. And exception, as it is said, 'always proves the rule'.

Conclusion

Nancy Botwin is a multifaceted, ambivalent figure, hard to locate within clear-cut categories or along fixed gender lines. We are faced with a powerful character, endowed with a viral charge that is able to contaminate and transform contemporary TV portrayal of gender and gender issues.

Nancy seems to attack popular culture's 'immune system' from many directions: in addition to transgressing the law, as a pot dealer, and gender norms, as aberrant mother and sexual predator, Nancy also violates narrative norms. She evades the majority of tropes and rhetoric configurations commonly found in mainstream representations of women who cross borders – criminals included – that are deployed precisely in order to domesticate these figures.

To continue with this metaphor, many of the antibodies the system-series specifically develops with the aim of curtailing Nancy's power are seen to work only partially. For instance, it is true that Nancy is recast with traditional femininity by depicting her as a woman in need, albeit subconsciously, of a Prince Charming to rescue her, but this prince never arrives. At the end of the series, after multiple sexual and sentimental incursions, Nancy still retains the same status she had at the beginning: she is alone. Women who do not end up in a romance display the most disruptive power: love is reassuring as it feeds the myth of complementarity between men and women, and 'complementarity allows us to believe in the social order precisely because the opposition between male and female stands in for the social antagonism' (Neroni 2005: 1439).

'Really Good At It': The Viral Charge of Nancy Botwin in *Weeds*

In *Weeds*, a constant oscillation is found between oppression and liberation, radicalism and reactionary implications, gender conformism and female agency. I believe it worthy to make a final point on those which remain as problematic aspects and on their relationship to wider sociocultural forces. The emergence of transgressive women is a result of the new environment that the feminist movement created, where 'women could adopt more aggressive roles' (Inness 2004: 6), albeit played by frequently hyper-sexualized feminine figures. Forty years later, the female lead's body and, more generally, her sexuality, still constitute the dimensions where representational policies show their most regressive, conservative vocation. Nancy's non-normative sexual conduct clearly is one of her most liberating traits – and even more so as she is a mother – yet sexuality is also (a) the weapon the series uses to blunt Nancy's antagonistic potential, (b) the weapon Nancy herself uses to control her male business partners, as well as (c) to delegitimize her female rivals.

These three uses of sexuality, in my view, stem from and reinforce patriarchal systems of control and regulation. As for the first one, I have showed how gender and social deviance, sexuality and crime interact in ways that serve systematically to make Nancy's gender visible: on the one hand, this produces an abrupt essentialist 'slip' in line with post-feminist texts' vocation to reassert sexual difference (Gill 2007: 157); on the other, it marks Nancy as an exception in her field of play.

Let us make clear that it is an exception that does not last forever: in the end, Nancy realigns with narrative trajectories coded for female (anti)heroines that are 'carefully exported out of the plot' (Schubart 2007: 529). Some do so in a traumatic way, by committing suicide and passing from tough female heroes to 'sacrificial heroes' (a transformation in which scholars see the endorsement of patriarchal oppression [Crosby 2004: 176]); others benefit from softer exit strategies: Teresa Mendoza in the last episode quits the field, accepting an immunity deal with DEA; Nancy, too, is exported out of the drug world, as she sells her franchise to Starbucks. In both cases, the norm of male control of the drug business – although completely legalized in that of Nancy's – is indirectly reasserted.

Patriarchal forces are also seen at work in Nancy's use of sex to secure her business, because she willingly participates in her own self-exploitation, and because her sex appeal takes the MILF form with all the attached implications in terms of control over female life-cycle/subjectivity.

Finally, when Nancy wants to be fierce towards other women, she hits them in the sexual sphere: she disregards the two girls Shane loses his virginity to, calling them 'young whores' ('Head Cheese' 2008), showing no empathy towards these pre-adolescents depicted as daughters of careless mothers. The same thing happens with Emma, a girl who has tried to neutralize a competitor, Silas, by having sex with him and by playing unfairly (what Nancy herself does on a regularly basis!). She calls Emma a 'cheap whore' and claims her superiority on the grounds of her status as mother ('System Overhead' 2011). Nancy appears to be completely co-opted into patriarchal logic in her use of female sexuality as a social control device, deployed to distinguish between good and bad women, and – *divide et impera* – to counter-pose them to one another.

There is no sisterhood for Nancy Botwin, incapable of making female friends and clearly disinterested in doing so. The final scene epitomizes this: Nancy, finally resolved to sell her chain of marijuana shops, sits on the porch steps, surrounded by Doug, Andy and her three sons, who have joined her one by one. There she is, 'retired' and comforted by the hug of the only relations she was ever able to maintain: those with men produced either by her seductive or reproductive power. The last images of Teresa Mendoza are even more explicit in re-positioning her in a 'natural' feminine role: she has changed life, moved to the seaside and smiles happily while caressing her seven-month pregnant belly.

One of the research questions underpinning this book concerns the 'condition of possibilities' of the reconciliation 'between a male genre and a female gender long considered incompatible'. Despite *Weeds*, a dark comedy, clearly not being an expression of a male TV genre, Nancy's role and the environment she moves within definitely are. This series seems to warn us that such reconciliation is possible, and women are allowed to behave badly only under precise conditions: the traditional gender order has to be (at least partially) restored; the heroine needs to abdicate her unconventional role in the end; the heroine has to pay the price of being isolated from individuals of her own gender. To me, this is the most problematic and saddest aspect, one that confers on the series an aftertaste of post-feminism understood as a backlash to feminism. There must still be something scary and forbidden about the idea of (strong) women tied to one another.

References

'A Beam of Sunshine' (2012), Micheal Trim, dir., *Weeds*, Season 8, Episode 2, 8 July, New York: Showtime.

'A Hole in Her Niqab' (2011), David Holstein, dir., *Weeds*, Season 7, Episode 4, 18 July, New York: Showtime.

'All About My Mom' (2009), Scott Ellis, dir., *Weeds*, Season 5, Episode 13, 31 August, New York: Showtime.

'A Yippity Sippity' (2010), Tate Donovan, dir., *Weeds*, Season 6, Episode 3, 30 August, New York: Showtime.

'A Shoe for a Shoe' (2010), Micheal Trim, dir., *Weeds*, Season 6, Episode 6, 27 September, New York: Showtime.

Beck, B. (2012), 'Mother courage and her soaps: *Incendies, Weeds, Nurse Jackie*, and daytime drama', *Multicultural Perspectives*, 14: 1, pp. 28–31.

'Bill Sussman' (2007), Craig Zisk, dir., *Weeds*, Season 3, Episode 5, 10 September, New York: Showtime.

Besson, L. (1990), *Nikita*, France: Gaumont.

Bradshaw, L. (2013), 'Showtime's "female problem": Cancer, quality and motherhood', *Journal of Consumer Culture*, 13: 2, pp. 160–177.

Brown, J. A. (2011), *Dangerous Curves: Action Heroines, Gender, Fetishism, and Popular Culture*, Jackson: University Press of Mississippi.

Buonanno, M. (2014), 'Donne al comando fra action e melodramma. Il caso di *Squadra Antimafia*', in M. Buonanno (ed.), *Il prisma dei generi. Immagini di donne in TV*, Milano: FrancoAngeli, pp. 49–77.

Cameron, J. (1986), *Aliens*, Brandywine Productions: Marshall, MI.

Clover, C. (1992), *Men, Women, and Chain Saws: Gender in the Modern Horror Film*, London: BFI.

Coppola, F. F. (1972), *The Godfather*, USA: Paramount Pictures.

Crosby, S. (2004), 'The cruellest season: female heroes snapped into sacrificial heroes', in S. A. Inness (ed.), *Action Chicks: New Images of Tough Women in Popular Culture*, New York: Palgrave MacMillan, pp. 153–178.

Demme, J. (1991), *The Silence of the Lambs*, USA: Strong Heart/Demme Production.

'Dead in the Nethers' (2005), Arlene Sanford, dir., *Weeds*, Season 1, Episode 5, 12 September, New York: Showtime.

'Dearborn-Again' (2010), Scott Ellis, dir., *Weeds*, Season 6, Episode 10, 25 October, New York: Showtime.

D'Enbeau, S. and Buzzanell, P. M. (2014), 'The erotic heroine and the politics of gender at work', in N. Jones, M. Bajac-Carter and B. Batchelor (eds), *Heroines of Film and Television: Portrayal in Popular Culture*, Lanham: Rowman and Littlefield, position 80–409 (Kindle edition).

'Do Her/Don't Do Her' (2011), Micheal Trim, dir., *Weeds*, Season 7, Episode 13, 26 September, New York: Showtime.

Early, F. and Kennedy, K. (eds) (2003), *Athena's Daughters: Television's New Women Warriors*, Syracuse: Syracuse University Press.

'Fashion of the Christ' (2005), Burr Steers, dir., *Weeds*, Season 1, Episode 4, 29 August, New York: Showtime.

Forster, D. E. (2013), 'Drugs, racial stereotypes, and suburban dystopia in Showtime's Weeds', in *The Asian Conference on Cultural Studies 2013*, Osaka, Japan, 24–26 May, Nagoya, Japan: IAFOR.

'From Trauma Cometh Something' (2011), Micheal Trim, dir., *Weeds*, Season 7, Episode 2, 4 July, New York: Showtime.

'Gentle Puppies' (2011), Scott Ellis, dir., *Weeds*, Season 6, Episode 8, 11 October, New York: Showtime.

Gill, R. (2007), 'Postfeminist media culture: Elements of a sensibility', *European Journal of Cultural Studies*, 10: 2, pp. 147–166.

Gillota, D. (2012), '"People of color": Multiethnic humor in *Harold and Kumar Go to Castle* and *Weeds*', *Journal of Popular Culture*, 55: 5, pp. 960–978.

Giomi, E. (2007), 'Lara Croft: Ein Neues Vorbild für Actionheldinnen und Frauen?', in L. Mikos, D. Hoffman and P. Winter (eds), *Mediennutzung, Identität und Identifikationen*, Weinheim: Juventa Verlag GmbH, pp. 67–82.

Gjelsvik, A. and Schubart, R. (eds) (2016), *Women of Ice and Fire: Gender, Game of Thrones and Multiple Media Engagements*, London: Bloomsbury.

'Glue' (2009), Micheal Pressman, dir., *Weeds*, Season 5, Episode 12, 24 August, New York: Showtime.

'Good Shit Lollipop' (2005), Craig Zisk, dir., *Weeds*, Season 1, Episode 3, 22 August, New York: Showtime.

'Grasshopper' (2007), Perry Lang, dir., *Weeds,* Season 3, Episode 6, 17 September, New York: Showtime.

'Head Cheese' (2008), Craig Zisk, dir., *Weeds,* Season 4, Episode 11, 25 August, New York: Showtime.

'I Am the Table' (2008), Adam Bernstein, dir., *Weeds,* Season 4, Episode 8, 4 August, New York: Showtime.

'If You Work for a Living, Then Why Do You Kill Yourself Working?' (2008), Craig Zisk, dir., *Weeds,* Season 4, Episode 13, 15 September, New York: Showtime.

Inness, S. A. (1999), *Tough Girls: Women, Warriors and Wonder Women in Popular Culture*, Philadelphia: University of Pennsylvania Press.

—— (2004), 'Boxing gloves and bustiers: New images of tough women', in S. A. Inness (ed.), *Action Chicks: New Images of Tough Women in Popular Culture*, New York: Palgrave Macmillan.

'It's Time (Part 2)' (2012), Micheal Trim, dir., *Weeds,* Season 8, Episode 13, 16 September, New York: Showtime.

Jaramillo, D. (2013), 'Narcorridos and newbie drug dealer: The changing image of the Mexican narco on US television', *Ethnic and Racial Studies*, 37: 9, pp. 1587–1604.

Jones, N., Bajac-Carter, M. and Batchelor, B. (eds) (2014), *Heroines of Film and Television: Portrayal in Popular Culture*, Lanham, Maryland: Rowman and Littlefield.

La Reina del Sur/The Queen of the South (2011, USA: Telemundo).

'Last Tango in Agrestic' (2006), Bryan Gordon, dir., *Weeds,* Season 2, Episode 3, 28 August, New York: Showtime.

'Machetes Up Top' (2009), Micheal Pressman, dir., *Weeds,* Season 5, Episode 2, 15 June, New York: Showtime.

Mattei, B. (1990), *Terminator 2*, USA: Carolco Pictures, Pacific Western Production.

McCaughey, M. and King, N. (eds) (2001), *Reel Knockouts: Violent Women in the Movies*, Austin: University of Texas Press.

McRobbie, A. (2004), 'Postfeminism and popular culture', *Feminist Media Studies*, 4: 3, pp. 255–264.

Mercille, J. (2014), 'The media-entertainment industry and the "war on drugs" in Mexico', *Latin American Perspectives*, 41: 2, pp. 110–129.

'Mother Thinks the Birds Are After Her' (2008), Craig Zisk, dir., *Weeds,* Season 4, Episode 1, 16 June, New York: Showtime.

'Mrs. Botwin's Neighborhood' (2006), Craig Zisk, dir., *Weeds,* Season 2, Episode 5, 11 September, New York: Showtime.

Negra, D. (2009), *What a Girl Wants? Fantasising the Reclamation of Self in Postfeminism*, London and New York: Routledge (Kindle edition).

Neroni, H. (2005), T*he Violent Woman: Femininity, Narrative, and Violence in Contemporary American Cinema*, Albany: State University of New York Press.

'No Man is Pudding' (2008), Craig Zisk, dir., *Weeds,* Season 4, Episode 5, 14 July, New York: Showtime.

Nurse Jackie (2009–2015, USA: Showtime).

Owen, S., Stein S. R., and Vande Berg, L. R. (2007), *Bad Girls: Cultural Politics and Media Representations of Transgressive Women*, New York: Peter Lang Publishing.

'Release the Hounds' (2007), Ernest Diuckerson, dir., *Weeds*, Season 3, Episode 9, 8 October, New York: Showtime.

Roberts, R. (1993), *A New Species: Gender and Science Fiction*, Urbana: University of Illinois Press.

'Risk' (2007), Paul Feig, dir., *Weeds*, Season 3, Episode 13, 5 November, New York: Showtime.

'Saplings' (2012), Micheal Trim, dir., *Weeds*, Season 8, Episode 9, 26 August, New York: Showtime.

Schubart, R. (2007), *Super Bitches and Action Babes: The Female Hero in Popular Cinema, 1970-2006*, Jefferson: McFarland (Kindle edition).

Scorsese, M. (1990), *GoodFellas*, USA: Warner Bros.

Snyder, K. (2014), 'Burn one down: Nancy Botwins as (post)feminist (anti)heroine', in N. Jones, M. Bajac-Carter and B. Batchelor (eds), *Heroines of Film and Television: Portrayal in Popular Culture*, Lanham: Rowman and Littlefield, position 413–723 (Kindle edition).

Squadra Antimafia/Antimafia Squad (2009–ongoing, Italy: Canale 5).

'Suck 'n' Spit' (2009), Micheal Trim, dir., *Weeds*, Season 5, Episode 9, 3 August, New York: Showtime.

'Su-Su-Sucio' (2009), Lesli Linka Glatter, dir., *Weeds*, Season 5, Episode 3, 22 June, New York: Showtime.

'Synthetics' (2011), Micheal Trim, dr., *Weeds*, Season 7, Episode 8, 15 August, New York: Showtime.

'System Overhead' (2011), Scott Ellis, dir., *Weeds*, Season 7, Episode 10, 29 August, New York: Showtime.

Tarantino, Q. (2003), *Kill Bill vol. 1*, USA: A Band Apart.

—— (2004), *Kill Bill vol. 2*, USA: A Band Apart.

Tasker, Y. (1993), *Spectacular Bodies: Gender, Genre and the Action Cinema*, New York: Routledge.

Tasker, Y. (1998), *Working Girls: Gender and Sexuality in Popular Cinema*, London: Routledge.

The Big C (2010–2013, USA: Showtime).

'The Brick Dance' (2007), Lev L. Spiro, dir., *Weeds*, Season 3, Episode 3, 27 August, New York: Showtime.

'The Godmother' (2005), Lev L. Spiro, dir., *Weeds*, Season 1, Episode 10, 10 October, New York: Showtime.

'The Punishment Light' (2005), Robert Berlinger, *Weeds*, Season 1, Episode 8, 26 September, New York: Showtime.

The United States of Tara (2009–2011, USA: Showtime)

'To Moscow, and Quickly' (2010), Micheal Trim, dir., *Weeds*, Season 6, Episode 9, 18 October, New York: Showtime.

'Vehement v. Vigorous' (2011), Scott Ellis, dir., *Weeds*, Season 7, Episode 7, 8 August, New York: Showtime.

'You Can't Miss the Bear' (2005), Brian Dannelly, dir., *Weeds*, Season 1, Episode 1, 8 August, New York: Showtime.

Walters, S. D. and Harrison, L. (2014), 'Not ready to make nice: Aberrant mothers in contemporary culture', *Feminist Media Studies*, 14: 1, pp. 38–55.

Weeds (2005–2012, USA: Showtime).

'Wonderful Wonderful' (2009), Scott Ellis, dir., *Weeds,* Season 5, Episode 1, 8 June, New York: Showtime.

'Yeah. Like Tomatoes' (2006), Craig Zisk, dir., *Weeds,* Season 2, Episode 11, 23 October, New York: Showtime.

Yaquinto, M. (2004), 'Tough love: Mamas, molls, and mob wives', in S. A. Inness (ed.), *Action Chicks: New Images of Tough Women in Popular Culture*, New York: Palgrave Macmillan, pp. 207–230.

Chapter 6

Really Bad Mothers: Manipulative Matriarchs in *Sons of Anarchy* and *Justified*

Amanda D. Lotz

Given the centrality of maternity in societal constructions of womanhood, both the mandate to become a mother and directives regarding maternal behaviour have been central to the policing of women's identities. Feminist movements across history and around the globe have sought to deconstruct the perceived biological imperative linking womanhood with motherhood that has constructed women who are incapable of bearing children as well as those simply not desiring to do so as failed women. Indeed, the very nature of how one engages and performs the tasks of motherhood remains highly fraught in both cultural imaginations and individual women's psyches. Key battle lines over gender equity have revolved around assumptions that a woman's presence in public life must necessarily come at the detriment of her maternal duties. And given the charged nature of the politics of motherhood in society, it is of little surprise that depictions of motherhood in popular media have been similarly contested and controversial (Douglas and Michaels 2004).

Because patriarchal power structures have so emphasized motherhood as a primary component of the value it affords to women, being a bad mother represents an act of significant transgression. Though this collection explores a multitude of ways in which women can be seen behaving badly in contemporary television series, by the measure of many societies, the bad mother occupies the status of the ultimate bad woman. Bad mothers are not uncommon media objects, though the ways in which they are bad have been narrowly defined. Traditionally, the bad mother embodies the pinnacle of villainy, although some contemporary bad mothers challenge that categorization.

This chapter focuses on two bad women who are also bad mothers: Gemma Teller (Katey Segal), the matriarch of *Sons of Anarchy* (FX, 2008–2014), and Mags Bennett (Margo Martindale), the second season antagonist of *Justified* (FX, 2010–2015). In the same way as a character such as Tony Soprano spreads his influence through a mix of benevolence and fear within his community with his patriarchal control that extends beyond blood relations as some sort of royalty, the matriarchal control of these two women exerts a similar reach. Although this chapter could explore their antiheroic attributes in their manipulation of their communities and acts that make them antiheroes through acts of crime, as the collection of chapters here suggests, such female characters become less exceptional in television dramas in the early twenty-first century. Uncommon among the other antiheroines, however, is their status as mothers, and both series' exploration of antiheroic characters that extend their malevolence into acts of parenting provides a distinctive lens through which to examine these characters and their stories.

The narratives considered here are unequivocal; Gemma and Mags clearly hold the power over their respective domestic and illicit entrepreneurial regimes. This chapter explores the matriarchal control inflicted by these characters, how they challenge established norms of maternal portrayal, and how they deviate from women who only commit bad acts outside of their familial role.

Gemma and Mags defy conventional female portrayal in many ways. Unlike the dominant trope of depicting mothers as selfless and commonly willing to martyr themselves for their children, Gemma and Mags act with cool ambivalence to their offspring, often willingly using them as pawns in their larger plans, though also adequately performing maternal love to a degree that allows their children to believe they are safe in their care. In teasing apart their distinction from other compelling but bad characters, the chapter also examines whether their greatest crimes are those they commit in 'business' or against family and what this suggests about the access to power contemporary television imagines for women.

Gemma and Mags also defy common characteristics of the male 'antihero' characters common in cable series at this time (*Breaking Bad*; *The Shield*; *Dexter*; *Rescue Me*) – including those series in which the women appear. These characters were developed for US cable television at a time when male protagonists defying the common narrative of a 'hero's journey' were all the rage, though efforts to develop female characters with similar heroic ambiguity stumbled. The chapter places these characters within the nexus of simultaneous storytelling about bad men who are fathers to explore how the women manipulate expectations of them as women and as mothers to become the controlling force in their respective narrative universes.

As characters, Mags and Gemma were largely unprecedented on US television, but foreshadowed in early seasons of *The Sopranos* that hinted that Tony's mother Livia (Nancy Marchand) exerted invisible but significant power both within the family and the family business. Feminist film scholar E. Ann Kaplan describes the monstrous mother common in film as taking two different forms: either the 'fusional' mother who is possessive, destructive and all devouring, or the mother who becomes monstrous through her over-indulgence and her efforts to 'live through' the child (Kaplan 1992: 27–29). Neither monstrous types characterize Gemma and Mags well. To some degree they resemble the fusional mother, but motherhood is central to the identity of the film characters Kaplan considers while Mags' and Gemma's acts of manipulation often involve goals unrelated to family.

Walters and Harrison (2014) identify the emergence of the 'aberrant' mother in television of the early 2000s and assess her ideological significance. They describe her as

> not quite a twenty-first century feminist heroine but she does upend more traditional depictions of maternal identity. Unabashedly sexual, idiosyncratic to a fault, and seriously deleterious in her caretaking skills, she seems to live largely in the high end of popular culture.
>
> (Walters and Harrison 2014: 40)

The trope of 'aberrant' mothers – a form of bad motherhood that is more neglectful than monstrous – that Walters and Harrison explore begins with Showtime's *Weeds* in 2005, which traces the descent of Nancy Botwin (Mary-Louise Parker) from suburban mom to drug dealer and presents Botwin as an uncommonly neglectful mother (examined in detail in Chapter 5). Though she initially engages in drug dealing under the justification of providing for her family after her husband's death, she performs few acts throughout the series that suggest the well-being of her children rates a comparable priority to her own desires – although the comedic tone of the show discourages substantial reflection on this aspect of her character.

'Bad' television mothers are more often neglectful than monstrous. Though still 'bad', a merely neglectful mother can be more benign; she fails by not providing whatever emotional and physical sustenance is culturally expected. Constructions of neglectful mothers who fail to provide for children are most common in news and crime genres. Until the aberrant mother, the 'neglect' of the working mother appeared frequently and functioned as a regulating representational trope.

The subscription-cable channel Showtime followed *Weeds* (2005–2012) with the tonally and thematically similar *Nurse Jackie* (2009–2015) and *United States of Tara* (2009–2011), which both offered significantly flawed mothers who deviated substantively from the struggling-but-functional mothers otherwise common on broadcast network dramas (*Judging Amy*; *Good Wife*). As primarily dark comedic case studies of the protagonists, *Weeds*, *Nurse Jackie* and *United States of Tara* exhibited fair similarity, though there are also significant differences among them with regard to how and why the women defy conventional expectations of motherhood. In all cases, the women performed a spectrum of neglect, but were not monstrous.

Also debuting in the early twenty-first century, the legal thriller *Damages*, produced first for FX and then DirecTV, merits mention for its unapologetically non-maternal, but not quite monstrous protagonist Patty Hewes. Shows including *Damages* (2007–2012), *The Killing* (2011–2014) and *Homeland* (2011–ongoing) all presented narratives that primarily told the story of their protagonists' professional lives, but occasionally acknowledged these women were also mothers – though struggling with those responsibilities. Like the others, Hewes neglects her son, but in a way that recalls cultural anxiety of the 1980s executive working woman and related fears of 'women in power'. Her behaviour towards her junior associate Ellen Parsons is indeed monstrous, but is more accurately considered as monstrous mentorship rather than motherhood.

AMC's *The Killing* and later seasons of Showtime's *Homeland* also reintroduced the spectre of the female professional who cares more for her career than her child. Both of these shows re-enact this work/home negotiation faced by women in a manner distinctive from tropes typical until the 1990s. Neither Sarah Linden (Mireille Enos) nor Carrie Mathison (Claire Danes) so much choose their greater devotion to work, as carry some psychic damage that prevents her from more fully inhabiting her role as mother.[1]

But this chapter focuses on two characters who are bad mothers in ways entirely different from those discussed so far. Mags – a smaller consideration here, given her single season of narrative – runs a family marijuana business that dominates the trade in rural, eastern Kentucky. She assumes leadership of the business after her husband's death and uses her three sons as muscle to enforce her will and prevent competition or challenge to her enterprise.

Gemma is the mother of Jax, whose journey the seven seasons of *Sons of Anarchy* explores. Jax is heir to the leadership of an outlaw motorcycle club in rural California that supplements income from an auto repair shop by fencing illegal guns supplied by a Northern Ireland cartel. Jax's father, John Teller (JT), founded the club with his friend Clay Morrow. After the death of Jax's father in a motorcycle accident when Jax was still young, Gemma marries Clay. Though not a member of the men-only motorcycle club, Gemma has fully embraced the life of illicitly gained means. Despite the macho-environ of its motorcycle club setting, melodrama provides most of the suspense and action in *Sons of Anarchy*. The ever-shifting allegiances, secrets and betrayals that drive episodic plot action afford Gemma an uncommon position of behind-the-scenes power.

Gemma and Mags are women behaving badly in ways similar to characters considered in other chapters. This chapter, however, largely sets their 'professional' villainy aside and explores their crimes against their families. Though both are extraordinary television characters on account of the rarity with which women are depicted as the masterminds of illegal enterprises (or legitimate ones, for that matter), these women manipulate and deceive their children just as other bad women behave towards those in their 'professional' world. The relationship dynamics between mother and son in Gemma's case and mother and sons in Mags' is complicated. The women claim they love their children and appear to believe they act in the best interest of family, though their actions suggest otherwise.

One reason Gemma and Mags stand out so profoundly among other contemporary series is because of their contrast to narratives exploring the illicit behaviour of male 'antihero' characters that attempt to redeem them by constructing them as good fathers. From *Breaking Bad*'s Walter White to *The Shield*'s Vic Mackey, the surprising rise of seemingly good men doing illegal things as the subject matter of cable dramas consistently finds its root in their need to provide for or restore their families (Lotz 2014). Much more so than in the construction of previous male characters, these men are characterized as fathers who seek to be active and engaged in their children's lives. At this time in which the role of fatherhood is uncommonly narratively central to stories television explores about male characters, female characters in comparable shows shirk maternal duties, or in the case of Gemma and Mags, use their children to achieve desired ends.

I emphasize the industrial specificity of 'cable' – particularly channels such as Showtime, AMC and FX – throughout these paragraphs, and it is a distinction requiring more explicit comment. The women (and men) behaving badly considered here all seem worthy of analysis at least in part because they are so different than nearly all characterizations US television has previously offered. Importantly, it is not US television that has changed so much as that a separate and distinctive sector of television storytelling emerged at the beginning of the twenty-first century: series created for cable channels. Those who watch these series outside of the United States may understandably wonder what this distinction involves, as outside of the United States, these series are not industrially sequestered in the same way. The economic model for US-originated content involves two entities: the studio that makes the content and the broadcast network, cable channel or broadband portal (Netflix, Amazon) that pays to license that content in its first window of availability; a licence fee that typically covers 60–70 per cent of the production costs at the start of a series.[2]

For decades, the US broadcast networks were the only US entities with enough financial resources to afford original scripted series. The limited competition among the few networks (three for most of television history) led to remarkable consistency in the types of series produced and to the perception that only a narrow range of content was commercially viable. The business of television until the 1990s was one of aggregating a mass, heterogeneous audience. Television content was consequently designed to be palatable to as many as possible, although achieving this broad palatability led it to also be passionately loved or despised by few.

The expansion of competition within the US market, first with a slow trickle and then a steady stream of cable channels beginning in the early 1980s, gradually adjusted the competitive dynamics of the business. Subscriber-supported channels HBO and Showtime began financing the production of original series in the early 1990s, though did not achieve profound success until later in the decade with *Sex and the City* (1997) and *The Sopranos* (1998). Significant experimentation with original narrative series was evident on advertiser-supported cable channels in those same years, though the most notable success and the establishment of a distinctly 'cable' series sensibility does not emerge until *The Shield* in 2002.

The practice of cable channels licensing original content then exploded and substantially altered expectations of television series because the cable channels had a business model based on dual revenue streams; advertiser-supported cable channels are funded fairly equivalently by advertising and by the fees cable service providers pay each month per subscriber in order to include the channel in its offerings. None of the series discussed in this chapter could have been produced for the mass audience required by broadcast economics. The advent of series developed for cable channels is thus critical for explaining why so many protagonists that defy the conventional hero's journey emerge in US television series at this time.

Sins of the Mother

Mags Bennett emerges unexpectedly as the primary antagonist in the second season of *Justified*. The six seasons of *Justified* primarily follow US Marshal Raylan Givens as he returns to his birthplace in rural Kentucky and pursues the criminals he finds there. In the first season, the series lacked a cohesive narrative and followed more of an episodic, criminal-of-the-week organization. With the introduction of Mags and her family – antagonists that span the entire second season – the series began to cohere around an increasingly serialized, season-long form of story construction.

Though onlookers might regard Mags as merely a tough woman – a necessity for a widow in rural Appalachia running an extensive marijuana trade – superficial appearances conceal a lot. Mags is succinctly described as a mountain woman. In her late fifties with grown children, she appears without make-up and is clad in oversized men's shirts that conceal her large figure. Mags cultivates an identity of community matriarch, but behind closed doors, she treats her own children poorly. She is verbally, emotionally and physically abusive. This is most evident when she crushes her son Coover's hand with a hammer when she learns he's been cashing the unemployment checks of an employee she killed as punishment for alerting authorities about a sex offender in their midst. (It is not that she condoned the sexual predator, but that involving outside legal authorities introduced a threat.) The facts that Coover, larger and stronger than his mother, submits to the punishment and that his brother watches and allows it to happen suggest the extent of the history of abuse. It is clear that Mags has used extreme acts of violence – both within the home and community – to cow others in fear.

Beyond the example of physical abuse, Mags controls her children by treating them inequitably and fostering an environment of jealousy and competition for her love, which allows her considerable latitude in manipulating them. Mags takes in Loretta, the pre-teen daughter of the employee she kills, in the first of her episodes and lavishes attention on her in a way that appears honestly loving. It may indeed be genuine affection as Mags enjoys the prospect of now having the daughter she never had, but Loretta's presence also fuels the sibling rivalry. Mags quickly affords Loretta privileges Coover never achieved – such as responsibility for watching over the family's general store – and Coover overhears Mags telling Loretta about her disappointment and embarrassment over his dimness (Mags seems unaware he hears, but it would be consistent with her psychological abuse to deliberately perform this disavowal).

Mags' regime of abuse ensures that her sons will do her bidding. She demands they enforce her will and presents her machinations as best for her family and community, but they are always to advance her self-interest. A secondary plotline throughout the season follows the efforts of a mining company to come into the community and buy up land from Mags and others to create a new mine. Mags initially refuses and makes an impassioned public plea to others not to sell their land, reminding the community of its deep historical roots and how it would be disastrous to sell. She later changes her mind when the price for her land becomes extraordinary. She realizes the financial windfall would allow her to move her son Doyle – the county sheriff – and his family away from Appalachia's poverty and disadvantage.

Her reversal undercuts the matron of the community identity Mags has cultivated, and reveals the true self-interest of her character. She is unwilling to help her two more derelict sons, Coover and Dickie, leaving them with the marijuana business, and otherwise disowning them. Various plot complications ensue, and Mags' story ends when she takes her life after Coover and Doyle are killed in confrontations with law enforcement and Dickie is bound for jail; though it seems the greatest motivation for her suicide is the despair she feels when confronted by Loretta who figures out Mags was responsible for her father's death. In the end, the deal with the mining company falls through, and all that remains of the long-storied Bennett family is the incarcerated Dickie.

Mags' relatively compact storyline makes constructing her maternal failings and general status as a bad woman easier to explain than Gemma's. Mags' story is told in a mere 13 episodes and Raylan's dealings with Bennett's amount to only a third of narrative time. In contrast, Gemma is a primary character throughout the seven seasons of *Sons of Anarchy*, and a contradictory and evolving one. Generically, *Sons* functions primarily as a melodrama with key plot tensions built on truths, lies, who knows those truths and when, and for what reason they share them, which provides rich narrative engagement, but is difficult to contain in succinct analysis.

Other scholarly considerations of Gemma explore the contradictions at play between her outlaw identity and the non-traditional femininity it encompasses in comparison with the way in which the character displays a traditionally 'feminine' set of priorities based on doing all and anything for her family. Gemma is perennially clad in skin-tight pants, high-heeled boots, and low-cut blouses that reveal a scar on her chest from heart surgery for the congenital defect that killed her brother and one of her sons; she carries a gun in her purse – and uses it on occasion – regularly smokes cigarettes and marijuana, and drinks extensively. Though not actually a member of the motorcycle club, she is deeply involved in its life and generally privy to and complicit in its illegal dealings. The club's involvement in pornography and escorts means Gemma is surrounded by sex workers, though she works as the business manager of the automotive business. These outlaw attributes are then contrasted with Gemma's self-construction as a matriarch whose raison d'être is care and maintenance of her family.

As literary scholar Kerry Fine describes,

> This combination of familial protection, outlawry, and instrumental aggression subverts the role of the outlaw hero by expanding it to include maternal protection, redefining that traditionally masculine power in a distinctly feminine way. Gemma's identification as a mother categorizes her as feminine – in other words, she is more than a figurative male – but at the same time, she undermines the traditionally masculine nature of heroism.
> (Fine 2012: 170)

Fine explores whether Gemma can be argued to be a feminist character; however, analysis of Gemma as a bad woman requires interrogating whether Gemma is as vigilantly maternal as she professes and apparently desires to believe.

Gemma is not easily categorized as a bad mother. Indeed, a surface reading of the series makes readily available an understanding of her as a fierce matriarch.[3] Throughout the series, she speaks of 'her boys' as her primary purpose and motivation – whether the boys she bore – Jax and Thomas (who died in childhood) – or her grandsons, Abel and Thomas. But the 'boys' she does not acknowledge in this claim are the boys of the motorcycle club. Although it is often the case that the interests of the club and of her family are the same, it is when these interests do not align that melodrama, violence and vengeance rage after

Gemma unilaterally determines what is in the best interest of her bloodline regardless of her son's desires.

In many ways, Gemma struggles with the same paradox that drives the series' primary narrative: Jax's conflict in negotiating the interests of the family of the club with the family composed of his wife and sons. We first meet Jax and Gemma on the day his son is born and he is already in the midst of an existential crisis regarding the club and his role in it. He has come across a manuscript written by the father he never really knew. Though his father John Teller (JT) co-founded the club, Jax finds that just before his death, he came to question what the club had become and had endeavoured to detach the club from the illegal arms dealing that had become a significant part of its existence. The series' seven seasons trace Jax's efforts to right the way of the club and fulfil his role as father and husband in a manner different from his own father. The disparity between what Jax and Gemma determine as best for Jax's boys leads Jax's story – in its final seasons – to transition from one of melodrama to one of outright tragedy.

Dramatic tension throughout the series is as driven by interpersonal conflict – given the incompatibility of Jax's goals with Gemma and Clay's priorities – as by the adventure and complicated dealing among gangs and factions with which the club deals. Either his family or the club faces constant threat: kidnapping, incarceration and efforts by various law enforcement units to destroy the club; in the end, though, the greatest threat comes from within the family. By the series' conclusion, the club is at last clear of guns dealing, but Jax's family is largely destroyed – and Jax has had to choose between them many times over.

Likewise, although never acknowledged by the character, Gemma struggles with conflicting loyalty and priority. Her words speak constantly of the importance of family, but her actions belie the priorities of the club. From the start, the conflict between Gemma's lifelong devotion to the club and the needs of her son is clear. Gemma is very much the 'mother' of the club – an 'old lady', in the vernacular – to all club members, in a manner similar to the way Mags is a community matriarch, though Gemma is far more committed to her clan. She 'founded' the club alongside JT, and the series suggests she conspired in JT's demise when he began to doubt the path of the club and sought to end the gun dealing. By this point he was also engaged in an extramarital affair with a woman in Belfast, and Gemma consequently conspired with JT's best friend, club co-founder, and her new love interest, Clay, to kill him.

Once Clay assumed presidency of the club, she became the none-too-subtle power behind the throne, able to manipulate Clay in a way the series suggests was less possible with JT. Reflecting on Gemma, series creator and writer, Kurt Sutter acknowledges, 'I had always envisioned Gemma as sort of being like the Nancy Marchand character in *The Sopranos* – kind of in the background and kind of pushing buttons and pulling strings, but not necessarily the key manipulator' (quoted in Deggans 2014). Jax's loyalty to the club is critical to Gemma because it ensures her continued access to the seat of power. Before all manner of complications begin to impede the club's operation, Gemma relates her concern about Jax's introspection to Clay – asking him to keep Jax close. Clay's arthritic hands number the days of his leadership, and Gemma is desperate for Jax to assume its leadership when Clay steps down.

Gemma is intricately bound up in the series – and its central problematic – because of her prioritization of the club as it is and because Jax ultimately endeavours upon a plan to shift the club back towards brotherhood and away from its illegal dealings. For Jax, this is a question of family and of being the man, husband, father, and friend he seeks to be. He recognizes that the way of the club, as it is, will leave his own boys as he was left, without a father – whether by death or incarceration. Moreover, just as he is uncertain about the legacy he has assumed, he is uncertain of similarly preordaining this path for his sons.

Gemma does not see how the life of the club poses such a threat to the life Jax desires and he does not confide either his concerns or plan in her. Gemma interprets his actions as Jax being misled down his father's path and experiences Jax's desire to leave the club and consequently the rural California town of Charming as an act against her and the performance of 'family' she idealizes. Although this interpretation is understandable, Jax does not seem to intend his questioning of the club as a refutation of Gemma or in any way an act against his mother. Her failing as a mother – and what leads her to become a bad woman – is engaging in manipulations in order to assert her will that he prioritize the club and reproduce his childhood inside the club for his sons over Jax's efforts to opt out of this life.

In early seasons, Gemma's actions are more benign and can nearly be rationalized – as she seems to – as actions taken for the good of her family. From the first episodes, she meddles with Jax's private life: she nearly kills his heroin-addicted, ex-wife Wendy by telling her she'll never see the child she bears in pre-term labour and leaving her with a loaded syringe. Wendy survives the overdose, and Gemma later tries to reinstate her as Jax's love interest once she detoxes and proves a more malleable partner than Jax's first love, Tara, who returns to Charming and encourages Jax's questioning. Tara left Charming to pursue her education and tried to convince Jax to come with her, but broke his heart by leaving. Tara's earlier act of trying to take Jax from Charming and then causing her son's heartbreak provokes Gemma's maternal fierceness.

Beyond manipulations to distance Tara and Jax, Gemma's primary machinations in the early seasons result from her fears that the truth of JT's demise will come to light. Apparently realizing the wisdom of keeping enemies close and lacking success in discouraging Tara from being in Jax's life, Gemma is forced to confide in and build a relationship with Tara when Gemma is gang-raped at the start of the second season and requires Tara's medical help. A new club foe attacks Gemma to 'send a message' to the club, but Gemma keeps the message to herself through most of the season, trying to stake claim to this trauma as hers alone and prevent it from being visited upon the club and her family. Tara becomes increasingly entrenched in the club as her medical skills are constantly needed and Gemma begins mentoring her. In the end, Gemma must share the truth of her assault to preserve her family and keep Clay from running the increasingly defiant Jax off to a different club. She first tells Clay and Jax about the assault, and they are immediately reunited by the need to exact vengeance. Once shared, Gemma's trauma becomes a violation of her family and the club, motivating the club's efforts to eliminate this group that introduced new drug trade within Charming.

The paradoxes that force prioritization of family over club keep emerging. A few episodes after the resolution of rape vengeance, Gemma is arrested to cover up an ATF agent's bad kill; Gemma was in the same location as the agent and killed a different person – the woman who had lured her to her assault. The ATF offers Gemma a deal that forces her to either turn on the club and implicate its members or consign herself to the risk of the death penalty and be prevented from seeing the biological family that she claims to prioritize during a lengthy prison sentence. Jax negotiates a different deal with the corrupt agent and keeps it from Gemma, who is afraid his actions to protect her will hurt the club. Ultimately Jax double-crosses the ATF, which saves Gemma and secures short prison sentences for him and several members of the club involved in a shooting. Their interests aligned, Gemma and Tara continue to grow close and Gemma helps care for the children while they await the men's release from a 14-month imprisonment (Tara bears Jax a second son, Thomas, while he is incarcerated).

When the men are released, Gemma learns that JT's Belfast mistress has given Jax the letters JT wrote her, letters that threaten anew to reveal Gemma and Clay's complicity in JT's death. The threat of this discovery incenses Clay, who is increasingly embattled as club president and has been forcing the club into transporting drugs in hopes of a big pay day that will allow him to retire comfortably. Jax never sees the letters, but Gemma learns Tara read them, which forces Tara back into Gemma's, and now Clay's, crosshairs. Fearing that Tara or another senior club member who has learned of the letters will hold him to account, Clay murders the club member and hires a team of assailants who attempt to abduct Tara. Jax prevents the abduction, but Tara's hand is severely broken imperilling her ability to continue in her vocation as a neo-natal surgeon.

Gemma is distraught that Clay would hurt Tara, after promising not to, because she believes she can control Tara without disrupting Jax's family. After learning of Clay's actions and receiving a beating when she confronts him, Gemma goes to Jax and gives Clay up. She gives Jax evidence of a half-truth that implicates Clay, but not her, in JT's death, knowing Jax will recognize it is his burden to kill Clay. This is a manipulation on multiple levels. Jax and Tara had announced plans to leave Charming, and this forces them to stay. The selective presentation of facts also somewhat immunizes Gemma from being suspected of involvement in JT's death. Though Tara has read the letters and knows Gemma too is implicated, she also knows that without the other letters, Jax would not likely believe Gemma was involved even if Tara tells him.

As always, club-related complications prevent Jax from extricating himself quickly and he must keep Clay alive as part of his plan to end the gun trade. Gemma begins having steady clashes with Tara and Jax as they prepare to leave Charming. Gemma bristles at parenting choices Jax and Tara make that decrease her role in the boys' lives. In an attempt to regain more control, she tells Wendy (Jax's now sober ex-wife) she suspects Tara has been abusing painkillers prescribed for her broken hand, as well as other subtle manipulations. Tensions build as Tara prepares to leave Charming with the boys without Jax, as well as to assign custody to Wendy to get the boys away from Gemma and the club as she begins to fear she'll be arrested as an accomplice to the club. Both her decision to leave without Jax and to pass custody to Wendy (rather than Gemma) in case of their deaths or incarcerations incenses Jax, who still believes the family might escape intact.

That possibility is eliminated when Tara is arrested, and the penultimate season traces her withdrawal from Jax and internal debate over entering witness protection. By this point it is clear that Jax cannot extricate himself from the club. Jax crafts a deal with law enforcement that would send him to jail in exchange for the dropping of all charges against Tara, and he tells Tara she can take the boys wherever she wants. But Gemma, not privy to Jax's deal making and suspicious that Tara is about to testify against the club and flee with the boys into witness protection, kills Tara and pins the murder on an Asian drug cartel.

This action – not just the murder, but a cover-up that leads to countless deaths as Jax attempts to enact retribution – secures Gemma's unequivocal status as bad woman. Both within the rules of the club life and the norms of conventional society, her family is lost if Jax learns the truth, so despite the exponential body count produced by her lie, she stays the course. Eventually Jax learns the truth and is faced with the burden of the only action available to him. His family destroyed and the club in equally dire straits as a consequence of Jax's wrongly targeted campaign for vengeance, Jax tracks down Gemma. Only after she tells him, '[...] [y]ou have to do this; it's who we are, sweetheart. It's okay, my baby boy. It's time, I'm ready', shoots her ('Red Rose' 2014). At this point, Jax is planning his own death as the only way to save what remains of his club and his family, but in the process also divorces the two once and for all.

Both Mags and Gemma are bad in multifaceted ways and their dealing in drugs and weapons alone warrant their consideration within an investigation of television's antiheroines. They commit multiple illegal deeds, including taking the lives of others, but from the vantage point of assessing them as gendered television characters, their biggest transgressions are in the actions they take against their children. Mags' crimes go far beyond neglect. Though she is not directly responsible for the death of either of her boys, it is circumstances that she puts in motion that lead them to their fate. Gemma presents a case of the worst possible fusional mother – possessive, destructive and all-devouring. Her possessiveness and her unwillingness to allow Jax to leave Charming ultimately results in the deaths of both mother and son.

Returning back to the broader range of antiheroines who cohabited television screens along with Gemma and Mags, it is also worth considering the particular class status of these women and their families. Unlike the relative privilege of characters such as *Weeds'* Nancy Botwin or *Nurse Jackie's* Jackie Peyton that struggle amidst conditions of relative affluence, Gemma and Mags give voice to women who occupy a very different social world. Importantly, both series so richly inhabit their milieu – whether Appalachian Kentucky or rural California – that the vindictive and manipulative actions of Gemma and Mags don't take on the weight of representing all women lacking economic privilege. However, their class status – in conversation with those of the women throughout the collection – speaks to the ways in which these shows explain the transgressions of their bad women relative to economic privilege and opportunities.

Mags and Gemma are not bad women or mothers because they are poor. The paucity of opportunities to provide a good life for their families – or even for themselves – does, however, lead them to desperate acts more quickly than likely the case for women of greater privilege. Working class characters remain exceptional on US television, and Gemma and Mags as rare exceptions – despite their monstrous acts – are worth noting.

Significant, as well, is the degree to which the series do not invite identification with the characters or their struggles. Admittedly, they are not titular characters and their presence in the narratives is as a threat or foil to male protagonists at the centre of the series. Both are compelling characters – well written and skilfully acted – such that watching them on screen is richly pleasurable. This is in contrast to the difference in the allowances contemporary series provide for male and female characters who deviate from the predominant heroic journey of television protagonists. The acts of *Breaking Bad*'s Walter White and even Jax Teller are as depraved and destructive as those of Mags and Gemma, except that their manipulations are not enacted upon their family and are often enacted upon others in perceived duty to family.

There is more to be written on the monstrous motherhood increasingly on display in television melodrama. Indeed, Gemma and Mags appear different and draw our attention more due to genre bending than gender bending. *Sons of Anarchy* has been widely considered through the same lens as protagonist-centred dramas such as *The Sopranos*, *Breaking Bad* or *Deadwood*, although it has always been better understood as melodrama. Confusingly far removed from melodrama's traditional inhabitation of feminine spaces and signifiers, *Sons*' melodramatic excess in the world of motorcycles, drug trade and patriarchal masculinities is delightful for its genre play. In this light, a character such as Gemma is easily considered amongst a long history of manipulative matriarchs on US daytime television. Melodrama has been less common in US prime time, but her lineage connects her with 1980s prime-time soaps such as *Dallas* and *Dynasty* and, more recently, *Revenge* or even a character such as Cersei in *Game of Thrones*.

At the core of some of the most compelling contemporary television are simple struggles between familial and professional duty, loyalty and the complicated political machinations to which characters subject those around them to achieve desired ends. Of interest to critical gender scholars is mapping whether male and female characters are held to similar standards in regard to their actions as bad mothers and fathers and how those actions position them as heroes or villains in their narrative worlds. Gemma and Mags extend the transgressions of other male and female antihero characters as characters who ensnare their children in their illegal enterprises and not simply neglect, but destroy their offspring in the process.

References

Deggans, E. (2014), '*Sons of Anarchy* ends as a macho soap opera often anchored by women', *NPR, All Things Considered*, 9 December, http://www.npr.org/2014/12/09/369263143/sons-of-anarchy-ends-as-a-macho-soap-opera-often-anchored-by-women. Accessed 2 June 2016.

Douglas, S. J. and Michaels, M. W. (2004), *The Mommy Myth: The Idealization of Motherhood and How it Has Undermined Women*, New York: Free Press.

'Red Rose' (2014), Paris Barclay, dir., *Sons of Anarchy*, Season 7, Episode 12, 2 December, Los Angeles: FX.

Fine, K. (2012), 'She hits like a man, but she kisses like a girl: TV heroines, femininity, violence, and intimacy', *Western American Literature*, 47: 2, pp. 152–173.

Justified (2010–2015, USA: FX).

Kaplan, E. A. (1992), *Motherhood and Representation: The Mother in Popular Culture and Melodrama*, London: Routledge.

Lotz, A. D. (2014), *Cable Guys: Television and Masculinities in the 21st Century*, New York: New York University Press.

Sons of Anarchy (2008–2014, USA: FX).

Walters, S. D. and Harrison, L. (2014), 'Not ready to make nice: Aberrant mothers in contemporary culture', *Feminist Media Studies*, 14: 1, pp. 38–55.

Notes

1. A handful of female protagonists who were not mothers that were characterized with uncertain likeability also emerged at this time: Brenda Leigh Johnson, *The Closer* (TNT, 2005–2012); Grace Hanadarko, *Saving Grace* (TNT, 2007–2010); and Sonya Cross, *The Bridge* (FX, 2013–2014), though these protagonists did adhere to a more conventional hero's journey. Given its popularity, it is also worth mentioning that *Mad Men* with Betty Draper and her particular version of bad motherhood was also produced for a cable channel in this period. Set in the gender dynamics of 1960 and constructing Betty as at-best a secondary character in later seasons, her character's failed motherhood is certainly a distinctive phenomenon.
2. The models of Netflix and Amazon are newer and less certain. Netflix began with a similar model as networks and channels, while Amazon created its own studio, and like more recent Netflix productions is experimenting with more of a cost-plus funding model that allows it ownership of the series.
3. Notably, the cited scholarship did not have the benefit of working with a completed series and the last two seasons are particularly critical of assessments of Gemma.

Chapter 7

La reina del sur: Teresa Mendoza, a New *Telenovela* Protagonist

Yeidy M. Rivero

In 2011 a multinational television collaboration introduced viewers of *narco telenovelas* and series to something new. Since the creation of the narco subgenre in Colombia in 2006 (*Sin tetas no hay paraíso/Without Tits There is no Paradise*, Caracol network, 2006–2010), *narco telenovelas* and series had narrated tales of drug violence that made these shows synonymous with Colombia and its brutal male drug kingpins.[1] Then *La reina del sur/Queen of the South* (Telemundo, 2011) a co-production with RTI (Colombia), Telemundo/Argos (United States/Mexico) and Antena 3 (Spain), moved these dramas of violence and the drug trade out of Colombia and presented audiences with a female drug lord as the lead. An adaptation of Spaniard Arturo Pérez Reverte's novel with the same title, *La reina del sur* tells the story of Teresa Mendoza, a Mexican woman who became a powerful drug queen figure in the south of Spain. In many respects, this dramatic series, which shifts the action between Mexico, Spain, Africa, Colombia and the United States, reflects the realities of the contemporary global drug trade. It implicitly recognizes Mexico's current dominance in drug smuggling, the powerful position some women have acquired in Mexico's drug business and the deterritorialization of drug trafficking.[2] In doing this, *La reina del sur* altered the gender, geographical and cultural backdrop of the *narco telenovela* and series narratives.

Yet, *La reina del sur*'s uniqueness goes beyond the incorporation of a woman as a drug smuggler and the representation of the transnational geo-political and economic elements of the contemporary narco world. Teresa Mendoza, aka La Reina del Sur not only was a successful drug dealer in a business dominated by men, she was also a woman who fervently cared for and supported other women. By selecting (and being loyal to) a woman as her business partner, by creating a family structure with female friends and by allowing herself to love another woman, *La reina del sur* created a new *telenovela* leading character.

In this chapter, I analyse the representation of women's relationships and sexuality in *La reina del sur*. The depiction of Teresa Mendoza's power within a male-dominated structure and, more importantly, her love for other women, were groundbreaking elements in this *narco telenovela*. Even as some men were important in Teresa Mendoza's life and even though the narrative limited sexual relationships to normative expectations (all bisexual and lesbian characters had been conveniently eliminated by the end of *La reina del sur*), her female friends occupied the centre of her selected family. Teresa Mendoza was a woman who loved women. Therein lies the uniqueness of this character and of this *narco telenovela*, suggesting that we should look more closely at the depiction of women and sexuality in *La reina del sur*.

As an expensive co-production that broke ratings records in Colombia, Mexico and the United States, *La reina del sur* has been the topic of several academic articles. Scholars have examined the *telenovela*'s articulation of the narco imaginary, the representation of Mexicanness in relation to drug trafficking and the *narcocorridos* (a Mexican folk music genre that narrates stories about drug trafficking across the Mexico-US border and that served as the inspiration for Pérez Reverte's novel) and the economic forces shaping this commodified cultural product.[3] The original novel and the televised adaptation also generated much discussion within the media. Journalists and writers have been especially interested in Arturo Pérez Reverte's immersion into Mexico's drug underworld to develop the character of Teresa Mendoza and in the similarities between the principal character and the real-life Mexican drug dealer Sandra Ávila Beltrán, aka La Reina del Pacífico [the Queen of the Pacific] (see, for example, Benavides 2008; Mondaca Cota 2004; Scherer García 2008).[4] Contributing to these dialogues, I am particularly interested in the construction of Teresa's transgressive behaviour, of how she was – to borrow a phrase from this anthology's title – 'behaving badly'. Was she behaving badly by regularly engaging in illegal activity that included not only drug trafficking but also murder? Was she behaving badly by intruding in and transforming what many considered a masculine workspace? Or was she behaving badly by developing a strong sentimental bond with another woman?

As I explain in the following pages, the answer is all of the above. Similar to the fictional women/characters who populate many *narcocorridos*, Teresa is an antiheroine. Echoing the personality traits of some *narcocorrido jefas* (bosses), Teresa is a beautiful, intelligent and courageous warrior who is also morally ambiguous and vindictive (Mondaca Cota 2004: 90). As a 'bad woman', a key aspect of her antiheroic persona comes not only from her questionable ethics, but also from her love for another woman, a sentimental attachment that can be interpreted as crossing the parameters of heterosexuality. As Alicia Gaspar de Alba notes regarding the typology of the 'bad women' in the context of Mexican culture (which can also be transposed to other Latin American cultures), 'A "bad woman" defies these limited/limiting roles – virgin, mother, whore – and spurns the duty of her sex to provide pleasure for the husband, solace for the son and heirs for the father. A "bad woman" is dangerous, contagious, viral' (Gaspar de Alba 2014: 8). Teresa Mendoza, as a twenty-first-century *narco telenovela* protagonist, could challenge some of the conservative gender norms imposed on women in Latin America. Nonetheless, there were limits to her defiance, particularly regarding sexual desire. The demise of bisexual and lesbian characters situates challenges to heterosexual norms as culturally unsustainable and thus an unacceptable antiheroic feature for a *narco telenovela* protagonist. Hence, to understand *La reina del sur*'s narrative parameters for Teresa's antiheroism, it is necessary to provide an overview of how she became involved in the world of drugs and emotionally close to women.

La reina del sur: Teresa Mendoza, a New *Telenovela* Protagonist

The New Narco Female Lead

La reina del sur narrates the story of Teresa Mendoza, a beautiful, smart and initially poor and innocent woman from Culiacán, Mexico whose romantic association immersed her in the world of drug trafficking. Packed with action-adventure and tragic romance, the narrative begins with Teresa receiving a phone call alerting her to the assassination of 'El Güero Dávila', the love of her life and a Sinaloa Cartel member (later in the narrative the audience learns that he was an undercover Drug Enforcement Administration [DEA] agent). His death not only destroys Teresa emotionally; it also forces her to run away from members of the Sinaloa Cartel. After fleeing, hiding and being raped by a cartel thug, Teresa begs Epifanio Vargas, the head of the Sinaloa Cartel, for her life. He lets her live, sends Teresa to Spain, and she ends up in the city of Melilla, working at the Yamila, a disreputable bar and brothel. While working at the bar, first as a waitress and later as a bookkeeper (Teresa, as we soon discover, is a math whiz), she befriends Fatima Mansur, a Moroccan prostitute, and the two women develop a sisterly bond. In addition, Teresa develops close relationships with other prostitutes. In Melilla, she also becomes romantically involved with Santiago 'El Gallego', a man who smuggled hashish by boat (by now it should be evident that Teresa has a certain *je ne sais quoi* that attracts drug dealers). To make a long story short, Teresa and her boyfriend move to Algeciras, Spain, she begins working with him and learns the business, her boyfriend is killed doing one of their jobs and she survives but is sent to prison. In prison Teresa meets the woman who will radically transform her life: Patricia O'Farrell.

Patty is a strikingly beautiful, sophisticated, well-educated and capricious bisexual woman. Bored with her opulent life (she was born with a silver spoon in her mouth) and, while only mentioned once in the narrative, traumatized by the sexual abuse of her father, she is drawn to drugs, alcohol and men involved in illegal activities. Found guilty by association and for refusing to provide information about the whereabouts of her dead boyfriend's cocaine supply, Patty is incarcerated. During Teresa's two years in prison, she and Patty are inseparable. Patty also provides the principal capital (via her boyfriend's stolen cocaine) for what becomes the most successful drug trafficking business in the South of Spain. An important aspect of their friendship and business association is Patty's love for Teresa, an unrequited love that is a central romantic storyline in *La reina del sur*. Although, for a while, their cohabitation prompted rumours in the drug and police worlds about a possible romance, they were never sexually intimate. Teresa and Patty, nonetheless, kissed in prison – an experience that enthused Patty's hope for a future with Teresa.

Over time, Teresa and Patty's business (Transer Naga) took control over the drug trafficking in the Mediterranean Sea, which led in part to the creation of Teresa's nickname – La Reina del Sur. This success, however, came with a price. Teresa had many enemies in the drug world and the Spanish and US authorities pursued her relentlessly. Meanwhile, Patty, unable to let go of her romantic feelings for Teresa, turned increasingly to drugs and alcohol. Depressed by her unrequited love and by being misled emotionally by a Teresa look-alike DEA agent, Patty committed suicide. After losing all the people she loved, Teresa negotiated her immunity with the DEA by testifying against Epifanio Vargas (the mastermind behind the death of El Güero), who was running for the presidency of Mexico. The last shot of the series shows Teresa, living in a luxurious villa in an unknown place, pregnant (from a relationship with a man who turned out to be a traitor), at peace with herself and staring at the sea.

One of the most captivating aspects of *La reina del sur* and its protagonist is Teresa's strength that allows her to subvert the narco patriarchal system without losing her humanity and her empathy for others, *specifically women*. Teresa does not come from the same line of cruel and inhuman narcos and hit men depicted in Colombian narco series and *telenovelas*.[5] Although she eliminates her enemies, these murders (committed by others) are presented in the narrative as the only way for Teresa to survive and retaliate for the atrocities done to her. As audience members we root for vengeance for Teresa, which comes in the killing of those who physically abused her and robbed her of her family and of her innocence. We empathize and support Teresa, despite her myriad drug trafficking-related faults because she is a melodramatic antiheroine. 'What makes the female public like this heroine is her complicated personality. On the one hand, she is courageous and, on the other hand she is shy, weak, and fragile' (Mainhold and Sauter de Mainhold 2012: 82). *La reina del sur* distances itself from its Colombian *narco telenovela* and series predecessors via its melodramatic tone, emotionally appealing protagonist and its somewhat happy ending. This narconovela is a hybrid cultural product whose narrative was shaped by the transnational cultural, industrial and economic forces behind its production (Piñón 2014; Rincón cited in Reforma 2012). And it is precisely this transnational melange, I contend, that allowed for the creation of a new *telenovela* protagonist.

La reina del sur and its protagonist, Teresa Mendoza, are products of four primary forces. The first influence clearly comes from Arturo Pérez Reverte's creation. In the novel, Teresa is a strong young woman who uses drug trafficking to liberate herself from male oppression and to obtain economic independence (González Flores 2010). In addition, the patriarchal system motivates her to develop a strong alliance with Patty.[6] Hence, the essence of the televised Teresa comes from the literary Teresa. Interconnected to Pérez Reverte's novel and character are the *narcocorrido* and its female protagonists. In *narcocorrido* songs, women are brave, intelligent, loyal and cruel; they are also respected, admired and feared by men in the drug trafficking world (Mondaca Cota 2004). Given that Pérez Reverte was inspired by the *narcocorrido*, one could argue that some of Teresa's personality traits migrated from the *narcocorrido*, to the novel, to the *narco telenovela*. Still, Teresa's audacity, along with the backbone of some of *La reina del sur*'s secondary female characters, was also shaped by another factor: the Colombian *telenovela*.

Representations of strong women who are in charge of their life are defining characteristics of the Colombian genre. In the words of Omar Rincón and María Paula Martínez, '[…] [i]n Colombia's *telenovela*, women are warriors. The woman is not going to be saved by a man, so in order to succeed she'll need to struggle at work. In the end, she is the one who saves the men' (Rincón and Martínez 2014: 177). The forceful women who were part of Colombian hits such as *Señora Isabel* (Canal A, 1993–1994), *Café con aroma de mujer/ Coffee with a Scent of a Woman* (RCN, 1994–1995) and the gruesome *narco telenovela Rosario Tijeras/Rosario Scissors* (RCN, 2010) – the first Colombian drama that depicted a woman as a vindictive hit man – permeate the creative universe that moulded Teresa and other characters. This influence comes not only through RTI (Colombia), one of the production companies behind *La reina del sur*, but also through Telemundo (US) which has appropriated the creative style of the Colombian *telenovela* product.

The last element shaping *La reina del sur*, Teresa and the relationships among women is the imagined audience. In recent years, Latin American and US Spanish television networks have invested in the quality of *telenovelas* and series to tap into the global market while also maintaining the local one (Hopewell 2015). *La reina del sur* is part of this trend. The objective behind its co-production, as Juan Piñón (2014) notes, was to develop a high-quality product capable of attracting large segments of the Latin American, Spanish and global markets while preserving the profitable US Hispanic market. Comprised of immigrants from Latin America and the Spanish Caribbean and first- and second-generation US-born individuals, the US Hispanic audience is 'transnational, multicultural, and mostly bilingual' (Piñón 2014: 5). Since 2011, Telemundo has aggressively invested in local, Miami-based productions to compete with rival Univision and conquer the Hispanic market, particularly targeting individuals born and raised as Latinas/os. As former Telemundo president Emilio Romano remarked,

> The core of Telemundo Media's mission is to be the best producer of original Spanish content for the world [...] We are slowly but steadily building an environment that allows producers and talent relevant to the U.S. Hispanic market to bring new waves of ideas and different products to the screen.
>
> (Littleton 2013)

Having what Romano describes as 'US sensibilities', Telemundo began to capitalize on the visual and narrative quality of its products and to include more risqué topics. For *La reina del sur*, the racy subject entailed not only a female narco, but also the possibility of a bisexual *telenovela* protagonist.

Teresa and Gendered Spaces

> No, you are not the first one. The first ones were some guys from the barrio, when I was fourteen years old. There were around six [...] they were my firsts. Does that count? Because if it doesn't, we can think of the jerk who gave me the exchange of currency job on Juárez Street and who later charged me [sexually] for the favor.
>
> ('Correr para vivir' 2011)

This was Teresa's response to El Güero when he asked why she was reluctant to become intimate with him, a reluctance that made him think she was a virgin. This is also how, during the first episode and via a flashback (El Güero only appeared during Teresa's recollections of the past), the audience learns about Teresa's difficult relationships with men. Indeed, men were present in Teresa's life, but, with few exceptions, most behaved like beasts towards her. They were individuals capable of committing horrendous crimes to eliminate their enemies and/or competitors who, in the drug world, belonged in the same category. Raped on multiple occasions before meeting El Güero and afterwards (as noted previously, by a member of the Sinaloa Cartel), Teresa found it difficult to trust men and to be emotionally and physically intimate with them. Conversely, she was at ease with women, seeing them as allies, and she did everything in her power to aid and protect them. Thus, it should not come as a surprise that the places where Teresa was most comfortable were those in which she was near women. She also felt calm at the Mediterranean Sea, a place that was like home for her.

The principal spaces where Teresa established close associations with women were the bar Yamila, the prison and the house she shared with Patty. The first location, the bar, was socially constructed as a masculine space. As geographer Daphne Spain writes, "gendered spaces" separate women from knowledge used by men to produce and reproduce power and privilege' (Spain 1992: 30). Located in Melilla, a border city with Morocco, this bar was linked to illegality. The inhumane transporting of Africans to Spain, prostitution, drug trafficking and corrupt political deals were some of the arrangements that materialized at Yamila.

At first glance, there would seem to be few substantive differences between Melilla and Culiacán, Mexico, Teresa's city, a space that was also constructed as masculine. Like Melilla, violence, drugs and political corruption characterized Culiacán. For Teresa, though, the Mexican city awakened drastically dissimilar feelings. It was in Culiacán that she experienced her first true love, but it was also the place where she was objectified, used, sexually and physically abused and basically dehumanized. Her city-home-country 'failed to provide [...] safety, sustenance, and livelihood' (Benavides 2008: 157–158). Both Culiacán's and Melilla's patriarchal structures somewhat delimited Teresa's actions; however, it was in the Spanish city that Teresa began to take control of her life.

At the bar Yamila, Teresa reinvented herself professionally, found a new love and, more importantly, created a group of female friends who provided unconditional support. In return, Teresa protected her friends from the abuses of men (clients or otherwise) and helped those in powerless positions. For example, Teresa crossed the border and brought Fátima's son from Morocco ('We Mexicans specialize in crossing borders' ['Pesadilla de tráfico' 2011]), risking her life to save her friend's child. She also convinced the bar owner to let Fátima work as a waitress so she could earn a living to raise her son. While initially Teresa clashed with one of Yamila's prostitutes, and she endured discrimination for being Mexican, little by little, she gained the women's trust and created a solid community of female friends. In some ways, the strong bond between Teresa and the women who worked at Yamila altered the spatial gendered-coding and created a safer space for them.

It should be clear that during Teresa's time at Yamila, her behaviour and attitudes were not fully liberated from the patriarchal system in which she grew up. While the strong, independent and sure-of-herself Teresa began to emerge at the bar, the desire to support her man at any cost still motivated some of her actions. For instance, to help El Gallego (her second boyfriend) access the trafficking of hashish, Teresa slept with the man who controlled the business. While Teresa had ulterior economic motives, her behaviour at this stage reproduced the conduct of someone who had been physically and emotionally abused. The fact that Santiago was sometimes physically aggressive with her, and that she stayed with him regardless of his explosive temperament, is another behavioural trait associated with abused women. In the narrative, nonetheless, their relationship is primarily depicted as passionate (as cued via the cheesy music).

Besides sex, alleged love and sporadic tantrums (which on one occasion came with a slap in the face and on another with a rape attempt), Santiago taught Teresa the twists and turns of drug trafficking across the sea. From him she learned how to drive and fix a boat, the fastest and safest routes to transport drugs, the geography of the region and the tricks to escape the coast guards. This learning was instrumental to her future economic independence. Still, without the friendships and life experience Teresa established in prison, it would have been impossible for her to become La Reina del Sur.

Prison was obviously far from an ideal place for Teresa. She almost lost her life, was treated with prejudice because of her nationality and was victimized by her unscrupulous lawyer who stole all of her and Santiago's money. Yet, despite Teresa's ordeals, prison was important for her. She met 'La Conejo', a woman who, like Fátima, would become part of her family of friends, and Patty, who turned into her best friend, educator and business partner – a woman she loved deeply.

Teresa and Patty became friends while sharing a cell and their relationship grew organically over their years in prison. Thanks to Patty, Teresa 'La Mexicana' (her prison nickname) discovered the world of literature and became an avid reader ('a book is the door to many paths', Patty told Teresa). Alexander Dumas's *The Count of Monte Cristo*, the first book Patty gave Teresa, became Teresa's favourite novel, a literary reference that would always make her think of Patty. The highly educated Patty also introduced Teresa to Mexican literature (Octavio Paz and Juan Rulfo), an important reconnection to a place Teresa wanted to forget. While incarcerated and after their release, 'La Teniente' (the lieutenant, Patty's prison nickname) also taught Teresa about culture, manners and how to look professional and elegant, knowledge that came in handy when dealing with drug lords (principally, the more stylish heads of the Russian and Italian mafias). She also risked her life to save Teresa from a fire that almost cost La Mexicana her life.

Teresa and Patty were each other's shadow. Patty, madly in love with Teresa, did everything to please her and make her life more pleasant. Teresa, on the other hand, felt great admiration for Patty. She was mesmerized by her knowledge of the world, culture and refinement. Teresa also considered Patty stunningly attractive. It is not totally surprising then, that in prison – a women's space sexually coded as lesbian – they kissed.

Geographer Emiel Maliepaard observes, 'Space, or the sexual coding of space, impacts the sexual identity negotiations of sexual subjects as well as sexual identity negotiations influence the sexual coding of space' (Maliepaard 2015: 149). After the kiss, the spaces where both Patty and Teresa cohabited (prison and, later, their home), together with the *telenovela* genre's tradition of narrating stories about impossible love, make it possible to read their relationship as a love story. Whereas Teresa's heterosexuality was quickly and constantly asserted after the kiss (she made Patty promise not to talk about the incident ever again), the narrative also provided spaces for spectators to interpret her as bisexual and their relationship as romantic, yet platonic. Teresa's unconditional love, support and loyalty to Patty even in moments when her drug addiction threatened her business and her own well-being, in addition to Teresa's jealousy towards one of Patty's girlfriends (after prison, Patty mostly slept with women and had a steady relationship), hinted that Teresa's love for Patty might have been more than that of a friend. Still, in the context of the Latin American *telenovela* genre and the region's conservative culture, an openly romantic relationship between Teresa and Patty would have been difficult to showcase.

In his analysis of Arturo Pérez Reverte's novel, Hugo Benavides ponders whether Teresa and Patty's impossible love might have been 'less a problem of sexual preference than of the impossibility of love under postcolonial conditions' (Benavides 2008: 153). While this reading could be transferred to the *telenovela*, I suggest that in the context of television, the unfeasibility of the women's love was sociocultural and economic. That is, the industry's fear of alienating segments of the imagined audience and the economic consequences associated with censorship most likely constrained the fulfilment of Patty and Teresa's love. As Samantha Nogueira Joyce writes regarding the heteronormativity that characterizes Brazilian *telenovelas*, the power of the Catholic Church and the conservatism that is part of Brazilian culture have delimited gay and lesbian representations on Brazilian television (Nogueira Joyce 2013). The same logic can be used for the *telenovela La reina del sur*. For example, Mexican network Televisa (owners of Galavisón, the sister network that aired *La reina del sur*) deemed the Teresa and Patty storyline too *risqué* for its audience and censored the kissing scene. In a more drastic move, the Chilean television channel Megavision eliminated all scenes that addressed lesbianism (Rubio 2011; Tavira 2011). Based on these actions, it appears that, according to the industry, Latin American audiences could not digest seeing a *telenovela* protagonist being in love with another woman.

At the same time, however, the television text was more accommodating to homoeroticism, opening the possibility for a variety of readings based on the spectators' positionality. As Maria San Filippo astutely observes regarding textual representations and spectators' reading of bisexual moments, '[a]dmittedly, the act of reading bisexually is often prompted by the undecidability of an image or instance in question – that is, textual resistance to pinning characters or narrative elements down as *either* straight *or* gay/lesbian in persuasion or perspective' (San Filippo 2013: 31). Different from the novel, the *telenovela La reina del sur* provided a series of character attitudes and behaviours that visually foregrounded a relationship that was more than a simple friendship. For instance, contrary to the novel wherein Patty initiated the kiss, in the *telenovela* it became a shared and reciprocated experience. The television text also highlighted Teresa and Patty's constant physical affection with one another, adding another dimension to the description of their relationship in the novel.

Most likely influenced by the 'American sensibilities' of the US Hispanic market, *La reina del sur*'s production team might have wanted to create a balance to please middle-ground conservative and liberal segments of their rather broad regional and local audiences. Nonetheless, regardless of the production's actual intentions, the narrative resulted in stereotypes and predictable outcomes when depicting those who, unlike Patty, felt exclusively attracted to other women. In *La reina del sur*, lesbians were a detriment to feminism and womanhood.

Reproducing the images present in the women in prison film genre where 'lesbianism is usually either marginalized, pathologized, [...] and lesbian characters usually face grim futures or suffer violent death' (Herman 2003: 143), the lesbians in prison with Teresa and Patty were depicted as a major threat to other women. As La Conejo told Teresa, 'they are like sharks', doing everything possible to get what they wanted regardless of the consequences. The leader of the lesbians was Trinidad Sánchez, alias 'La Macoqui', a butch from Colombia (most of the lesbians in prison were Colombian, a skewed demographic characteristic that makes one wonder if the country's principal export is lesbians instead of coffee). La Macoqui was the most malevolent prisoner, using violence and threats to terrify all women. If an inmate challenged her, as was the case with Teresa, she did not hesitate to try to kill her. In fact, La Macoqui's level of cruelty and inhumanity was such that the method she used in her failed attempt to kill Teresa was burning her to death.

Based on *La reina del sur*'s narrative, being attracted to another woman was acceptable as long as men were still seen as objects of sexual desire. Bisexuals, such as Patty, were manageable because, in the eyes of Teresa, her sexual desires towards women were a product of her 'crazy personality'. Since Patty never acted on her feelings after the kiss, Teresa felt comfortable around her knowing that she would never mention the incident. Furthermore, contrary to La Macoqui (and the other lesbians in prison), Patty was a beautiful and feminine woman whose cheerful personality enchanted everyone, including heterosexuals such as La Conejo. In fact, in terms of bodily performance, manners and behaviour, Teresa was the more 'butch' of the two, adopting a stronger, detached and somewhat masculine persona in prison, a personality trait that intensified when she began to deal with drug lords. By the time Teresa and Patty were released from prison and had decided to work and live together, all traces of the young, innocent and fragile Teresa were gone.

Teresa, Patty, Fátima and her son Mohammed lived together briefly in a mansion in Málaga, Spain. For Teresa, it was important to have people she considered her family under the same roof. She saw herself as the main provider and protector of her family; thus, having them close, she thought, was the best way to help them. Teresa was happy sharing her space with her two friends and Mohammed, who called her aunt and whom she adored. While Patty did not like the idea of others living in the house, she agreed to Teresa's wishes.

For outsiders, there was no doubt that Teresa and Patty were an item, and in reality, their living arrangements followed that of a traditional heterosexual couple. Patty adopted the rich housewife persona with which she was familiar, taking care of the house and social events and keeping everything in order and ready for Teresa – from dinners, to decorations, to clothing. Teresa became the breadwinner, working hard for her family and keeping track of her own and Patty's money and investments. For the time that it lasted, all were happy.

Time spent in the shared living space, nonetheless, was short. Teresa discovered that having her loved ones near could cost them their lives. Both Fátima and her son were killed in retaliation for Teresa's expansion of her business into areas originally controlled by others. Thus, to protect Patty's life, Teresa moved away to Marbella, Spain, and distanced herself; thereafter, mostly maintaining a professional relationship. Little by little, Teresa's detachment and the impossibility of receiving her love destroyed Patty, until she committed suicide.

Besides the bar, prison and home, spaces where Teresa created a strong bond with women, the other space where Teresa was calm and content was at the Mediterranean Sea. Opened to an array of possibilities, the sea provided Teresa with the opportunity to reinvent herself in ways she had never imagined. The anonymity offered by the sea, its lack of societal, ethnic and gendered hierarchical structures and its vastness, allowed Teresa to obtain power that few women had ever acquired. At the sea, Teresa could prove her superiority in the drug trafficking business, beating her competitors with her innate intelligence, sagacity and experience. Each trip she made with her cargo from one point of the Mediterranean to another was a way to prove that, by far, she was the best in the business. She was the Queen of the South, a pseudonym achieved thanks to her talent near and on the Mediterranean Sea.

For Teresa, the sea was her home, a space without constraints or rules, where she was able to be herself. It should come as no surprise then that it was at sea, first when Teresa was sailing, trying to recover from the pain of losing Patty, and later, when she was dispersing Patty's ashes, that she finally grasped her immense love for Patty. Via flashbacks, Teresa remembered all the moments they shared, including the kiss. Playing 'their song', the one Patty dedicated to Teresa the day they kissed, Teresa said farewell to her friend.

Did Teresa realize that she was in love with Patty after she died? Was Patty Teresa's second big love? The narrative provides no definite answers. Nonetheless, the YouTube videos dedicated to their relationship do. With a variety of clips depicting moments between Teresa and Patty and with musical backgrounds that include Patty and Teresa's love song as well as other romantic ballads, fans depict the relationship between these two female characters as the central love story in *La reina del sur*. Thus, even though the *telenovela*'s last shot shows Teresa looking at the sea with her and El Güero's love song as background music (thus reasserting Teresa's heterosexuality), the YouTube videos created a different ending. As Maria San Filippo writes, 'Screen media's bisexual spaces are those that represent and appeal to interstitial, fluid spectatorial identifications and desires, and thus have the potential to subvert, or "unthank," monosexuality' (San Filippo 2013: 17–18). The videos dedicated to Teresa and Patty's relationship demonstrate that, for some viewers, Teresa's sexuality was more fluid than the final scene allowed.[7] For some fans Teresa Mendoza was not only the first *narco telenovela* leading lady, she was also the first bisexual *telenovela* and series leading character.

Conclusion

In January 2015, Telemundo began to broadcast *Dueños del paraíso/Masters of Paradise*, a narco-themed 'super series' co-produced by Telemundo and the Chilean network TVN.[8] Considered Telemundo's most expensive co-production to date, *Dueños del paraíso* centred on Anastasia Cardona, a 'ruthless narco queenpin who turns Miami into her territory' (De Pablos 2015). Following the tradition from Colombian narco series and *telenovelas* of mixing reality and fiction, this production is set in Miami in the late 1970s and early 1980s, a time when this culturally diverse city endured a high drug-related crime rate that led to its designation as the murder capital of the United States. Like *La reina del sur*, *Dueños del paraíso* is anchored by a strong female lead. Nonetheless, beyond their positions as drug queen pins, Teresa Mendoza and Anastasia have little else in common. Unlike Teresa, Anastasia is not afraid to take justice into her own hands, killing her enemies herself without any remorse. This new narco antiheroine has more in common with her Colombian male and female predecessors than with Teresa, although in contrast to the Colombian drug dealers and hit men who usually travelled 'to the other side', Anastasia escaped the authorities and enemies, spending the rest of her life hiding with her 'man'. Her vindictive and cruel nature made her a bad woman, yet not as bad as Teresa Mendoza, whose flexible sexuality crossed the boundaries of the genre's traditional heteronormativity.

Unlike Anastasia's criminal behaviour, Teresa's sexual behaviour had consequences. Even though she was allowed to live, her punishment left her alone and pregnant – relegating her to a traditionally defined gendered role. Her future job as a mother left her void of sexual pleasure. The fact that other characters who dared to express sexual desire for other women and who acted on those desires were conveniently killed presents a rather grim picture for those whose erotic sensibilities transcend the confines of heterosexuality. Patty committed suicide. Her DEA Teresa look-alike lover died in a car accident. The evil Colombian lesbian butch vanished; who knows where, but definitely far away, to the margins of society. Neither a poise and charm course nor a makeover could save La Macoqui. As characterized in *La reina del sur*, a *narco telenovela* antiheroine can sell and transport drugs, kill and be vindictive, but she cannot be in love with or act on her desire for another woman. Constructed as an unpalatable antiheroic trait for the *narco telenovela*'s imagined audience, sexually active bisexuals and lesbians were prone to tragedy.

Nonetheless, despite its problematic representations, *La reina del sur* was revolutionary. Influenced by aggressive competition between television networks, the availability of alternative platforms to access content, and the need to attract local, regional and global audiences, *La reina del sur* presented a new type of *telenovela* protagonist. Teresa's strength, her success in a male-dominated business and her support for women introduced a unique antiheroic heroine who attracted a variety of audiences. The question is: How much risk is the industry willing to take to broaden its market? Will television networks represent a really 'bad' woman who, despite the Roman Catholic Church and the conservative culture, would dare to openly love other women? Maybe it is written in the stars but regardless of how television officials proceed, audiences are creating their own stories. As one of *La reina del sur* fans wrote in her YouTube video scene collage, 'One day I will make a video which presents a happy ending for this couple'. Perhaps, without realizing it, she and other fans have already rewritten Teresa and Patty's love story.

References

Benavides, O. H. (2008), *Drugs, Thugs, and Divas: Telenovelas and Narco-dramas in Latin America*, Austin: University of Texas Press.

'Correr para vivir' (2011), Mauricio Cruz and Walter Doehner, dir., *La reina del sur*, Episode 1, 28 February, US: Telemundo.

De Pablos, E. (2015), 'Latin American High-end TV Drama Co-prods Prosper Under Prexy Marcos Santana', *Variety*, 14 April, http://variety.com/2015/tv/global/mip-tv-telemundo-international-puts-faith-in-super-series-1201471979/. Accessed 15 June 2015.

Dueños del paraíso (2015, US: Television Nacional and Telemundo).

Gaspar de Alba, A. (2014), *[Un] framing the 'Bad Woman': Sor Juana, Malinche, Coyolxauhqui, and Other Rebels with a Cause*, Austin: University of Texas Press.

González Flores, F. (2010), 'Mujer y pacto fáustico en el narcomundo: Representaciones literarias y cinematográficas en *La vendedora de rosas* de Víctor Gaviria, *María llena eres de gracia* de Joshua Marston y *La reina del sur* de Arturo Pérez Reverte', *Romance Quarterly*, 57: 4, pp. 286–299.

Herman, D. (2003), '"Bad Girls Changed My Life": Homonormativity in a women's prison drama', *Critical Studies in Media Communication*, 20: 2, pp. 141–159.

Hopewell, J. (2015), 'Latin America Broadcasters Play up Drama With High-end Event Series', *Variety*, 3 April, http://variety.com/2015/tv/global/latin-america-broadcasters-play-up-drama-with-high-end-event-series-1201464801/. Accessed 7 May 2015.

Jaramillo, D. L. (2014), 'Narcocorridos and newbie drug dealers: the changing image of the Mexican Narco on US television', *Ethnic and Racial Studies*, 37: 9, pp. 1587–1604.

La reina del sur (2011, US: Telemundo).

Littleton, C. (2013), 'NBC Universal Bets Big on Original Spanish-Lingo Productions', *Variety*, 30 July, http://variety.com/2013/tv/news/nbcuniversal-bets-big-on-original-spanish-lingo-productions-1200569558/. Accessed 3 May 2015.

Maliepaard, E. (2015), 'Bisexuals in Space and Geography: More-Than-Queer?', *Fennia-International Journal of Geography*, 193: 1, pp. 148–159.

Mainhold, G. and Sauter de Mainhold, R. M. (2012), 'Capos, reinas y santos–la narcocultura en México', *México Interdisciplinario*, 2: 3, pp. 32–45.

Martín-Barbero, J. and Rey, G. (1999), *Los ejercicios de ver: Hegemonía audiovisual y ficción Televisiva*, Barcelona: Gedisa.

Mondaca Cota, A. (2004), *Las mujeres también pueden: Género y narcocorrido*, Sinaloa, Mexico: Universidad de Occidente.

Nogueira Joyce, S. (2013), 'A Kiss is (not) Just a Kiss: Heterodeterminism, Homosexuality and TV Globo Telenovelas', *International Journal of Communication*, 7: 19, pp. 48–66.

Páez Varela, A. (2007), 'Historias del narcotráfico', *Letras Libres*, http://www.letraslibres.com/revista/convivio/historias-del-narcotrafico. Accessed 12 May 2015.

Payán, T. (2006), *The Three US-Mexico Border Wars: Drugs, Immigration, and Homeland Security*, Westport: Praeger Security International.

'Pesadilla de tráfico' (2011), Mauricio Cruz and Walter Doehner, dir., *La reina del sur*, Episode 10, 11 March, US: Telemundo.

Piñón, J. (2014), 'Corporate transnationalism', in A. Dávila and Y. Rivero (eds), *Contemporary Latina/o Media: Production, Circulation, Politics, Contemporary Latina/o Media: Production, Circulation, Politics*, New York: New York University Press, pp. 21–43.

Reforma (2012), 'El amor en los tiempos del narco', 13 March, http://www.zocalo.com.mx/seccion/articulo/el-amor-en-los-tiempos-del-narco. Accessed 27 February 2015.

Rincón, O. (2011), 'New Television Narratives: Entertainment Telling Citizenship Experimental', *Revista Comunicar*, 18: 36, pp. 43–50.

Rincón, O. and Martínez, M. P. (2014), 'Colombianidades Export Market', in A. Dávila and Y. Rivero (eds), *Contemporary Latina/o Media: Production, Circulation, Politics, Contemporary Latina/o Media: Production, Circulation, Politics*, New York: New York University Press, pp. 169–185.

Rubio, C. (2011), 'Califica autor de hipócrita censura a *La reina del sur*', *Reforma*, 7 May, p. 3.

San Filippo, M. (2013), *The B Word: Bisexuality in Contemporary Film and Television*, Bloomington: Indiana University Press.

Scherer-García, J. (2008), *La reina del pacífico: Es la hora de contar*, Mexico City: Grijalbo.

Spain, D. (1992), *Gendered Spaces*, Chapel Hill: University of North Carolina Press.

Tavira, A. (2011), 'La Reina del Sur y los 9 escándalos que provocó en México', *Animal Político*, 1 June, http://www.animalpolitico.com/2011/06/la-reina-del-sur-y-los-9-escandalos-que-provoco-en-mexico/. Accessed 13 March 2015.

Notes

1 In the case of the Colombian narco series and *narco telenovela*, it is almost impossible to separate fiction from reality. Since the genre's birth in 2006, narco series and *narco telenovelas* have been intrinsically interconnected to reportage about drugs and violence in Colombia. As communication scholar Omar Rincón notes, 'Narco-soap operas are testimonial television […] their authenticity is aesthetics – aesthetics that document a way of thinking and popular taste' (Rincón 2011: 47). Following the tradition of the Colombian *telenovela*, which since the mid-1960s had captured the characters, themes and realities of the nation-state and its citizens (Martín-Barbero and Rey 1999), the narco series and *narco telenovelas* present a thorny aspect of Colombia's violent past and the continuance of violence in the present.

2   During the 1980s, the drug trafficking business began to change. The United States' Drug Enforcement Administration and the Colombian government began dismantling the Colombian cartels and their businesses in Miami, the main entry point for cocaine into the United States. In response to law enforcement tactics, Colombian drug dealers initiated business relationships with the Mexican cartels, which, since the 1960s, had been trafficking marijuana and heroin to the United States, the main buyer in the region (Payán 2006: 28–29). For information on women's role in Mexican drug cartels, see Alejandro Páez Varela's (2007) essay 'Historias del narcotráfico'.

3   For example, in their examination of the narcoculture in Mexico, Gunther Mainhold and Rosa María Sauter de Mainhold (2012) explore the ways in which *La reina del sur* articulated elements of the narco imaginary while concomitantly transforming some of the *telenovela* genre's narrative traits. As the authors observe, in *La reina del sur*, the heroine continues to suffer; however, the suffering takes place in an 'exotic and tropical atmosphere, among dollars, bullets, and blood' (82). Also focusing on textual representations of elements associated with the narco culture, Deborah Jaramillo (2013) examines *La reina del sur* in the context of US commercial television, comparing the *telenovela* to *Weeds* (Showtime, 2005–2012) and *Breaking Bad* (AMC, 2008–2013), critically acclaimed shows that depict drug trafficking. Jaramillo argues that although these three series do not transgress the long-standing Hollywood depiction of Mexicans as drug dealers, they nonetheless create more complex representations of Mexicanness, resembling those of *narcocorridos*. Juan Piñón (2014) takes a different approach by focusing on the new economic forces and transnational business affiliations shaping US Spanish-language and Latin American television. He characterizes *La reina del sur*'s production and themes as examples of the new strategies used by television networks to expand their audiences.

4   The association between *La reina del sur*'s character and Mexican drug dealer Sandra Ávila Beltrán also derives from the *narcocorridos*. *Contrabando y traición/Contraband and Betrayal*, a Los tigres del norte's song, was the inspiration for Pérez Reverte's protagonist. The song tells the story of a gutsy woman who crossed the Mexico-US border smuggling drugs with her lover and who then kills him after learning that he had another lover. After Pérez Reverte's novel was published, Los tigres del norte wrote a song titled *La reina del sur* that narrates the adventures of Pérez Reverte's fictional character.

5   For example, in the televised adaptation of Gustavo Bolívar's non-fiction book, *Sin tetas no hay paraíso*, one witnesses a young woman's painful journey to improve her economic condition by becoming the lover of a brutal drug lord. In *Rosario Tijeras*, based on Jorge Franco's novel (RCN, 2010), we see a poor young woman who, after being gang raped, drastically transforms her life and becomes a hit man for drug cartels. In the *narco telenovela Pablo Escobar, el patrón del mal/Pablo Escobar, The Drug Lord* (Caracol, 2012), adapted from Alonso Salazar's biography, *La parábola de Pablo*, the audience vicariously experiences the atrocities committed by Pablo Escobar, head of the Medellín Cartel and one of Colombia's most powerful and vindictive drug kings. Similarly, in a script originally written for television, *Alias el mexicano* (RCN, 2013–2014) captures the life of narco José Gonzalo Rodríguez Gacha, another powerful and violent member of the Medellín Cartel.

6　In her essay, González Flores briefly refers to Adrienne Rich's 'concept of the *continuum*' to explain female bonding in *La reina del sur* and other novels. Curiously, Flores omits the *lesbian* connected to Rich's *continuum*, which is key to Rich's theorization of women's relationships, and which provides a useful analytical tool to examine the liaison between Teresa and Patty (González Flores 2010: 292).

7　See, for example, https://www.youtube.com/watch?v=Mu55QcgEhzI; https://www.youtube.com/watch?v=juywtgIORBs; https://www.youtube.com/watch?v=1_oAESVmVFA; https://www.youtube.com/watch?v=b2IXbD4BQd4

8　Since 2015, *La reina del sur* is being referred to as a 'super series' instead of a *telenovela*. Super series is a marketing term used by the industry for high-quality and expensive series that follow many of the *telenovela* genre traits, but they have fewer episodes than a *telenovela* (around 60 or less) and their narratives highlight action-adventure. In several articles covering Telemundo's 2015 super series *Dueños del paraíso*, *La reina del sur* is mentioned as the first super series even though, when this product was released in 2011, it was being advertised as a *telenovela*. In this chapter I refer to *La reina del sur* as a *telenovela*, as both industry officials and audiences referred to it when it was released (De Pablos 2015).

Part III

Women in Prison

Chapter 8

Blurred Lines: The Queer World of *Bad Girls*

Vicky Ball

New Girls on the Block

Bad Girls is a British women-in-prison (WIP) drama that ran for eight seasons between 1999 and 2006. Produced by Shed Productions for ITV, the UK's commercial network, the series offers an insider's view of prison life from the perspective of female inmates and 'screws' of the fictitious G-Wing, Larkhall Prison.

While there have been various cycles of the WIP film since the form emerged in the 1920s (Zalcock 1998: 19), *Bad Girls* remains only the third WIP drama to be produced for television after the British *Within These Walls* (Thames Television for ITV, 1974–1978) and the Australian *Prisoner: Cell Block H* (Network Ten, 1979–1986). The scant production of WIP dramas is perhaps telling regarding the spaces and discourses that female characters have been allowed to inhabit on television. As such, the appearance of *Bad Girls* in the late 1990s in the United Kingdom can be perceived to signal particular shifts to the construction of femininity in the context of late modernity.

To be sure *Bad Girls*' focus upon 'women behaving badly' follows on from a much longer lineage of unruly women characters that have populated television screens since the medium's early years and via texts such as *I Love Lucy* (CBS, 1951–1957) and the British sitcom *The Rag Trade* (BBC, 1961–1963). Blending the conventions of WIP film and soap opera, *Bad Girls* is reminiscent of its television forerunners *Within These Walls* and *Prisoner: Cell Block H*. However, as its title indicates, *Bad Girls* also gave a knowing wink to the more cult and 'trashy' exploitation cycle of the WIP genre in the 1970s through its explicit sex (including lesbianism), violence, camp and irony. As with exploitation films and *Prisoner* before it, *Bad Girls* enjoyed cult status in the United Kingdom, with a spin-off book, musical and over 100 websites run mostly by its legion of lesbian fans (Millbank 2004: 163).

The cult status and huge lesbian following of *Bad Girls* owes much to the central narrative arc of the first three series featuring the love affair of G-Wing Governor Helen Stewart and prisoner Nikki Wade. Unlike *Prisoner*, however, which was relegated to a late night slot in the United Kingdom, *Bad Girls* enjoyed prime-time positioning, occupying the coveted 9–10 p.m. slot on ITV. The first three series averaged seven million viewers, 40 per cent of whom were the schedulers Holy Grail of 16–34 year olds (Midgley 1999). Series viewing peaked at 9.4 million during seasons 2 and 3. The text went on to enjoy international distribution in 16 countries and the producers were also in talks with FX and HBO to produce an American version.

It is reviewing the success story of *Bad Girls* that signals how the text's constructions differ or indeed go beyond previous televisual constructions of female unruliness. The unruly and morally ambivalent bad girl figures that populate the text engage not only with questions of gendered but also sexual 'transgression' that, as I will explore further below, was unusual for British terrestrial television up until the late 1990s. Yet, it is through such characterizations that such femininities would appear to embody the characteristics of the antiheroine.

This position is evident in the research of *Bad Girls* that has already been carried by scholars within the disciplines of Law and Social Policy (Herman 2003; Millbank 2004). Both Herman and Millbank discuss *Bad Girls* precisely because of what they see as the text's distinctive and oppositional representations of the female criminal and the institution of prison.

The accounts of both Herman and Millbank, for instance, discuss the significance of *Bad Girls* in terms of the way it counters heteronormative representations of lesbians on television. At issue here is not only how 'heteronormativity' constructs heterosexuality as natural and normal, but also that it is an epistemological project: 'it shapes what we know and how we know it'. In other words, 'it also provides the prospective through which we know and understand gender and sexuality in popular culture' (Herman 2003: 144). Heteronormativity informs the lack or visibility of representations of lesbian and gay identities historically on television and indeed the wider popular culture. When gay/lesbian characters in mainstream texts such as *Ellen* (ABC, 1994–1998) or *Will and Grace* (NBC Studios, 1998–2006) do appear, they can also be perceived to embody heteronormativity 'in that the sexuality of the gay characters is on display for the scrutiny/pleasure of a predominantly straight audience' (Herman 2003:144). Thus, gayness is presented as either an issue (*Ellen*), or a sense of humour (*Will and Grace*) and, at best, is confined within a liberal, heteronormative place of tolerance (2003: 144).

Millbank's discussion of the regimes of heteronormative representations is sobering regarding the symbolic violence that is cast upon lesbians. Given the dualisms on which heteronormative ideology is based, lesbians are placed on the negative side of the good/bad distinction and are frequently characterized not only as criminals but also as violently transgressive (Millbank 2004: 156). As Millbank suggests, lesbians are characterized as being closely associated with film noir, WIP and horror genres where they 'often symbolise the abject, the depraved, the anti-social' (2004: 156). The issue here is not only how heteronormativity reinforces certain ideological and cultural norms within the realm of representation, but how such representations have real effects. As Millbank's account charts, hegemonic imagery of 'insanely aggressive lesbians' produces real material effects on how lesbians are treated within the criminal justice system (2004: 156).

Countering such heteronormative representations, Herman and Millbank discuss how *Bad Girls* not only places lesbians at the centre of its narrative, but also 'validates and normalizes lesbian sexuality' (Herman 2003: 141) via the Helen Stewart/Nikki Wade storyline. While at the outset of the narrative Helen is characterized as heterosexual, the three series charts her blossoming lesbian relationship before the two characters are eventually united on the 'outside' after Helen helps Nikki to win her appeal at the end of season 3. Nikki is serving ten years for stabbing a police officer whom she found raping her partner; a narrative that would appear to perpetuate the association of lesbians with criminality. However drawing on the work of Ruthann Robson (1992), Millbank argues that Nikki, as well as the representations of other transgressive lesbianism within *Bad Girls,* needs to be contextualized in relation to the domestification of lesbian and gay political struggles with an almost exclusive emphasis upon assimilation through marriage, family and capitalist relations. For Millbank, building on Herman's analysis, the 'anti-social' representation of lesbianism in *Bad Girls* (2004: 158) is one that embodies the figure of the lesbian outlaw (2004: 159). This figure is one that returns our attention to both the *lesbian* and the *law* and in so doing opens space to revisit the long-lost quest of liberation that has been elided through our focus on assimilation (2004: 159).

Significantly in this respect, Nikki's crime involved violence, but as Millbank argues, the narrative interrogates the circumstances, rather than simply 'portraying violent, irrational or out of control lesbians' (2004: 164). Consequently, sexuality is implicated in Nikki's crime, 'but it is not posited as causal' (2004: 164). Nikki is not simply excused for being violent, 'but she is frequently portrayed as heroic' (Millbank 2004: 165); a leader amongst the women who uses force if necessary to care and protect the more vulnerable inmates such as the 'new fish' Rachel Hicks in episode 1 who is being bullied by the notorious inmate Shell Dockley and sexually exploited by Senior Prison Officer Jim Fenner.

Constructed as both the moral and political conscience of the text, Nikki is used by the writers to comment on a range of issues affecting women in prison, 'including prison healthcare, the incarceration of women forced to abandon vulnerable children and the treatment of non-English speaking inmates' (Herman 2003: 146). By way of comparison to Nikki, Helen's heroism is founded particularly in a 'Cagney and Lacey' style and is most assuredly not in the WIP genre – she is a feminist crusader, seeking personally to break the glass ceiling in the prison service, and politically to force the service to respond more effectively to inmates' needs (Herman 2003: 146). Indeed, it is Nikki and Helen's feminist politics that creates an initial bond between them: Helen asking for Nikki's help in countering 'the old boys' network' and scuppering the plans of corrupt officers that attempt to undermine her authority and plans for reform (Herman 2003: 146).

Whilst Herman and Millbank's readings of *Bad Girls* are useful for exploring constructions of the morally complex lesbian outlaw figures that populate the series, their accounts subsequently marginalizes an analysis of the 'straight' female characters that make up this female ensemble drama. The latter characters – prostitutes, gangsters, sociopaths, bullies, shoplifters, fraudsters, bigamists, murderers – are constructed as being just as morally ambivalent 'outlaws' as their lesbian counterparts; their criminality positioning them as deviating and disrupting the norms of conventional (heteronormative) femininity. It is such ambivalent characterizations of femininities, as Milly Buonanno discusses in the introduction to this collection, that makes it difficult to categorize them as heroines or as antiheroines. Rather their complexity defies categorization and thus disrupts gendered dualisms that govern constructions of femininity.

This chapter supplements Herman and Millbank's reading of *Bad Girls* by exploring the construction of the transgressive and morally ambivalent femininities that make up the community in *Bad Girls*. I will explore how such ambivalent femininities within *Bad Girls* makes strange – and thus queers – the penal system and women's position within it. This reading will encompass not only how gender and sexuality are represented within *Bad Girls*, but also how the text can be read as offering a commentary on the relationship between gender, sexuality and the imperatives of British television at the turn of the millennium.

Critical Contexts

The emergence of *Bad Girls* and its constructions and celebration of transgressive femininities in the prime-time slot in 1999 is suggestive of the 'feminization' and 'sexualization' of television schedules within this period. The 'feminization' of television was perceived to manifest itself via the increased visibility of female experience as well as in the discourses and spaces associated with women and feminine-gendered fiction in prime-time slots (Brunsdon 2000; Moseley 2000; Ball 2012). The concern with the domestic lives of male as well as female characters in television dramas ranging from *Casualty* (BBC, 1986–ongoing) to *Wallander* (Yellow Bird and Left Bank Pictures for BBC, 2008–2010) and participants in makeover programmes also translates into a concern with the personal and emotional 'life politics' (Creeber 2004: 118) of individuals.

Intersecting with the feminization of British television, the late 1990s also saw a proliferation of sexual discourses and identities on television across both factual and fictional genres. In the area of British television drama, for instance, texts such as *Oranges are Not the Only Fruit* (BBC, 1990), *Portrait of a Marriage* (BBC, 1990), *The Buddha of Suburbia* (BBC, 1993), *This Life* (World Productions for BBC2, 1996–1997), *Band of Gold II* (Granada for ITV, 1996), *Real Women* (BBC One, 1998), *Playing the Field* (Tiger Aspect for BBC One, 1998–2002), *Tipping the Velvet* (Sally Head Productions for BBC One, 2002) and *Queer as Folk* (Red Production for CH4, 1999–2000) represented the proliferation of gay, lesbian and queer identities on British television and, crucially, a dispersal of 'moral and ideological positions from which events and issues are debated and evaluated' (Arthurs 2004: 2).

While I have separated out the two shifts for the purposes of clarification, they do, as I will illustrate with *Bad Girls*, intersect in particular ways. Both of these shifts can be usefully understood as an attempt to attract audiences within a period marked by the waning of traditional ways of being, and where notions of 'lifestyle' and neo-liberal 'choice' dominated schedules and narratives in the increasingly deregulated, competitive and commercialized contexts of broadcasting. This movement away from traditional ways of being in both broadcasting and subjective terms also had palpable effects on the aesthetics of television that foregrounded a postmodern sensibility – self-reflexivity, intertextuality, performance, irony and camp. However, as this list suggests, the values that came to dominate television in the 1990s also embody a queer sensibility, given the way these aesthetics draw attention to their own constructedness and thus hold potential for playing with cultural codes of gender and sexuality.

However, in the United Kingdom, it is texts that focus upon masculinity such as *The Buddha of Suburbia* and *Queer as Folk* that have been discussed as embodying a queer sensibility. Analyses of British texts that engage with feminine identity in relation to concepts of lifestyle, sexuality and performativity tend to be explored with recourse to the concept of post-feminism, resulting in the queer potential of these texts being overlooked. At issue here is the differing politics that underpins these two concepts. Both post-feminist and queer politics advocate a freeing of agency from structure (whether this be gender or sexuality) and privilege the concept of lifestyle in terms of building meaningful identities. In this way, both concepts have been perceived as being complicit with consumer culture by privileging notions of style, performance and individualism over an analysis of the structural inequalities and factors that continue to inform sociocultural identities within the context of late modernity. What marks these two sensibilities apart is the way in which post-feminist texts often involve scenarios of retreatism and a re-traditionalization of gender (Ball 2012). This is the antithesis of queer politics. Consequently, the ways in which discourses of post-feminism and queer collide, collude or contrast within British feminine-gendered fictions of the late 1990s have yet to be teased out.

Queer Feminism

This queer feminist reading of *Bad Girls* is an attempt to tease out the gender and sexual politics at play within British texts produced in the late 1990s. As the accounts of Herman and Millbank suggest, the construction of gender and sexuality in *Bad Girls* is interesting to explore due to its embodiment of outlaws and antiheroines. Before exploring these constructions of femininities in *Bad Girls*, it is necessary to clarify what is referred to here by queer feminism. Following Marinucci in *Queer Feminism*, 'queer feminism is the application of queer notions of gender, sex, and sexuality to the subject matter of feminist theory, and the simultaneous application of feminist notions of gender, sex, sexuality to the subject matter of queer theory' (2000: 1961).

However, this 'queer feminist' reading of *Bad Girls* may appear to be an oxymoron: 'In so far as feminism is referential of the existing sex and gender binaries, it might seem to be at odds with the rejection of binary forms of categorization' (Marinucci 2000: 2026) that underpin the queer project. Yet, as Marinucci also argues:

Retaining 'feminism' [...] reminds readers that despite intentions to the contrary, the world just so happens to be structured in binary terms, and people assigned as female or feminine are often disadvantaged as a result. Until or unless the 'feminism' in 'queer feminism' is rendered meaningless through major linguistic and conceptual transformation, the 'feminism' in 'queer feminism' will remain relevant.

(2000: 2043)

By suggesting that *Bad Girls* can be read queerly, I am referring to the way in which the text offers a place for the expression of what Doty refers to as 'non-, anti-, or contra straight' (1993: 3) reading of these criminal femininities.

I want to explore this point further with reference to the opening scenes of season 1 of *Bad Girls* ('Them and Us' 1999). The text opens with the soundtrack of N-Trances' remix of the Bee Gees disco classic 'Stayin Alive'. The black-and-white title sequence is replaced with several differing femininities performing to the song: two middle-aged white women in sparkly wigs and costumes dancing, a younger mixed-race 'butch' woman in a transparent red hoodie and combat trousers and finally a white woman in the style of a beauty queen strutting her stuff. Excerpts of each of these performances are intercut with shots of a black woman in a room, bleeding and crying out in physical pain. The setting and relationship of these differing women is not revealed until the song finishes. At which point the lights come up and we find we have witnessed the inhabitants of G-Wing (the two Julies, Denny and Shell Dockley) performing a dress rehearsal of a fashion show; the other woman is Carol, an inmate experiencing a miscarriage alone in her prison cell.

Within these 70 seconds, the text's particular brand of 'infotainment' is vividly established. It is one in which the 'realities' of life in a woman's prison are played through the heightened codes of melodrama and camp. In this way, the text is not so different from *Prisoner: Cell Block H*. The first episode of *Bad Girls* received scathing reviews akin to *Prisoner* in the British press:

> No cliché is too cheap. We have got the troublemaker, the bully, the enforcer, the victim, the male warden who thinks he's in a harem, the other male warden who is handsome and innocent, the embittered female warden and, of course, all the serious pretensions to meaningful drama which will justify the salacious scenarios.
>
> (Hennessey 1999: 38)

Yet, while *Bad Girls* does trade on stereotypes and clichés of the WIP genre, it does so in a very knowing way. Following the postmodern turn in television drama in this period, the opening scenes of the fashion show and Carol foreground the performative aspects of identity. There is, for instance, the drawing on the 'performance-within-a-performance' trope of the fashion show and the range of stereotypes that are paraded for both 'us' the viewers at home as well as the imagined audience of prison inhabitants within the diegesis: female friends (two Julies), the butch (Denny), the femme (Shell Dockley), the suffering woman (Carol). Both scenes are also marked by the aesthetics of excess – the carnivalesque fashion show and the horrors taking place in Carol's cell. The heightened aesthetics of these scenes and the rapid cutting between them serves to create an ironic distancing from which to view these performances of femininity.

In this vein, the codes and conventions of *Bad Girls* work similarly to the exploitation cycle of WIP films of the 1970s. To be sure, the exploitation cycle of texts enjoy only low cultural status because it is 'essentially a commercial category, a market term for those films produced at minimum cost for maximum return which 'take up, "exploit" the success of other films – replaying the themes, star-stereotypes and genres of more lavish, up-market productions' (Cook 1976: 122). However, the exploitation film's fetishized images of women as sexual object, seemingly produced by men for the male market, have been interesting to feminists precisely because of the way in which their hallmarks – bad acting, crude stereotypes and schematic narrative – work to denaturalize and thus disturb the 'patriarchal myths of women on which the exploitation film itself rests' (Cook 1976: 127). In a parodic nod to the exploitation film, the exaggerated 'excessive' opening scenes of *Bad Girls* makes visible how popular cultural texts 'exploit' the female body via their narratives of surveillance (Mayne 2000: 117).

For Mayne, the WIP film thematizes in a very pronounced way the capacity of the cinema not only to objectify the female body, but also 'create dramas of surveillance and visibility' (2000: 117). Mayne thus cites Foucault's influential work regarding the Panopticon as being central to feminist understandings of the relationship between the gaze and power. Originating with Jeremy Bentham, the Panopticon is a model for a prison system in which the prisoners are dispersed around a central tower, from which they are always in a state of potential surveillance by the authorities located in the tower (Mayne 2000: 117). Citing Doane, Mellencamp and Williams' feminist reading of the Panopticon, Mayne suggests that the sense of permanent visibility may provide a fitting metaphor for the relationship between women, the gaze and power within culture (2000: 117).

The WIP film disturbs the presumption that it is the male spectator of cinema who occupies the authority figure in the central tower of the Panopticon. Rather, as Mayne argues, what is 'quite striking' about the WIP film is the way the male figures, who provide 'patriarchal authority', tend to be marginal to plots, and how 'thoroughly surveillance involves women watching other women; women objectifying other women' (2000: 118). In the world of the WIP it is differences between women that 'take the place usually occupied by gender': these are differences not only in terms of sexuality, butch and femme personas, but also differences in terms of race, class, age, 'the types of crime (particularly prostitutes versus everything else), and physical differences' (Mayne 2000: 127).

Similarly to Stephen Maddison's discussion of the British soap opera *Coronation Street* and the female ensemble films of Pedro Almodovar,[1] *Bad Girls*, and the WIP genre more generally, can be perceived to enact 'gender dissent' in the way they privilege 'heterosocial bonds':

> Heterosocial bonding is a reversal of the discourse of homosociality. If homosocial relations strive towards an appropriate masculinity by suppressing women they also instate a faggot-other disavowed through misogyny. We could suggest that such relations produce a condition of gender dysphoria for straight women, lesbians and gay men, where their gender is culturally organised in such a way as to facilitate their exclusion, oppression, humiliation and powerlessness. [...] Narratively, social bonds are often concerned with displacing the dominance of homosocial representations of women and queers, which constitute male subjectivity, by foregrounding bonds that express our interests.
> (Maddison 2000: 275)

It is via the privileging of heterosocial bonds that *Bad Girls* queers the perspective from which we are 'normally' offered the opportunity to view female criminals. To explore this point, I want to zoom out from the analysis of *Bad Girls* for a moment and explore the ideologies of heteronormativity that inform and shape understanding of female criminals within western patriarchal cultures.

Crossing the Line

The slang term 'bent' in popular culture is used to refer to homosexuality but also to the other so-called 'deviant' identity of 'the criminal'. In both cases, the term 'bent' applies to identities that have been 'othered' in culture, those which act as the constitutive outside to the so-called 'normal', 'straight' (heterosexual, law-abiding) identities.

Heteronormative ideology of gender emerged in the nineteenth century and placed great emphasis on 'separate spheres' for women and men in western cultures (Heidensohn 1996: 163). The appropriate spheres for men and women to control and influence are, for men, the realm of public life, while women should be confined to their 'proper' place, the home. Yet, as Heidensohn has argued, 'the concept of separate spheres was not merely a pretty Victorian conceit. It served to rationalise both the prevailing sex-role division of tasks and power' (1996: 164). Thus women's role, and respectability, was accorded to their roles as wives and mothers within the private sphere. Along with domestic care, protection and education of children, women were constructed as the purveyor of moral values and civilizing influence on both children and men. For women to be 'unchaste, unfaithful, unseemly, vain, or frivolous' (Elshtain 1981: 161), their 'behaviour would be suffused with public implications namely the stability of society itself' (165).

While women's role within the private sphere functions as a form of social control of children and men, it also serves to shape and indeed constrain their own behaviour. In their feminist polemical article 'The coercion of privacy', Dahl and Snare argue that 'the nuclear family represents a prison comparable to the public institution carrying this label' (1978: 22):

> It can be argued that women are segregated and locked in their 'cells', the nuclear family, where they are hindered from having their own personal life due to lack of mobility, cash and free time. In particular a housewife with small children can not regulate her own time [...] one can propose that through material and ideological bonds, women are kept 'out of circulation' [out of] [...] a life in the public sector where men [of the ruling class] are now in control!
>
> (Dahl and Snare as quoted in Heidensohn 1996: 175)

Although '"prison" is perhaps a more meaningful metaphor for women's domestic position than actual description of it' (Heidensohn 1996: 176), Dahl and Snare's account does still resonate today where women remain primary care givers according to the law and within the domestic sphere. Moreover, nineteenth century ideologies continue to inform contemporary perceptions of crime and deviance. They have constructed a double standard in which men who commit crime are perceived to be capable of reform but where women continue to be stigmatized. Indeed women who commit crime are seen as being doubly deviant: offending 'both [...] society's behavioural rules about property, drinking, violence and also [...] the more fundamental norms which govern sex-role behaviour' (Heidensohn 1996: 134). Such ideologies have real effects and account for women's conformity to prescribed roles and thus the small number of women who commit crimes within culture (Heidensohn 1996: 10).

The 'other' status occupied by the criminal may account for the popularity and fascination with crime narratives on television. Docker suggests that the enduring appeal and cultural fascination with crime narratives is due to the way they personify 'the intersection where personal and private become social and public: where private passions erupt in to public knowledge, debate, contestation, judgement' (1994: 262). To be sure, the genres of law and order have been central to British television schedules historically, whether this be police procedural (*Z Cars* [BBC, 1962–1978], *The Bill* [Thames TV, 1984–2010]), detective and special forces (*The Sweeney* [Euston Films, 1975–1978], *Luther* [BBC, 2000–2010]), courtroom dramas (*Justice* [Yorkshire TV, 1971–1974], *Trial and Retribution* [Isle of Man Prod. for ITV, 1997–2009]) or indeed criminal communities (*Widows* [Euston Films for BBC One, 1983], *Mad Dogs* [Left Bank Pictures for Sky, 2011–ongoing]). But as this list of texts suggest, there has been a distinct lack of dramas that engage with life behind bars. By way of comparison to the multiple crime narratives that populate British television on a weekly basis, the total number of prison dramas that have been produced for British television since its inception in the 1930s can be counted on one hand. They are *Within These Walls* (Thames TV for ITV, 1974–1978), *Scum* (BBC, 1977), *The Governor* (La Plante Productions, Samson Films and Yorkshire TV for ITV, 1995–1996), *Buried* (World Productions for Channel 4, 2003) and *Bad Girls*.[2]

A closer look at the differences between the prison drama and other crime-based genres provides some clues as to their different positioning and status on television. The police or crime series has been traditionally informed by a crime-chase-arrest narrative structure. Such crime narratives stage particular anxieties regarding law and order that are relevant to specific sociocultural contexts. Narrative closure, traditionally culminating in the arrest of criminals, has been aligned with ideological closure and the re-assertion of patriarchal authority and law (Skirrow 1985: 175). It is presumed that criminal characters will be punished appropriately by the criminal justice system but this part of the narrative tends to be understood rather than dramatized. Thus while crime and criminality form the subject of dramatic fiction, convicted criminals of television fiction, like those in society, largely fall from public view.[3]

As Wilson and O'Sullivan have argued, prisons 'are deliberately constructed not just to keep prisoners in, but also to keep the public out' (2004: 8). This extends to the production of fictions of those worlds, whereby 'the authorities believed that prison should be a secret world, of which the public enjoyed a fearful ignorance' (Wilson and O'Sullivan 2004: 36). It is precisely because of the status of prison as a 'closed institution' (Wilson and O'Sullivan 2004: 38) that television and film 'are important sources of people's implicit and commonsense understandings of prisons and prisoners' (Wilson and O'Sullivan 2004: 8).

As with the crime series, the prison drama can be perceived to occupy 'a privileged relation to reality' (Brunsdon 1997: 71). In the British context, the codes of realism have been synonymous with 'quality', radical drama *a la* Ken Loach and Tony Garnett. Yet, it is precisely the attempt to show the 'realities' of prison life that has proved problematic for television. For instance, *Scum*'s attempt to critique the violence of the borstal system by showing it was considered too brutal and subsequently banned until 1991 when it was shown on Channel Four as part of a season on the theme of censorship (Hobday 2014). Similarly, Roy Battersby's drama-documentary *Five Women*, a play that dramatized the testimonies of female prisoners captured in Tony Parker's book of the same name, caused some controversy at the BBC because it 'had crossed an unacceptable line between "drama" and "documentary"' (Hill 2013: 134). The edited version of the play, eventually broadcast under the title *Some Women* (BBC One, 21 August 1969), removed the plays most controversial character, the 'lesbian drug-addict':

> While this was justified on the basis that the original version was too long (and it was impossible to shorten the original version without removal of an entire section), the cut did succeed in encouraging speculation in the press that the decision had been made on moral, rather than artistic grounds.
>
> (Hill 2013: 135)

To extend Hill's point, it is to suggest that dramas depicting the realities of prison life that engage with violence, drugs and lesbianism are not considered appropriate material for consumption by television audiences, as conceived historically by television institutions: namely, middle-class families with traditional patterns of gendered behaviour (Arthurs 2004: 1).

Attempting to construct the realities of prison life on television is problematic and subject to censure; it is the attempt to construct the female prisoner, as the example of *Five Women* illustrates, which appears particularly problematic for television. This is because femininity represents the antithesis of criminality within western cultures (Smart 1977: 182). It is pertinent at this point to bring *Within These Walls* into the discussion. As stated in the introduction to this book, this is the only other WIP drama to be produced in the British context until the appearance of *Bad Girls* in 1999. It is also the series that is credited with inspiring the Australian production *Prisoner*. As with *Prisoner*, *Within These Walls* did attempt to engage with the realities of life in a women's prison. The creators drew on professional 'insider' advice and each episode engaged with a contemporary issue such as drugs and bullying.

However, *Within These Walls* differs from *Prisoner* in the way it reverses the conventions of the WIP so that the experience of the 'new fish' that the text privileges is actually that of the recently appointed prison governor Faye Boswell (Googie Withers), rather than the experience of the prisoners per se. Each episode foregrounds Boswell's care of a particular prisoner; her attempts to understand their motives of crime, as well as to advocate that prison should be a space for rehabilitation rather than punishment. Produced within a context in which concern was building regarding prison officer brutality, prison governor Faye Boswell is constructed as a caring, matriarchal figure, in the mould of Mrs Benton in *Caged*, a governor who does her best to balance discipline with reform. The only whiff of corruption comes from the prisoners themselves, such as Lily the bully or Martha Kyle, a political activist.

If the construction of a feminine, caring prison service is one informed by the turbulent context of the 1970s in which it is produced, it also serves to reposition women in relation to traditional discourses of femininity. Thus, we have the caring governor, akin to Tania Modleksi's ideal mother of American soap operas such as *Days of Our Lives* (NBC, 1965–ongoing) (1981: 92), who nurtures and reforms her problematic 'children' in order that they take up their 'rightful' place as women within the contexts of home and family. Conversely, *Bad Girls* is more akin to the *Prisoner: Cell Block H* with respect to the contra-straight position it offers of female criminals.

Out of the Closet

As the opening scene involving the fashion show illustrates, *Bad Girls* takes the viewers behind the closed doors of the prison and 'outs' the experience of women with the penal system. British soap operas such as *Coronation Street* and *Crossroads* have long been celebrated for the way in which they privilege matriarchal communities of strong-minded and resilient women (Geraghty 1991: 135), but these focus upon femininities in the private sphere of home, family and in relation to their trials and tribulations as wives and mothers. British soap operas such as *Coronation Street* have long made explicit the labour that is carried out in the domestic sphere (Thumim 2002: 214) and thus blur the public/private dualism that informs gendered divisions of labour. At the same time, they have found it more challenging to accommodate the career woman, a figure who is defined in relation to the masculine public sphere because it 'challenges the basis of home and community' on which the British soap rests (Geraghty 1991: 135). By focusing on the private lives of incarcerated women within the public institution of the prison, *Bad Girls* queers the conventions of British soap opera. To extend a point made by Geraghty, by being down among the criminal women (Geraghty 1991: 47), *Bad Girls* offers an alternative vantage point from which to view these subaltern and stigmatized identities.

The construction of transgressive femininities found with the WIP genre follows a long tradition of unruly figures that Natalie Zemon Davis traced back to early modern Europe

(1975). These are figures who approach the female equivalent of the male tradition of Robin Hood, Dick Turpin, Rob Roy: 'figures who could inspire fear as well as admiration' (Docker 1994: 262). The prison space, as indicated by the opening scenes of *Bad Girls*, is characterized as an unruly, carnivalesque space. In *Rabelais and his World*, Bakhtin describes medieval carnival as the second world and second life of the people, organized on the basis of laughter and that which 'celebrated a temporary liberation from the prevailing truth and from the established order; it marked the suspension of all hierarchical rank, privileged norms and prohibitions' (1984: 10). In *Bad Girls*, the characteristics of the carnivalesque can be perceived not only in its characterization of unruly femininities, but in the way it 'brings down low' the representatives of law – the prison guards, the governor and the penal system.

In *Images of Incarceration* (2004), Wilson and O'Sullivan identify four character types that populate *Bad Girls*. These include the 'pantomime baddies' and 'goodies', 'soap opera style players', 'players in a prime drama' and 'dramatic approximations' of the kinds of women who actually populate prison. Wilson and O'Sullivan distinguish between these character types in order to illustrate how they are used in the text to generate an eclectic mix of storylines and scenarios that range from the cartoonish to the serious. But Wilson and O'Sullivan's account is also relevant to this analysis of the carnivalesque characteristics of *Bad Girls* in the way their typography exemplifies how it is not only the prisoners who could be described as contra-straight.

As their discussion of each of the character types suggests, it is the guards and wing governor as much as the convicted inmates who are implicated in criminal activity. Conversely, some of the inmates (the two Julies) as well as the guards (caring Dominic McAllister, Lorna Rose as well as Wing Governor Helen Stewart) are categorized as 'the goodies'. Yet, as familiarity with these characters attests, it is more often the case that the line between who is good and bad is, for the most part, blurred. For instance, even the 'good' officer Dominic McAllister kisses inmate Zandra Plackett. Rather than suggesting Dominic is a reprehensible character for this transgression, the storyline is used to explore the complexities of human relationship across the dividing line between prisoner and guard. A similar dynamic is at work with the love affair between Nikki and Helen. As Herman and Millbank have suggested, rather than punishing Helen for her transgression, the text celebrates the love affair between the two women. For Millbank the love story between Nikki and Helen 'suggests lesbianism as a rupture that crosses, and thereby dissolves, the hierarchical lines of gaolor and prisoner – both literally and figuratively freeing the woman imprisoned' (2004: 159). As this point of Millbank suggests, the contra-straight carnivalesque characters that populate *Bad Girls* can be seen as embodying a queer sensibility. Yet, it is not only the representatives of the law that are brought down low in *Bad Girls*.

In keeping with the text's cultural inversions, it is the penal system's treatment of women rather than the women themselves that is under scrutiny and found wanting in the text. According to the text's creator and producer, Ann McManus, the series was deliberately 'issue led' (McManus in Midgley 1999). Discussing this point in the book that accompanied the series, *Bad Girls: The Inside Story*, the Shed production team stated that the storyline involving Jim Fenner and his abuse of female inmates was used to exemplify some of the consequence of having male officers in women's prison, which was ironically a result of equal opportunities legislation (Reynolds and McCallum 2001: 111).

The second issue that the production team wanted to explore was the way in which the imprisoning of women often punished whole families by separating mothers from their children (Reynolds and McCallum 2001: 111). This theme is introduced from episode 1 of the first series via Monica Lindsey, a middle-class woman convicted of fraud and whose disabled son, Spencer, dies while she is in custody. But other related storylines include the neglect of pregnant women; women who are forced to give up their newborn babies; the difficulty of sustaining relationships with existing children and a concern for the safety of children held in social care for the duration of the mother's term in prison.

Conversely, the text also illustrates the ways in which the penal system fails women who end up in prison after being abused. Denny Blood's reunion with her alcoholic mother Jessie Devlin in G-Wing puts this issue in sharp focus. The text explores how Jessie became an alcoholic after being sexually abused by her own father. Denny subsequently set fire to the children's home in response to being sexually abused at the hands of her so-called carers. Such storylines serve to highlight the way in which the penal system exasperates the positioning of such abused women, who are subjected to further abuse and punishment rather than care and counselling at the hands of the state.

The queer feminism of *Bad Girls* is evident in its consciousness-raising regarding the positioning and experience of women within the penal system. It is also embodied in the support that the inmates give to one another in the face of such conditions. It is the relationships between women in *Bad Girls* that are paramount: the community of women inmates functions as a real family, 'providing warmth, support, and in some cases, mothering that the prisoners have not experienced on the outside' (Herman 2003: 152).

It is this aspect of the text that for Herman exemplifies a lesbian feminist construction of family 'evidenced by the fact that lesbians are at the heart of the community – not outside of it, opposed to it, to taking advantage of it' (2003: 152). Conversely, apart from the 'idealized' heterosexual relationship between two black characters, Crystal and Josh, Herman suggests that a large proportion of *Bad Girls*' representations of heterosexuality could be said to inhabit the violent, spectral place that is usually the province of lesbianism within popular culture (2003: 154). This is most telling in the case of senior prison officer Jim Fenner. Unlike the WIP film where male characters tend to be marginal to storylines, the centrality of Jim Fenner 'is central to the "othering" of heterosexuality' (Herman 2003: 155). All of Jim Fenner's sexual relationships (with his wife and four other women) are embedded within scenes of violence, abuse and exploitation, or at best, deception and manipulation.

Herman's reading of the sexual politics of *Bad Girls* has, however, been problematized by Wilson and O'Sullivan. They argue that, rather than straightforwardly normalizing and valuing same-sex desire and problematizing heterosexuality, the text problematizes and comments on all forms of sexual desire (2004: 133). For Wilson and O'Sullivan, sexual desire is represented as being problematic and is always implicitly contrasted with platonic friendships. Sexual desire is constructed in the text as leading to jealousy, possessiveness and clouding judgement. This is as true of Helen and Nikki's relationship wherein Nikki reacts to prison officer Dominic McAllister's interest in Helen. In turn, 'nice guy' Dominic McAllister 'loses something of his quiet confidence and becomes (mildly) inappropriately pushy when he starts to see Helen as a potential partner' (2004: 133). Conversely, Wilson and O'Sullivan suggest that Josh and Crystal's relationship is not disparaged because their relationship is motivated by a genuine concern for each other. Sex only becomes part of their relationship once trust has been firmly established between them (2004: 133).

The problematizing of all sexual desire is in keeping with the text's queer feminist sensibility, one in which it is '[p]latonic relationships (whether lesbian or straight) that are always represented as good and valuable, as being non-instrumental and as having the potential to achieve a genuine altruism' (Wilson and O'Sullivan 2004: 133).

Thus, *Bad Girls* can be seen to embody a queer construction of the family via their focus upon a polymaternal community, for instance, it is not only lesbians who are central to the caring, support network in the text. Gangster's moll Yvonne Atkinson frequently acts as mother figure to Denny, Shazza and Charlotte. In this instance, polymaternal kinships embody a queer sensibility 'in the way they resist (although not entirely transcend) normative familial configurations and normative domestic patterns' (Parks 2013: 317).

While the community that is constructed in *Bad Girls* is inclusive of women of different ethnicities and social classes, the text does not present these femininities as equal in status. It is this point that marks the limits of the text's queer and contra-straight positioning.

Although the majority of characters in *Bad Girls* occupy a working-class subjectivity, it is a white, middle-class feminist perspective that is privileged in the text. Thus, narrative authority is aligned with Nikki and Helen. As Herman has argued, 'While the class backgrounds of Nikki and Helen are ambiguous, Helen is university educated and Nikki soon will be. They share an interest in "good" literature and Nikki is often found in the library' (2003: 146). But a middle-class validation of female prisoners is also evident in Monica Lindsey's speech to the press, on her release from prison:

> I imagined that criminal women were monsters or lunatics. I was wrong. Most of the women I met and without whom I could not have survived are warm, intelligent, funny. Many will have been separated from their children. Some, like me, will lose them forever. Many are drug addicts that need rehabilitation; many are the victims of abusive men. They need love and support, not strip searching and bullying. In my opinion, prison as punishment, only makes bad situations worse. Thank you.
>
> ('Love Hurts', 3 August 1999)

Monica's speech is the most didactic of the series and is utilized here to communicate the perspective of the text's producers (themselves white and middle class).

Heroines or Antiheroines

As I have suggested, criminal women are perceived to represent the antithesis to femininity within western patriarchal culture. And yet if, as Snyder has suggested, a heroine is someone 'who acts courageously for the sake of others' (2014: 19) then the femininities in *Bad Girls* would appear to fall into this category. Moreover, and via the construction of 'caring matriarchs', *Bad Girls* could be understood as recuperating these transgressive femininities in relation to normative gender roles.

Rather than personifying a post-feminist-style narrative that often presents marriage and motherhood as 'the' life choice for women, the foregrounding of mothering and feminine discourses of care in *Bad Girls* is a political strategy and an antidote and commentary on the lack of these noble qualities within the patriarchal prison system. The drama politicizes the plight of women for whom the role of mother is idolized in culture and who are responsible in law for the protection and care of children but who are removed from their off-spring by this arm of the state.

At the same time, I would argue that the femininities in *Bad Girls* pose a challenge to the traditional ways of representing women characters similarly to the career woman in British soap opera. Femininities in *Bad Girls*

> [p]ropose a model in which women act rather than react; a model in which it is necessary for a woman to be self-assertive rather than continually absorbing the pain and punishment on behalf of other members of the family or community.
>
> (Geraghty 1991: 139)

In this respect, not all actions of the women are sympathetic, selfless or noble. The femininities in *Bad Girls* are not romanticized; the threat of violence and intimidation from both inmates as well as guards means that the women have to rely on their fists as well as their wits to enable them to survive within the prison system. In keeping with the queer sensibility of the text, the construction of femininities in *Bad Girls* is fluid and one in which the dialectic between heroine and antiheroine is kept continually in play. Significantly, it is not the morality of these criminal femininities that is found reprehensible in the text, but rather the patriarchal prison service that is marked out as the real villain of the piece.

References

Arthurs, J. (2004), *Television and Sexuality: Regulation and the Politics of Taste*, Milton Keynes: Open University Press.

Bad Girls (1999-2006, United Kingdom: ITV).

Bakhtin, M. (1984), *Rabelais and His World*, London: Bloomington.

Ball, V. (2012), 'The "feminization" of British television and the re-traditionalization of gender', *Feminist Media Studies*, 12: 2, pp. 248–264.

Brunsdon, C. (ed.) (1997), *Screen Tastes*, London: Routledge.
—— (2000), 'Not having it all: Women and film in the 1990s', in R. Murphy (ed.), *British Film of the 90s*, London: BFI.
Cook, P. (1976), '"Exploitation" films and feminism', *Screen*, 17: 2, pp. 122–127.
Dahl, T. S. and Snare, A. (1978), 'The coercion of privacy', in C. Smart and B. Smart (eds), *Women, Sexuality and Social Control*, London: Routledge and Kegan Paul.
Davis, N. Z. (1975), 'Women on top', in N. Z. Davis (ed.), *Society and Culture in Early Modern France*, California: Stanford University Press.
Doane, M. A., Mellencamp, P. and Williams, L. (1984), *Revisions: Essays in Feminist Film Criticism*, Maryland: University Publications of America.
Docker, J. (1995), *Postmodernism and Popular Culture: A Cultural History*, Cambridge: Cambridge University Press.
Doty, A. (1993), *Making Things Perfectly Queer*, Minneapolis: University of Minnesota Press.
Elshtain, J. B. (1981), *Public Man, Private Woman*, Oxford: Martin Robertson.
Geraghty, C. (1991), *Women and Soap Opera*, Cambridge: Polity Press.
Heidensohn, F. (1996), *Women and Crime*, (2nd ed.), Hampshire and London: Macmillan Press.
Hennessey, S. (1999), 'All Barr reality', *Scotland on Sunday*, http://www.scotsman.com/. Accessed 22 June 2015.
Herman, D. (2003), '"*Bad Girls* Changed My Life" homonormativity in a woman's prison drama', *Critical Studies in Media Communication*, 2: 2, pp. 141–159.
Hill, J. (2013), 'From five women to Leeds United!: Roy Battersby and the politics of "radical" television drama', *Journal of British Cinema and Television*, 10: 3, pp. 130–150.
Hobday, J. (2014), 'Scum', http://www.screenonline.org.uk/tv/id/439310. Accessed 22 June 2015.
'Love Hurts' (1999), Mike Adams, dir., *Bad Girls*, Season 1, Episode 10, 3 August, London: ITV.
Maddison, S. (2000), 'All about women: Pedro Almodovar and the heterosocial dynamic', *Textual Practice*, 14: 2, pp. 265–284.
Marinucci, M. (2010), *Feminism is Queer: The Intimate Connection Between Queer and Feminist Theory*, London and New York: Zed Books (Kindle edition).
Mayne, J. (2000), *Framed: Lesbians, Feminists, and Media Culture*, Minneapolis: University of Minnesota Press.
Midgley, C. (1999), '*Bad Girls* given a second chance', *The Times*, http://www.thesundaytimes.co.uk/sto. Accessed 22 June 2015.
Millbank, J. (2004), 'It's about This: Lesbians, prison, desire', *Social and Legal Studies*, 13: 2, pp. 155–190.
Moseley, R. (2000), 'Makeover, Takeover on British Television', *Screen*, 41: 3, pp. 299–314.
Parks, S. M. (2013), *Mothering Queering, Queering Motherhood*, Albany: State University of New York Press (Kindle edition).
Prisoner: Cell Block H (1979-1986, Australia: Network Ten).
Reynolds, J. and McCallum, J. (2001), *Bad Girls: The Inside Story*, London. HarperCollins.
Robson, R. (1992), *Lesbian (Out)law: Survival Under the Rule of Law*, Michigan: Firebrand Books.
Skirrow, G. (1985), 'Widows', in M. Alvarado and J. Stewart (eds), *Made For Television: Euston Films Limited*, London: BFI in association with Thames Television International Ltd and Methuen.

Smart, C. (1977), 'Criminological theory: Its ideology and implications concerning women', *The British Journal of Sociology*, 28: 1, pp. 89–100.

Snyder, K. (2014), 'Burn one down: Nancy Botwin as (post) feminist (anti) heroine', in N. Jones, M. Bajac-Carter and B. Batchelor (eds), *Heroines of Film and Television: Portrayals in Popular Culture*, Maryland and Plymouth: Rowman and Littlefield, pp. 17–29.

'Them and Us' (1999), Mike Adams, dir., *Bad Girls*, Season 1, Episode 1, 1 June, London: ITV.

Thumim, J. (2002), 'Women at work: Popular drama on British television c1955-60', in J. Thumim (ed.), *Small Screens, Big Ideas: Television in the 1950s*, London and New York: I.B. Tauris, pp. 207–222.

Wilson, D. and O'Sullivan, S. (2004), *Images of Incarceration: Representations of Prison in Film and Television Drama*, Winchester: Waterside Press.

Within these Walls (1974–1978, United Kingdon: ITV).

Zalcock, B. (1998), *Renegade Sisters: Girl Gangs on Film*, London and San Francisco: Creation Books Limited.

Notes

1 Maddison discusses Almodovar's *Women on the Verge of a Nervous Breakdown* (1988) and *All About My Mother* (1999) in this respect.
2 If we include imported prison dramas such as *Prisoner: Cell Block H* and *Oz* (HBO, 1997–2003), the list would expand to seven.
3 La Plante's *Trial and Retribution* took viewers from the crime committed to the prosecution.

Chapter 9

Top Dogs and Other Freaks: *Wentworth* and the Re-imaging of *Prisoner Cell Block H*

Sue Turnbull

In all the excitement about the emergence of a new female antiheroine in the post-*Sopranos* quality TV present moment, I want to make a case for recognizing the antiheroines of the past. Delighted as I was, and still am, about the female detectives in the Scandinavian crime series, *Forbrydelsen* (*The Killing*) and *Bron/Broen* (*The Bridge*), I could not help but think of them as the flawed and complex 'daughters of Jane Tennison' in Charlotte Brunsdon's terms (2012). As Deborah Jermyn has already reminded us, when Tennison first appeared, 'the sheer originality of a female cop as driven and yet as nuanced as Tennison' took audiences and critics entirely by surprise (2010: 3). Contradictory, selfish and aloof, Tennison was also vulnerable, empathetic, ambitious and smart. Thus equipped with a rear-view mirror, when the prison drama *Orange is the New Black* appeared courtesy of Netflix in 2013, I could not help but think of Australian television's own early foray into this genre, the now cult soap opera, *Prisoner* (Network Ten, 1979–1986), in which there was not one antiheroine but many, encompassing both the prisoners and their guards, whose narrative trajectories over the course of a long-running soap opera were at least as complicated as those of such recent criminal bad boys as Dexter Morgan (*Dexter*) or Walter White (*Breaking Bad*). Although *Prisoner* has been in syndication ever since, in 2012 (just ahead of *Orange is the New Black*), *Prisoner* was revisited in what producers Lara Radulovich and David Hannam described as a 're-imagining' of the series for the Foxtel Pay TV network in Australia (McTighe 2015: 52), where it proceeded to gather critical accolades, awards and a whole new generation of fans.

In order to address the lineage of the female antiheroine in the prison drama, this chapter will therefore consider the different cultural and social contexts in which both *Prisoner* and *Wentworth* emerged, not just in terms of the changing representation of women but also in relation to the evolution of the television landscape over time. Given that *Prisoner* is an Australian TV series that has arguably attracted more academic attention than any other in Australia's TV history (including *Neighbours* also created by Watson, the producer of *Prisoner*), this literature will be re-visited in order to identify the key issues about the show that were raised at the time (McKee 2001: 184). The relevance of these concerns with respect to *Wentworth* will then be discussed in the light of current debates about the portrayal of women on television with specific attention to sex, violence and power.

Inspiration

In the week in which I commenced this exploration of *Prisoner: Cell Block H* and the re-imagined *Wentworth* (Foxtel SoHo, 2013–ongoing,), there was a vivid reminder of just how pertinent such prison dramas continue to be. Faced with a ban on smoking in the state of Victoria's prisons (and quite possibly the issue of over-crowding, although this was barely touched on), 300 prisoners at the Ravenhall Remand Centre in Melbourne broke into the main control room and lit fires in what was described in the media as a 'protest' against the impending ban (Ferguson 2015). In the expectation of further trouble, the nearby Port Phillip prison instituted a 'lock down' of prisoners in their cells. During the ensuing days, there was further speculation in the media about whether similar disruptions might occur in the neighbouring state of New South Wales where a similar smoking ban was about to be implemented. Watching reports of the incident at Ravenhall on the nightly news was not unlike watching one of the now iconic riot scenes from *Prisoner* or *Wentworth*, as billowing smoke appeared above the grim prison buildings and stern police in combat gear armed with water cannons, tear gas and shotguns swarmed in the foreground. Meanwhile, helicopters and reporter drones furnished somewhat contradictory aerial shots of prisoners wandering aimlessly about their exercise yard. There were, however, a number of significant differences between reality and fiction – none of the rioting prisoners was female and there was a distinct absence of melodrama. The very fact that women were conspicuously absent from these reports points to one of the key reasons why both the original drama series *Prisoner* and its 're-imagining', *Wentworth*, continue to be significant both in the history of Australian television and the representation of women more generally: they put women behaving badly on the public agenda.

To return to its moment of origin, at the time when *Prisoner* was first conceived, Australia's third and youngest commercial television station, Channel Ten, was looking for a series to help recover the ground the network had lost since the demise of its earlier extremely successful and groundbreaking serial drama, *Number 96* (1972–1976). This latter series was exceptional for its frequent nudity and sex scenes, and for introducing what many claimed was the first ongoing, sympathetic homosexual male character on television (McKee 2001: 101). By the end of the 1970s, Channel Ten was keen to embark on another 'hard-hitting' contemporary series to try and win back its ratings and its reputation for 'edgy' and confronting drama (Bourke 1990: 8). *Prisoner* was intended to fulfil this role.

When it first appeared on Channel Ten in Australia in 1979 as a one-hour weekly drama, what was deemed extraordinary, and what inspired so much debate about the original *Prisoner*, was indeed the portrayal of the women, both the guards (the 'screws') and the inmates of Wentworth Detention Centre. Although the treatment of women in prison on screen was not in itself a new phenomenon, given that there had been a number of feature films over the years, including *Caged* (Cromwell, 1950), *Women's Prison* (Seiler, 1955) and *Caged Heat* (Demme, 1974), *Prisoner* was clearly different, despite the fact that it drew on a number of familiar tropes.

In their overview of the women in prison sub-genre, Zalcock and Robinson (1996) identify a number of stock characters and familiar narrative moves. These include the figure of the corrupt and repressed warden, the naive new inmate, the mad/bad lesbian stirrer, as well as the kind-hearted and the 'wise and worldly "top-dog" who rules the roost (1996: 90–91)'.

They also note the recurring tropes of the shower scene, the confrontation in the dining hall, the pervasive sadism and violence and the device of a riot as violent denouement (Zalcock and Robinson 1996: 91). But *Prisoner*, as they suggest and as many others have concurred, was different, mainly because it did not appear to pander to the 'male gaze' in its portrayal of women. Unlike other popular female action heroines of the 1970s who had appeared on Australian television, such as *Policewoman* (NBC, 1974–1978) or *Charlie's Angels* (ABC, 1976–1981), the women in *Prisoner* were presented as decidedly 'unglamorous', coming in all shapes and sizes rather than conforming to current notions of female beauty (McKee 2001: 166). As Zalcock and Robinson (1996: 89) suggest, these women were 'homely' with a kind of 'realism about them – they sweat, they have wrinkles, some of them are overweight'.

As a TV series, the creation of *Prisoner* is usually attributed to producer Reg Watson, who was born in Brisbane but acquired his television production experience in the United Kingdom. Whilst in Britain, Watson had had a number of significant successes, including the creation of the long-running British TV series, *Crossroads* (ITV, 1964–1988), set in a motel (Bourke 1990: 8). In 1978, Watson returned to Australia to work for the independent production house headed by Reg Grundy who together with Ian Holmes (who as former head of Channel Ten had been instrumental in getting *Number 96* on air) was interested in putting together a women's prison drama (Bourke 1990: 9). This interest had apparently been sparked by a number of recent events, including the reporting of prison riots in rural New South Wales at Bathurst Gaol; the Nagle Royal Commission into NSW prisons in 1976 and 1979; as well as the founding of the organization 'Women Behind Bars' in 1975. With 1979 declared as the year of the women, the timing for a drama about women in prison appeared right. Watson was also informed by an earlier British television series, *Within These Walls* (ITV, 1974–1978), which had focused more on those in charge of the prison than the inmates. Watson, however, always considered the more interesting stories were those of the prisoners (Bourke 1990: 8).

In the development of *Prisoner*, Watson therefore recruited Australia's longest serving female prisoner, Sandra Willson, who had recently been released following a very visible and sustained public campaign. Willson, who had been imprisoned for 18 years for the murder of her abusive husband, went on to become an advisor on *Prisoner*, and in his invaluable popular history of the show, Terry Bourke accords Willson the final word in testifying to the 'authenticity of the show':

> A number of long-term prisoners who had been released from prison, including myself, were interviewed for authentic material. [...] Although the general warning 'no resemblance to the living or the dead' is always screened, there were real characters and factual events beneath the cosmetic, artistic and condensed versions being aired.
>
> (Bourke 1990: 120)

As Willson goes on to explain, the story of Karen Travers (Peta Toppano), whom we meet in the first episode of the show, was based on Willson's own experience, as was the narrative trajectory of sympathetic inmate, Judy Bryant (Betty Bobbitt), who goes on to run a halfway house for prisoners, as did Willson herself. There were, however, limits to the show's documentary truth. While some viewers might have thought the show 'raunchy', Willson suggests that the reality of life in prison was even 'worse'. This points to the fact that the portrayal of sex and violence, including lesbian sexuality, had been considerably toned down for television to the extent that, as one of Alan McKee's correspondents noted: '*Prisoner* was exciting [but] I don't think I realised they were lesbians for quite a while' (McKee 2001: 167). The same could not be said of the 're-imagined' *Wentworth*.

Prisoner: Reception and Popularity

In a telling endnote to his discussion of *Prisoner* and its popularity, McKee suggests that from an academic point of view, the show would appear to have been of most interest in terms of its audience, and lists a number of significant 'ethnographic' studies devoted to the show (2001: 184), which include Thomas 1980; Turnbull 1984; Palmer 1986. All of these studies focused on teenage girls who were considered a particularly vulnerable audience, as I myself discovered when I conducted my own research into the reception of the show (Turnbull 1984). Although this research was not published, it did achieve some private circulation as a conference paper in a pre-Internet age. Here I will revisit the reasons why I embarked on this investigation at the time as this may help to illuminate the perceived impact of the show that was firmly located in its portrayal of women as antiheroines, while also offering a basis for a comparison with the reception of the re-imagined *Wentworth*. I might note that this original research was hardly 'ethnographic' in the anthropological sense of the term, involving simply a short period of observation and some semi-structured interviews.

In 1984, I arrived in Australia to take up an International Postgraduate Scholarship at La Trobe University in Melbourne. With two degrees in English Literature, specializing in Anglo-Saxon poetry and archaeology, I had trained as a secondary school teacher of English and Drama and had taught these subjects in high schools in the United Kingdom and America for ten years before deciding to return to study. Initially enrolled in a Master's programme in Media and Education, I had become increasingly interested in the role of popular culture in the lives of young people, and the then current interest in resistance that had been sparked by work at the Birmingham Centre for Contemporary Cultural Studies, in particular the publication of the collection *Resistance Through Rituals* in 1975 (Hall and Jefferson). While this collection had focused on aspects of male youth resistance, with the exception of the essay by Angela McRobbie and Jenny Garber on 'Girls and subcultures', I was inspired by the latter to explore how young women might be using the media in their resistance to school. By 1984, *Prisoner* had already achieved some notoriety in the press as a show adored by young people, with moralists frequently expressing anxiety about its negative impact, especially on girls who might be influenced by the bad behaviour of the female protagonists.

I was therefore immediately intrigued when I was informed by my then academic supervisor that in the process of one of his own research projects, he had come across a letter in the files of Channel Ten from the headmaster of a local co-educational secondary school objecting to the portrayal of women in the series *Prisoner*. The show, the headmaster argued, was having a direct and detrimental effect on the behaviour of a number of female students in his school. In the headmaster's opinion, the girls were 'modelling' the language of *Prisoner* (referring to their teachers as 'screws'), ganging up on others, and there had been two recent incidents, including an assault in a public toilet, which he directly attributed to the representation of violence in *Prisoner*. Also on file was an account of the response from the management of Channel Ten in Melbourne who had sent a producer of the show, and one of the actors, Betty Bobbit (Judy Bryant), to the school in costume to talk to the group of offending girls about the difference between fiction and reality in order to try and remedy their behaviour. As it happened, this visit coincided with the delivery of a video camera to the school, and the media teacher had made a film of the event that I was later to view. Having rediscovered, in the writing of this current chapter, my handwritten field notes written 31 years ago, I discovered that I had noted at the time that the tone of the documentary was heavily 'moralistic' in its presentation of both the female characters on the show, the girls' imitative behaviour and the event itself. I also speculated that the headmaster, the media teacher and indeed Channel Ten had failed to understand why the girls had identified so strongly with the series, and had apparently 'used it' in acting out their opposition to the values of both the school and society in general in terms of 'appropriate' behaviour for girls.

When I visited the school in 1984, a year after the visit of Bobbit and the Channel Ten producer, *Prisoner* was still in its initial broadcast run. At this time, I was granted permission to interview each of the remaining girls in the school who had been singled out for the 'special' treatment. Having recorded and transcribed these 11 interviews, my findings suggested that there were a number of ways in which the girls apparently 'identified' with the experience of the prisoners at Wentworth Detention Centre. These included the parallels in their relationship to authority, regimentation and containment. In other words, both the prison and the school sought to control the ways in which the girls and the prisoners dressed (uniform), behaved (in particular the expression of their sexuality), the use of their time and the kinds of work they undertook. The girls considered their school work as irrelevant and boring as that of the prisoners in the laundry at Wentworth, and their own aggressive language and behaviour to be a response to the authority of the middle-class teachers whom they delighted in outraging as a group.

There was, however, no indication that the girls considered that *Prisoner* was 'real'; their written comments about the various characters revealing that they were well aware that this was a constructed television drama featuring 'goodies' and 'baddies'. Given that this group of girls were identified as troublemakers, it is interesting to note that for the most part, the characters they liked best were the more sympathetic prisoners and guards who embraced the female characteristics of looking out for others. There was however, one exception. This was the character of the female guard, Joan Ferguson (Maggie Kirkpatrick), aka 'The Freak', who had joined the series in 1982 and whom Bourke describes as 'a malevolent force of terrifying moods and evil desires' (1990: 79). One of the students whom I interviewed wrote in answer to the question about her favourite characters, 'I like The Freak because she is a good actioner'. What I particularly love about this neologism is that it works on a number of levels, signalling a recognition that this is a character who makes things happen, and that the student recognizes her narrative function.

The Freak was also the favourite character of British schoolboy Peter McTighe, who would go on to become one of the scriptwriters of the re-imagined *Wentworth*. As McTighe recalls:

> Most teenage boys had Samantha Fox on their walls. I had Maggie Kirkpatrick (Joan 'The Freak' Ferguson). My mother was slightly confused ('She's not even attractive') and at the time was clearly missing the bigger picture.
>
> (2015: 33)

As McTighe explains, the bigger picture was the fact that as 'a young lad from Manchester', he 'loved' the show even though its setting in an Australian women's prison was as alien as a distant planet compared to *Doctor Who* or *Blake's 7*, his other favourite shows of the time. Nor was McTighe alone. Although *Prisoner* did not screen in the United Kingdom until 1984 and then only on regional networks, the show was only 29 episodes down the track in Australia when it first screened in the United States, on KTLA-5 Los Angeles on 8 August 1979.

Here I might note another earlier personal encounter with the series. In 1980, I was teaching in a senior high school just outside Philadelphia when it came to my attention that my American students were avid fans of a daytime soap opera called *Cell Block H* on KYW-TV which they told me was 'British', just like me. Their failure to recognize the show as Australian, and the confusion of a Northern English accent (mine) with the Australian (most of the prisoners), was hardly surprising, given that so little Australian television had been seen at that time in America or in the United Kingdom for that matter. It was, of course, only a matter of time before *Neighbours*, another Watson/Grundy creation, would change that situation and become a global phenomenon, although it would fail to win over a cult American audience as *Prisoner* had (Cunningham and Jacka 1996: 121). An evidence of this, I might note that by June 1980, *Cell Block H* had attained an avid (and loudly cheering) lunchtime viewing audience in the school cafeteria to the bemusement of the teaching staff who thought it 'crude' by American production standards in terms of its wobbly sets, 'gritty' aesthetic and lack of glamour. As for other American viewers, a critic in the American industry publication *Variety* described the show as 'a gritty and gripping drama series', noting that 'the yarn has a lot sharper focus than would be likely in a US production', while the National Organisation of Women (NOW) objected to *Prisoner*'s excessive violence and depiction of women in general (Bourke 1990: 74). Despite such objections, there was another segment of the American audience who responded to the show in immediate and very positive ways.

Terry Bourke begins his book on *Prisoner* with an account of the moment on 10 January 1980, when 50 women motorbike riders converged on the offices of KTLA-5 on Sunset Boulevard in Los Angeles in a scene that resembled 'the classic 1953 Marlon Brando movie *The Wild One*' (Bourke 1990: 7). The women were there to pay homage to the character of Franky Doyle (Carol Burns), the lesbian prisoner who had been shot by police while trying to escape during a riot the night before. According to Bourke, this group of bikers was only a small contingent of the 3000 lesbian biker fans of Doyle who would hold wakes for their favourite character across Los Angeles on that day. Although Franky only appeared in the first 20 episodes of the show, she had clearly made her mark. While the original outline for the series described her as 'a vile, bullying, loud-mouthed, troublemaking tattooed lesbian with a bikie gang background' (1990: 13), when called in to discuss the role, actress Carol Burns is quoted as saying:

> Great role folks. But she's a dog, too nasty, too evil. I can see the hate mail pouring in already. Now justify her behaviour, pull her back a little, and I'll do it.
>
> (Bourke 1990: 14)

This, the writers and the producers proceeded to do, with the result that with her mix of violence and vulnerability, as a female antiheroine, Franky Doyle rapidly acquired an avid fan base, not least because she was one of only a few gay characters to appear on television. The portrayal of the character of Franky therefore bears some further investigation, especially when this is compared with that of the re-imagined Franky Doyle in *Wentworth*, as such a comparison helps to mark some of the major shifts in the cultural contexts and the television landscapes of 1979 and in 2013.

Franky Doyle: Then and Now

In the first episode of *Prisoner* ('Episode 1' 1979), we meet Franky Doyle 13 minutes into the drama as we hear her raucous laughter in the corridor just before she appears in the doorway of the cell recently assigned to new inmate, Karen Travers (Peta Toppano). This cell, Franky and Karen are to share with Franky's current 'girlfriend', Doreen, though there will be no overt suggestion of any sexual activity between the two. It was, as indicated by the comment above, quite possible to miss the carefully coded lesbian implications of their relationship. Franky is dressed in denim dungarees, and a drab khaki tee shirt. Her hair is cut short, her face devoid of make-up and she is by no means conventionally attractive. Adopting a swagger, she leans against the doorframe and draws on her cigarette, in what might best be described as a parody of an aggressive 'masculine' pose. Meanwhile, her gaze is on the attractive Karen who is seated on her bed, dressed neatly in a denim pinafore dress and green collared shirt, the very model of a well-turned-out prisoner. 'Well well', observes Franky before cutting to the chase, 'You're beautiful. I love beautiful things'. Karen looks aghast as Franky asks her what she is in for. Karen rallies and replies somewhat defiantly, 'I stabbed someone, to death'. This show of bravado causes Franky to smile as she enters the room with the comment: 'Always like a challenge'.

Franky draws closer to Karen, until their faces are almost touching, in an intimidating display of power during which the following exchange, laden with double entendre, takes place:

FRANKY:	We'll have a happy time together Karen. It's up to you love. You can really enjoy yourself here if you put your mind to it.
KAREN:	I'm not like that, Franky.
FRANKY:	You're going to have to be and anything you don't know I'll teach you.
	(Franky grabs Karen by the arm)
KAREN:	Get your hand off me!
FRANKY:	Don't say anything you might regret, Karen. We're going to be in here night after night for years and years and years.

At this point, Karen wrenches free from Franky's grasp and exits the room, heading straight for the Governor's office to demand a cell of her own. In the corridor, she bumps into sympathetic guard Meg Jackson (Elspeth Ballantyne), announcing 'I won't share with that animal'. Having overheard Karen's comment, a furious Franky appears behind them with the challenge 'Animal, am I?' Meg shakes her head regretfully at Karen as she comments, 'You stupid girl'. Evidently, Karen has just managed to make an enemy of one of the most dangerous prisoners in the jail. As evidence of the danger posed by Franky, later in the same episode we witness her violent temper as she destroys the women's recreation room in a furious rage after she learns that she is to be separated from Doreen. The episode concludes with Franky in solitary confinement. Over the course of the next 19 episodes, there will, however, be a rapprochement between the two that further humanizes Franky after Karen discovers that she is illiterate and offers to teach her to read. Their developing friendship thus forms part of the backdrop to the first major story arc involving a battle for 'top dog' status between Franky and another long-term inmate, Bea Smith (Val Lehman). It is this storyline that will culminate in the prison riot in which Franky is shot and dies.

This opening scene is very different from that which introduces Franky Doyle (Nicole Da Silva) some 34 years later in *Wentworth*. In a tricky move, which, as writer Peter McTighe notes (2015: 54), would make it clear to fans of the original series that the scriptwriters of *Wentworth* were not 'wed' to the original storylines, the new inmate whom we follow as she is admitted into prison is the character of Bea Smith (Danielle Cormack), who in the original is already well-established as 'top dog'. Like Karen Travers, the new Bea is in prison for attacking her abusive husband, the difference being that, in this case, he has survived and she is on remand awaiting trial. After a traumatic admission process, Bea is escorted to her cell and left to her own devices, only this time the private cell is in an accommodation block, with the women's cells clustered around a shared living space. Upon opening the door of her assigned cell in order to deposit her belongings, Bea is confronted by the sight of a naked Franky lying on her bed with an Asian woman, engaged in what is clearly mutually pleasurable sex. The slim, attractive Franky with her well-cut hair and carefully applied heavy eye make-up turns to look over her tattooed shoulder at the stricken Bea in the doorway. Smiling, Franky observes somewhat ambiguously: 'All yours when we are done'. As Bea continues to stand there transfixed, Franky adds, 'What, you like to watch do yer?' She then pointedly licks her fingers, and resumes operations with the comment 'We're just getting started'. Franky then continues to maintain eye contact with Bea as her partner moans in appreciation of her ministrations. Bea backs away into the shared community room where she sinks down dejectedly over her belongings.

During the next ten episodes of the first season of *Wentworth*, Franky will subsequently manipulate Bea into smuggling drugs into the jail, engage in a battle for power with the current 'top dog', Jacs Holt (Kris McQuade) and openly flirt with the governor of the jail, Erica Davidson (Leeanna Walsman), who in episode 5 is revealed to be having sexual fantasies featuring Franky. This episode also openly features numerous references to, and depiction of, masturbation, given that this is the subject of frequent talk between the women who discover much to their amusement that Bea has never attempted this. We even 'see' (this is implied rather than graphically depicted), Davidson masturbating while seated at her office desk as she watches surveillance footage of Franky and her girlfriend making out in a corner of the exercise yard. This episode concludes with Bea engaging in her first attempt to masturbate after being told by fellow inmate Liz Birdsworth that there is nothing wrong with 'making yourself feel good'.

As this comparison reveals, while it might have been possible to miss the fact that Franky was a lesbian in the early days of *Prisoner*, this would be impossible in *Wentworth*, which is much more explicit in its depiction of sex, including sex between women, women and men and indeed masturbation, than the earlier series. While this openness can certainly be attributed to changing cultural attitudes to sexuality and to its depiction on-screen, the overt portrayal of Franky as a lesbian, and indeed the more graphic sex and violence in *Wentworth*, can also be seen as a factor of a number of other changes to the television landscape. Significantly, this would include the move from a free to air broadcast environment to the more niche market afforded a subscription television service in what has been described as a TVIII era dominated by the 'cable sector' and digital distribution (Reeves et al. 2011: 83).

Changing Television Landscapes

While *Prisoner* was made available to anyone with a television set at that time, *Wentworth* was produced by FremantleMedia and Screen Australia for the pay television network, Foxtel, which was reported to have only 2.6 million subscribers in Australia by the end of 2014 (Davidson 2015). Nevertheless, according to Giles Hardie (2013), *Wentworth* made history when it was first screened on the SoHo Foxtel channel in April 2013 as Foxtel's most watched Australian drama series premiere ever, with a grand total of 240,000 viewers (Hardie 2013). This tiny audience is, however, merely the tip of the iceberg when it comes to judging the commercial value of the series in the global market place, including its potential 'long tail' in repeat syndication on Foxtel internationally and DVD releases. According to journalist Andrew Hornery (2015), by May 2015, *Wentworth* had been sold by its parent company, FreemantleMedia, into 87 different territories, including the United States. In the United Kingdom it was shown on Channel 5 in company with long-running Australian stablemate *Neighbours* which it soon overshadowed becoming the most popular Australian drama since 2002. Meanwhile, the Dutch and the Germans produced their own licensed versions, *Celblok H* and *Block B: Unter Arrest* respectively (Hornery 2015). Evidently, *Wentworth* had managed to find a new audience, capitalize on the global success of the original *Prisoner* and take advantage of the opportunities afforded by the different regulatory environments of subscription television.

As Amanda Lotz (2007: 216) suggests, it was precisely because of the relative freedom of subscription television during the last decade of the twentieth century that HBO were able 'to push the boundaries even further' in series such as *Sex and the City*, confident that their 'niche' audience would not be offended by explicit depiction of sex, including sex between women and female masturbation. And indeed, such explicitness rapidly became part of HBOs recognition as 'quality' TV. As Janet McCabe and Kim Akass have observed, in this environment:

> [...] [P]ushing the limits of respectability, of daring to say/do what cannot be said/done elsewhere on the networks, is entwined with being esoteric, groundbreaking and risk-taking.
>
> (McCabe and Akass 2011: 67)

Thus in 2004, when the American cable network Showtime was seeking to emulate HBO in the quality stakes, it did so by taking on the production of *The L Word*, which they promoted as a lesbian version of *Sex and the City* (Himberg 2014: 293). As one industry commentator informed Julie Himberg, 'markets drive social change' (2014: 298): a comment implying that the constitution and taste of a perceived 'niche' and economically attractive audience may well be a key factor in determining what will make it on to television. At the same time, Himberg notes that the portrayal of lesbians and lesbian sexuality on-screen was perceived by the industry practitioners to whom she spoke 'as a significant method for creating "edgy" programming and attracting a wide range of viewers to cable TV' (2014: 289). This notion of 'edgy' recalls the original moment of *Prisoner*, when Channel Ten was looking for 'edgy' programming to win back its audience, the term synonymous with explicit sexual content that may not be altogether 'straight'. Given that the ongoing success of the original *Prisoner* had demonstrated the existence of an audience interested in non-normative representations of women, it is therefore quite possible that the potential for rendering lesbianism more explicitly on-screen may well have been a key factor in the proposal to 're-re-imagine' *Prisoner* as *Wentworth* for subscription television in the expectation that the new show would attract the kind of 'niche' audience for earlier shows dealing more explicitly with sex such as *Sex and the City* or the *The L Word*.

Reception and Popularity of *Wentworth*

While some Australian viewers were guarded in their initial response to *Wentworth*, as ABC Radio National TV reviewer and blogger David Knox reported, many took to Twitter when the first episode was screened offering such appreciative comments as:

> #wentworth not better than #prisoner – but definitely on a par with atm [atmosphere?]. Roll on Wednesday #Imhooked.
>
> (Knox 2015)

and

> OMG ... TOTALLY LOVE #Wentworth. Was shocked by some of the character reversals but it is great!!! Can't wait for next Wednesday!!!
>
> (Knox 2015)

After it was shown in the United States, some American bloggers were swift to draw a comparison with the Netflix drama also set in a women's prison, *Orange is the New Black*, which had launched earlier in the year. *Bitch Flicks* blogger Amanda Roderiguez suggested that *Wentworth* was 'much grittier, darker and more realistic' than the Netflix show because the 'over-the-top-zany approach to characterization' for comedic effect lessened the impact of *Orange is the New Black*. In her opinion, *Wentworth* was superior because it took

> [...] a no-holds-barred approach to subjects like officer sexual exploitation of prisoners, turf wars and hierarchy, sexuality, the intimate code of silence, gang beatings, gang rapes, prison riots, and the brutality of the crimes that landed these women behind bars.
>
> (Rodriguez 2013)

Meanwhile, on the award-winning lesbian website *Autostraddle* in a post entitled '10 reasons why your next favourite lesbian prison show is *Wentworth*', Franky as played by Nicole Da Silva is identified as the most attractive lesbian character on the small screen, and as much more aggressive and unpredictable than her *Orange is the New Black* counterpart, Shane (Gabrielle 2015).

Perhaps what is most interesting about the reception of both *Orange is the New Black* and *Wentworth* was the absence of any public outcry about the representation of sex, violence and women behaving badly, even though poster Gabrielle went on to observe about the latter that:

> There is physical brutality, there is torture, there is rape and abuse and substance abuse and there were times when I had to take a lot of deep breaths to get through. This is not a show to watch when you're looking to lift your spirits, in my experience, this is a show that makes us examine our own dark potentials, our own fears and boundaries and where those boundaries can be broken.
>
> (Gabrielle 2015)

Clearly, within the new television landscape of niche programming, what would once have caused offence and a public outcry appears invisible to those who might have been offended. What is more, *Wentworth* went on to win a number of Australian television awards that were widely reported in the mainstream press and on television. This included the Logie Award for most Outstanding Drama series in 2015 (Idato 2015).

Plus ca Change..?

While the absence of moral outrage and concern about the possible effects of portraying women behaving badly in *Wentworth* on a young, female audience was one major difference in the reception of the two series some 36 years apart, there were other differences of both lesser and greater importance. For example, there was a major difference in the production values of the two shows, with the 're-imagined' *Wentworth* benefiting from advances in media technology to create a more visceral and realistic experience of both the setting and the action. This included the memorable experience of 'toilet-cam', as a camera positioned in a toilet (with a glass screen on top, thankfully) offered a confronting point of view as Bea Smith vomited up a contraband delivery of drugs in Episode 1. Also gone are the shaky sets of the original, with a much larger and more convincing construction that looked rather more like the real thing, including an outdoor exercise yard. The bars, however, were the same.

There were also many differences between the remake and the original *Prisoner* characters, including their back-stories and narrative trajectories. For example, in *Prisoner*, Franky has been convicted of armed robbery and murder and is serving a life sentence, while in the update, she is in prison for throwing a pan of boiling oil over a cooking show host who mocked her during her appearance on a reality TV show, the kind of crime that while horrific is also laughable in a reality TV moment dominated by such cooking shows as the global franchise *Masterchef*. Furthermore, while the original Franky is illiterate and dies in episode 20, in the remake she has recently passed her HSC (with the assistance of Erica Davidson), and is planning to undertake a law degree, thereby obtaining valuable information about legal matters that she passes on to her fellow inmates. The updated Franky clearly foresees a future for herself, one in which she sees no need to hide her sexuality. In this way, although the portrayal of lesbianism on-screen might have been deemed 'edgy', by 2013 it may have become somewhat less so. Indeed, what was perhaps most 'edgy' about *Wentworth*'s sexual politics in 2014 was the introduction in season 2 of Maxine, a male-to-female transgender character at a moment when transgender characters appeared to the latest *vogue* in television drama series seeking to break down gender barriers. However, while *Orange is the New Black* featured the character of Sophia, played by transgender actress and advocate Laverne Cox who went on to become the first openly transgender person to be featured on the cover of *Time* magazine. In *Wentworth*, Maxine was played by Australian male actor, Socratis Otto, who has not been accorded the same media attention and accolades.

While the sets and the characters may have changed over the intervening years, what unambiguously has not is the familiar battle for power enacted on a number of different fronts. These include the competition for the status of 'top dog' between Jacs Holt (who has ruled the roost for seven years) and Franky Doyle in which the unfortunate Bea becomes first a pawn and then a player. Paralleling this struggle is the competition for leadership between guard Vera Bennett and Erica Davidson following the death of Governor Meg Jackson in episode 1. Nor can one ignore the ongoing battle for control enacted between the prisoners and the staff, with each side attempting to manipulate the other. What is most interesting about these various battles is that they depend not so much on violence and strong-arm tactics (although these are certainly present) as on knowledge: who knows what about whom and how will they use it. For example, Jacs is able to control prison guard Vera because Jacs knows that Vera initiated the riot in which Meg Jackson was killed in an endeavour to prove her own mettle as a guard. Jacs also knows that guard Will Jackson has a drug problem and uses this to control him, too. Strutting around the prison with her perfectly blow-waved hair and gravelly authoritative voice, Jacs therefore appears indomitable as she wields her symbol of 'top dog' status, the steam press in the laundry. In the DVD extras to season 1, actor Kris McQuade has described how she modelled her performance on that of Clint Eastwood as the man with no name in his spaghetti western era.

Franky, on the other hand, is all lightness and fire, nimble on the basketball court and nimble at taking advantage when she can find it. Franky is therefore able to bring about the end of Jacs' reign by divulging to Bea that Jacs is directly responsible for the death of her 16-year-old daughter as a result of a heroin overdose administered by Jacs' son Braydon on his mother's orders. This is the knowledge that turns all of the other inmates and guards against Jacs since killing another woman's child is clearly a step too far. In this way, although the moral universe of the prison is murky, with the guards' misdemeanours laying them open to the manipulations of the prisoners while the prisoners themselves are hardly above reproach, there is a sense of right and wrong, a moral code operative that encompasses both guards and prisoners in this world within a world. In this way, Franky ends the first season as the rightful 'top dog' by manipulating Bea who has been so horrendously wronged by Jacs, thereby setting up another potential power battle in season 2 between Franky and Bea.

As in the original *Prisoner*, the violence enacted within the prison is revealed to be an echo of the violence both the women and the guards have experienced in the outside world. For example, guard Vera Bennett is a victim of the psychological damage inflicted on her by her appalling mother. The violent outbursts and drinking of male guard Fletch are revealed to be reaction to his military service in East Timor. Many of the female prisoners are victims of domestic violence and assault at the hands of their partners and, like Bea, are in prison because they have fought back. While in prison, some of them are also the perpetrators of violence against other women. This would include a particularly brutal 'ganging' in which Bea is beaten up on Jacs' orders in episode 7. In this way, *Wentworth*, like *Prisoner* before it, does not shy away from the violence inherent in the everyday experience of women in prison, either as victims or as perpetrators. In each case, such violence is revealed to be a product of the circumstances in which these women find themselves. Neither the women nor the guards are either all bad or all good; they are indeed all antiheroines doomed to make bad choices most of the time.

While the drama of *Wentworth* might therefore appear to be somewhat overwrought, the portrayal of women as victims is not far from the truth. According to the Australian feminist website *Destroy the Joint*, currently waging a campaign to end violence towards women, from January to July 2015, 52 women died in Australia as a result of an assault, many of them killed by their partner (Facebook 2015). Even more shocking was the news tucked away in a corner of the *Sydney Morning Herald* that a number of indigenous mothers in the state of Victoria were being placed in a maximum security prison on remand for minor offences to protect them from their partners because emergency accommodation options were so limited (Perkins 2015). With indigenous women being 34 times more likely to experience domestic violence, and less likely to report this for fear that their children might be taken away from them, these figures point to a reality that a show like *Wentworth* can hardly begin to encompass. As the Melbourne *Herald Sun* reported (Morris-Marr 2015), while the vernacular inside the Dame Phyllis Frost women's prison in Melbourne might read 'like a script from TV prison drama *Wentworth*', there is still more 'drama' going on inside the prison than could ever be shown on TV.

Wentworth, however, like *Prisoner* before it, is not intended as a documentary but as a melodramatic drama series that works on a number of different levels: as an entertainment featuring strong female characters who vie for power and control and as an insight into the lives of women who for one reason or another fall foul of the law and are rendered invisible in the process. In *Wentworth* as in *Prisoner*, behaving badly on-screen frequently looks like a reasonable option for women in a social context where the dice are still so heavily loaded against them. No wonder we continue to cheer them on. Also true is the fact that the antiheroines of *Wentworth* are just as complex and multifaceted as their forebears in *Prisoner*, even though there is a tendency to condescend to the past as a simpler time. Although the humble soap opera is no longer the focus of contemporary television scholarship, given the ways in which characters may continue to shapeshift over time in order to accommodate new storylines, I suspect that as a genre it may have much more to tell us about the contemporary female antiheroine than we might suppose. She has not come from nowhere.

Acknowledgement

The author would like to thank Jessie Hunt for her invaluable assistance in the research for this chapter.

References

Batty, C. (2014), 'Why *Wentworth* is raising the bar in Australian TV drama', *The Conversation*, 6 May, https://theconversation.com/why-wentworth-is-raising-the-bar-in-australian-tv-drama-25598. Accessed 17 July 2015.

Bourke, T. (1990), *Prisoner: Cell Block H, Behind the Scenes*, London: Angus and Robertson.

Brunsdon, C. (2012), 'Television crime series: "Women, police and fuddy-duddy feminism"', *Feminist Media Studies*, 1: 1, pp. 1–20.

Cunningham, S. and Jacka, E. (1996), *Australian Television and International Mediascapes*, Cambridge: Cambridge University Press.

Curthoys, A. and Docker, J. (1989), 'In praise of *Prisoner*', in J. Tulloch and G. Turner (eds), *Australian Television: Programs, Politics, Pleasures*, Sydney: Allen and Unwin, pp. 52–69.

Davidson, D. (2015), 'Foxtel ramps up subscribers by 4.7pc', *The Australian*, 12 February.

'Episode 1' (1979), Arthur Graeme, dir., *Prisoner*, Season 1, Episode 1, 27 February, Australia: Reg Grundy Organisation.

Facebook (2015), *Counting Dead Women Australia 2015*, 21 July, https://www.facebook.com/notes/destroy-the-joint/counting-dead-women-australia-2015-we-count-every-single-death-due-to-violence-a/905594706154941. Accessed 21 July 2015.

Ferguson, J. (2015), 'Inmates riot at Melbourne's Ravenhall Remand Centre ahead of smoking ban', *The Australian*, 30 June, http://www.theaustralian.com.au/news/nation/inmates-riot-at-melbournes-ravenhall-prison-ahead-of-smoking-ban/story-e6frg6nf-1227421822467. Accessed 3 July 2015.

Gabrielle (2015), '10 reasons why your next favourite lesbian prison show is *Wentworth*', *Autostraddle*, 2 September, http://www.autostraddle.com/10-reasons-why-your-next-favorite-lesbian-prison-show-is-wentworth-193341/. Accessed 21 July 2015.

Hall, S. and Jefferson, T. (eds) (1975), *Resistance Through Rituals*, Birmingham: Centre for Contemporary Cultural Studies, Birmingham University.

Hardie, G. (2013), '*Wentworth* breaks out with a bang', *Sydney Morning Herald*, 17 July.

Himberg, J. (2014), 'Multicasting: Lesbian programming and the changing landscape of cable TV', *Television and New Media*, 15: 4, pp. 289–304.

Hornery, A. (2015), 'Australian TV shows prove popular in global market', *The Sydney Morning Herald*, 31 May.

Idato, M. (2015), 'Logies 2015: Carrie Bickmore claims Gold Logie', *Sydney Morning Herald*, 3 May, http://www.smh.com.au/entertainment/tv-and-radio/logies-2015-carrie-bickmore-claims-gold-logie-20150503-1mz331.html. Accessed 21 July 2015.

Jermyn, D. (2010), *Prime Suspect*, London: British Film Institute.

Knox, D. (2015), 'Twitter loves *Wentworth*', *TV Tonight*, 2 May, http://www.tvtonight.com.au/2013/05/twitter-loves-wentworth.html. Accessed 21 July 2015.

Lotz, A. D. (2007), *The Television will be Revolutionized*, New York and London: New York University Press.

McCabe, J. and Akass, K. (2011), 'Sex, swearing and respectability: Courting controversy, HBO's original programming and producing quality TV', in J. McCabe and K. Akass (eds), *Quality TV: Contemporary American Television and Beyond*, London and New York: I.B. Tauris, pp. 62–76.

McKee, A. (2001), *Australian Television: A Genealogy of Great Moments*, South Melbourne, Vic: Oxford University Press.

McTighe, P. (2015), 'Behind the bars: Writing *Wentworth*', *Storyline*, 33, pp. 52–56.

Morris-Marr, L. (2015), 'Behind the bars of hell', *Herald Sun*, 26 July.

Palmer, P. (1986), *Girls and Television*, Ministry of Education, NSW, Sydney: Social Policy Unit.

Perkins, M. (2015), 'Aboriginal mothers kept in jail "for their own safety", family violence hearing told', theage.com.au, 20 July, http://www.theage.com.au/action/printArticle?id=998451220. Accessed 21 July 2015.

Prisoner: Cell Block H (1979–1986, Australia: Network Ten).

Reeves, J. L., Rogers, M. C. and Espetin, M. M. (2011), 'Quality control: The daily show, the peabody and brand discipline', in J. McCabe and K. Akass (eds), *Quality TV: Contemporary American Television and Beyond*, London and New York: I.B. Tauris, pp. 79–97.

Rodriquez, A. (2013). '*Wentworth* makes *Orange is the New Black* look like a middle school drama', *Bitch Flicks*, 11 September.

Thomas, C. (1980), 'Girls and counter-school culture', in D. McCallum and U. Ozolins (eds), *Melbourne Working Papers 1980*, Melbourne: University of Melbourne.

Turnbull, S. (1984), '*Prisoner*: Patterns of opposition and identification', unpublished paper, Department of Media Studies, Melbourne: La Trobe University.

Wentworth (2013–ongoing, Australia: Foxtel SoHo).

Zalcock, B. and Robinson, J. (1996), 'Inside *Cell Block H*: Hard steel and soft soap', *Continuum*, 9: 1, pp. 88–97.

Note

1 *Counting Dead Women Australia 2015*, 21 July 2015, https://www.facebook.com/notes/destroy-the-joint/counting-dead-women-australia-2015-we-count-every-single-death-due-to-violence-a/905594706154941. Accessed 21 July 2015.

Chapter 10

Lesbian Request Approved: Sex, Power and Desire in *Orange is the New Black*

Suzanna Danuta Walters

Even in an era of a supposed renewal of feminist energies, one is hard pressed to find many cultural representations that speak to a wide range of female identities and pleasures. In other words, the old binary of virgin/whore – and the insistence that 'bad women' get punished (while 'bad men' get revered as iconic forms of a new masculinity) – remains with us to this day. The antiheroes of *Breaking Bad* and *Mad Men* easily adhere to older noir tropes that valorize a kind of strong but broken lone wolf who simply can't play by the rules, rules often signified as enforced by a nagging feminine presence. Because male criminals and antiheroes could be both 'bad' and attractive at the same time, the assumed contradiction (e.g. a hero who does bad things) was undermined by the appeal of errant masculinity.

Not so for women. The cultural insistence that women's 'likeability' as characters was non-negotiable rendered the possibility of a female 'antihero' slim indeed. Appropriate and normative femininity depended on likeability or, alternately, a female villain (often a negligent mother or sexual adventurer) to round out the limited range of representational options. Happily, recent years have seen a shift as a variety of non-traditional and decidedly unlikeable female characters have moved into public purview. Some of them are mirror images of the 'bad boys' of high-end cable, but others (such as the decidedly unlikeable women of HBO's *Girls* and the criminal mama of *Weeds*) have pushed into substantive new territory, creating images of women – sexual, criminal, idiosyncratic – that we have just not seen before in mainstream popular culture. These new antiheroines are not merely criminal outliers who are villainized and extruded from the body politic, but rather represent the development of a substantive – and new – imagery of female power and subjectivity as iterated through the trope of 'antihero', a framing typically reserved for male characters.

None has achieved this with such verve as *Orange is the New Black*. Netflix's critically acclaimed series, adapted from a bestselling memoir by Piper Kerman, premiered in 2013 and quickly became both a darling of the critics and a site of frenzied fandom and analytic interest. Created by Jenji Kohan, the daring mastermind behind Showtime's *Weeds*, it focuses here not on a suburban mom turned drug dealer, but on a diverse and quirky group of women in a minimum-security prison. Centring on the story of Piper – an upper-class Smith college grad jailed for her involvement in drug smuggling – the series is explicit about sex, violence, corruption and racial and ethnic divisions within the prison system even as it mines those tropes for humour.

Orange is the New Black (*OITNB*) has entered our cultural imaginary as a multivalent and symptomatic text. In other words, unlike most television programmes (streaming or network), *OITNB* signifies wide and deep, prompting endless Internet chatter, media reflection, encomiums on the realities of prison life etc. A large and active fan community tracks every episode and has helped to make stars out of many of the actors in the series. The 'extra-textual' meanderings of *OITNB* have circulated widely: actors have been featured in LGBT pride parades, Facebook pages and tumblrs abound, and you can follow just about everyone on Twitter. If you have a hankering for bad food you can buy cookbooks from 'Litchfield Federal Prison' and you can go to your next *OITNB* party sporting a tee shirt featuring 'Crazy Eyes' proclaiming her love. Academics and culture critics have been no slouches here and have added to the mix by analysing the racial politics of the show, comparing the depiction of prison life to the real thing and deconstructing the ethics of a comedy about incarceration. Like other signal cultural representations (I think here of *Girls, House of Cards, Mad Men*), *OITNB* iterates in ways that engage viewing publics in larger conversations about a variety of pressing social and political issues. While this is all to the good – and recent high-end cable and streaming TV has certainly pushed the envelope of representational options – it also puts enormous pressure on any individual series. Because *OITNB* shows us something rarely seen in popular culture (a multiracial, class diverse, sexually variant group of women who primarily relate *to each other* and not to men), critics and fans alike both expect more and are disappointed more deeply. This brings to mind the experience of a much lesser series – Showtime's *The L Word* – which carried the burden of a pent-up lesbian desire for sexually open and frank representations of a community largely invisible or limited to tired stereotypical dismissals.

This is all by way of saying that both the fan-mania of adoration and the angry tone of the critical naysayers need perhaps to be put in some context, a context in which these types of images are so few and far between (still, yes, in 2015) that we both over-invest and over-critique. Which is not to say, of course, that much of the criticism is not on target – and I will be engaging some of that criticism in this chapter – rather, it is to suggest that alongside the criticism we maintain a simultaneous recognition that the problems of an OINTB are of a different order than the problems of, say, a *Seinfeld* or any other iconic (white, male, monied) cultural object in which the absence of difference almost sucks the air out of the critical room. Those of us perennially marginalized in cultural life (or ghettoized, or tokenized, or vilified, or stereotyped) often seem caught between two analytic magnets, pulling us in the direction of unalloyed celebration or (alternately) a bitter regret that the seams of sexism, racism, homophobia are still showing. In the desire for both verisimilitude and recognition, critics can sometimes misdirect their ire, and therefore miss the fact that something like *OITNB* (as flawed as it is, as flat footed) is attempting *something* – in seemingly good faith – that most mainstream media producers do not even think about, much less substantively address. *OITNB* speaks to, for, about people and identities and institutions that are largely ignored in mainstream media production. It seems both pointless and churlish, for example, to condemn *OITNB* because it does not (didactically) declare the overthrow of the prison industrial complex. When Eric Stanley (2014) takes *OITNB* to task by arguing that, '*Orange*'s powerful critique of imprisonment maintains the inevitability of the [Prison Industrial

Complex] by closing the spaces where the viewer might imagine something else beyond the frame', he both misses the point and mistakes this for a documentary. To complain, as Stanley (2014) does, that *OITNB* is a tool of 'the system' because '[…] we learn that Sophia was sent to prison for the credit card fraud that was necessary to fund her transition […] [but] instead of pushing us to understand issues of medical access or the fraud of credit, the narrative collapses into moralism', misreads the complexity of Sophia's narrative arc. In fact, there are a few precious moments of 'moral progress' in *OITNB*, and Sophia's trajectory is depicted precisely as cathected to a system that does not provide the resources she needs, as we see early on in her battle to get her hormone treatments. Indeed, the privatization of the prison that haunted season 3 – and the futility of reform efforts by (relatively) well-meaning wardens – pushes *OITNB* away from overly optimistic prognostications. It might be helpful, therefore, to invoke that old adage: the perfect is the enemy of the good. And *OITNB* is very good.

Really, what is there not to like about a dark comedy set in a women's prison, especially one that features hot sex in a chapel, Russian mobsters with a yen for haute cuisine, Shakespeare quoting inmates, a memorial for a lost library and Lea DeLaria? The world of Litchfield is multiracial, class variant and sexually heterogeneous without treating those markers as empty signifiers of something else. *OITNB* brashly displays enduring stereotypes, yet slyly and consistently overturns them at every step. So the crazy Suzanne quotes Shakespeare and comes from a white, bourgeois family; the butch bulldyke Big Boo is not only stereotypically predatory but also the one character to really exhibit feminist solidarity; the seemingly angelic Morello is a lying stalker.

While many commentators seem to find the prison memoir by Kerman preferable to the series, I am convinced that the television rendition is superior in just about every way. One thing that surprised me (given all the talk of 'real' prison vs TV prison) was how much more feminist, queer and racially interesting the TV show was than the (curiously) much-acclaimed prison memoir by Piper Kerman. Most importantly, while Piper remains the narrative centre, she is regularly pushed aside as multiplying plotlines fill in and the backstories of other inmates figure centrally in each episode.

More to the point, Kerman's memoir is devoid of the raunchy and ribald sexuality that has emerged as one of the key flashpoints of debate. Along with depictions of race and class, the sexual terrain of *OITNB* has been variously described as exoticized, refreshingly frank and unnecessarily unusual. It is to this sexuality that I now turn, in part, to unpack the ways in which sexuality is always refracted in and through specifically racialized identities.

Pulp Frictions

OITNB comes to the screen with a fair amount of representational baggage. The women's prison trope has long been a site of feminist and queer fascination. As Heather Love (2014) points out, 'Like boarding schools, convents, rooming houses, and brothels, prison is a classic setting for scenes of lesbian eroticism'. Mostly low budget and firmly exploitative – and filled with the stock stereotypes, patriarchal reformism and heterosexual redemption – it occasionally morphed (particularly in the 1970s) into more fantastical proto-feminist narratives of sisterly solidarity and ass-kicking rebellion.

One of the things that has always been intriguing about the 'women-in-prison' trope is that, besides the fun of the explicit lesbian sexuality, it often laid bare what more genteel forms of popular culture cover up: abusive guards, sexual assault, injustice and structural discrimination and – to a lesser extent – racial and ethnic battle lines. More rarely (and here I think of a wonderfully proto-feminist pulp film of the 1970s, Jonathan Demme's *Caged Heat*), women's prison dramas are downright utopian, rallying (interracial) cadres of prisoners in an explosive act of female solidarity against the brutalizing Man.[1]

OITNB is both a homage and a send-up (and possibly even a critique) of the largely exploitative B movie 'women-in-prison' genre. Not only does the venue of streaming TV render *OITNB* more homey and prosaic than its foremother films, but the intended audience is surely *not* the voyeuristic male getting off on the shower scenes and nudity of the earlier films. Nevertheless, *OITNB* shares some interesting parallels with the more utopian and even proto-feminist examples of that genre, most especially Jonathan Demme's *Caged Heat* (Walters, 2001). Unlike most of our popular culture – which either depicts all-white worlds, hides racial tensions behind a veneer of Kumbaya diversity or presents racial tensions in a social problem mode – *OITNB* (and *Caged Heat* before it) openly displays the deep and abiding rifts of gender and race. Race, sex and class – usually so submerged within narrative niceties – are here on the bubbling, crackling, corroding surface. As critic Tope Fadiran Charlton notes,

> From the moment Piper steps foot in Litchfield – *OITNB's* fictional prison, which is based on the Danbury women's prison in Connecticut, where Piper Kerman served time – *OITNB* makes clear that this is a world where no veneer of polite colorblindness papers over racism and racial prejudice. Piper is rudely awakened to this reality when Lorna Morello, a fellow white inmate, concludes Piper's orientation with a smiling comment: 'We look out for our own'. Piper's visible horror at this candid statement of racist preference is met with amusement: 'Oh, don't get all PC on me. It's tribal, not racist'.
>
> (2013)

Curiously perhaps, *OITNB* does not really explore the fantasy of interracial female solidarity nor depict a vibrant interracial lesbian sexuality, both characteristics of (some) of the earlier filmic versions of the prison narrative such as *Caged Heat*. Perhaps this is a nod to the realities of mass incarceration, not really the status quo during the heyday of the women's prison film, although the absence of sex workers among the Litchfield population is a stark omission and the earlier films often did serve up 'vice' as a form of titillating prison drama. On the other hand, *OITNB* makes visible the clear racial lines that segregate prisoners – in stark contrast to the almost utopian vision of interracial sisterhood offered in some 1970s women's prison exploitation films.

Rightly heralded for openly depicting the multiracial, multi-sexual milieu of prison life, and for slyly upending the melodramatic and redemptive tenor of earlier women-in-prison films, *OITNB*'s depiction of prison life is not without its problems. First, in an era of rampant mass incarceration marked by profound racial and class inequities, a quirky and comic take on prison life is hard for many to swallow. Certainly, the critique of *OITNB* as not sufficiently attuned to the realities of mass incarceration and the prison-industrial complex – such as as positing the prison population as filled with women who make 'bad choices' instead of women caught up in a sexist and racist structure – has some merit. While it is true that the discourse of 'bad choices' permeates *OITNB*, a counter-narrative is equally present: backstories repeatedly show women entangled in the drug business of their men, snared by intractable systems and ground down by poverty and the lack of meaningful options.

Other critics, such as April Bernard (2014) writing in the *New York Review of Books*, find themselves torn between the (new) pleasures of the show and the ambivalence of becoming a 'tourist of suffering' by laughing at/with incarcerated women. Current and former inmates have been trotted out to challenge the veracity of this depiction of a federal prison, arguing that both the everyday boredom and ever-present aggression are underplayed, resulting in an airbrushed summer camp tableau instead of the raw and rough realities of incarceration.

And because it is, somehow, a comedy (in other words, not its most obvious televisual analogue, *Oz*), moments of uplift and improbable triumph creep in. As Bernard (2014) notes, '[…] many of the baddest guys – the rapist guard, the thieving warden, the heroin dealer – are miraculously defeated by the ingenuity of the inmates provid[ing] a completely fantastic, *Hogan's Heroes* sort of vibe'.

All are vital points of critique, but I am less interested in the 'realism' debates (this is, after all, TV where even so-called 'reality' is scripted and orchestrated) than in the types of identities, bodies, solidarities engaged in and through the series. And here is where a surprising problem sets in: curiously, the open sexuality that is one of the hallmarks of the show, is restricted largely to the white inmates. This cannot be a mere oversight, particularly in a series that is so profoundly engaged with questions of race, class and sexuality. *OITNB* revels in a nose-thumbing display of female bodies, female sexualities, female desires that push against normative ideas of both beauty and sex. So we see all kinds of bodies in all kinds of hues and shapes but sex itself seems reserved for the white women. Indeed, as feminist critic Yasmin Nair (2014) points out, the rare moments of black sexuality are too often reliant on stereotypical tropes, as when Piper is leered at by a black male inmate at the Chicago prison. Many have bemoaned the continuation of sexual double standards in *OITNB*, manifest not only in the focus on the bodies of thin, white, normatively beautiful women, but on the ways in which white women's breasts are 'artfully covered' while women of colour are displayed more openly (Nair 2013). Others have bemoaned the nudity double standard, where we see plenty of Piper's 'TV titties' but the butcher and less TV friendly bodies are generally in less fulsome display.

My read on the sexual double standard is this: in the effort to avoid the exoticization and hyper-sexualization that plague minority representations in mainstream popular culture, Jenji Kohan (the showrunner) has avoided Black and Latina sexuality almost completely, unwittingly perhaps replicating other stereotypes such as the mammy character (Taystee?) and the tragic mulatto (here played by 'Crazy Eyes/Suzanne' – not herself visibly light-skinned but raised in a white family).

Some of this is assuredly tied to the narrative centrality of the tempestuous 'love story' between Piper and Alex. We see them in flashback and in various prison iterations, going at it in high romance mode in a luxurious hotel suite and like furtive rabbits in prison chapels and bathrooms. But given that the white women of Litchfield (Big Boo, Morello, Nicky) have been given a wide sexual berth, the absence of sex among the Black and Latina prison populations is noticeable. Moreover, this restriction further heterosexualizes the women of colour or, when they evince some Sapphic inclinations, thwarts those inclinations at every turn.

We see this trend from the beginning. In early episodes, Crazy Eyes/Suzanne latches on to newcomer Piper and declares her devotion in ways both humorous and, in the end, pathetic. When her desire for a 'chocolate and vanilla swirl' with her blonde 'dandelion' is firmly rejected (and rejected by reference to Piper's commitment to her male fiancée), she promptly pees outside Piper's bunk, a move that further establishes her mental instability but also puts her even more definitively outside the realm of potential sexual partners. Curiously, homophobic counsellor Healy denies her request to bunk with Piper ('lesbian request denied') by wrongly reading Suzanne as a 'stud' and as butch. Not only is she misread and thwarted, but it is revealed in season 3 – when she is courted by a new white inmate – that she has never actually had a girlfriend. While the tide appears to be turning for virginal Suzanne – and we can anticipate the potential for romance with Maureen, her biggest fan – their courtship (like her desire for Piper) is depicted in infantilized ways, ways that speak to the fragile mental conditions of both women but that also avoid locating African American women as adult agents of their own (lesbian) desires.

Similarly, lesbian Poussey's only luck with the ladies is in flashback. An Army brat, we see her in a passionate affair with the (white) daughter of a German officer (interestingly one of the few moments of interracial lesbian sexuality and one that is both sexy and funny in its mockery of the ludicrous fantasy that 'scissoring' is actually a thing lesbians do) that is brutally broken up, setting the scene for her prison character as perennially lonely and thwarted. Once in prison, her desire for Taystee is (gently) rejected and Taystee serves instead as a loving friend who helps navigate her away from her incipient alcoholism.

The Latina women are even less able to indulge in Sapphic prison delights, although they are not wholly desexualized as we see in Daya's relationship with the boyish prison guard John Bennett. When Maritza and best bud Flaca lock lips in a passionate kiss, we anticipate (finally) some sexuality between the Latina women but they quickly dissolve in giggles and pull apart. Lesbian sex – even for the time served – is not for them.

So the women of colour are either signified heterosexually or desexualized or, alternately, existing in an endless state of thwarted desire. They do not have sex with each other nor do they have sex with different 'tribes'. Indeed, one of the very few instances of interracial sexuality is riven with abuse and subterfuge, when the women unite to pin Daya's pregnancy on Pornstache by getting him to have sex with her, or when Nicky 'scores' with Soso in her epic battle of sexual one-upmanship with Boo.

Interestingly, the moment of interracial sexual solidarity is a highly mediated one, itself a meta-commentary on the (male, pornographic) voyeuristic uses of 'traditional' women's prison tales. Spurred by the new counsellor's attempt to engage the women in creative writing exercises, Crazy Eyes/Suzanne discovers she has a gift for penning pornographic sci-fi and has the whole campus eagerly awaiting the next instalment of her polymorphously perverse tale, *The Hump Chronicles*, described by her as not just sex: 'It's love. It's two people connecting…with four other people…and aliens'. Here, then, the stymied desire of the black lesbian takes artistic form, a form that does what little else can do in the prison: cross racial, age, class and sexuality boundaries. As Suzanne herself proudly states, 'The universality of my work unites all the races'. This may be cold comfort for those of us who would like to see a more robust and diverse queer sexuality spread around Litchfield, but it is – I am convinced – a (perhaps failed) strategy to avoid the dilemmas of hyper-sexualization that so often plague the depiction of women of colour.

Butch Realness and Gay All the Way

If *OITNB* stumbles in its differential treatment of the sexuality of white women and women of colour, it charts brave new territory in its embrace of the butch. And they have a lot to work with here: star Lea DeLaria (Big Boo) brings a downtown cult sensibility and queer activist cred to her take no prisoners butch swagger, and Natasha Lyonne (Big Boo's softer butch buddy) has achieved a certain renown for her role in the cult queer classic *But I'm a Cheerleader* and, unfortunately, her own well-publicized drug issues. More to the point, prison narratives have long relied on the predatory butch figure as warning sign of what women's power and autonomy can breed and as a counterpart to benevolent patriarchal figures who rescue women gone wrong. More broadly, butch figures – from 1960s paragons such as evil and dumpy *Sister George* and the suicidal soft butch of the *Children's Hour* to the crazy butch stalker of 2006's *Notes on a Scandal* – have been signs of disorder and danger, often the implied dangers of a world in which gender normativity gets shaken up.

In one of the most daring moves of all three seasons, *OITNB* not only upends the stereotypes of butchness (self-loathing, woman-hating, bitter, destined to kill or be killed), but places the feminist crown firmly on the head of short, stout, proudly butch Big Boo, a crown previously worn almost exclusively by the almost transcendently good transgender character Sophia.[2]

Importantly, butchness here (in both its 'hard' and 'soft' version) retains its attachment to sexual power and desire but – particularly in the figure of Big Boo – gets reattached to an eloquent sisterhood and feminist ethics. We see hints of this butch solidarity in season 2, with a narrative arc that traverses several episodes. Here, Big Boo and Nicky (with the help of scorekeeper Chang) engage in a 'bang-off' to see not only who can score higher on the sexual conquest chart but, significantly, who can provide the most orgasms. Once again, *OITNB* overturns type and foregrounds female sexual agency as not the simple inverse of male agency. In other words, women's sexual prowess here is not at the *expense* of the pleasure of the other but rather dependent upon it. In the episode where the 'bang-off' begins, Big Boo confronts Nicky for 'picking all the peaches' and then discovers Nicky's 'fuck book' and calls her a junkie. 'It's not an addiction, it's a collection', Nicky demurs. 'Some people collect buttons, Taco Bell Chihuahuas, I collect orgasms. I'm all about giving. I'm like a bean flicking Mother Teresa… I'm a sexual Steve Jobs', she explains. While Big Boo and Nicky's much maligned 'bang-off' may seem to some as a 'girls can be as gross as boys' sexism, it conversely can be read as signalling a humorous and unusual depiction of female sexual agency (Nair 2014). In addition, the competition is narratively situated in an interesting way, on the heels of an 'our bodies/ourselves' moment when Sophia schools the women (replete with revelatory hand-mirrors) on the intricacies of female genitalia, thus linking sexual knowledge with sexual agency.

Even more powerfully, the competition does not get in the way of the solidarity between Nicky and Big Boo (they simultaneously call it off when they tie at 36 and sweetly wrap arms around each other) nor does it get in the way of the insistence on the humour and quirkiness of sex. Nor do we see these women and their conquests as temporarily queer. While the book configures Piper as predominantly heterosexual (and wholly unengaged in 'gay for the stay' prison sex), the TV series in fact moves in a different direction. Early on, we see Piper taken in and swept off her feet by the glamorous and sexually adventuresome Alex, and her commitment to her male fiancée and heterosexuality more generally is further undermined by this passionate and deeply ambivalent attraction to her, especially when she joins and then re-joins Piper in the prison (a twist away from the memoir). Interestingly, if the book paints a more traditional narrative of heterosexual redemption (and Alex/lesbianism as a phase, and a bad phase at that), the series more firmly roots our heroine in queerness. Indeed, lest we think Chapman is only gay for Alex, her unambiguous desire for the gorgeous new inmate Stella (played by out model Ruby Rose) dispels that particular mythology.

OITNB thus puts a queerer riff on the 'gay for the stay' trope about prison life. As Hannah McIlveen points out,

> Several points on the LGBT spectrum are represented, putting to rest any notion of heterogeneity in prison with characters like male-to-female transgender character Sophia (Laverne Cox), butch dyke 'Big Boo' (Lea DeLaria), and celibate nun Sister Ingalls (Beth Fowler). Sex is seen to serve different purposes for different people, too – for Morello, it seems a matter of convenience; for Nichols, it's a definite pleasure. The takeaway?

People's sexuality is never as simple on the inside as it looks from the outside. And if your perspective is too rigid, you may come off sounding like ignorant Mr. Healy.

(2013)

One of the most appealing aspects of *OITNB* is that sex is depicted as the complex thing it surely is: sometimes it is done for love, sometimes for recreation, sometimes for power, sometimes for competition, sometimes simply to relieve the boredom. Often it is funny, even when we imagine it not to be (nothing is funnier than the 'hate sex' between Alex and Piper in season 3). Often it is sad (nothing is sadder than Pennsatucky's rape – and her response to it – in season 3). Occasionally it is moving (Poussey and her German paramour). And every once in a while it knocks it out of the park. One of the most controversial episodes – in which a screwdriver goes missing – hilariously overturns our anticipation of violence by revealing that said screwdriver has been pressed into masturbatory service (pleasure) and not into the service of violence (danger).

Sisters are (Kinda) Doing It for Themselves

OITNB is no more a feminist Valhalla than a real panopticon. But it has its moments. Season 3 – the bleakest but also the most intricately drawn – reveals more of the darkness of prison life and the corporations that profit from the carceral state at the same time that unlikely pairings and incongruous identities continue to break down bordered identities. The Piper/Alex and Daya/Bennett pairings irritated some critics because of the centralizing of white femininity and the romanticizing of prisoner/guard sexuality, but both are firmly dismantled in this season. The 'hate sex' between Piper and Alex is cringe-worthy and laughable, and Piper's (rather unbelievable but still…) transformation into prison kingpin makes her even less likeable and sexually unappealing. Indeed, her pseudo-feminist jump-on-a-table speech enticing the women into her business plan is revealed as less sisterly communalism and more robber baron capitalism. The white knight (Bennett) gets out of Dodge and the real heroines are a bulldyke and her white trash buddy. The nonsexual friendship between atheist, feminist, resolutely queer Big Boo and bible-thumping, homophobic, former meth addict Pennsatucky sidles up to you, hits you like a thunderbolt, and then explodes into scenes of feminist solidarity worthy of that great 1980s underground feminist film *Born in Flames*.

If *OITNB* has, in previous seasons, skirted around sexual violence (and the percentages of women both assaulted while in prison and victims prior to incarceration are high enough to make this omission noticeable), in this season it is in full and ugly bloom. The rape of Pennsatucky by the new guard Coates (like Bennett, another 'seems nice' young white guy whose true colours are quickly revealed) and her prior sexual victimization are heartbreaking, particularly since the filming of both scenes is so similar: the camera moves in quietly on her blank, resigned, pained face and the assailants (random douchebag, random arm of the state) merge seamlessly one into the other. Here, too, *OITNB* paints a more complex and intricate picture of gendered violence: as implicated in the sexualized parenting of little girls (Pennsatucky's mother 'schools' her when she gets her period at the age of ten years. 'Now', she says, 'you're like a case of pop. You've got value… best thing is to go on and let them do their business baby…'), in the everyday expectations of boys and men, and in institutional regimes of gendered power.

But in the next episode, Boo becomes aware of Pennsatucky's assault and what ensues is about as moving and feminist a moment ever to hit television. Pennsatucky has so internalized her own self-hatred and worthlessness that when Boo asks her if she was forced ('you know there's a word for that, right?') she can only protest that, 'no, it's not his fault. I was flirting too much, I was smiling, and I was really confusing'. The bulldyke as rape crisis counsellor – and moreover as counsellor to a homophobe who calls her a 'munchmuffer' – is surely a rare sight in popular culture. Boo is horrified by Tucky's refusal to name her assault and stands up in pure grief as she come face to face with what used to be called 'male-identification' or the internalization of patriarchal ideologies, ideologies Boo has assiduously rejected.

In an incredible follow-up scene, Boo comes into Tucky's cubicle and dumps an armload of candy on her bed and demands she go down on her. This 'tough love' lesson in bodily integrity and self-worth comes not from any crisis counselling handbook but from the political integrity of the character most boldly sexually promiscuous if not 'aberrant'. Ending in tears ('I wanted it to stop. I wanted it to stop so bad. I wanted him to stop), hugs and Boo's insistence that 'we're going to get that motherfucker', this scene is made more meaningful by the arc it shares with the unionizing efforts of the guards and Piper's increasingly vicious and self-serving rejection of communal interest. The fact that the two of them can't go through with Boo's plan of 'Girl with the Dragon Tattoo' revenge (as Pennsatucky says, 'I don't have rage. I'm just sad') may be disappointing to those who want to see Coates brutalized, but it serves to further unite this strange pair as it resists the desire for redemption and progress.

It humanizes, but without the detritus of a limp humanism, rendering the tough women as (anti)heroic figures of a quirky women's world. As Rebecca McLennan so powerfully argues in a roundtable discussion on *OITNB*,

> *Orange* shows how the banalities of institutional life make the prison system by turns soul crushing, counter-productive, unjust, and fiscally wasteful. But more importantly, it puts a face – or, more accurately, many faces – on the prison statistics. And rather than soft-pedaling the fact that prisoners (like all human beings) can be threatening, violent, and petty, the show initially portrays many of the inmates in a rather unsympathetic light, before presenting the backstory of how one or other came to be incarcerated. In repeating this narrative structure, *Orange* undoes, episode by episode, an essential part of the apparatus of alienation that has so successfully disappeared offenders from their communities and from middle-class consciousness. Giving back the prisoner her pre-prison home, her childhood,

her neighborhood, her story – even so much as her first name – opens a vital space for social empathy and, potentially, political mobilization. Given the drought of human feeling towards offenders these past few decades, that's no mean feat – and it's a necessary, if not a sufficient, condition for change.

(2014)

Amen. Or should I say, 'lesbian request approved'.

References

Allen, S. (2014), 'How *Orange is the New Black* tokenizes transgender people', *The Daily Dot*, 13 June, http://www.dailydot.com/opinion/oitnb-tokenizing-transgender-laverne-cox. Accessed 1 June 2015.

Berlatsky, N. (2014a), 'Orange is the new caged', *Public Books* Roundtable, 15 May, http://www.publicbooks.org/artmedia/virtual-roundtable-on-orange-is-the-new-black. Accessed 1 June 2015.

—— (2014b), 'A lewd reminder of how tame *Orange is the New Black* really is', *The Atlantic Online*, June, http://www. theatlantic.com/entertainment/archive/2014/06/caged-heat-the-lewder-crazier-more-political-precursor-to-orange-is-the-new-black/361796. Accessed 1 June 2015.

—— (2014c), '*Orange is the New Black*'s irresponsible portrayal of men', *The Atlantic Online*, June, http://www.theatlantic.com/entertainment/archive/2014/06/why-it-is-a-bad-thing-that-orange-is-the-new-black-leaves-men-out/373682. Accessed 1 June 2015.

Bernard, A. (2014), 'Caged laughter', *New York Review of Books*, 6 June, http://www.nybooks.com/blogs/nyrblog/2014/jun/06/caged-laughter. Accessed 1 June 2015.

Bogado, A. (2013), 'White is the new white', *The Nation Feminism Blog*, 16 August, http://www.thenation.com/article/white-new-white. Accessed 1 June 2015.

Bordt, R. (2012), 'From Angela Davis to the long island Lolita: An analysis of contemporary Women's Prison Narratives', *Women and Criminal Justice*, 22: 2, http://dx.doi.org.ezproxy.neu.edu/10.1080/08974454.2012.662125. Accessed 1 June 2015.

Carman, C. (2013), 'Orange humor', *The Gay & Lesbian Review Worldwide*, 20: 6, http://go.galegroup.com/ps/i.do?id=GALE%7CA348330296&v=2.1&u=mlin_b_northest&it=r&p=AONE&sw=w&asid=73335cea47bdc931f6e8c680fd9ab84e. Accessed 1 June 2015.

Charlton, T. F. (2013), '"Orange is the New Black", and how we talk about race and identity', *RH Reality Check*, 3 September, http://rhrealitycheck.org/article/2013/09/03/orange-is-the-new-black-and-how-we-talk-about-race-and-identity. Accessed 1 June 2015.

Coker, H. C. (2014), 'An ex-con reviews *Orange is the New Black* and calls bullshit, mostly', *Jezebel*, 26 June, http://jezebel.com/an-ex-con-reviews-orange-is-the-new-black-and-calls-bul-1596441167. Accessed 1 June 2015.

Comfort, M. (2014), 'The two pipers', *Public Books* Roundtable, 15 May, http://www.publicbooks.org/artmedia/virtual-roundtable-on-orange-is-the-new-black. Accessed 1 June 2015.

D'Addario, D. (2014), '"Orange is the New Black" Husband Larry Smith seems like a nice guy: Why is his TV self such a jerk?', *Salon*, 16 July, http://www.salon.com/2014/07/16/orange_is_the_new_black_husband_larry_smith_seems_like_a_nice_guy_why_is_his_tv_self_such_a_jerk. Accessed 1 June 2015.

Diaz, V. (2013), 'Why *Orange is the New Black* is so addictive', *ColorLines*, 2 August, http://www.colorlines.com/articles/why-orange-new-black-so-addictive. Accessed 1 June 2015.

Dockterman, E. (2015), 'How TV sex got real', *Time blog*, May, http://time.com/how-tv-sex-got-real. Accessed 1 June 2015.

Dubois, L. (2014), 'Haiti on the small screen', *Public Books* Roundtable, 15 May, http://www.publicbooks.org/artmedia/virtual-roundtable-on-orange-is-the-new-black. Accessed 1 June 2015.

Edelman, R. (2014), 'It gets better: The evolution of "Queer TV"', *Los Angeles Review of Books*, 21 July, http://lareviewofbooks.org/ essay/gets-better-homosexuality-seen-tv. Accessed 1 June 2015.

Gittell, N. (2014), 'The one thing keeping *Orange is the New Black* from being the most feminist show on TV', *Mic*, 10 July, http://mic.com/articles/93117/the-one-thing-keeping-orange-is-the-new-black-from-being-the-most-feminist-show-on-television. Accessed 1 June 2015.

Hedges, I. (2014), 'Prison films: An overview', *Socialism and Democracy*, 28: 3, http://dx.doi.org/10.1080/08854300.2014.963955. Accessed 1 June 2015.

Herman, D. (2003), '"Bad Girl's changed my life": Homonormativity in a women's prison drama', *Critical Studies in Media Communication*, 20: 1, http://dx.doi.org.ezproxy.neu.edu/10.1080/07393180302779. Accessed 1 June 2015.

Hopkins, M. (2013), '"You can say it: Abortion": Reproductive justice in *Orange is the New Black*', *Soapbox Inc.*, 3 September, http://www.soapboxinc.com/2013/09/you-can-say-it-abortion-reproductive-justice-in-orange-is-the-new-black. Accessed 1 June 2015.

Iannacci, E. (2014), 'A revolutionary moment': From Laverne Cox to Sons of Anarchy, TV is in the grips of a "trans"-formation', *Maclean's*, 16 June, http://go.galegroup.com.ezproxy.neu.edu/ps/i.do?id =GALE%7CA371687330&v=2.1&u=mlin_b_northest&it=r&p=AONE&sw=w&asid=3e81e173cf5bcbbfd20a11eaf5cf6054. Accessed 1 June 2015.

Janeczko, J. (2013), 'Books behind bars: The literary world of *Orange is the New Black*', *Bitch Magazine*, 22 August, http://bitchmagazine.org/post/books-behind-bars-the-literary-world-of-orange-is-the-new-black. Accessed 1 June 2015.

Krischer, H. (2014), '*Orange is the New Black*'s trailblazing portrayal of foster care', *Salon*, 19 June, http://www.salon.com/2014/06/19/orange_is_the_new_blacks_trailblazing_depiction_of_foster_care. Accessed 1 June 2015.

Landsverk, K. (2014), 'Doing time', *Public Books* Roundtable, 15 May, http://www.publicbooks.org/artmedia/virtual-roundtable-on-orange-is-the-new-black. Accessed 1 June 2015.

Lang, N. (2014), 'Op-ed: *Orange Is the New Black* proves to be the model of queer TV', *The Advocate*, 30 June, http://www.advocate.com/commentary/2014/06/30/op-ed-orange-new-black-proves-be-model-queer-tv. Accessed 1 June 2015.

Law, V. (2013), 'Three real life prison issues shown in *Orange is the New Black*', *Bitch Magazine*, 12 August, http://bitchmagazine.org/post/ three-real-life-prison-issues-shown-in-orange-is-the-new-black-feminist. Accessed 1 June 2015.

Liss-Schultz, C. (2013), '"Orange is the New Black": Taking privilege to task', *Ms. Magazine Blog*, 17 July, http://msmagazine.com/blog/ 2013/07/17/orange-is-the-new-black-taking-privilege-to-task. Accessed 1 June 2015.

Love, H. (2014), 'Made for TV', *Public Books* Roundtable, 15 May, http://www.publicbooks.org/artmedia/virtual-roundtable-on-orange-is-the-new-black. Accessed 1 June 2015.

McHugh, K. A. (2015), 'Giving credit to paratexts and parafeminism in *Top of the Lake* and *Orange is the New Black*', *Film Quarterly*, 68: 3, http://www.jstor.org/stable/10.1525/fq.2015.68.3.17. Accessed 1 June 2015.

McIlveen, H. (2013), 'New Netflix show "Orange is the New Black" is a complex look at sex, gender and prison', *Bitch Magazine*, 10 July, http://bitchmagazine.org/post/new-netflix-show-orange-is-the-new-black-is-a-complex-look-at-sex-gender-and-prison. Accessed 1 June 2015.

McLennan, R. (2014), 'Why prison stories matter', *Public Books* Roundtable, 15 May, http://www.publicbooks.org/artmedia/virtual-roundtable-on-orange-is-the-new-black. Accessed 1 June 2015.

McNutt, M. (2013), 'The race to address race in *Orange is the New Black*', *Cultural Learnings*, 22 August. http://cultural-learnings.com/2013/08/22/the-race-to-address-race-in-orange-is-the-new-black. Accessed 1 June 2015.

Mead, R. (2014), 'Office hours', *The New Yorker*, 27 October. http://www.newyorker.com/magazine/2014/10/27/office-hours. Accessed 1 June 2015.

Moore, T. (2014), '*OITNB*: Today's best black show has a white star', *The Root*, 5 June, http://www.theroot.com/articles/culture/2014/06/ orange_is_the_new_black_best_black_show_has_a_white_star.html. Accessed 1 June 2015.

Mu'min, N. (2014), '*Orange is the New Black* rewrites the 'Bad Prisoner' stereotype', *Bitch Magazine*, 9 June, http://bitchmagazine.org/post/ orange-is-the-new-black-rewrites-the-bad-prisoner-stereotype. Accessed 1 June 2015.

Nair, Y. (2013), 'White chick behind bars', *In These Times...*, 18 July, http://inthesetimes.com/article/15311/white_chick_behind_bars. Accessed 1 June 2015.

——— (2014), 'The reign of Whitey is never over', *In These Times...*, 11 June, http://inthesetimes.com/article/16819/the_reign_of_ whitey_is_never_over. Accessed 1 June 2015.

Najumi, M. (2013), 'A critical analysis of *Orange is the New Black*: The appropriation of women of color', *The Feminist Wire*, 28 August. http://www.thefeministwire.com/2013/08/a-critical-analysis-of-orange-is-the-new-black-the-appropriation-of-women-of-color. Accessed 1 June 2015.

National Public Radio (2013), '"Orange" creator Jenji Kohan: "Piper Was My Trojan Horse"', *Fresh Air*, 13 August, http://www.npr.org/2013/08/13/211639989/orange-creator-jenji-kohan-piper-was-my-trojan-horse. Accessed 1 June 2015.

Nussbaum, E. (2013), 'Vice Versa: God and bad in *Oranges is the New Black* and *Ray Donovan*', *The New Yorker*, 8 July, http://www.newyorker.com/magazine/2013/07/08/vice-versa-2. Accessed 1 June 2015.

——— (2014), 'Lockdown: The lessons of *Orange is the New Black* and *Louie*', *The New Yorker*, 7 July, http://www.newyorker.com/magazine/2014/07/07/lockdown-2. Accessed 1 June 2015.

Orange is the New Black (2013–2015, USA: Netflix).

Paige, A. (2014), 'Seeing Orange', *Fourth Genre: Explorations in Nonfiction*, 16: 1, https://muse.jhu.edu/journals/fourth_genre_ explorations_in_nonfiction/v016/16.1.paige.html. Accessed 1 June 2015.

Peterson, L. (2013), 'Mistakes, Huh? Watching *Orange is the New Black*', *Racialicious*, 14 August, http://www.racialicious.com/2013/08/14/mistakes-huh-watching-orange-is-the-new-black. Accessed 1 June 2015.

Quinlan, C. (2013), 'Bisexuality on TV: It gets better', *The Atlantic Online*, October, http://www.theatlantic.com/entertainment/archive/2013/10/bisexuality-on-tv-its-getting-better/280850. Accessed 1 June 2015.

Rivera, G. (2013), '*Orange is the New Black*: Seven Things we should talk about', *Autostraddle*, 21 July, http://www.autostraddle.com/orange-is-the-new-black-7-things-we-should-talk-about-186228. Accessed 1 June 2015.

Ross, K. B. (2013), 'Why orange is not the new black', *Racialicious*, 26 November, http://www.racialicious.com/2013/11/26/why-orange-is-not-the-new-black. Accessed 1 June 2015.

Rose, R. (2014), '*OITNB*'s real-life Alex is also writing a book about her prison time', *Jezebel*, 19 August, http://jezebel.com/oitnbs-real-life-alex-is-also-writing-a-book-about-her-1623740635. Accessed 1 June 2015.

San Filippo, M. (2014), 'Doing time: Queer temporalities and *Orange is the New Black*', *In Media Res*, 10 March, http://mediacommons. futureofthebook.org/imr/2014/03/10/doing-time-queer-temporalities-and-orange-new-black. Accessed 1 June 2015.

Saraiya, S. (2014), 'The year in hair: How afros, wigs, and extensions took over pop culture', *Salon*, 27 December, http://www.salon.com/ 2014/12/28/the_year_in_hair_how_afros_wigs_and_extensions_took_over_pop_culture. Accessed 1 June 2015.

Sered, S. (2014), 'What Pennsatucky's teeth tell us about class in America', *Bitch Magazine*, 1 July, http://bitchmagazine.org/post/what-pennsatucky's-teeth-tell-us-about-class-in-america. Accessed 1 June 2015.

Smith, A. M. (2015), 'Orange is the same white', *New Political Science: A Journal of Politics and Culture*, 37: 2, http://dx.doi.org/10.1080/07393148.2014.995401. Accessed 1 June 2015.

Smith, M. D. (2014), '*Orange is the New Black*'s accurate portrayal of men in a story about women', *Feministing*, 15 July, http://feministing.com/2014/07/15/orange-is-the-new-blacks-accurate-portrayal-of-men-in-a-story-about-women. Accessed 1 June 2015.

Stanley, E. A. (2014), 'Abolition and trans resistance', *Public Books* Roundtable, 15 May, http://www.publicbooks.org/artmedia/virtual-roundtable-on-orange-is-the-new-black. Accessed 1 June 2015.

Stoeffel, K. (2013), 'Five formerly incarcerated women on prison, relationships, and *Orange is the New Black*', *New York Magazine Online*, 19 August, http://nymag.com/thecut/2013/08/former-prisoners-watch-orange-is-the-new-black.html. Accessed 1 June 2015.

Sullivan, M. J. (2014), 'Piper's adventures in blackness', *Public Books* Roundtable, 15 May, http://www.publicbooks.org/artmedia/virtual-roundtable-on-orange-is-the-new-black. Accessed 1 June 2015.

Tillet, S. (2013), 'It's so not *Oz*: Netflix's *Orange is the New Black*', *The Nation Feminism Blog*, 23 July, http://www.thenation.com/article/its-so-not-oz-netflixs-orange-new-black. Accessed 1 June 2015.

Trier-Bieniek, A. M. (2015), 'Introduction: Finding feminist fandom in *Orange is the New Black*', in A. M. Trier-Bieniek, *Fan Girls and the Media: Creating Characters, Consuming Culture*, Lanham: Rowman and Littlefield. pp. xi–xix.

Villarejo, A. (2014), *Ethereal Queer: Television, Historicity, Desire*, Durham: Duke University Press.

Walters, S. D. (2001), 'Caged heat: The (R)evolution of women-in-prison films', in M. McCaughey and N. King (eds), *Reel Knockouts: Violent Women in the Movies*, Austin: University of Texas Press, pp. 106–123.

Ziegler, K. (2013), '*Orange is the New Black* and its new black trans narrative', *blac(k)ademic blog*, 22 July, http://blackademic.com/orange-is-the new-black-and-the-new-trans-narrative. Accessed 1 June 2015.

Notes

1 See my article 'Caged heat: The (r)evolution of women-in-prison films' in *Reel Knockouts: Violent Women in the Movies* for a more developed discussion of this theme.

2 The complication of the Sophia character in season 3 is equally daring. Not only did her sympathetic portrayal of a transgender prisoner jolt actor Laverne Cox into superstardom and national and beloved trans spokesperson, but critics and fans alike are unanimous in their praise, even when dismissing the series as a whole. But in season 3, Sophia is given some of the complexity of other characters. Her much vaunted feminism is undermined by her sexual advice to son Michael to '[f]ind a real insecure girl and practice on her. That way, when you meet a girl you really like, you'll be good at it', Sophia relays. When Michael asks, 'Do you really want to be a lady in a world where men do that?' Sophia takes not the high road but the road of normative femininity, 'God help me, I do', she replies. If Sophia served as the voice of clarity, empathy and even feminism in season 1, by season 3 this has shifted. Her halo is quite tarnished (from her sexist advice to her son and from her refusal to correct the record with Gloria when she realizes that it was Michael and not Gloria's son who got in trouble) and her victimization at the hands of other prisoners and the system provides a locus of sympathy but not necessarily of full-on redemption.

Part IV

Villainesses and Anti-antiheroines

Chapter 11

Women and Criminality in Brazilian *Telenovelas: Salve Jorge* and Human Trafficking

Samantha Joyce and Antonio La Pastina

The traditional melodramatic formula used in Latin American *telenovelas* often includes a villainous woman, willing to engage in criminal activities to thwart the happiness of the leading couple, but they are usually not professional criminals. Crime is a by-product of their evil nature, or the desire for vengeance, not their way of living; it is the melodramatic leitmotif that propels most *telenovelas*. However, a recent (2012–2013) *telenovela* in Brazil, *Salve Jorge/Hail George*, written by Glória Perez, introduced a new type of villainess: a mobster. Although this type of programming is known for having female characters in leading roles – the heroine and the villainess – the gangster story, the epitome of the male-dominated crime genres, has not traditionally been a part of these narratives. In *Salve Jorge*, Glória Perez presented a new type of villainess: Lívia Marine, the boss of an international human and drug trafficking organization who deceives women promising them a better life as waitresses and/or models in Turkey, but instead forces them into slavery, working as 'drug mules' and prostitutes. Although writer Glória Perez has a long history of engaging with complex social issues in her *telenovelas*, in *Salve Jorge*, for the first time, she fully developed a female character that embodied the power and strength of a crime boss. In this essay we approach this melodrama from a critical and feminist position, investigating how Glória Perez structured a criminal female lead and how this subversion of the traditional structure of women villains in Brazilian melodramas is in tune with other recent globally circulating representations of women criminals.

Crucial to Lívia Marine's characterization as a new type of villainess is not just the fact that she is 'evil' or 'ill intentioned' against a heroine or antiheroine. The very nature of her (masculine) evil acts are noteworthy: much like Toni Soprano, she is a vicious murderer and the boss of a criminal enterprise, but also an upstanding member of society promoting philanthropic causes. She is the perpetrator of heinous crimes against women. She traffics and enslaves them and instructs her thugs to drug and rape them in order to control their bodies and spirits more efficiently. Although she is clearly marked as the villain of the narrative, she is nonetheless well liked by a portion of the public, fascinated by her elegance and power, who desire to emulate her through acts of consumption. For example, throughout the programme's broadcast, TV Globo's customer service often received inquiries regarding the products associated with her such as the clothing manufacturer and lipstick color and brand (Bittencourt 2013: 36).

Salve Jorge, a production of Globo Network, Brazil's largest media conglomerate, is akin to recent US television series and serials such as *Weeds* and *Orange is the New*

Black that portray female leads 'doing crime', as they are implicated in various roles and positions in the illegal business of criminal organizations (mafia, drugs cartel, weapons trafficking and so forth). As the other chapters in this book attest, in the post-network era, the trend of more nuanced representations of women varying in race, sexuality, profession and their choices between illicit/licit activities is a global one. TV dramas such as *Salve Jorge* offer an opportunity to engage with complex questions regarding constructions of gendered others by appropriating characteristics such as power, money, violence and crime, traditional pillars of the male-dominated hyper-masculine criminal world of fictionalized TV serials. Also noteworthy is the fact that the *telenovela*, which is traditionally seen as a 'women's genre' has put forth this peculiar character and storyline in such a distinct manner: not only do we have a female boss of a crime organization, but the product that she illicitly distributes is enslaved women. According to data on judicial proceedings on human trafficking in Brazil, 43.7 per cent of those charged with the crime are women (Ferlin 2014). Glória Perez, as in many of her previous works, uses an innovative strategy to document the reality of contemporary urban life while using her characters to challenge established systems of oppression.

Telenovelas: Lachrymose Romantic Spaces of Oppression or Heterotopic 'Other Spaces'?

As a narrative mode, melodramas have been dismissed as politically alienating, especially due to their association with the superficiality of the mass media and their reliance on a dominant aesthetic that prescribes classic narrative forms (Gutiérrez-Albilla 2010: 144). Additionally, as John King (1990: 155) argues, the melodrama is 'a genre usually condemned by Latin American critics as deploying a false, lachrymose consciousness'. However, it is important to understand that *telenovelas*, as melodramatic as they may be, are not purely hegemonic patriarchal sites of alienation and oppression. By taking into account Martín-Barbero's (1997) perspectives on melodramas as spaces of contestation and negotiation, we can understand melodramas as a heterotopic space, as described by Foucault (2009).

Telenovelas are a complex site of mediations/representations. Martín-Barbero (1997) argues that, although melodramas may function as an ideological opiate, they also retain the traces of a popular culture that has resisted the direct imposition of dominant forms. As we will discuss later in this chapter, because of their immense popularity, Brazilian writers (or auteurs) have leeway to break new ground with innovative representations, contesting traditional hegemonic beliefs and offering a space where alternative models of 'masculinity' and 'femininity' can be imagined.

Martín-Barbero (1997) and Foucault (2009) offer unique perspectives to investigate *telenovelas* as complex spaces for understanding identity and, more specifically, the changes in representation of female identity, especially in recent TV shows where women engage in criminal activity. In *From Media to Mediations* (1997), Martín-Barbero investigates the social construction of identity by individuals influenced by the media, due to its immense penetration within their social and individual spaces – especially those who watch *telenovelas*. Martín-Barbero (1995: 71) understands communication processes as 'phenomena of production of identity, reconstitution of subjects, social players'. The author adds that as a means of communication they 'are not a pure commercial phenomenon, not a pure phenomenon of ideological manipulation; they are a cultural phenomenon through which one person or many persons live the constitution of the meaning of their lives.'

Perez (2009: 1) brings attention to 'melodrama's ability to mediate a range of identities, especially its capacity for opening a space for marginalized subjectivities to play on a national or even world stage'. While Gutiérrez-Albilla (2010) argues that although the melodramatic mode has been conventionally associated with a 'textual effect that implies a closeness, an immediacy and hence an uncritical spectator – one who is taken in, often to the point of tears, entailing a loss or fading of subjectivity in the process of signification' (Doane 2004: 14), we should not, and cannot so easily dissociate it from a 'rational' political project.

We propose that Brazilian *telenovela* writers such as Glória Perez use these programmes as heterotopic spaces. Foucault (1984/1999) discusses heterotopic spaces while attempting to explain the range of cultural, institutional and discursive spaces that are different, disturbing, contradictory and transforming, in other words, those places and spaces that function in non-hegemonic conditions. Thus, *telenovelas* such as *Salve Jorge* – especially through the villainess Lívia Marine – act as a space that transgresses gender norms that are upheld by hegemonic discourses on femininity and womanhood. Due to their immense popularity, authors have freedom to represent alternative views, so *telenovelas* can become heterotopic spaces[1] 'because they can act as "other spaces" for expression and for creativity'.[2]

Foucault (2009) used the mirror as a metaphor for the duality and contradictions, the reality and the unreality of utopian projects. Thus, the mirror is used as a metaphor for utopia because the image that one sees in it does not exist; and because the mirror is a real object that shapes the way one relates to his/her own image. Thus, we can argue that the television image, or the image within the screen, and more specifically the changing image of women (i.e. Lívia Marine) in specific *telenovelas* can be seen as heterotopia.

In a discussion about the movie *Avatar* (Cameron, 2009) and heterotopia, Gomes poses that Foucault

> makes reference to the theatre and to the cinema as examples of heterotopia: Thus it is that the theater brings onto the rectangle of the stage, one after the other, a whole series of places that are foreign to one another; thus it is that the cinema is a very odd rectangular room, at the end of which, on a two-dimensional screen, one sees the projection of a three-dimensional space.
>
> (Gomes 2010: 48)

Salve Jorge, like *Avatar*, 'works as a mirror, giving us a vision of ourselves, or of our culture' (Gomes 2010: 43). A few other Brazilian *telenovelas*, especially those associated with long-time established 'hit-makers' like Glória Perez, have also worked as heterotopic spaces. Due to their immense popularity and high ratings, and akin to American cable TV shows, such as *Weeds*, that do not suffer as much pressure from advertisers as those programmes on traditional networks, these *telenovelas* can act more creatively and in non-hegemonic ways, in other words, as 'other spaces' for the representation of non-traditional, 'masculine', criminal women.

TV Globo's *Telenovelas*, Social Merchandizing and Glória Perez

Brazilian *telenovelas* last on average 150 episodes and have been the staple of TV programming for over six decades. Audiences follow the stories for several months and they have in fact become an integral part of Brazilian culture (Hamburger 2005; La Pastina 2004; Porto 2012). Starting in the early 1950s, serial dramas such as *telenovelas* evolved first from a Cuban melodramatic template, relying on narratives that were either based on classical novels or exotic tales set in distant lands (Fernandes 1994). In the 1970s, the genre began to evolve to incorporate a local vernacular and urban locations. Brazilian writers, many trained in theatre, started to incorporate real-life social-economic-political problems to the plots as a way to encourage the audiences' critical thinking. Even under the military dictatorship that lasted from 1964 to 1985, authors were able to bypass censorship by carefully articulating metaphorical situations to address concrete problems of an increasingly urban society. After the re-democratization process in the late 1980s and early 1990s, issues that had been previously deemed off limits, such as racism, homosexuality and land reform, started to appear in prime-time *telenovelas*. Contemporary programming invariably will include pro-social content, from minor insertions to complex narrative arches, such as the case in *Salve Jorge* (Xavier 2007: 193).

Globo's *telenovelas* operate in a transnational space, as they are exported to over 140 countries worldwide (Telles 2004). Thus, not only do they have to be successful at home, but they also must increasingly maintain a market abroad. It seems that Glória Perez is both responding to these transformations and adapting her traditional strategy to use *telenovelas* to engage in social issues that affect women's lives and rights. Through this recent women/drug trafficking storyline she has not merely accorded diegetic centrality to the women involved in the business of crime, thus giving rise to compelling figures of antiheroines, she has also brought awareness to this very real global issue.

A key aspect of Brazilian *telenovelas* that has distinguished it from other producers in the region is its consistent inclusion of social merchandizing (La Pastina, Patel and Schiavo 2003). Until the 1990s, the inclusion of socially relevant issues was always the result of a writer's social and political agenda. Starting in the 1990s, Globo network began to articulate strategies for the insertion of social merchandizing in partnership with the writers, allowing for their ideas to be supported by relevant research and infrastructure to maximize the impact of the message (La Pastina, Patel and Schiavo 2003). Over the past decades, it has promoted causes that are deemed important to writers and producers, such as racism, homophobia, disease prevention and family planning (Joyce 2012).

Glória Perez's career at TV Globo goes as far back as 1979. She has written several TV series and serials since then and is notorious for her history of including social awareness and social merchandizing in her narratives and subsequently to the everyday lives of Brazilians. What Mattelart and Mattelart wrote in *The Carnival of Images* is still the case today:

> In the press, discussion on the *novela* is not limited to specialized magazines that are of minor importance in Brazil. All press genres – daily, weekly, monthly, for all readerships – speak abundantly of telenovelas, including interviews with authors, actors, directors, producers and viewers, roundtables on themes, reviews by specialized journalists, academic analysis, humor, and gossip in the tittle-tattle press. On top of the copious press dossiers prepared by Globo and weekly programme bulletins it publishes, most Brazilian magazines devote extensive articles to novellas that serve as veritable national events, continually reiterated [...] A history of the social impact of a telenovela could be written through its echo in the press. The sheer volume of articles on the novela is without echo in Europe.
>
> (1990: 79–80)

Glória Perez's 1995/96 *telenovela Explode Coração/Exploding Hearts* used social merchandizing by wedding real-life events with fictional ones. In one of the storylines, Odaísa's (actress Isadora Ribeiro) son Gugu disappears, and from this starting point, the author tells the real-life drama of mothers who lost their children. Real mothers appeared in the *telenovela* showing pictures of their missing children. The programme was credited with reuniting 64 missing children to their parents (Xavier 2007: 196–198).

In 2001/02 Glória Perez's *O Clone/The Clone*, one of the most successful Brazilian *telenovelas* to date, debuted a series of stories with a multicultural perspective and transnational locations. *O Clone*, partly set in Morocco, discussed topics relating to Islamic culture, drug and alcohol addiction as well as ethical issues regarding human cloning (Teledramaturgia 2010). Once again, the writer used real-life addicts to tell their stories of struggles and relapses.

Salve Jorge follows a similar pattern, with the author incorporating a serious social and political issue into a transnational context relying on the conventions of *telenovela* melodrama. *Salve Jorge* travels between Brazil and Turkey and is engaged with an increasingly global social crisis: the trafficking and enslavement of women.

Salve Jorge/Hail George

The 179 episodes of the prime-time *telenovela Salve Jorge* aired Monday to Saturday from 2 October 2012 to 17 May 2013. The main plot involved the protagonist Morena (actress Nanda Costa), a poor young mother living in the well-known *Morro do Alemão*, a real-life favela (slum) in Rio de Janeiro, notorious for its violence and drug trafficking. The line between reality and fiction is quickly crossed in the first few minutes of the broadcast, when audiences see real and fictional footage of the process of 'pacification'[3] of that favela by the *Unidade de Polícia Pacificadora/Pacifying Police Squad*. Morena not only lives in this community, but was born there and is portrayed as a hard-working and ethical single mother who was abandoned by her drug trafficking boyfriend after she got pregnant.

Morena lives with her mother Lucimar (Dira Paes) and meets her love interest – Théo (Rodrigo Lombardi) – within the first few episodes of the broadcast and spends the duration of the programme jumping through hoops to finally have her happy ending at the end of the *telenovela*. Although the audience knows and expects this, what was innovative was that the villainess Lívia and her sidekick Wanda (Totia Meireles) impede the lovebirds from being together not for revenge, but for money. They trick Morena into sex-slavery and drug trafficking with promises of a good paying job abroad.

In the first moments of the broadcast, the audience is introduced to the villainess who will be the driving force behind the main actions of the programme. As Brandão and Moreira (2013: 13) state, Lívia Marine poses as an esteemed professional in the fashion world and, due to the fact that she is an elegant woman with several personal contacts in politics and showbiz, no one suspects her of illicit activities. She moves freely and swiftly through Rio de Janeiro's high society. In this first introductory scene to Lívia's character (on the first day of the broadcast), she is seen leaving a restaurant and is immediately surrounded by paparazzi.

Brandão and Moreira (2013: 13) point out that Lívia is charismatic and manipulative, but also cold and cruel. She is in charge of her 'model agency', but is also able to eliminate those who are onto her by murdering them with a lethal syringe with high doses of heroin, which made the character popularly known as 'A vilã da seringa' ('The syringe villainess').

Lívia is a charming predator who takes advantage of poor young women. This is how she is able to lure Morena into her sex-slavery scheme. Disillusioned by her army-captain boyfriend Théo (a literal and figurative knight/prince charming on a horse), broken and jobless, Morena meets Wanda (who is Lívia's recruiter) and is tricked into going to Turkey under the false pretence of being a waitress/dancer and making lots of 'dollars' to help her family. In reality, to everyone's surprise – Morena and the audience – she is entrapped at a brothel disguised as a dance club. And thus begins her saga as a trafficked sex-slave.

In Turkey we meet two other key players of the human trafficking organization: Irina (actress Vera Fisher) who works as an accountant at the dance club and Russo (actor Adriano Garib) the thug who intimidates the entrapped women by threatening their families, beating and even raping them. The triad Wanda, Irina and Russo follow Lívia's orders, the do-gooder businesswoman and philanthropist who uses her role in the fashion industry to seduce the girls with hopes of a better life as a dancer/waitress abroad. Lívia is frequently referred to as 'chefa' the female version of *chefe*/boss in the Portuguese language.

Writer Glória Perez spends several episodes explaining how human trafficking works – by showing the personal struggles of these young women – especially Morena's – with money, family, broken hearts and dead ends, due to a lack of education and opportunities – until we see them locked up without their passports in a dungeon-like room. In search for a better life for her son, Morena makes the hard, but pragmatic decision to leave him with her mother Lucimar for a few months in order to work abroad and receive 'in dollars' the equivalent of over one year's salary as a sales clerk at a local mall.

Glória Perez shows that these girls receive cash up front, new clothes and a complete makeover, since it is explained to them by the 'recruiter' that their 'good appearance' will be key in their role as waitresses/dancers. They are told that the money used to finance the makeover is a salary advance and that in time they will pay 'the agency' back. Perez uses these narrative strategies to clearly mark these women as victims and not prostitutes, because they did not choose to sell their bodies for money. They are sex-slaves who are forced to sell their bodies to survive.

In Turkey, Morena meets three other entrapped women: Jéssica (Adriana Dieckman), Rosângela (Paloma Bernardi) and Waleska (Laryssa Dias) who have also been duped by Lívia and Wanda. From this point on in the story, the narrative shows their struggles to survive and to break from captivity, such as when Morena and Jéssica are sent back to Brazil as drug mules and are even able to visit their families, but are too afraid to turn the criminals in to the authorities because they worry about what might happen to their families and the stigma of having become 'prostitutes', even if against their free will.

In March of 2013, while *Salve Jorge* was still on air, the weekly television programme *Fantástico* (akin to CBS's *60 minutes*) showed an investigative report that illustrated how the Brazilian and Spanish Federal Police worked together in an investigation on human sex trafficking and slavery in Salamanca that freed seven women from various countries including Brazil and Colombia from a Spanish brothel. According to authorities, the operation could not have been possible without a tip from the mother of one of the enslaved women, who told the Brazilian police she only understood what was happening to her daughter after she watched *Salve Jorge* (Fantástico 2013).

According to a report by the Brazilian weekly newsmagazine *Isto é*, data by the Brazilian Federal Police indicates that about 70,000 Brazilians have been sent abroad, victims of trafficking/sexual exploitation, mostly women and children, to countries such as Germany, Spain, the United States, Italy and Turkey (Torres and Costa 2011). Interestingly enough, according to the São Paulo's Ministry of Justice, *Salve Jorge* greatly influenced Brazilian society, at least in the following way: data indicates that in the first four months of 2013 the number of complaints about trafficked Brazilians grew by 106 per cent as compared to the number of complaints during the same period in the year prior to the broadcast (Racy 2013).

Women Committing Crime: A Radical Transformation of *Telenovela*'s Leitmotif

By taking into account Foucault's (1984/99) premise of fluid identities and heterotopia, we can understand the *telenovela* as a rich environment to examine how the programme constitutes the female identity, and more importantly, how unique representations of women contribute to reveal other types/spaces of representation and identification of new identities. While being a vicious mobster and assassin as well as a drug trafficker may be simplistically understood in a dichotomous scale of a 'good' or a 'bad' kind of representation, this unconventional female identity can be said to exert power in the Foucauldian sense, as it sets things into motion by opening up new types of representation/identification of *telenovela*/real-life women.

According to Matos (2006) although some *telenovelas* present audiences with complex roles for female characters, the majority of women are still portrayed in traditional gender roles and cannot be described as 'modern'. The author argues that in *telenovelas*' narratives the most striking distinctions in gender roles have to do with the clearly demarcated domestic and public spheres starkly separated as 'home' and 'work' (such as in sales or medical field) where the social and economic status differ according to gender: we have the male bosses and the businessmen versus the secretaries and the maids.

This is more alarming when we take into account the fact that research indicates that for many women in Brazil, television is still the primary form of entertainment and thus, looking at how women are represented in the most watched genre in that country, is imperative because *telenovelas* tend to reproduce the traditional female model where motherhood and marriage are still the female priorities. Thus, media discourses about what it means to be a woman reinforce stereotypes perpetuated by other social institutions – that help shape a norm for female identity. By looking at the most watched TV programme in Brazil, we can then see how at times women take pleasure and are complicit in their own subordination as demonstrated by Sifuentes and Ronsini (2011: 138).

Additionally, the authors state that *telenovelas*

> reproduce the same model which has changed very little throughout the decades, for 50 years. Thus, many young women […] watch telenovelas from infancy, and although they participate in a negotiation of meanings while decoding these products, they are educated by them, as they are by school, their family and other social institutions. Thus, by presenting basically the same types of female representations, the melodrama genre throughout the years constitutes an important female ideal.
>
> (Sifuentes and Rosini 2011: 140)

While traditionally such a female ideal was understood as being associated with the private sphere, family and motherhood, with Lívia Marine we have a complete reversal, as this female leading character is an unwed mature woman in her forties, a criminal who exploits other women and who makes no excuses for it – making this *telenovela* a heterotopic space, as previously argued. She is not acting for revenge or vengeance, the traditional leitmotif of *telenovela* melodramas. She is driven by power and money. While this may not be an ethical and moral ideal, it is important to stay away from the previous stereotypes, as Sifuentes and Ronsini (2011) have shown, media portrayals serve to organize and to create cognitive schemes that are responsible for defining 'what it means to be' a woman. In the case of

Brazilian commercial media, in most of its history it has worked to produce a representation of women as young, attractive, motherly and so forth.

Here, Lívia Marine's criminality becomes subversive. She is elegant and powerful. She is not a whining villainess who resents the heroine or seeks revenge for an imagined wronged past. She wants power and money and is willing to do what it takes to get it. She is attractive, but she is neither motherly nor submissive. She is not fragile or in despair. She operates as feminine and as a woman, committing crimes as a woman, using female spaces to create opportunities to subvert power structures that will enrich her while reinforcing patriarchal structures oppressing other women.

Lívia's transgressions subverting the black/white/good/evil dichotomy also operate at the visual level. As Faria and Fernandes (2013: 13) point out, Lívia is 'always wearing white, the color of purity'. Her role is also transgressive because, as the authors have suggested, the villainess is also seen as the traditional 'heroine': 'spirited and articulate, she spares no charm or visual aids such as clothing, hairstyles, makeup and even costly high fashion brand name shoes – in fact Lívia was recognized by one of her victims due to the remarkable pair of heels she wore during an event she was promoting'.

Faria and Fernandes (2013: 14) also point out that at times, the villainess is 'sensitive and soft, as the great divas of the cinema, but when [her] evil actions are hanging by a thread and are about to be discovered by the police, [she] does not hesitate to take up arms, run over her victims with their cars, threaten them with knives, needles with lethal doses of drugs or whatever it takes to get the job done'.

The *telenovela*, and more specifically *Salve Jorge*, is understood as an institution capable of creating favourable conditions for the construction of new identities, particularly through the representation of specific female portrayals (Haerter et al. 2008). Lívia did not just live and work in the public sphere; she operated between the public and the underground spheres: philanthropy in the public eye, and criminality in the down low, moving an underground economy. Glória Perez, who declared she was a fan of the American show *Dexter*, could not escape comparisons between her cruel syringe-killer villain and the American (male) counterpart. Several times during the broadcast audiences witnessed Lívia Marine kill/attempt to kill her enemies by giving/attempting to give them a lethal injection, including Jéssica (Carolina Diekman) who was Morena's best friend amongst the trafficked young women; or trying to kill a police officer by planting a bomb in her car. But the writer declared that even though she was a *Dexter* fan, her inspiration for Lívia Marine started during the research stage of the production. According to Perez,

> I am his fan as I have stated. But when I did research on trafficked people, I found that this is the kind of thing they do to kill people. This is not hard to understand, since the traffickers want to get rid of a foreigner who is giving them trouble, and with the syringe, you can fake an overdose. I was inspired by a real life drama for the Morena's story (Nanda Costa), a real person who lived all that, and whose friend died that way.
>
> (Castro 2014)

In addition to being a skilful killer, Lívia is extremely rich, having at her disposal not just money, but the means to transport the women, the drugs and to build and maintain her international enterprise. Her public life career lends legitimacy to her 'talent-scouting', enticing her victims with promises of fashion shows, fame and money. But her wealth does not come from her honest job, but rather from her illegitimate human-trafficking enterprise. According to the International Labor Organization (ILO), the annual profit made from human trafficking reaches $ 31.6 billion. The United Nations Office on Drugs and Crime Survey (UNODC) also shows that the profit of criminal networks for every human being taken from one country to another can reach $30,000 per year (Communicação de Interesse Público 2009).

Lívia Marine used her job as fashion insider to disguise her illicit activities. For example, when talking on the phone with one of her 'contacts', she asks whether her latest 'collection has been delivered', objectifying the enslaved women both physically and symbolically. Lívia's enterprise, however, is dependent on her side kick Wanda (actress Totia Meireles), who is her main 'scout'. Wanda is the one responsible for taking the protagonist Morena to Turkey, with the false promise of work in a restaurant. She is a polite, vibrant and manipulative woman in her forties who preys on young vulnerable women, preferably in their late teens, early twenties. Although Wanda's character is not the focus of our analysis, to a lesser extent her character also attests to the fact that this particular *telenovela* stands in for a heterotopic space. Wanda has a lot of the same characteristics as Lívia Marine, and although she is not the main villain she certainly operates in the same way.

Lívia Marine represents a radical transformation of *telenovela*'s leitmotif. Recent research (Brandão and Moreira 2013; Hummell and Alvetti 2007; Sá Santos 2014) identifies a shift of focus from heroine to villainess in *telenovelas*, but Lívia Marine was the first one involved in organized crime. Sá Santos (2014: 186) states that starting in the 1990s, the villainess has the key function of setting the main plot of the programme into motion, in addition to, as with Lívia's case, functioning as the purveyor of socio-educational messages. The villainess continues to seek power and create obstacles to the heroine in the traditional melodramatic mode, but her attitudes now have educational features. Lívia is attractive and dangerous, and contributes to the naturalization of subjects not known by the general public through social merchandising.

Hummell and Alvetti (2007) state that the villain oftentimes becomes more important and famous than the heroine. They argue that there is a gender performance that makes the audience remember the villainess more. For Hummell and Alvetti, gendered villainy has changed in melodramas:

> First, because as the characteristics of melodramas change, they lead to a change in the characteristics of the villains. Second, society's moral values, in which lies a balance of the gender roles have changed. And finally, although transgression is still uncommon, it is clear that in the villainess's role there is a clear space for questioning, which makes the

character a little more nuanced, sometimes more ambiguous, bringing it closer to the present reality.

(Hummell and Alvetti 2007: 257)

The authors conclude that the role of the villainess is not to simply counteract the heroine protagonist. When it comes to Lívia, Brandão and Fernandes (2013: 10) agree that she is more than a counterpoint to Morena and suggest that in the melodrama she serves the function of bringing forth issues that tend to cause ethical and moral discussions to the public agenda, generally triggered by the struggle of good versus evil.

Lívia Marine enslaves women, uses them as drug mules and orders them to be raped – for example when she ordered Russo to sexually assault Morena's friend Jéssica in order to control her psychologically as well as physically. As Brandão and Fernandes (2013: 10–11) argue, Lívia and her partner Wanda

are contemporary primetime villainesses that rely on impulsivity, lack of guilt or remorse, violation of social norms and a complete lack of guilt when causing pain to others in order to get what they want immediately. This is in tune with our current society's culture of individualism that preaches self-fulfillment and self-satisfaction at the expense of obligations to other people. The authors add that Lívia Marine 'rose a rung on the ladder of villainy in television fiction, in addition to lying, they cheat for money and power, and dominate an international network of trafficked people'.

(2013: 13)

Furthermore, as far as this new type of representation of women in *telenovelas* – the crime boss – is concerned, it is interesting to highlight that such a different portrayal of a woman came through the writing of the only female writer in the 8 p.m. timeslot (Castro 2014). When asked how she chose the theme of human trafficking for the plot, the author stated that it all started when she saw pictures of a human-trafficking campaign at an airport and wondered why that was the only place where she had ever seen the campaign, and that she wanted to 'give visibility to the invisible, to give a voice to the voiceless'.

She did just that, she created a narrative that explicitly forced millions of viewer in Brazil and abroad to engage with the problematic representations of women exploiting women; and of women trafficking and subjugating women, but she also created an 'other space' for complex and powerful representations of women who have agency and who are driven by power and not emotions.

But at the end of the story, Morena slowly but successfully devises a plan to bring the trafficking ring down and to reunite her family. Following a melodramatic and highly improbable explosion, the heroine is able to escape captivity, and to find refuge at a village in Cappadocia. There, Morena contacts the Brazilian police (more specifically Helô, her detective friend) via the Internet and serves as an important informant and a key player in

Lívia's arrest on the last day of the broadcast. The success of Lívia as a villain is consequently thwarted at the end of the narrative to create a semblance of order as expected by the traditional *telenovela* viewing public.

Conclusion

As we have demonstrated, TV Globo's *telenovelas* operate in a transnational space and have to be successful not only at home but must increasingly maintain a market abroad. With this new type of representation of women – the mobster Lívia Marine as well as her accomplice Wanda – it seems that Glória Perez is in tune with other productions that place women in this traditionally male-dominated position, such as Nancy Botwin in *Weeds*. Thus, we suggest that Glória Perez is both responding to these transformations that have accorded diegetic centrality to women involved, in various ways, in the business of crime, giving rise to compelling figures of antiheroines. Furthermore, Perez is adapting her traditional strategy to use *telenovelas* to engage in social issues that affect women's lives and rights.

As previously stated by Sifuentes and Ronsini (2011: 144) we contend that although *telenovelas* are fictionalized stories, they play a major role in expanding the range of female representations, fleeing the simplified images that reduce women to the still hegemonic private sphere – and thus contributing to a more equal relationship between genders. Brazilian *telenovelas* are a powerful mechanism in the formation of opinions and in the construction of identities in contemporary Brazil. They support the definition and the flexibility of the social roles assigned to men and women, reconfiguring the pre-conceived ideas about the 'house wife', the 'successful professional' or the 'prostitute', forging new identities, roles and values (Haerter et al. 2008: 6).

Ultimately, as Martín-Barbero (1997) demonstrated, *telenovelas* are a site of mediations, of multiple readings and meanings, a space for struggle for signification that goes beyond a simplistic but very lucrative marketplace. They are a powerful venue that can activate new knowledge, discourses and dialogue in the social production of meaning. Criminality and human slavery are real global problems gaining visibility not only in the media, such as in *Salve Jorge*, but also in social media campaigns such as #enditmovement that encourage social media users to shine a light on the lingering problem of slavery by posting a selfie with a red 'X' on their hands to their social media pages with the hashtag 'enditmovement'.

Although melodramas and *telenovelas* have been traditionally dismissed as politically alienating due to their lachrymose nature and dominant classic narrative form and aesthetic (Gutiérrez-Albilla 2010: 144), we must understand *telenovelas* as a complicated site for negotiating identity. As melodramatic as they may be at times, this type of programming is not a purely hegemonic patriarchal space of alienation and oppression and can act as 'other spaces' in the Foucauldian sense.

By combining Martín Barbero's (1997) perspectives on melodramas as spaces of contestation and negotiation with Foucault's concept of heterotopia (2009), we showed that *Salve Jorge* and its crime boss Lívia Marine help us understand certain melodramas as a heterotopic space, a complex 'other space' to portray and understand identity formation, and more specifically, the changes in representation of female identity, especially in recent television productions in different parts of the world where women engage in criminal activity. Shows such as *Weeds*, *La reina del sur* and *Salve Jorge* act as a space/'other space' that transgresses gender norms traditionally upheld by hegemonic discourses on femininity and womanhood.

References

Beck, B. (2012), 'Mother Courage and her soaps: Incendies, Weeds, Nurse Jackie, and daytime drama', *Multicultural Perspectives*, 14: 1, pp. 28–31.

Bittencourt, V. M. (2013), 'O meio é a mensagem? Estudo sobre o merchandising da marca Kia via a personagem Rosângela na novela Salve Jorge', http://repositorio.uniceub.br/handle/235/4034. Accessed 6 February 2016.

Brandão, M. C. and Moreira, G. (2013), 'A Vilania Feminina na Telenovela: Alianças com o Banditismo', http://www.intercom.org.br/papers/nacionais/2013/resumos/R8-1767-1.pdf. Accessed 18 June 2015.

Castro, N. (2014), '"Escrevi para continuar vivendo", afirma Glória Perez sobre a volta ao trabalho após a morte da filha', Oglobo.com.br, 27 April, http://oglobo.globo.com/cultura/revista-da-tv/escrevi-para-continuar-vivendo-afirma-gloria-perez-sobre-volta-ao-trabalho-apos-morte-da-filha-12301173#ixzz3S94YRZKY. Accessed 18 February 2015.

Cameron, J. (2009), *Avatar*, USA: Twentieth Century Fox.

Comunicação de interesse publico (2009), 'Mídia criativa denuncia tráfico de seres humanos no Quênia', Cip.ig.com.br, 11 December, http://cip.ig.com.br/index.php/2009/11/12/midia-criativa-denuncia-trafico-de-seres-humanos-no-quenia/. Accessed 18 February 2015.

Doane, M. A. (2004), 'Pathos and pathology: The cinema of Todd Haynes', *Camera Obscura*, 19: 3, pp. 1–21.

Fantástico.com.br (2013), 'Mãe de prostituta explorada na Espanha ajuda polícia a desmontar tráfico de mulheres. Segundo a Polícia Federal, a novela "Salve Jorge" encorajou a mãe a pedir ajuda pelo serviço Ligue 180', 2 February, http://g1.globo.com/fantastico/noticia/2013/02/mae-de-prostituta-explorada-na-espanha-ajuda-policia-desmontar-trafico-de-mulheres.html. Accessed 11 February 2015.

Faria, M. C. B. de and Fernandes, G. M. (2013), 'A Vilania Feminina na Telenovela: Alianças com o Banditismo', Intercom.org.br, http://www.portcom.intercom.org.br/navegacaoDetalhe.php?id=53890. Accessed 20 June 2015.

Ferlin, D. (2014), 'Brasil: O berço do tráfico de mulheres e da exploração sexual', Jurisway.org.br., 14 April, http://www.jurisway.org.br/v2/dhall.asp?id_dh=4386. Accessed 25 February 2015.

Fernandes, I. (1994), *Telenovela Brasileira: memória*, São Paulo: Editora Brasiliense.

Foucault, M. (1984/1999), 'The Foucault Reader', in P. Rabinow (ed.), *Michel Foucault: The Foucault Reader*, New York: Pantheon.

—— (2009), 'Estética: literatura e pintura, música e cinema', in M. Foucault, *Ditos e Escritos III* (2nd ed.), Rio de Janeiro: Forense Universitária.

Gomes, M. R. G. (2010), 'Avatar: Between utopia and heterotopia', *Matrizes*, 3: 2, http://www.revistas.usp.br/matrizes/article/view/38257. Accessed 20 June 2015.

Gutiérrez-Albilla, J. D. (2010), 'The gender ethics and politics of affection: The "feminine" melodramatic mode in Walter Salles' Central do Brasil', *Bulletin of Latin American Research*, 29: 2, pp. 141–154.

Hamburger, E. (2005), *O Brasil antenado. A sociedade na novela*, Rio de Janeiro: Jorge Zahar Editor.

Haerter, L., Germano, R. P. and Da Silva, M. F. S. (2008), 'O papel da mulher na novela das oito: uma análise acerca das personagens femininas em Duas Caras e das construções identitárias que as perpassam', http://www.fazendogenero.ufsc.br/8/sts/ST8/Haerter-Germano-Silva_8.pdf. Accessed 18 February 2015.

Hummell, R. and Alvetti, C. (2007), 'Apontamentos sobre a imagem da vilania: uma leitura do horário nobre', *Revista Estudos de Comunicação*, 8: 17, pp. 255–261.

Joyce, S. N. (2012), *Brazilian Telenovelas and the Myth of Racial Democracy*, Washington: Lexington Books.

King, J. (1990), *Magical Reels: A History of Cinema in Latin America*, London: Verso.

La Pastina, A. (2004), 'Selling political integrity: Telenovelas, intertextuality, and local elections in rural Brazil', *Journal of Broadcasting & Electronic Media*, 48: 2, pp. 302–325.

La Pastina, A., Patel, D. and Schiavo, M. (2003), 'Social merchandising in Brazilian telenovelas', in A. Singhal, M. J. Cody, E. M. Rogers and M. Sabido (eds), *Entertainment-Education and Social Change: History, Research and Practice*, New York: Routledge.

Martín-Barbero, J. (1995), 'Secularización, desencanto y reencantamiento massmediatico', *Revista Dia-logos de la Comunicación*, 41, pp. 71–81.

—— (1997), *Dos meios às mediações. Comunicação, cultura e hegemonia*, Rio de Janeiro: UFRJ.

Matos, P. (2006), 'A mulher moderna numa sociedade desigual', in J. Souza (ed.), *A invisibilidade da desigualdade brasileira*, Belo Horizonte: Editora UFMG.

Mattelart, M. and Mattelart, A. (1990), *The Carnival of Images: Brazilian Television Fiction*, New York: Bergin and Garvey.

McLaughlin, L., Steiner, L. and Carter, C. (2014), *The Routledge Companion to Media and Gender*, London: Routledge.

Mead, W. R. (1995/96), 'Trains, planes, and automobiles: The end of the postmodern moment', *World Policy Journal*, 12 : 4, pp. 13–31.

Perez, H. (2009), 'Alma Latina: The American hemisphere's racial melodramas', *The Scholar and Feminist Online*, 7: 2, http://sfonline.barnard.edu/africana/perez_01.htm#text2. Accessed 14 May 2015.

Porto, M. (2012), *Media Power and Democratization in Brazil: TV Globo and the Dilemmas of Political Accountability*, New York: Routledge.

Racy, S. (2013), 'Jorge Salva', *Estadao.com.br*, 16 May, http://blogs.estadao.com.br/sonia-racy/jorge-salva/. Accessed 18 February 2015.

Sá Santos, L. (2014), 'A Representação dos vilões através das fases da telenovela brasileira, Cambiassu', 14, http://www.cambiassu.ufma.br/cambi_2014.1/representacoes.pdf. Accessed 18 June 2015.

Salve Jorge/Hail George (2012–2013, Brazil: Globo Network).

Sifuentes, L. and Ronsini, V. (2011), 'O que a telenovela ensina sobre ser mulher? Reflexões acerca das representações femininas', *Revista FAMECOS*, 18: 1, pp. 131–146.

Sood, S., Menard, T. and Witte, K. (2004), 'The theory behind entertainment-education', in A. Singhal, M, Cody, E. Rogers and M. Sabido (eds), *Entertainment-Education and Social Change: History, Research, and Practice*, New York: Routledge, pp. 117–145.

Teledramaturgia.com.br. (2010), 'Glória Perez', http://www.teledramaturgia.com.br/tele/gloria_perez.asp. Accessed 9 February 2015.

Telles, L. (2004), 'Teledramaturgia ganha caráter científico com trabalho do Núcleo de Telenovelas/Teledramas gain cientific carácter with the work of the telenovelas group', http://www.usp.br/agenciausp/repgs/2004/pags/007.htm. Accessed 9 February 2015.

Torres, I. and Costa, F. (2011), 'Tráfico de pessoas. Dados do Ministério Público e da Polícia Federal revelam que o número de brasileiros levados para o Exterior por traficantes já soma 70 mil. ISTOÉ mostra como funciona e quais são as principais rotas do esquema, *Istoé.com.br*, 21 October, http://www.istoe.com.br/reportagens/170188_TRAFICO. Accessed 18 February 2015.

Xavier, N. (2007), *Almanaque da telenovela brasileira*, São Paulo: Panda Books.

Notes

1 Utopia is a place where everything is good; dystopia is a place where everything is bad; and heterotopia is the place where things are different (Meade 1995: 13).
2 For a discussion of other (mediated) spaces, see McLaughlin, Steiner and Carter (2014: 236).
3 The real-life occupation by the military police in *Morro do Alemão* happened in November 2010. The operation was considered a success by the government and the local media since a large quantity of illegal drugs, weapons and money was confiscated from drug traffickers and the community and the city are deemed safer 'pacified' places.

Chapter 12

'Your Turn, Girl': The (Im)Possibility of African American Antiheroines in *The Wire*

Bruce A. Williams and Andrea L. Press

Introduction

The almost entirely unsaid and unnoticed truth about crime – particularly the most grisly, outrageous crimes – is that they are committed overwhelmingly by men. Criminality is inherently bound up, culturally, with masculinity. Criminologists agree on this issue; crime statistics indicate that in every category except prostitution and 'running away from home', men far outnumber women in perpetrating crime (Britton 2000: 60).

This sociological reality, however, and the way public debate over criminality ignores the issue of masculinity, has not prevented feminist criminologists from critiquing the way the field of criminology has differentially treated female criminals. Female criminals do exist, and they are analysed quite differently from men in the criminology literature as feminist scholars have illustrated (Britton 2000). Most notably, they are analysed through a series of ideological lenses, which construe women who commit crimes as either the extremely passive victims of their male partners, or as the highly stylized 'evil women' we've become familiar with in popular culture. Both frames ignore the specific structural conditions that affect women who enter criminal life, just as they affect men.

This stereotyping of the female criminal, and of women's access to criminal life, pervades not only the social scientific study of criminology, but our popular media products as well. The television show *The Wire* is now widely appreciated for its highly realistic portrayal of drug dealers in Baltimore and the institutions that police them. As Potter and Marshall note, 'Its stories scream of verisimilitude' (2009: 8–9). Prominent race scholars Chaddha, Wilson and Venkatesh (2008) note, '*The Wire* is an accurate depiction of life in the inner city during the drug war'. Following from this assessment, college courses focused entirely on *The Wire*, and the world it portrays, have become commonplace, with the most publicized course offered at Harvard by the sociologist of race William Julius Wilson.

While we agree that *The Wire* is a remarkable show, and pathbreaking in its representations of race, class, the drug trade and inner-city life, it is disappointing in its representations of women, especially so in its treatment of women of colour in the 'underclass' it portrays. *The Wire*'s leading men fit Mittell's (2013) definition of the 'antihero' to a tee: in his view, the antihero is a character who serves as the audience's 'primary point of ongoing narrative alignment, but whose behavior and beliefs provoke ambiguous, conflicted, or negative moral allegiance'. Yet, throughout the five seasons and 60 episodes of *The Wire*, the morally ambiguous behaviour of African American women does not serve as points of audience identification in the ways that have largely come to define the dramatic antihero in television's 'third golden age'. This is not to say that the representations of women in *The Wire* do not substantively differ from television's typical gendered representations.

Indeed, 'The female characters featured on *The Wire* provide the kind of diversity' that was largely absent in 'past decades of network television' (Press 2009: 146). Nonetheless, the question remains: why do the strong and complex African American women of *The Wire* fail to provoke the same sort of conflicted moral allegiance as their male counter-parts? To begin to answer this question, this chapter reviews scholarship addressing women in *The Wire* and common understandings of post-network television's antiheroes to foreground the analysis of three characters in particular: Briana Barksdale, De'Londa Brice and Donnette. We conclude with a theorization of this pervasive problem of the biased and simply 'non'-heroic representation of underclass women in television.

The Wire, developed in 2002 by David Simon based on his experiences working as a police reporter in Baltimore and his co-author Ed Burns' experience as a homicide detective and later a middle-school teacher, is a remarkable television show that is often cited as one of the best shows that has ever aired (Carey 2007; Kennedy and Shapiro 2012; Miller and Traister 2007; Olmstead 2011; Roush 2013). In addition to its reliance on an in-depth, ethnographic knowledge of Baltimore based upon the careers of the two creators, the show frames its narrative with a sophisticated institutional and structural perspective, with each season highlighting a different set of institutions and showing how they structure the lives of the characters affected by them. This attention to the operations of specific institutions and broader structures of opportunity is one of the greatest achievements of *The Wire*. It invites a predominantly white and middle-class audience to understand the actions (often criminal) of many of the show's characters as resulting not from evil or amoral personalities, but rather from the ways in which social, political and economic institutions shape their perspectives and choices. Consequently, the show operates as a powerful critique of what is more common in popular media: the demonization of inner-city men and women of colour. Rather, the perspective most viewers would find dominant in *The Wire* argues that the problems of the characters we encounter do not stem from them being 'different' from average middle-class Americans. Instead, the representations illustrate that the lower-class individuals depicted – called the 'underclass' in sociological terminology – often share middle-class values, but exist within a radically different set of institutional structures from that encountered by most middle-class HBO viewers.[1]

Nowhere is this achievement more apparent than in the many memorable and nuanced inner-city black men the show represents. These men combine heroic with decidedly antiheroic qualities, given that they are enmeshed in criminal activities. Stringer Bell, second-in-command of the Barksdale drug family who attends night college business classes to learn how to better run his own business, runs his gang's meetings according to Robert's Rules of Order, collects modern art and has Adam Smith's *The Wealth of Nations* on his bookcase. President Obama's favourite character (on what he also says is his favourite television show), Omar Little, the gay 'stick-up boy', seeks revenge when his lover is brutally tortured and killed by the Barksdales. Also notable are Michael, Dukie, Namond and Randy, the four middle-school students whom we follow throughout season four's focus on the public school system. Yet, despite the many male characters on both sides of the law and the smaller number of memorable female characters in the criminal justice system, there are no similarly sympathetic and nuanced female characters among the street characters. In their case, the unattractive features of criminal personalities are stressed and detailed, and there is no concomitant idealization, sexualization or romanticization of their characters above and beyond the criminal elements portrayed.

The 'Wild Women' of *The Wire:* A Classed Presentation?

There is little doubt that *The Wire* creates several nuanced and thoroughly unique portrayals of women. But we argue in this chapter that the most interesting female characters in *The Wire*, and in fact, the 'wildest', most sexual and 'coolest' figures offered as objects of identification, are confined perhaps ironically to the women on the 'right side' of the law. These police officers, lawyers, politicians and campaign consultants are a diverse group: African American and white, lesbian and straight, married and unmarried, with and without children; but they are all respectable citizens. In contrast to their general competence on the job, much of their 'wildness' consists of their sexual behaviour – cheating on their partners, brief hook-ups with colleagues and abandoning their parental responsibilities. To be sure, the focus on these characters' sex lives also serves to provide ample opportunity for the show to exploit the freedom of pay-cable to show explicit sex scenes, arguably gratuitous, and so exploit the difference between censored broadcast and basic cable shows. Yet, as we'll argue, showing the unruly sex lives of these otherwise career-oriented, successful women creates complicated and fully drawn characters.

In contrast to their law-abiding counter-parts, the female characters on *The Wire*'s 'street', involved directly or indirectly in the drug trade, are, with few exceptions, more stereotyped and unidimensional, offering viewers little opportunity for empathetic identification. Most troubling, these women continue a cultural tradition of 'mother blaming', laying blame for the ills of society squarely on the shoulders of mothers – stereotypical thinking that has particularly stalked the African American community since before the days of the Moynihan Report in the 1960s.[2]

Law Abiding Not Quite 'Antiheroines'

Main *The Wire* male character Detective 'Jimmy' McNulty is perhaps the prototypical 'antihero' of crime drama, the lone male of film noir and other crime films with whom we have become familiar with in popular culture. Though in *The Wire* he is portrayed as perhaps more morally ambiguous than heroes like Humphrey Bogart's Philip Marlowe of *Maltese Falcon* (1941) fame, or Robert Mitchum's Jeff Bailey in the iconic film noir *Out of the Past* (1947), we nevertheless enjoy McNulty's character, identify and sympathize with his problems and his reluctance to fully identify with the police establishment.

McNulty is a 'wild man' par excellence, both in his approach to police work and his personal life. He begins the series as a talented homicide detective, frustrated with the bureaucratic politics of the Baltimore Police Department. He violates the 'chain of command' by speaking with a judge about his frustration with the failure of his department to pursue the Barksdale gang that controls much of the city's drug trafficking and the associated killings. Acting on McNulty's complaints, the judge embarrasses the department and forces the creation of the special unit that becomes the permanent Special Crimes Unit and the focus of the show for all of its five seasons. McNulty is punished for his disloyalty to the police as an organization and is punished by being transferred to the Harbor Unit, his least preferred assignment. By the fifth season, McNulty has been promoted and demoted several times and become so frustrated that he engineers a truly wild scheme by inventing a serial killer who preys on the homeless of Baltimore in order to divert the funds allocated to finding the imaginary killer to the pursuit of the drug gang led by Marlo Stansfield that has replaced the Barksdales. McNulty ends the series in disgrace, forced to leave the police department.

McNulty's loose canon approach to his professional life is mirrored in his personal life. In addition to having a drinking problem, he is a divorced father of two who maintains a tense, often jealous relationship with his ex-wife and endangers his two young sons by using them to help trail a criminal suspect. He is selfish and unreliable in two sexual affairs he carries on, the first with attorney Rhonda Pearlman (Dierdre Lovejoy) in season 1, and the second with Beatrice 'Beadie' Russell (Amy Ryan), a Port-of-Baltimore police officer and single mother of two. Yet, despite or perhaps because of his wild actions, McNulty is always charismatic, an antihero with whom we are invited to identify.

McNulty's female associates, though interesting in many ways, are not afforded the same opportunities for 'antiheroic' status. Rather, on the job they are dedicated, competent professionals who, though often sympathetic to McNulty's frustration with the criminal justice system, never undermine or circumvent the rules (formal and informal) of the organizations within which they work. Instead, their rebellious or 'wild' sides are entirely restricted to their personal life, especially their sex lives.

Particularly notable is Detective Shakima 'Kima' Greggs (Sonja Sohn), one of the main characters throughout the series. We meet Kima in the very first episode when she is in charge of a drug bust and, after the dust settles, shows her two subordinates (also continuing characters – Herc and Carver) that they have missed a loaded gun in their search of the dealer's car. As the episode continues, we see her in a number of situations such as joking back and forth with Herc and Carver as they fill out paperwork, and working with her immediate superior Cedric Daniels (Lance Reddick) to figure out how to respond to demands from higher ups in the Baltimore Police Department's chain of command. The result is that we quickly understand that Kima is a supremely competent detective who has the well-deserved respect of both her superiors and subordinates.[3]

While the portrayal of a female professional as being uber-competent and respected is hardly groundbreaking,[4] later in season 1 we also get a more nuanced perspective on why she is respected by fellow police. After the police have staged a drug raid and lined up 'the usual suspects,' i.e. young black street-level dealers, one of them (Bodie, also a continuing character) hits one of the officers, who happens to be an older alcoholic burnt-out. The police immediately throw Bodie to the ground and begin beating him savagely. Kima sees what is happening and begins running to the scene of the beating. Everything about the scene leads us to believe she is going to restrain the other officers and stop the beating; instead she enthusiastically joins in, showing us that she is 'one of the guys', she's a cop, she's an insider.

The difference between the antihero McNulty and the more unambiguously admirable Kima is most clearly established in the penultimate episode of the entire series. When she discovers that McNulty's serial killer is an invention, she refuses to help and rejects his argument about this being the only way to get the resources needed to do 'real' police work. Instead, in an act of loyalty to 'the-chain-of-command' and her own moral compass, Kima reports the fraud to her boss Daniels, an act that quickly leads to McNulty's dismissal from the force.

That Kima is an 'out' lesbian in a lesbian relationship, which is foregrounded in the show, also serves to contrast her with the more typical female cops in television. As so often happens on HBO series, we see explicit (by television standards) sex scenes between Kima and her partner, establishing the pleasure both get from sex. On the one hand, this is a convenient plot device; since Kima is upfront with her sexuality, the show never needs to deal with questions of wanted or unwanted advances by her mostly male partners.[5] On the other hand, the series offers a nuanced exploration of the evolving relationship between Kima and her partner Cheryl (Melanie Nicholls-King), an African American lawyer. Again, in this instance, by focusing on the ways individuals respond to the institutional incentives they face, the series explodes many gender as well as racial stereotypes.

For example, at the beginning of season 2, both Kima and Daniels are off the street: Kima because she was shot in season 1, and Daniels because of bureaucratic politics that consign him to a dead-end assignment. Both have promised their partners that they will not return to the assignments that cost them so dearly.[6] Both couples struggle with a much-used trope in television cop shows: the police officer whose craving for the excitement and danger of the street leads to family crisis. Yet here, in a memorable scene, Kima and Daniels are shown in parallel shots telling their partners over dinner that they are returning to their old assignments. The scene cuts back and forth between the two couples as the camera circles the dinner tables until both Cheryl and Marla put down their utensils and angrily leave the table.

Over the course of its five seasons, *The Wire* continues to challenge gender stereotypes as it follows the arc of Kima and Cheryl's relationship. In one narrative, primarily at Cheryl's insistence the couple decide to have a child, which Cheryl carries. During the pregnancy, Kima – acting like a stereotypical male cop – becomes bored with the increasing domestic responsibilities, and alienated from Cheryl and the baby. She begins to pick up women in lesbian bars and becomes closer to McNulty as the two become prototypical 'drinking buddies', and in drunken conversations they express frustration with their 'civilian' partners (in McNulty's case, his ex-wife). We see Kima in sexual one-night stands, similar to the way men are more normally portrayed; and we see McNulty in these situations as well. Here again, the explicit scenes that accompany one of Kima's one-night stands chronicle the pleasure of sex for her (and us).

Assistant State's Attorney Rhonda Pearlman is another main female character whose transgressions are limited to her personal life. From the first episode of season 1, Pearlman, like Kima, is shown to be an exceptionally competent and well-respected professional. Throughout the series, she is the prosecutor who works with the Major Crime Unit to guide them through the process of obtaining the necessary warrants for the various surveillance strategies necessary to gather legally admissible evidence against the targets of their investigations. She often acts as a mediator between more conservative members of the detail and the more free-wheeling (and legally dubious) approach of McNulty. In variants of this scene throughout the series, Rhonda plays a sort of 'mommy'-figure to the unruly and fighting children of *The Wire*.

Like Kima, Rhonda expresses the frustration of trying to do good work in a highly flawed institutional setting, but also understands the informal rules of her position that can be strategically used to her advantage. In one memorable scene, she uses the sexism of her superiors to advantage, as when making a plea for resources to a lecherous judge in a suggestive short skirt, she repeatedly crosses and uncrosses her legs. Paralleling Kima's arc, Rhonda is competent, respected and professionally ambitious. By the series' end, she has been promoted to the position of Maryland's chief prosecutor for violent crime.

Similar to Kima, Rhonda's personal life is unsettled and she transgresses against the competence and control exercised in her professional life entirely in the realm of her relationship to men. Initially, she is involved in an on-again, off-again, but primarily casual sexual relationship with McNulty. There are hints that they had a more serious relationship in the past, but when we meet them in season 1, McNulty shows up at Rhonda's apartment late at night, drunk, seeking companionship and sex. Initially reluctant to let him in, she is offended that he expects her to be available for both with no explanation or commitment. In the end, though, she gives in and we are treated to an HBO explicit sex scene that makes clear how much pleasure she herself gets from sex. Over the course of the series, Rhonda ends her relationship with McNulty and begins one with the more stable Lieutenant Cedric Daniels (Lance Reddick), now separated from his wife Marla. More HBO explicit sex scenes follow, re-establishing her sexual pleasure. It is difficult to know what precisely to say about the fact that Daniels is black and Pearlman is white, but clearly this adds to the frisson of their sex scenes.

There are other memorable women on *The Wire* but none who break the new ground of Kima or Beadie. We appreciate that unusually, these two are 'wild women' indeed who offer the possibility of identification, though not quite at the 'antiheroic' level of McNulty. What's most interesting for our analysis here, however, is the way these characterizations contrast with those of the African American underclass women portrayed. The latter women, paradoxically, are portrayed more puritanically – perhaps in reaction to a history of the stereotyping of African American women as 'oversexed' (Bogle 2001). Yet their characters are also more flat, 'evil' people rather than the 'antiheroes' we see with some of the more notable men of quality television (Mittell 2013; Shafter and Raney 2012).

The Wire's Female Underclass: Anti-antiheroines

As we've noted elsewhere (Williams and Press, forthcoming), there is a disappointing, fundamental gender blindness in *The Wire* generally, as acknowledged by Laura Lippman (2009), David Simon's best-selling crime novelist wife. Though Lippman lauds the treatment of many female characters on the series, she attributes many of *The Wire*'s blind spots to the paucity of women in creative positions on the show: in the first two seasons, only one woman wrote for the show at all, and only three directed episodes. As Lippman notes, the world described on *The Wire* is 'starkly masculine' (2009: 55). She goes on, in effect, to apologize for this, stating, 'Yes, many of the women in *The Wire* appear in secondary roles, but that is a simple truth about the world it portrays…' (2009: 60). The sentence continues tellingly, however: '– and the point of view through which it is filtered'. Admission of this filter is key to our own critical perspective on the series. What we are shown on *The Wire* is a penultimately *male* perspective, a male filter; and this, unfortunately, makes the show mundane, no different from the vast majority of popular television and film to which *The Wire* has often been compared so favourably.

What we would like to emphasize here, however, is the stark contrast between the social classes of the female characters who *are* included. This does not parallel the representation of men on the show: in fact, as has often been noted, one of the central achievements of *The Wire* is a sympathetic, almost heroic representation of the African American male underclass.

While the middle-class professional women are represented with some of the empathy afforded the central antihero McNulty – and some of the African American drug-lord leads – the African American female underclass is not represented with this level of sympathy. In fact, most of these characters embody a kind of 'evil' in their personalities that does not transcend current stereotypes of African Americans more generally in popular entertainment. This is particularly evident in the representation of African American mothers, who are some of *The Wire*'s basest characters, and indeed embody a kind of 'mother-blame' for producing underclass men that we have become familiar with in popular culture and in popular sentiment more generally. In the remainder of this chapter we focus on three main underclass African American females: De'Londa Brice (Sandi McCree), Brianna Barksdale (Michael Hyatt) and Donnette (Shamyl Brown).

De'Londa Brice is the mother of Namond Brice (Julito McCullum), one of the four middle-school students in season 4. While not married to him, De'Londa has taken the last name of Namond's father, Roland 'Wee-Bey' Brice (Hassan Johnson), a fearsome hit man for the Barksdale drug family. As Stringer Bell (Idris Elba), second in command of the Barksdale gang, says to Wee-Bey, 'You so evil, you have to count up the number of people you've killed on the fingers of both hands; even you don't know how many people you've killed'. When arrested, to avoid the death penalty, Wee-Bey pleads guilty to many unsolved murders (even some he didn't commit); in return he asks for a pit beef sandwich with extra horseradish from his favourite restaurant. As with so many other characters, despite his horrific actions, Wee-Bey is treated with a good deal of sympathy, though probably does not achieve 'antihero' status as do some of the other African American male criminal drug lords. We learn, for example, that he keeps tropical fish as a hobby and is worried about who will care for them while he's in prison. He brings a toy fish-tank to prison and we sympathize with him when it is smashed by an angry prison guard.

In season 4, Wee-Bey is in prison, and De'Londa is essentially single parent to Namond. She lives with her son in a nice (although gaudily furnished) apartment, buys him nice school clothes and, of the four young friends, he is the only one with a parent watching out for him. Namond's fate turns on the conflict between De'Londa and Howard 'Bunny' Colvin (Robert Wisdom), who is helping lead an intervention programme for at-risk kids in which Namond is enrolled. Bunny is, for *The Wire*, an almost saintly figure. We meet him in season 2 as a Major in the Baltimore Police, who is deeply troubled by the department's punitive and statistics-driven approach to the drug war. In season 3, he risks his career by establishing, on his own, a zone in his district where drug dealing will essentially be legalized. By confining the drug trade to this one small area (called Hamsterdam), crime and violence in the rest of the district declines and ordinary residents are seen reclaiming their streets. The experiment is shut down, however, and Bunny loses his job after Hamsterdam becomes a political football in the mayoral elections. He eventually finds a rewarding job working with a Johns Hopkins professor on the intervention programme where he meets Namond.

While Namond's mother pushes him to become more like his father, i.e. to become more serious in his drug dealing in order to move up in the Barksdale organization, it takes Bunny – and not Namond's mother – to see a different set of possibilities. Bunny believes that Namond is a smart and sensitive young man, ill-suited to his underworld path. With the proper support, he believes Namond might actually escape the drug trade and the street. The conflict between the two adults comes to a head when Namond is arrested for drug dealing and Bunny intervenes to get him out of jail. When Bunny brings Namond home, De'Londa is outraged. She berates her son for being so weak that he cannot endure 'baby booking' and warns Colvin to stay away from her son.

Ultimately, Bunny and his wife decide they want to adopt Namond informally, but De'Londa resists giving up her son. Bunny goes to prison to talk to Wee-Bey and tells him that Namond is not a 'soldier' like his father. Rather, Namond can escape the streets and become anything he wants to be, 'maybe even president.' Convinced by Bunny, Wee-Bey tells De'Londa that he has decided that it's best for their son that he live with the Colvin's.

When De'Londa is resistant, Wee-Bey chillingly threatens her, saying that even though he is in prison, there is nowhere she can hide where he cannot find her. Not only is De'Londa portrayed as an evil, inept parent: she is weak as well compared to Namond's more criminal father – who is portrayed, paradoxically and inexplicably, as the superior parent. We last see Namond enjoying a warm family dinner with Bunny and his family.

Throughout the season, the conflict between the two adults is presented in stark terms. De'Londa is portrayed as unsympathetic and self-interested; she is constantly pushing Namond to be more aggressive, more involved in the drug trade and focused on becoming a good earner for the Barksdales (and by implication for her as well). Bunny, on the other hand, is a warm, honest and generous figure (throughout all the episodes in which he appears), only interested in what is best for Namond, an escape from the streets.

Yet, if we use scholarly ethnographies of inner-city neighbourhoods, this stark contrast between 'street culture' and 'middle-class culture' is a vastly over-simplified portrayal of the situation facing De'Londa and Namond (e.g. Bourgois 2003; Goffman 2014; Leap 2012; Venkatesh 2008, 2009). Elijah Anderson's (1999) seminal ethnography of inner-city Philadelphia, for example, finds that anytime they venture outside, even children from solidly 'decent families' (as he labels them) must abandon the values they learn at home and negotiate a very different street culture. This requires of them a sophisticated ability to 'code switch' between the two sets of cultural values. In most ways, The Wire, especially in season 4, addresses the necessity of code switching, its difficulties and the psychic toll it takes on children trying to be decent. The issue we raise here is that the show's plotting makes Bunny the voice of decent values, and allows him to swoop in and remove Namond from the environment in which he and both his parents have always lived. This eliminates the whole issue of the difficulties of code switching and the life-and-death necessity of understanding the street-culture values voiced by De'Londa, and thereby reinforces this unflattering portrayal of yet another prototypically blameworthy black mother. It also leads to the unsettling portrayal of Wee-Bey as the 'good' parent who acts in Namond's interests, as opposed to his black single mother De'Londa.

Donnette (Shamyl Brown) is the 'baby Mama' of D'Angelo Barksdale, a major character in seasons 1 and 2. D'Angelo is Avon Barksdale's nephew and we first meet him in episode 1, season 1, where witness intimidation by the Barksdale gang gets him acquitted of a murder charge. D'Angelo's story arc shows what happens when a drug dealer, even one with familial connections to the leader of his gang, has a conscience. D'Angelo is shown having incredible guilt about the killing of one of the witnesses to his crime. This guilt is manipulated by the police. As we will see below, D'Angelo winds up agreeing to be sentenced to a long prison term for another crime in order to shorten the sentence of his uncle Avon Barksdale. He sacrifices for the family. And in fact, his mother does not come to his defense (as we discuss below).

Donnette is D'Angelo's girlfriend and the mother of his son. We first meet Donnette when D'Angelo takes her out to dinner at an expensive downtown Baltimore restaurant. In one of the more memorable scenes from The Wire, we see these two young African Americans from the inner-city ghetto being made to feel extremely uncomfortable in this setting. At first, we follow the camera and see only white faces in the establishment: initially, the issue is that they are the only black faces. After establishing this, the camera roams more thoroughly, revealing that there are also many middle-class black diners; at this point, the issue becomes the intersection of race and class, a central issue for the show. In this particular scene, it is D'Angelo who seems most uncomfortable and wonders to Donnette: 'Do they know where we are from; e.g. does it (our background) show?' Donnette, one of many harder female voices on the wrong side of the law, is not sympathetic to D'Angelo's social sensitivity. Basically, she tells him that the only thing that matters is the money he has. This establishes her as yet another female character on the wrong side of the law with eyes focused solely on the 'bottom line', while it's left to male characters to express the more subtle and emotional toll that blacks from inner-city Baltimore face in a variety of unfamiliar social settings.

We see Donnette again much later, in season 2, after D'Angelo has been sentenced and is already in prison. The Barksdale gang is worried that D'Angelo might give evidence about the family in exchange for a shorter sentence. Stringer Bell, Avon Barksdale's right-hand man and one of the more compelling and memorable villains in *The Wire*, pays Donnette a personal visit. He tells Donnette that she needs to visit D'Angelo more often in prison to make it clear that he is still 'in the family' and that the Barksdale organization is taking care of her and his son.

Donnette agrees to this, but then proceeds to allow herself to be seduced by Stringer. The seduction begins when Donnette asks Stringer if he wants a new sweater that has been bought for D'Angelo, even though it might be too small for Stringer (in a nod to his 'built' body and sex appeal; Idris Elba, who plays Stringer Bell, is much larger than Lawrence Gillard Jr, who plays D'Angelo). However, unlike in the case of the more law-abiding female characters, we never see the actual sex; therefore, we don't know if it's good, bad or indifferent sex, or whether she experiences any pleasure in the act. She's wild; but then again, she's not – at least, not in the way of the show's middle-class women, who have sex and like it. What we do see as the couple begins to kiss and touch, however, is the camera moving from them to a family picture of D'Angelo, Donnette and their son, sitting on the side table, underscoring how unfaithful she is being to her family unit and thus what a terrible mother and partner she is. The sympathy and, indeed, amused acceptance accorded McNulty's unfaithfulness, for example, is entirely absent in this portrayal.

In a second example, we consider the story of Brianna Barksdale, D'Angelo's mother and Avon Barksdale's sister. Brianna is never seen taking any pleasure, in sex or in any other area of life. After D'Angelo has been arrested for murder, the police offer to place him in the witness protection programme if he will testify against the Barksdales. D'Angelo is sorely tempted to take the deal because he sees that this is his only way out of a life that this introspective, sensitive and moral young man is ill-suited to lead. This would lead to the weakening and perhaps destruction of the entire Barksdale family and would certainly jeopardize his mother's position.

D'Angelo's mother Brianna realizes he is tempted to take the deal, and prefers to preserve her and her brothers' strength, from which she benefits, even though her son faces up to 20 years in prison if he does not turn evidence. She manages to find out where D'Angelo is being held by the police (who had attempted to keep it secret) with the help of the Barksdales. When she finally finds D'Angelo, she tells him that 'if he wants, Avon will "take the weight", and go to prison for decades', even though we know that there's actually no indication that Avon ever considered doing this, or would; but that if that's what D'Angelo wants, this would mean that he would have to become head of the Barksdale family, something both he and his mother know fully well he is completely unsuited to doing. In one of the more chilling scenes from the first season, Brianna convinces D'Angelo that entering the witness protection programme will mean he loses his family, and that if he loses his family, he loses all. Like De'Londa, Brianna is shown to be placing her own welfare above the welfare of her child.[7] She is a prototypically selfish mother.

While there are a lot of gratuitous shots of sex and nudity in *The Wire*, the only person on the wrong side of the law having what seems to be enjoyable and emotionally connected sex is Omar, the gay stick-up boy. Omar is shown naked in bed, soothing his lover, who is jealous of the two gay women stick-up 'boys' in the gang. Omar reassures him, saying 'he don't go that way', they engage in a long, lingering French kiss. Gender as well as sexuality matters, obviously, in these portrayals.

Class is central as well to the varying portrayals of women, even more so than race, as women on the 'right side' of the law, irrespective of race, are portrayed remarkably differently from the criminals. The former are permitted 'wild' behaviour vis-à-vis sexual activity in a way that the latter, inexplicably, are not. At several points in the show, we see the African American lesbian cop Kima having sex, which is filmed as eminently pleasurable with both her partner Cheryl (Melanie Nicholls-King) and co-parent, and later on with a one-stand night 'pickup'. Similarly, the prosecutor Rhonda Pearlman is pictured having very enjoyable wild sex with McNulty, and several seasons later, with the African-American police captain Cedric Daniels. Interestingly, though Daniels had been married to an African-American politician, we never see him having sex with his wife, and neither have we seen McNulty having sex with his ex-wife. And though McNulty is for a while in a stable relationship with Amy Ryan, single mother of two, they are never shown in sexual play. McNulty's more casual sexual encounters are continually hinted at, as he is shown often in pick-up bars (usually with the married Kima), and we do see him graphically enjoying his affair with Pearlman. In sum, there are plenty of 'wild times' on *The Wire* had by almost all – except underclass African American women.

Conclusion

Like many HBO shows, *The Wire* seems to delight in the ability of pay cable to show explicit sex and nudity, and to push the boundaries of how explicit the portrayal of sex can be on television. The show portrays plenty of wild times. Further, sex on *The Wire* is often transgressive: we see gay stick-up boys; lesbian police officers; and casual sex way outside marriage or commitment.

Gender as a category is also pushed to the limit in the character of Snoop, a gender-neutral stick-up person. Snoop is ordinarily a woman dressed in gender-neutral male attire; yet she calls attention to her liminal status in this wild scene. Felicia 'Snoop' Pearson's first lines in HBO's prime-time drama *The Wire* (2002–2008) in response to rising drug kingpin Marlo Stansfield's coded instructions ('Your turn, girl') are the reply, 'It's about time [...] for real' ('Back Burners' 2004) (Youtube 2009). In the next scene, the audience watches as Snoop approaches a corner controlled by the rival Barksdale organization on the back of a motorcycle disguised in a pink satin jacket and tight three-quarter length jeans. When the bike stops, she leans back, pulls out a semi-automatic handgun and begins spraying bullets. With two low ranking members of the Barksdale organization lying on the ground, the bike pulls off revealing hair adorned with pink bows. The femininity on display, both regarding her disguise and her position on the back of motorcycle, is particularly striking, given that her previous appearances were marked as masculine through body language, baggy jeans and over-sized tee shirts. Yet, beyond Snoop's gender ambiguity, it is difficult to read this murder of a largely anonymous soldier (another more familiar character was unharmed in the shooting) as an antiheroic act.[9]

Though in this scene Snoop murders, we never see her/him having much fun; nor is she portrayed as a sexual being. One of the unintended take-aways of *The Wire* is that people can have transgressive and enjoyable sex, but only when they are gay men, straight men or women on the 'right side' of the law. On the 'street', we almost never see explicit sex; even more scarce are women who enjoy it in this setting. Additionally, street mothers seem to take little pleasure from their maternal role; often, they are hardly maternal in any of their actions. Interestingly, they are shown as having *only* male children: a mainstay of the transgressive pleasures of the 'woman's film', there are no mother-daughter 'street' couples on *The Wire* (Kaplan 1990; Williams 1990). The women on the street remain 'guilty' – in their roles as sexual partners and as mothers. They gain status through their male partners and sons, but offer little loyalty or love in return. They have sex, but the consequence is betrayal or unwanted motherhood, rather than pleasure or love.

The male figure of the gay stick-up boy Omar is portrayed quite differently, as a devoted and tender lover. In his story, we begin to see what a more passionate portrayal of personal life on the street might look like. He launches one of the central plot-arcs, beginning a vendetta against the people he thinks are responsible for killing and torturing one of his treasured lovers. The underclass female characters are not afforded this position, however, and remain difficult for viewers to place as central objects of identification. Contrary to the typical protagonist of quality television, which Mittell argues serves as the audience's 'primary point of ongoing narrative alignment [...] but whose behaviour and beliefs provoke ambiguous, conflicted, or negative moral allegiance', these underclass African American women do not provoke ambiguous or conflicted moral allegiance at all: they are almost entirely negative characters in a moral sense and continue popular culture's unfortunate proclivity to portray the African American underclass with little sympathy, understanding or structural truth. We expected better from *The Wire*, but were disappointed.

References

Anderson, E. (1999), *Code of the Street: Decency, Violence, and the Moral Life of the Inner City*, New York: Norton.

Ault, E. (2012), '"You can help yourself/but don't take too much": African American motherhood on *The Wire*', *Television and New Media*, 14: 5, pp. 386–401.

'Back Burners' (2004), Tim Van Patten, dir., *The Wire*, Season 3, Episode 7, November 7, New York: HBO.

Bennett, D. (2010), 'This will be on the midterm: You feel me?' *Slate*, 24 March, http://www.slate.com/articles/arts/culturebox/2010/03/this_will_be_on_the_midterm_you_feel_me.html. Accessed 29 July 2015.

Bogle, D. (2001), *Toms, Coons, Mulattoes, Mammies, and Bucks: An Interpretive History of Blacks in American Films, Fourth Edition*, London: Bloomsbury Academic.

Britton, D. M. (2000), 'Feminism in criminology: Engendering the outlaw', *Annals of the American Academy of Political and Social Sciences*, 571, September, pp. 57–76.

Bourgois, P. (2003), *In Search of Respect: Selling Crack in El Barrio*, New York: Cambridge University Press.

Carey, K. (2007), 'A show of honesty', *The Guardian*, 13 February, http://www.theguardian.com/commentisfree/2007/feb/13/thewire. Accessed 29 July 2015.

Chaddha, A. and Wilson, W. J. (2010), 'Why we're teaching *The Wire* at Harvard', *The Washington Post*, 12 September, http://www.washingtonpost.com/wp-dyn/content/article/2010/09/10/AR2010091002676.html. Accessed 31 July 2015.

Chaddha, A., Wilson W. J. and Venkatesh S. (2008), 'In defense of *The Wire*', *Dissent*, 55: 3, pp. 83–86.

Dow, B. (1996), *Prime-Time Feminism: Television, Media Culture, and the Women's Movement Since 1970*, Philadelphia: University of Pennsylvania Press.

Goffman, A. (2014), *On The Run*, New York: Picador.

Itzkoff, D. (2014), 'For 'Game of Thrones', rising unease over rape's recurring role', *New York Times*, 2 March, http://www.nytimes.com/2014/05/03/arts/television/for-game-of-thrones-rising-unease-over-rapes-recurring-role.html?_r=0. Accessed 7 August 2015.

Kaplan, E. A. (1990), 'The case of the missing mother: Maternal issues in Vidor's *Stella Dallas*', in P. Erens (ed.), *Issues in Feminist Film Criticism*, Bloomington: Indiana University Press, pp. 126–136.

Kennedy, L. and Shapiro S. (eds) (2012), *The Wire: Race, Class, and Genre*, Ann Arbor: University of Michigan Press.

Koehler, S. (2014), 'The sexual politics of nudity on HBO's hit television shows', *Pacific Standard*, 30 June, http://www.psmag.com/books-and-culture/sexual-politics-full-frontal-nudity-hbos-hit-television-shows-84737. Accessed 7 August 2015.

Lauzen, M. M. (2015), 'It's a man's (celluloid) world: On-screen representations of female characters in the top 100 films of 2014', http://womenintvfilm.sdsu.edu/files/2014_Its_a_Mans_World_Report.pdf. Accessed 29 July 2015.

Ladd-Taylor, M. and Umansky, L. (1998), *'Bad' Mothers: The Politics of Blame in Twentieth-Century America*, New York: New York University Press.

Leap, J. (2012), *Jumped In: What Gangs Taught Me About Violence, Drugs, Love and Redemption*, Boston: Beacon.

Lippman, L. (2009), 'The women of *The Wire* (no, seriously)', in R. Alvarez (ed.), *The Wire: Truth be Told*, New York: Grove Press, pp. 54–60.

Lotz, A. D. (2006), *Redesigning Women: Television After the Network Era*, Urbana: University of Illinois Press.

Martin, B. (2013), *Difficult Men: Behind the Scenes of a Creative Revolution, From the Sopranos and The Wire to Mad Men and Breaking Bad*, New York: Penguin.

Miller, R. and Traister, R. (2007), 'The best TV show of all time', *Salon*, 15 September, http://www.salon.com/2007/09/15/best_show/. Accessed 29 July 2015.

Mittell, J. (2013), 'Complex TV: The poetics of contemporary television storytelling', http://mcpress.media-commons.org/complextelevision/serial-melodrama/. Accessed 7 August 2015.

Moore, M. H. and Braga, A. A. (2003), 'Measuring and improving police performance: The lessons of Compstat and its progency', *Policing: An International Journal of Police Strategies and Management*, 26: 3, pp. 439–453.

Moynihan, D. P. (1965), *The Negro Family: The Case for National Action*, Washington: Office of Policy Planning and Research, U.S. Department of Labor.

Newman, M. and Levine, E. (2011), *Legitimating Television: Media Convergence and Cultural Status*, London: Routledge.

Olmstead, K. (2011), *The Wire: The Untold History of Television*, New York: Harper Collins.

Paskin, W. (2013), 'Was 2013 the year the TV antihero died?', *Slate*, 25 December.

Potter, T. and Marshall, C. W. (eds) (2009), *The Wire: Urban Decay and American Television*, London: Bloomsbury Academic.

Press, A. (2009), 'Gender and family in television's golden age and beyond', *The Annals of the American Academy of Political and Social Science*, 625: 1, pp. 139–150.

Roush, M. (2013), 'Showstoppers: The 60 greatest dramas of all time', *TV Guide*, pp. 16–17.

Shafter, D. M. and Raney, A. A. (2012), 'Exploring how we enjoy antihero narratives', *Journal of Communication*, 62: 6, pp. 2018–2046.

Simon, D. and Burns, E. (1998), *The Corner: A Year in the Life of an Inner-City Neighborhood*, New York: Broadway Books.

Smith, S. L. (2008), 'Gender stereotypes: An analysis of popular films and TV', http://www.seejane.org/wp-content/uploads/GDIGM_Gender_Stereotypes.pdf. Accessed 29 July 2015.

The Wire (2002–2008, USA: HBO).

Ulaby, N. (2013), 'Working women on television: A mixed bag', *NPR Radio IQ*, 18 May, http://www.npr.org/sections/monkeysee/2013/05/18/184832930/working-women-on-television-a-mixed-bag-at-best. Accessed 2 August 2015.

Venkatesh, S. A. (2008), *Gang Leader for a Day: A Rogue Sociologist Takes to the Streets*, New York: Penguin Books.

——— (2009), *Off the Books: The Underground Economy of the Urban Poor*, Cambridge: Harvard University Press.

Wilde, J. (2007), '*The Wire* is unmissable television', *The Guardian*, 21 July, http://www.theguardian.com/culture/tvandradioblog/2007/jul/21/thewireisunmissabletelevis. Accessed 29 July 2015.

Williams, B. A. and Press, A. L. (forthcoming), 'Women of the *Wire*', *Intersections*, 1: 1.

Williams, L. (1990), 'Something else besides a mother: *Stella Dallas* and maternal melodrama', in P. Erens (ed.), *Issues in Feminist Film Criticism*, Bloomington: Indiana University Press, pp. 137–162.

Wilson, W. J. (1997), *When Work Disappears: The World of the New Urban Poor*, New York: Vintage.

Youtube (2009), 'The Wire – Snoop's Turn', http://www.youtube.com/watch?v=jTLhRojxEtk. Accessed 23 June 2016.

Notes

1 This approach is evident in the series' very first scene (based upon an actual story told to David Simon by Baltimore police). One of the main characters, Detective Jimmie McNulty (Dominic West), is interviewing a young black man who has witnessed the murder of another young black man who had ripped-off a crap game. He tells the detective that the dead young man had regularly played in the game and always tried to steal money. McNulty asks the young man why, if he always tried to steal the money, he was still allowed to play. 'Got to man, this is America man'.

2 The Moynihan Report was written in 1965 by Daniel Patrick Moynihan, Assistant Secretary of Labor under Lyndon Johnson. It chronicled the rise of black single-parent families and ghettos and blamed many of the ills of African Americans in our society on this family form (Moynihan 1965).

3 Indeed, later in the episode, Daniel tells his immediate superior that Griggs is the best detective he has.

4 See Ulaby (2013) on the increasing but mixed representation of professional women on popular television.

5 This reinforces the show's distressing failure to deal with rape or sexual assault, which we discuss below.

6 In Daniels' case, his wife Marla Daniels (Maria Broom) is an elected Baltimore City Council member.

7 Of course, this is one step up from Tony Soprano's mother, who seems to go along with ordering a hit upon her own son. Though this is a white family, this mother is truly a new low (Martin 2013).

8 We are indebted to Michael Wayne for bringing this incident to our attention, and for the discussion of many of the ideas in the broader paper.

Chapter 13

Taming Pussytown: How Post-feminism Domesticated *Underbelly: Razor*

Leigh Redhead

Australian Antiheroines

In 2011 the television trailers for the new season of the *Underbelly* franchise, *Underbelly: Razor*, were aired frequently on the commercial broadcast network, Channel Nine, revealing a colourful and glossy big-budget production. The minute-long advertisements were accompanied by contemporary songs – Adele's *Rolling in the Deep* and an industrial dance version of 1980s hit *Tainted Love* – and looked like music videos. Fast cuts revealed attractive actors in 1920s costume dancing, drinking and snorting cocaine. Glamorous, pin-curled prostitutes shimmied in silky lingerie and feather boas while men in hats and three-piece suits brawled and brandished guns and cut-throat razors. The words 'Two women rule' flashed up on the screen in a blood-spattered font, and the viewer was introduced to 'vice queens' Kate Leigh and Tilly Devine: beautiful young women clad in fringed dresses and cloche hats who were shown undressing seductively, screaming, sobbing and fighting each other in the street. 'But who', the titles ask, 'will conquer?'

As a crime author who likes to write and read about complex female characters, I was looking forward to *Underbelly: Razor*. I had heard of Kate Leigh and Tilly Devine, real-life characters who had run sly grog (illegal alcohol) shops and brothels in depression-era Sydney, and was aware the programme was being based on a meticulously researched book *The Razor Wars* by Larry Writer. I was also excited at the prospect of seeing transgressive female characters on-screen in leading roles with not one, but two women protagonists. Since the end of *Prisoner* (known in the United Kingdom and United States as *Prisoner: Cell Block H*), lead roles for women on Australian commercial television have been commonly confined to nurturing mothers, plucky police officers, caring nurses, crusading lawyers and professional women juggling careers and family while looking for love. It would be nice to see a couple of antiheroines on the screen for a change.

Australians have always had a soft spot for an antihero, from nineteenth-century bushranger Ned Kelly to fictional outlaw Mad Max. And while the television industry has depicted many female villains, the only notable antiheroine, before *Underbelly: Razor* (2011) and *Wentworth* (2013–2015), was *Prisoner* (1979–1986) character Bea Smith (Val Lehman). Bea was a double murderer and 'top dog' of Wentworth prison, and the character appeared in 376 episodes of the show from 1979 to 1983. She is a classic antiheroine, managing, like Tony Soprano, to be 'simultaneously charismatic and menacing [...]' (Paskin 2013). Viewers empathize with Bea when she targets drug dealers and child abusers, but are appalled by her actions when she goes too far. The scene where Bea burns the hands of a fellow inmate in the laundry steam press is still recalled with a shudder by those who watched the show as children in the late 1970s.

At first glance, the characters of Kate Leigh and Tilly Devine seem to fulfil the requirements necessary to achieve antiheroine status. As women controlling criminal organizations, they are flouting traditional gender roles and breaking the rules of both 'respectable' society and the underworld subculture. They have (criminal) agency at a time when most women, particularly working-class women, had no agency at all. However, a female antihero is not so much defined by her occupation as by her complexity, her dubious moral code and the way she challenges patriarchal values. Unlike a villain, the viewer generally desires for the antiheroine to succeed, except for those moments where she crosses a moral line, causing the same viewer to recoil, but only temporarily. After all, the antiheroine protagonist's ambiguous and often perverse ethical framework is fascinating to watch. These characters create a state of uncertainty in viewers who sometimes cheer on the antiheroine's actions, and at other times reject them.

While Kate and Tilly appear at first to be antiheroines, it soon becomes apparent that they are not antiheroic in any meaningful way. I will argue that the post-feminist sensibility that permeates the series robs the characters of any moral complexity, prevents any questioning of the patriarchal status quo and leaves the viewer with one heroine and one villainess, instead of two antiheroines.

Underbelly

The first season of *Underbelly* was based on a best-selling true crime book, *Leadbelly: Inside Australia's Underworld* by journalists John Sylvester and Andrew Rule. The show was set in Melbourne, and covered the period from the mid-1990s to 2004 when rival outfits battled to control Melbourne's drug trade. In all, more than 30 people were murdered in what the newspapers dubbed 'The Gangland War' (Australian Associated Press 2010a).

The show was a huge success, one of the highest rating Australian television programmes in history, despite being banned in Victoria for seven months while criminal trials involving the real characters concluded. The ban served to heighten interest in, and gain publicity for, the production. A trade in bootleg DVD copies sprang up and many Australians made their first foray into illegal Internet downloading to access the series (Gregg and Wilson 2010: 417).

The success of the first *Underbelly* has been attributed to a number of factors, including the contemporary nature of the events and the enthusiasm with which Australians have always celebrated criminal antiheroes such as Chopper Read, a notorious Australian villain who published his memoirs as popular true crime titles (Pickering 2014: 90). Gregg and Wilson ascribe *Underbelly*'s popularity to familiar locations and actors, and the fun of seeing the cast abandon their usual good-guy roles to play excessive, murderous and distinctly Australian suburban gangsters (417). Sue Turnbull also cites the 'pleasure of recognition'

(2014: 227) as a factor in the show's success. The aforementioned controversy around the banning of the series certainly played a role, as did the graphic scenes of sex and violence and the show's general 'voyeuristic appeal' (Kroenert 2009). The popularity of the first *Underbelly* paved the way for multiple seasons of the show, all focusing on different gangs and eras in Australia's true crime history.

I enjoyed the first season of *Underbelly*, but it was a guilty pleasure. Women were consigned to the background in most episodes, and apart from the wives and girlfriends of the gangsters, female characters were mostly strippers and prostitutes depicted in scenes that focused on sex and nudity. As a former sex worker, I am not at all opposed to sex and nudity on screen (or in real life), but as a feminist I am troubled when this is the only aspect of the sex worker experience that is portrayed. And while there were scenes with naked male actors, these were not as abundant as those featuring the female cast. As Turnbull put it: 'I expected the sex, I just did not expect quite so many gratuitous boobs and bums jiggling and bobbing up and down front and centre so obviously and so often' (2014: 227). Turnbull, citing Negra, has described *Underbelly* as 'the kind of post-feminist television crime show that had "just about forgotten feminism"' (Turnbull 2014: 226, citing Negra 2009).

I had hoped that *Underbelly: Razor*, with two female protagonists driving the action, would redress the original series' anti-feminist representation of women. Unfortunately, it was not to be. I watched the first few episodes of the show then turned off, having quickly lost interest. Fellow crime writer Angela Savage blogged that the show was anachronistic and the characters glamorized and sanitized. She posted mug shots of the real women to emphasize her point and wrote: 'The show is soap-opera with cut-throat razors. More entertaining was the commentary on Twitter' (2011). Savage also provided a link to a blog post by Jo Hilder titled 'How to make a TV series about two real middle-aged women without any middle-aged women'. Another author, Josephine Pennicott, blogged that she turned off after the first half hour because of the incongruous casting, historical inaccuracy (a sly grog club that looked like an American speakeasy with a lounge singer crooning a 1980s pop song), unconvincing sets and dialogue, and a style comprising fast cuts and voice-over exposition. 'It's really a video clip rather than a narrative experience' (2011). A review in the *Sydney Morning Herald* stated that 'these liberties and the pop-eye graphics deny *Razor* the realism, gravitas and feel for place offered by *The Wire*'s Baltimore, *Breaking Bad*'s New Mexico or *Boardwalk Empire*'s 1920s Atlantic City' (Burt 2011).

Although I agreed with these sentiments, most viewers did not, and *Underbelly: Razor*, while not as successful overall as the first series, rated highly with the first episode viewed by a record 2.8 million people (Turnbull, citing Throng 2014: 229). Watching the entire 13-episode season in preparation for writing this chapter, however, I became aware that something else was problematic besides the pop songs, MTV visuals and over-glamourized actors. Could it be the post-feminism of which Turnbull and Negra spoke?

Double Entanglements

Mizejewski argues that 'post-feminism' is not a descriptor for a specific era of feminism so much as a term that elucidates 'how filmmakers, audiences and the media may conceptualize certain characters and narratives' (2005: 121). Not a movement or even a direct backlash against feminism, post-feminism therefore constitutes a kind of cultural sensibility, particularly evident in media and popular culture, whereby the work of feminism is assumed to have been done. It implies that equality has arrived, sexism is a thing of the past, and as a result, women are free to throw off the prescriptive shackles of second-wave feminism with all of its negative connotations (shrill, disapproving, butch, boring, playing-the-victim) and embrace their femininity, sexuality and right to choose. Want to be a high flying executive? Kick-ass action hero? Stay-at-home mum? You go, girl! It doesn't sound too bad at first. However, at the same time as post-feminism is espousing certain tenets of feminist politics such as equality in the workplace, individual empowerment and sexual freedom, it is advocating a conformist, neoliberal consumer agenda that not only harbours elements of racism and classism, but also anti-feminism (Holmlund 2005; McRobbie 2007; Tasker and Negra 2007; Vered and Humphries 2014). Angela McRobbie has identified this phenomenon as a 'double entanglement' (2007: 28). For example, post-feminist media presents a discourse that is both 'empowering and objectifying' (Mizejewski 2005) as evident in many music videos featuring female singers in sexualized performances.

Like most dominant discourses, post-feminism is not found just in political rhetoric, but is embedded in all aspects of culture. Common post-feminist tropes include: the 'unquestioned expertise of a woman in a male profession' as exemplified by female action heroes and cops who have risen to the top of their occupations without having to deal with institutionalized sexism (Mizejewski 2005: 123); 'Confident, sexually assertive women [...]' who 'express themselves through private acts of consumption' (Vered and Humphries 2014: 157–158) as seen in *Sex and the City* and *Keeping up with the Kardashians*; and the ascendancy of a commercially constructed femininity that can be achieved with diet and exercise products, make-up, beauty salons and fashion.

Girl culture and youthfulness is also important and can be maintained by an increasingly mainstreamed cosmetic surgery industry. Makeover shows abound and it is interesting that many best-selling books with adult women protagonists have the word 'girl' in the title, while titles about adult men are not similarly infantilized. *Our Boy in Havana* doesn't have quite the same ring to it as *The Girl with the Dragon Tattoo*. Another trope is that of traditional sexual differences and the recurring theme that the pinnacle of female ambition is marriage and children. Much has been written about both the book and the film *Bridget Jones' Diary*, and contemporary dating programmes such as *The Bachelor* continue the refrain. The Australian reality show *The Farmer Wants a Wife* manages to combine this with the notion of 'getting back to basics' – women leaving unsatisfying, high-powered jobs in the city to find happiness baking and engaging in handicrafts. Much post-feminist media is also antagonistic to representations of women in power.

In this chapter, I will consider *Underbelly: Razor* in relation to a post-feminist media landscape and the then current Australian political situation. It might be noted that the show was produced and aired in the period 2010–2011, coinciding with the appointment of Australia's first female prime minister, Julia Gillard, who experienced a barrage of negative, gendered media representation. In the process, I will reveal how a television programme that masqueraded as feminist and transgressive was deeply conservative at heart. Post-feminist and anti-feminist sentiments infiltrate the show through dichotomous and stereotypical representations of women. Female characters are dis-empowered through dialogue and *mise-en-scène*, by a narrative focus on the domestic and maternal, and in the ways in which women and violence are depicted. Post-feminist tropes such as individualism and consumption are embedded in the ideological framework of the text that reflects the Australian media's problematic relationship with women in positions of power.

The Worst Woman in Sydney

Episode 1 was named 'the Worst Woman in Sydney', an ambiguous title that immediately sets up the women as rivals and begs the question: who is the worst woman?

The episode introduces the characters of Kate Leigh (Danielle Cormack) and Tilly Devine (Chelsie Preston Crayford), their families and associates. These include a fellow gangster named Phil 'The Jew' Jeffs (Felix Williamson), the police who are trying to stymie their criminal enterprises and an out-of-town standover man named Norman Bruhn (Jeremy Lindsay Taylor), who is intent on taking over and 'taming pussytown'. This episode will be considered in close detail as it is emblematic of the series as a whole and constitutes a template for subsequent episodes. Narrative elements introduced in the pilot are then repeated and reinforced as the series continues.

'The Worst Woman in Sydney' opens with a shot of a beautiful, dark haired woman who appears to be in her mid to late thirties, reclining in a bath. The female voice-over[1] declares: 'Once upon a time, there lived a beautiful queen called Kate'. Kate then opens her mouth to talk to her daughter, revealing a rough, ocker[2] accent that makes her sound more like a dock worker than royalty. She gets out of the bath and examines herself in the full length mirror. Her naked body is Hollywood-slim and toned. As Kate examines herself in the mirror, the voice-over continues: 'As far as Queen Kate was concerned, the world was very nearly perfect. There was only one small blot on the landscape, and that blot was young and blonde and pretty. She, too, was a queen, and her name was Tilly'. Cut to an image of Tilly Devine, aged in her mid-twenties and also beautiful, with pin-curled platinum blonde hair and heavy make-up. She is seated in a boudoir, wearing satiny lingerie, and looking at herself in the mirror. In a reference to *Snow White*'s evil queen she says, in a cockney accent: 'Mirror mirror on the wall, who's the most gorgeous tart and all?'

The fairy-tale references of this opening, which position both women as 'queens', serve a significant function, positioning the supposedly true crime narrative as untrue, as a story or fable. They also infantilize the account, making it childish and thus draining its potentially transgressive power. The women are not shown as powerful, intimidating crime bosses, but passive, unthreatening and distinctly sexualized: Kate is naked and Tilly wears lingerie. The bathroom and bedroom locations situate them firmly within the domestic sphere where they indulge in 'feminine' pursuits, or at least a male scriptwriter's fantasy of what women get up to in their private spaces: relaxing, grooming and admiring their reflections. Throughout the series, while the male characters are shown being active in public and outdoor areas, the female characters are more usually framed within domestic interiors and are depicted bathing, having sex, cooking, washing and folding clothes. They are rarely pictured in public spaces.

Marise Williams maintains that the domestic *mise-en-scène* in Underbelly: Razor helps to counter the masculine bias of the Underbelly franchise as a whole, and posits that these locations and 'the daily activity of women's domestic labour forms an important, contextualising visual backdrop, and the representation of a female gender economy' (Williams 2012: 18). On the contrary, I would argue that by focusing solely on the domestic, and not juxtaposing these scenes with images of criminal agency and public action, an opportunity has been lost. For example, the pleasure of watching recent male television antiheroes such as *Breaking Bad*'s Walter White frequently resides in discovering that the 'domestic scene [has been] refashioned to conceal a flow of alternative capital: weapons, crime trophies and cash' (Larabee 2013: 1131). This source of pleasure could have been garnered from Underbelly: Razor if we had been presented with the spectacle of watching these women as they organized their complex criminal empires from within their domestic environments.

Good Girl/Bad Girl

Throughout the series, the women are placed in opposition to each other, with Kate masculinized and portrayed as the hero and Tilly depicted as a feminized villain. Kate has many of the attributes of the 'classic' larrikin Australian hero, as celebrated in films such as *Crocodile Dundee*. Russel Ward sums up this type in *The Australian Legend*:

> According to the myth the typical Australian is a practical man, rough and ready in his manners and quick to decry any appearance of affectation in others [...] He is a 'hard case', sceptical about the value of religion and of intellectual and cultural pursuits generally. He believes that Jack is not only as good as his master but [...] probably a good deal better [...] He is a fiercely independent person who hates officiousness and authority [...] Yet he is very hospitable and [...] will stick to his mates through thick and thin [...] He swears hard and consistently, gambles heavily and often, and drinks deeply on occasion.
>
> (Ward 1965: 1–2)

Taming Pussytown: How Post-feminism Domesticated *Underbelly: Razor*

In *Underbelly: Razor*, Kate is ascribed all the qualities of the idealized Australian man (except for the drinking) as well as those of the idealized Australian woman. In a way she is a reworking of the 'bush mum' of literature from the early twentieth century. 'Women who were practical, blended the masculine with the feminine, and who conveyed a sense of classlessness and whiteness' (Gill 2012: 279).

Kate's maleness is first signalled by her speech that completely contradicts her femininity as revealed in the opening images in the bath. As soon as she speaks, the audience recognizes that her voice is deep, 'blokey' and 'ocker' – that of an Australian 'bushman'. Her use of the vernacular, 'not up the duff, are ya?' frequent humour and anti-authoritarian utterances mark her as a (culturally prized) Aussie larrikin type.

Kate's 'feminine' side is brought out in scenes of mothering and nurturing, and rather than the combined masculine/feminine traits indicating a complex character with a fluid relation to gender, the behaviours are read as stereotyped and reactionary: if Kate has acted in a masculine way in one scene, then the next will emphasize her femininity (which is synonymous with maternity) and vice versa. This back-and-forth behaviour, although it seems awkward on screen, actually makes sense when Australian cultural constructions of gender are taken into account.

> Women can be afforded status when they act in ways deemed masculine, but their behaviour will be acceptable within a total social network of meanings only if they remain true to what is believed to be their feminine nature [...] These attributes (being emotional, looking feminine, acting as if motivated by maternal instinct) are marks of femininity within a masculine economy.
>
> (Schaffer 1988: 14)

Schaffer also argues that to define Australian 'national character' is to compare it to 'what it is not'. And in many cultural products this opposition manifests itself in the 'male, Western, neo-colonial, Australian hero of the bush' versus 'the British parental authority representing old world bourgeois culture' (Schaffer 1988: 20). This dichotomy is particularly evident in the construction of Kate as hero and Tilly as antagonist, where Kate is set up as the unpretentious 'Aussie Battler' in the style of bushranger Ned Kelly or an ANZAC at Gallipoli, while Tilly's accent, pompous statements, obsession with King and Country, acquisition of cars and property, desire for veneration and general air of superiority mark her as the colonial overlord – often represented in Australian film and television as the colonial police who hunt Ned Kelly, or the British officers who sip tea, while sending young Australian soldiers to their deaths in the first world war.

As the series progresses, each episode contrasts the two characters, reinforcing Kate as a 'good' woman and Tilly as 'bad'. If Kate appears in her kitchen preparing food for her family, then Tilly is shown swearing and smoking cigarettes. Kate has sex with her de-facto partner Wally (John Batchelor) in the woman-on-top position, establishing her as a strong, sexual post-feminist woman and therefore 'good'. Soon after, Tilly is beaten by her husband when she confronts him about his infidelities. Tilly always forgives and makes excuses for her husband's violence, setting her up as weak and complicit in male aggression – not a post-feminist position at all. Tilly is shown attacking and biting one of Kate's female cocaine dealers, then the image cuts to Kate meeting a police officer in church, talking with him about god, and lighting a candle for the now-deceased Norman Bruhn. Kate, despite running sly grog shops, is a teetotaller, Tilly drinks and smokes to excess and snorts cocaine.

Other ways in which Tilly is set up as the 'bad girl' to Kate's good is her anti-maternal, non-'family values' depiction. In the first episode, Kate is in her kitchen, making scones for her family and a police officer. The next scene shows Tilly telling her husband Jim (Jack Campbell) to punch a pregnant prostitute in the abdomen so she'll abort her foetus. As he does so, she calmly discusses buying him a 'big, shiny new car'. Immediately, the image cuts to Tilly in a home for unwed mothers, recruiting young women who have just given birth to work in her brothels. Tilly's role as a 'bad mother' is further reinforced in 'Jerusalem Revisited' (2011) when it is revealed Tilly has a six-year-old son in care of her parents back in England. As Tilly tries to engage with the boy it is obvious he is frightened of her, yelling 'you're not my mother' and 'I hate you'.

Despite Writer (2009) stating that both of the women were devout Catholics, Tilly is never shown in church. She is in the brothel, the boudoir and her domestic labour is confined to folding satiny underthings. Tilly's background as a prostitute is mentioned often, and although the real Kate Leigh was also a prostitute working on the mean streets of Sydney for many years, this is not mentioned in the series. In Australian commercial television, graphic violence, nudity, sex scenes and sex worker characters are allowed, but a current or former sex worker as protagonist appears to be forbidden.[3]

Anachronism

After the initial introduction, the commentary explains who each of the women are (exposition and foreshadowing through voice-over and on-screen titles are a feature of all the *Underbellys*): Kate is the bootleg liquor proprietor and Tilly the brothel owner. In typical *Underbelly* style this is done with a series of fast cuts, using images of nightclub patrons drinking and dancing and prostitutes getting ready for the night ahead. The soundtrack to this is a song by Split Enz that was a hit in Australia in the 1980s – *The Nips are Getting Bigger*, performed in this instance by the 1920s nightclub band. This obvious historical anachronism situates the narrative in an ironic, postmodern space that is highly artificial and stylized, neither past nor present, resulting in a fantastic, dream-like feel. This effect is reinforced when the exterior scenes appear – the streets of Sydney's between-war slums are Disneyland clean and the computer-generated historical backdrops have a cloudy, painted look. The lack of verisimilitude contributes to the fairy-tale feeling, reassuring the viewer that women gangsters aren't real.

Taming Pussytown: How Post-feminism Domesticated *Underbelly: Razor*

The Feud

In a subsequent scene, Tilly is shown reading a newspaper in which Kate is described as the 'worst woman in Sydney'. Tilly is apparently jealous that Kate is getting more recognition than she is, and the voice-over states that 'even ninety years ago, the cult of celebrity was irresistible'.

The feud between Kate and Tilly is then explained through a short scene in which the women meet on a street and, with strained politeness, comment on the fluffy Pomeranian dogs each is carrying. Tilly's imperialist pretentions are revealed as she mentions 'the royal family have Pomeranians' while Kate displays her down-to-earth, antimonarchist persona by joking: 'Oh, for afternoon tea, you mean, on toast?' Kate agrees, however, to lend her stud dog to Tilly for breeding purposes. Tilly then decides she doesn't want to give him back, instead returning an inferior, infertile dog, disguised to look like Kate's original. This is the first of many scenes in which Tilly is associated with infertility and anti-maternal sentiment. When Kate confronts Tilly at her terrace house, calling her a 'thieving Pommy bitch', Tilly pours the contents of a bedpan over her head. The voice-over states 'And that's how Kate and Tilly's decade-long feud started – over nothing. Over a borrowed dog'.

This is presented as a flimsy premise for a bloody feud, and it once again suggests the women are childish, as though they don't have the serious concerns and high stakes of male gangsters. Walter White in *Breaking Bad* feuds with Mexican drug lords over control of methamphetamine manufacture and distribution and to protect his family, in *Boardwalk Empire*, Nucky Thompson's conflicts stem from a deadly bootlegging heist, Ray Donovan in the eponymous television show struggles with his father over murder, money and being abandoned to paedophile priests and in the original *Underbelly* the gang war is a result of factions battling to control Melbourne drug supply.

I wondered if the scene was included in a nod to historical accuracy, so checked the book on which the television series was based. According to Writer:

> [...] the women despised each other. Kate and Tilly's enmity was not totally professional, but also borne of a fierce personal rivalry. As the only two female arch-criminals in Sydney, each stove to outdo the other, to be richer, more powerful, more feared, dress more lavishly, and get more and bigger headlines in the papers.
>
> (2001)

Kate and Tilly would each give newspaper interviews castigating the other. In one, Kate said that she 'once loaned Tilly Devine a dog and that woman never returned it'. Tilly retaliated with '[...] never in my life did she give me a dog. They are my dogs!' (Writer 2001: 145).

While it may be the case that the women's feud included an exchange of Pomeranians, it is arguable that their 'fierce personal rivalry' could have been depicted in a more potent way. The sequence's purpose is therefore not to attain historical verisimilitude, nor is it to provide a comic breather between scenes of violent action. Instead its motivation appears twofold: to set up Tilly Devine as the antagonist and to undermine the power of the main female characters – portraying them as fluffy and unthreatening – just like the Pomeranians they're fighting over.

Gentle Sexism and 'The Unquestioned Expertise of Women in Male Profession'

Another feature of the first episode is the institution of a kind of 'gentle sexism' that, I will argue, is representative of post-feminism's repudiation of feminist inquiry. As with McRobbie's 'double entanglement', this mild chauvinism is actually disguised as critique, a sort of 'look at the sort of sexist things women had to put up with back then' that refuses to investigate deep structural and political inequities.

In 'The Worst Woman in Sydney', Norman Bruhn, the thuggish gangster, is on his way from Melbourne to Sydney to try and take over the sly grog and brothel game from the women. Norm and his criminal associate Squizzy Taylor (Justin Rosniak) refer to Sydney as 'Pussytown' and Squizzy instructs Norm to 'Kick Kate in the balls' for him. They think that seizing the criminal enterprises of a couple of women will be easy.

Although Australia was the second country in the world to legislate women to vote (unless they were indigenous), the 1920s and 1930s were hardly progressive as far as women's civic, social and political rights were concerned. However, these conditions, and the fact that Kate and Tilly rose to such powerful positions within them, are mostly overlooked by the series. It is as though the post-feminist 'all the gains have been made' argument has been transferred onto the interwar years, and there is very little mention of inequality. When it is mentioned, it is done so in a very mild and personal way: individual bad guys make sexist comments, or male police officers suggest their female counterparts should 'get a husband'. It is only in episode 5, 'The Darlinghurst Outrage', that any social inequality is addressed. This episode by female scriptwriter Michaeley O'Brien focuses on the gang rape case of a woman who (unusually for *Underbelly: Razor*) is a prostitute *and* a married mother of two. The episode deals with issues of class and consent, Williams describing it as 'a historical vignette which highlights the reality of working-class women's lives in the late 1920s and the pervasiveness of prostitution as a career and an occasional financial option' (2012: 20). Writing about the first season of *Underbelly*, Turnbull argues that the female narrator 'was clearly intended to counter accusations of the Channel Nine show's macho posturing' (2014: 226) and that episode 7, 'Wise Monkeys', which dealt with the experiences of female characters, 'went some ways to counter the masculine bias of the series as a whole' (227). I get the feeling that 'The Darlinghurst Outrage' is serving a similar function. It is as though women get one vaguely feminist episode per season of *Underbelly* – just enough to 'counter the masculine bias' – and by the next episode, the show is back to female sexualization and celebratory male violence.

Mizejewski writes of post-feminist female police characters played by Ashley Judd in *Twisted* (2004) and Angelina Jolie in *Taking Lives* (2004), who have reached the top of their profession without having to struggle against institutionalized sexism or the forces of patriarchy. She describes the position of the characters in these movies as 'posited on a 1970s equity-feminist assumption: the unquestioned expertise of a woman in a male profession' (Mizejewski 2005: 123). This is also apparent in *Underbelly: Razor*, where the women's rise to the top is unquestioned and unexamined 'with the postfeminist (actually, anti-feminist) implication being that this polished woman gained her authority on her own' (125).

In this way, the critical question remains unanswered: how did Kate and Tilly gain their authority and rise to the top of a criminal empire in an era when women were so socially disadvantaged? In a production inundated with post-feminist ideology it won't even be asked, nor will the characters be given any backstory that might reveal the answer. As Mizejewski elucidates, 'Cultural sources and narratives about exceptional women are more accessible than the history and discourses of feminism' (125). However, I cannot help but wonder how much more interesting *Underbelly: Razor* would have been if it had included Kate and Tilly's struggle for success.

Damned Whores and God's Police[4]

Two other key characters are introduced in 'The Worst Woman in Sydney', who seem tailor-made to provide a juxtaposition of post-feminism with outmoded second-wave feminism. Nellie Cameron (Anna McGahan) is a teenage prostitute picked up during a raid on the opening night of Tilly's new brothel. Lillian Armfield (Lucy Wigmore) is the arresting officer, apparently the first policewoman in Sydney, if not Australia. Nellie is beautiful, sixteen, educated, from an upper middle-class family and wants very much to work as a prostitute. Tilly and Jim try to dissuade her, but she pesters them until they let her work. When dowdy, middle-aged Lillian takes Nellie back to the station, she tries to 'save' her:

LILLIAN:	Nellie, it worries me when a girl like you finds herself consorting with ne'er-do-wells in a place like that. I've seen many a young girl stray, and I hope you're not one of them. It's all too easy to lose your reputation, and once it's gone, it is gone forever. Promise me you'll go home and forget about tonight's escapade.
NELLIE:	If I stay there, I suffocate. I just wanna live a little bit.
LILLIAN:	As a prostitute?
NELLIE:	Just wanna have some fun.

('The Worst Woman in Sydney' 2011)

Here, Lillian Armfield is standing in for what Charlotte Brunsdon identified as 'fuddy-duddy feminism' or 'feminism [...] perceived as a stern authority figure and an uptight prude' (Akass and McCabe 2006: 53). Variations on this conversation are repeated throughout the season, with Lillian trying to 'save' Nellie from sex work. Lurking in the background here is the sort of second-wave anti-pornography feminism exemplified by Andrea Dworkin and Catharine MacKinnon (and in Australia, Sheila Jeffreys) that equates sex work with rape and adopts a similar discourse to that of conservative, Christian ideologues (Levy 2010: 63–64).

In many ways, Nellie is the perfect post-feminist icon. She is a 'confident, sexually assertive wom[a]n' (Gill 2007: 74) and, at sixteen, still a girl. 'Empowered' by her choice of sex work she is independent of her parents and makes lots of money to spend on fashionable clothes. In a nod to raunch culture, Nellie loves her work as a prostitute and is not averse to a bit of S&M and striptease in her private life. She is in complete control of her older lovers and has a wonderful time playing them off against each other. She is often shown dancing, drinking, partying, having sex and wearing beautiful clothes or gorgeous lingerie. In contrast, Lillian is a staid, drab, teetotaller who dresses like an old fashioned suffragette and is single, possibly lesbian, certainly sexless, and often shown returning sadly to her lonely flat. She is post-feminism's 'single woman-as-lack' (Vered and Humphries 2014: 158) and her brand of prudish, victim feminism is rejected by Nellie and, by extension, the audience.

Prostitution

Underbelly: Razor's depiction of prostitution is certainly glamorized. Unlike the prostitutes and bordellos of, for example, *Deadwood*, everything is sanitized, attractively styled and looks like fun. The prostitution seems 'festive' and the sex workers look like models in a fashion editorial with a 1920s theme (Braham 2011: n.p.). In response, *The Sunday Telegraph* ran a headline: '*Underbelly: Razor*'s myth hides the ugly truth' and the right-wing opinion piece moralized about 'the horrible lie of glamorous sex work' stating that 'visiting prostitutes is wrong', while making a connection between the show and a political scandal involving a Labour Party minister alleged to have used union credit cards to pay for sex (Harvey 2011: n.p.). Australia, however, arguably does not suffer from a puritan hangover about sex (as does American society) and sex workers are not as likely to be depicted as villains unless, like Tilly, they try to gain power and rise above their stations. As Schaffer writes '[in Australia] sex is not an important cultural category of transgression' (1986: 64).

Turnbull argues that while the setting of the show, brothels, 'provided the producers with a legitimate reason for putting attractive women and sex on screen' (2014: 229), they did not have a legitimate reason to show strip clubs – a staple location of previous *Underbellys* – as none existed in the 1920s. However, that did not stop the producers from including a stripping scene in 'Jerusalem Revisited'. Here, a montage of images of police arresting criminals is intercut with a scene at Tilly's brothel, where, to the strains of another Australian 1980s hit *The Boys Light Up*, and for no apparent reason, the prostitutes are giving Jim Devine lap dances. The dancing suggests post-feminist raunch culture once again with the underlying message that sex workers are doing the job because it turns them on, rather than for economic reasons.

Violence

As with all the seasons of *Underbelly* – and indeed any crime show – violence is a key component of the narrative and usually reflects the underlying ideology of the production. Violent scenes are filmed in a stylized, Guy-Ritchie-movie way, with lots of slow motion and jump cuts. They are typically accompanied by Irish style music: an energetic jig for less serious fights; *Danny Boy* to accompany a large street battle in which several characters are seriously injured. This is the slick violence of feature films – exuberant, glossy and choreographed to resemble a kind of macho modern dance.

In *Underbelly: Razor*, the way in which male and female characters carry out violent action is markedly different. In each episode there is a scene of men being violent – punching, slashing or shooting each other – which usually takes place outside, in public spaces, and is brutal, graphic and effective. When not used in defence, the purpose of the violence is to intimidate, gain power or dispatch a rival. Very occasionally it is an expression of sadistic urges.

Men's violence towards women happens less often and includes Norman's S&M play with Nellie, which she enjoys; a gang member occasionally slashing the face of a beautiful prostitute (so that she suffers a post-feminist fate worse than death – becoming ugly and disfigured and losing her income and, by extension, her consumer power); Kate being attacked by a rival gang breaking into her home; Lillian getting randomly beaten on the street; and Jim hitting Tilly when she protests about his infidelity. Tilly always forgives him, however, and blames the other woman with statements such as 'don't you ever lead my husband astray' and 'don't you dare blacken that man's name'. This is another reason why she cannot be the heroine of the piece. A post-feminist protagonist, by her very nature, is too empowered to be a passive victim of domestic violence. Making excuses for a violent husband is the antithesis of 'girl power'.

A physical fight between men is a feature of every episode. While Kate and Tilly bicker verbally in each instalment, flinging comical epitaphs ('Guttersnipe moll', 'hairy clam'), physical fights between them and between other women are infrequent, occurring once every two or three episodes, and are dealt with differently. In 'The Worst Woman in Sydney', Kate and Tilly fight outside the courthouse. While this altercation appears quite violent, with punching, kicking and, finally, Kate brandishing a pistol, it is actually pacified by a number of manoeuvres. Firstly, the women throw infantile insults, screech and pull hair, signifying schoolgirls and catfights. Secondly, the music that accompanies the scene is comical and thirdly, the fight is watched by men – rival criminal Norman Bruhn and their partners Wally and Jim. Wally and Jim look at each other, grinning wryly and rolling their eyes, until Kate pulls out a gun. Once this phallic weapon is wielded, Kate has masculine authority and everyone finally takes the fight seriously – even the cheerful music is cut. The voice-over is prompted to muse 'taming Pussytown was going to be harder than Norman Bruhn thought'.

In 'Tripe and Brains', Nellie and another prostitute, Black Aggie (Emily Rose Brennan), have a topless fist fight in a pub. The reasons for both the fight and performing it with their breasts exposed are not entirely clear. Again, the scene is different to male fight scenes. There is the schoolgirlish scratching and hair pulling, the male audience who cheer and drink, treating it as an entertainment (jelly wrestling, topless barmaids and wet tee shirt contests are all evoked), and the comic music to signal that this violence is more entertainment than active gender transgression.

Compare the fights between Kate and Tilly and Nellie and Black Aggie to the season 1 finale of *Orange is the New Black*, where the protagonist, Piper (Taylor Schilling), battles her nemesis, the unhinged, Christian methamphetamine addict Doggett (Taryn Manning) 'beating (her) to a bloody pulp' (McHugh 2015: n.p.). The scene takes place out in the yard, away from the gaze of guards or other prisoners and is brutal and shocking. McHugh argues that Piper's transition from nice, middle-class girl to a character capable of excessive violence exposes the fact that her civility is a fact of her economic and social privilege (2015: n.p.). Most of the women's violence in *Underbelly: Razor* exposes the fact that in Australian cultural lore, violence between women is a product of petty female jealousy and performed for the gratification of the male onlooker.

There are two instances of violence by women against men, and they both end very differently while reinforcing the good mother/bad mother stereotype of Kate and Tilly. In 'The Sentimental Bloke', Kate is forced to shoot a young man who has forced his way into her house, violating the maternal heart of the home – the kitchen – and threatened her. Kate has a rifle and warns him to back off, or she will shoot. As he lies dying he cries 'I want my mum' and Kate kneels down and holds his hand, standing in for his mother. Once again, Kate's behaviour is only acceptable as long as she remains true to her 'feminine nature'. She can be the 'kick-ass' action heroine as long as it is for a defensive reason – to protect herself and her home in the absence of the husband/father – and as long as it does not interfere with her maternal positioning. It is interesting that this scene takes place after she has had a very oedipal (or, to use post-feminist parlance, Cougar or MILF-like) affair with a young man named Bruce (Lincoln Lewis) who she refers to as 'my beautiful boy'. The affair results in Bruce being slashed, disfigured and exiling himself in shame. Kate's cuckolded partner Wally is also shot, then leaves town in disgrace after informing on his shooter. Her affair has thus led to the degradation of both men and to her being alone, vulnerable and having to stand in for the man in order to protect the home. Her violence redeems her, however, allowing her to immediately regain her maternal status, first as she becomes the shot man's mother, and again at the end of the episode where she is shown cradling her daughter Eileen's (Izzy Stevens) baby.

Throughout the series, there are many scenes of bloody razor attacks. The splattering and pooling blood recalls the strategies of the slasher film and its underlying themes of gender and castration anxiety and the monstrous maternal (Creed 1986). In many scenes, the blood is suggestive of menstruation, birth and miscarriage both literally and metaphorically. For example, in 'A Big Shivoo' Tilly Devine wakes up in blood, having suffered a miscarriage that appears to be her punishment for a night of wild drinking, smoking and partying. Yet again, she is portrayed as the inadequate mother.

Gunshots in film and television are relatively bloodless compared to razor attacks, which cause men to bleed like women. It could be argued that the underlying ideology of *Underbelly: Razor* upholds that notion that women occupying positions of power will lead to the symbolic castration and emasculation and hobbling of masculinity. A footballer character is literally hobbled when his Achilles tendon is slashed by a razor. Powerful women also have a negative effect on the feminine as the razor war causes beautiful prostitutes (or handsome young men) to become disfigured and ugly and lose their sexual currency.

In the final scene of the last episode, 'Armageddon', Kate and Tilly meet at a graveyard and in an unsubtle nod to the notion that powerful women must be afflicted by penis envy, they point two large guns at each other. But the guns (penises) seem to cancel each other out and the series ends with a whimper, not a bang.

KATE: If we shoot each other, those blokes will take our place.
TILLY: And make a bloody mess of it.

So, who triumphs in the end? In a postscript, we find out that Lillian, the policewoman, died alone in a one-room flat (the inevitable fate of a childless feminist); Nellie committed suicide by putting her head in a gas oven at the age of 43 (without Botox, forty must have been the new sixty and her girlishness and sexual worth had vanished); Tilly and Kate both died broke, but no one came to Tilly's funeral (given she was un-mothering, stuck-up British bitch), while Kate (upholding the national allegory) had hundreds of mourners. She was a good mother, so she was liked, and that's the main thing a woman needs to be: Likeable.

The Australian Context

Australia has a long history of negating female experience (Schaffer 1988: 5–8) and this is particularly evident when it comes to filming true stories (biopics) that create and uphold national myths. Pickering argues that 'this process of myth-making favours the bushranger, the successful bloke and the battler – leading to a highly masculinised notion of Australianness' (2014: 88) and '[…] reflect(s) a very narrow definition of womanhood' (91). This definition is also a dichotomous one, as evidenced in *Underbelly: Razor*'s female roles:

Positive	*Negative*
Aussie Larrikin	Colonial Arriviste
Good 'Bush' Mum	Monstrous Maternal
Damned Whore	God's Police
Happy Hooker	Drab Housewife

Note that in *Underbelly*'s world, the prostitute is a positive figure who fits in well with the raunchy, sexually liberated post-feminist consumer – as long as she remains young and attractive and does not try to rise above her station and appropriate power from men.

Or, as Burt puts it in the *Sydney Morning Herald*, '[Channel] 9 will show women in leadership positions, provided somebody gets their gear off' (2011).

This fear of women in leadership became particularly evident when Julia Gillard became Australia's first female prime minister in 2010, at the same time as *Underbelly: Razor* was in preproduction. For the three years before she was ousted, she was constantly pilloried by the media, the opposition and the public in a highly gendered and sexualized way. She was called a witch, a bitch and a moll, specific mention was made of her body, sexuality, de facto relationship, appearance, atheism, Welsh birthplace and most of all her childlessness that other politicians – from both sides – focused on negatively and relentlessly.

> 'I mean anyone who chooses to remain deliberately barren [...] they've got no idea what life's about.'
> (Senator Bill Heffernan quoted in Kelly 2011: n.p.)

> 'To choose a career ahead of the opportunity of having children? I think [...] you haven't got as much love in your life if you make that particular choice [...] I've also had some experience where around small children she was wooden [...] Empathy around small children is a pretty good test of what sort of person you are in life.'
> (Former Labor leader Mark Latham quoted in Kelly 2011: n.p.)

> 'Julia Gillard, who [...] has chosen not to be a parent [...] shows that she just doesn't understand the way parents think about their children when they reach a particular age [...] she is very much a one-dimensional person [...]'.
> (Senator Brandis quoted in Maiden 2010: n.p.)

> 'Kevin Rudd, we were told by Labor frontbencher Kate Ellis, had denounced the prime minister as a "childless, atheist, ex-communist". He denies it but Ellis is adamant Rudd spoke those words.'
> (Guthrie 2012: n.p.)

The criticism of Julia Gillard was different to that of male leaders, and more vehement. When she brought attention to the sexism of the leader of the opposition in her famous 'Misogyny Speech' (lauded in the media everywhere except Australia) she was condemned for 'playing the gender card'. It quickly became apparent that chauvinism was still deeply entrenched in Australian society, perpetuated by what Ana Stevenson has called the media's 'post-feminist paradigm' within which 'the focus on Gillard's gender existed alongside the assumption that sexism and misogyny remain characteristics of an "unenlightened" past (2013: 54)'. Stevenson goes on to posit that underrepresentation of women in politics is seen 'not as the result of an ongoing patriarchal system or politics, but rather as the failure of individual women' (2013: 54). In this way, sexist slurs against Gillard were framed as isolated incidents rather than as part of a discourse discriminatory language (2013: 53–54). It's McRobbie's 'double entanglement' all over again.

Underbelly Razor not only reflects Australian culture's problematic relationship with powerful women, but is also complicit in upholding it, particularly in the characterization of Kate and Tilly. Many of the comments about Gillard are analogous to the gendered insults bandied about by the crime queens, where they insult each other according to appearance, marital status, mothering ability and age.

TILLY: I'm young, I'm rich, I'm beautiful [...] so I just want you to know one thing. I'm the winner.

KATE: You're not the winner, you stupid Pommy cow. This is my daughter, and this is my granddaughter. See, my blood flows through their veins. They're my legacy. And what about you? You're just a barren piece of shit with a murdering, cheating prick for a husband and nobody loves you – nobody even likes you.

('Jerusalem Revisited' 2011)

Female politicians and television antiheroines face similar problems. If a woman is nurturing and maternal, she succeeds as a woman but fails as a leader. If she is 'achievement-oriented, able to take charge, autonomous and rational' (Cannold 2014), then she's mannish and unlikeable. This is why Kate had to be an androgynous mix of idealized masculine and feminine 'Aussie' in order to be the protagonist, and why Tilly's villain status was constantly reinforced with references to her barrenness. It also points to why Julia Gillard garnered the same slurs as Tilly, as the Prime Minister was variously disparaged as a pom, an 'unproductive cow', 'deliberately barren' and unlikeable.

Conclusion

While Norman Bruhn may not have been able to 'tame pussytown', commercial television certainly did, and an opportunity to portray two exciting Australian antiheroines was lost. Through scripting, narrative choices, an anachronistic *mise-en-scène* and dichotomous gender stereotyping, the true story of two powerful, ruthless and feared female criminals was drained of its potentially transgressive power, the characters were domesticated and subdued.

Post-feminist and anti-feminist sentiments infiltrate the show through dichotomous and stereotypical representations of women. Female characters are dis-empowered through dialogue and *mise-en-scène* by a narrative focus on the domestic and maternal and in the sexist depiction of women and violence. Post-feminist tropes such as individualism and consumption are embedded in the ideological framework of the text that reflects the Australian media's problematic relationship with women in positions of power.

By overlaying myths of Australian nationalism with a post-feminist agenda, the programme reinforced patriarchal, phallocentric discourse while disguising it as female empowerment. In this instance, Australian commercial television, and Channel Nine in particular, failed to emulate such television shows featuring women in key roles as *Top of the Lake* and *Orange is the New Black*. While the Australian-produced Foxtel prison drama *Wentworth* (a remake of the earlier series *Prisoner*) seems as though it might be a step in the right direction, there is no indication that the commercial networks are ready to risk such feminist fare. And would Australian society take the psychic and political chance of another female prime minister? Perhaps if she was like *Underbelly: Razor*'s Queen Kate: equal parts lovable larrikin, bush mum, action hero and beauty queen. In other words, an Australian post-feminist fairy tale.

References

Australian Associated Press (AAP) (2010a), 'The gangland war', *The Age*, 19 April, http://www.theage.com.au/victoria/the-gangland-war-20100419-soql.html. Accessed 4 May 2015.

—— (2010b), 'Abbott accused of being "terribly old-fashioned" as he lets off steam', *Sydney Morning Herald*, 9 February, http://www.smh.com.au/national/abbott-accused-of-being-incredibly-oldfashioned-as-he-lets-off-steam-20100208-nnqr.html. Accessed 21 May 2015.

'A Big Shivoo' (2011), David Caesar, dir., *Underbelly: Razor*, Episode 8, 2 October, Sydney: Nine Network.

Akass, K. and McCabe, J. (2006), 'What has Carmela ever done for feminism?: Carmela Soprano and the post-feminist dilemma', in D. Lavery (ed.), *Reading The Sopranos: Hit TV from HBO*, Reading Contemporary Television, London: I.B. Tauris, pp. 39–55.

'Armageddon' (2011), Tony Tilse, dir., *Underbelly: Razor*, Episode 1, 21 August, Sydney: Nine Network.

Braham, S. (2011), '*Underbelly: Razor* recap – "The Worst Woman in Sydney"', *Pedestrian TV*, http://www.pedestrian.tv/entertainment/news/underbelly-razor-recap-the-worst-woman-in-sydney/51113.htm. Accessed 21 May 2015.

Brundson, C. (2013), 'Television crime series, women, police and fuddy-duddy feminism', *Feminist Media Studies*, 13: 3, pp. 375–394, http://dx.doi.org/10.1080/14680777.2001.652143. Accessed 8 November 2014.

Burt, D. (2011), 'Sex still sells as crime goes by', *Sydney Morning Herald*, http://www.smh.com.au/entertainment/tv-and-radio/sex-still-sells-as-crime-goes-by-20111019-1m6or.html#ixzz3a43FbQrG. Accessed 15 May 2015.

Cannold, L. (2014), 'Women in power stymied by gender bias', *The Age*, 25 January, http://www.theage.com.au/comment/women-in-power-stymied-by-gender-bias-20140124-31ehh.html. Accessed 21 May 2015.

Coulthard, L. (2007), 'Killing Bill: Rethinking feminism and film violence', in Y. Tasker and D. Negra (eds), *Interrogating Postfeminism*, Durham: Duke University Press, pp. 153–175.

Creed, B. (1986), 'Horror and the monstrous-feminine: An imaginary abjection', *Screen*, 27: 1, pp. 44–71.

Delaney, C. (2011), 'Hell razor: On the set of Underbelly's latest', *Encore Media, entertainment and the business of storytelling*, http://mumbrella.com.au/hell-razor-underbelly-9527. Accessed 21 May 2015.

Gill, F. (2012), '"Feminine women": Regional Australia and the construction of Australian femininity', in C. Elder and K. Moore (eds), *New Voices, New Visions: Challenging Australian Identities and Legacies*, Newcastle upon Tyne: Cambridge Scholars Publishing, pp. 277–288.

Gill, R. (2007), *Gender and the Media*, Cambridge: Polity Press.

—— (2011), 'Sexism reloaded, or, it's time to get angry again!', *Feminist Media Studies*, 11: 1, pp. 61–71.

Gregg, M. and Wilson, J. (2010), 'Underbelly, true crime and the cultural economy of infamy', *Continuum: Journal of Media and Cultural Studies*, 24: 3, pp. 411–427.

Guthrie, G. (2012), 'Put a stop now to the mother of all insults', *The Age*, 6 March, http://www.theage.com.au/it-pro/put-a-stop-now-to-mother-of-all-insults-20120305-1ue69.html. Accessed 15 April 2015.

Harvey, C. (2011), 'Underbelly razor myth hides the ugly truth', *The Daily Telegraph*, 28 August, http://www.dailytelegraph.com.au/news/opinion/underbelly-razors-myth-hides-the-ugly-truth/story-e6frezz0-1226123524269. Accessed 23 February 2015.

Holmlund, C. (2005), 'Postfeminism from A to G', *Cinema Journal*, 44: 2, pp. 116–121.

'Jerusalem Revisited' (2011), Shawn Seet, dir., *Underbelly Razor*, Episode 11, 23 October, Sydney: Nine Network.

Kelly, J. (2011), 'Mark Latham says Julia Gillard has no empathy because she's childless', *The Australian*, 4 April, http://www.theaustralian.com.au/national-affairs/mark-latham-says-julia-gillard-has-no-empathy-because-shes-childless/story-fn59niix-1226033174177. Accessed 16 July 2015.

Kroenert, T. (2009), 'Gangsters are people too', *Eureka Street*, 19: 5, 16 March.

Larabee, A. (2013), 'Editorial: The new television anti-hero', *The Journal of Popular Culture*, 46: 6, pp. 1131–1132.

Levy, A. (2010), *Female Chauvinist Pigs: Women and the Rise of Raunch Culture*, Melbourne: Black Inc.

Maiden, S. (2010), 'Childless Gillard can't speak on parental issues: Brandis', *The Australian*, 28 January, http://www.theaustralian.com.au/news/nation/childless-gillard-cant-speak-on-parental-issues-brandis/story-e6frg6nf-1225824139383. Accessed 15 July 2015.

McHugh, K. A. (2015), 'Giving credit to paratexts and parafeminism in *Top of the Lake* and *Orange Is the New Black*', *Film Quarterly*, Spring, 68: 3, pp. 17–25.

McRobbie, A. (2007), 'Postfeminism and popular culture: Bridget Jones and the New Gender regime', in Y. Tasker and D. Negra (eds), *Interrogating Postfeminism*, Durham: Duke University Press, pp. 27–39.

Mizejewski, L. (2005), 'Dressed to kill: Postfeminist noir', *Cinema Journal*, 44: 2, pp. 121–127.

Negra, D. (2009), *What a Girl Wants: Fantasizing the Reclamation of Self in Postfeminism*, London: Routledge.

Paskin, W. (2013), 'James Gandolfini, gone too soon', *Salon*, 20 June, http://www.salon.com/2013/06/20/james_gandolfini_gone_too_soon/. Accessed 14 March 2016.

Pennicott, J. (2011), 'A small slice of *Underbelly: Razor*', *Tale Peddler*, http://josephinepennicott.com/2011/08/24/a-small-slice-of-underbelly-razor/. Accessed 21 May 2015.

Pickering, K. (2014), 'Australia's sons: Looking for women in Australian biopics', *Metro Magazine: Media & Education Magazine*, 181, pp. 88–93, http://search.informit.com.au/documentSummary;dn=517913252727534;res=IELAPA. Accessed 21 May 2015.

Savage, A. (2011), 'Will the real Nellie Cameron please take a bath', *Angela Savage WordPress*, https://angelasavage.wordpress.com/tag/underbelly-razor/. Accessed 21 May 2015.

Schaffer, K. (1988), *Women and the Bush: Forces of Desire in the Australian Cultural Tradition*, Sydney: Cambridge University Press.

Stevenson, A. (2013), 'Making gender divisive: 'Post-feminism', sexism and media representations of Julia Gillard', *Burgmann Journal*, 2, pp. 53–63, http://eview.anu.edu.au/burgmann/issue2/pdf/ch08.pdf. Accessed 3 February 2015.

Tasker, Y. and Negra, D. (eds) (2007), 'Introduction: Feminist politics and postfeminist culture', in Y. Tasker. and D. Negra, *Interrogating Postfeminism*, Durham: Duke University Press.

'The Darlinghurst Outrage' (2011), Shawn Seet, dir., *Underbelly: Razor*, Episode 5, 11 November, Sydney: Nine Network.

'The Sentimental Bloke' (2011), Mat King, dir., *Underbelly: Razor*, Episode 10, 16 November, Sydney: Nine Network.

'The Worst Woman in Sydney' (2011), Tony Tilse, dir., *Underbelly: Razor*, Episode 1, 21 August, Sydney: Nine Network.

Trenoweth, S. (ed.) (2013), *Bewitched & Bedevilled: Women Write the Gillard Years*, Hardie Grant, Melbourne.

'Tripe and Brains' (2011), David Caesar, dir., *Underbelly: Razor*, Episode 7, Sydney: Nine Network.

Turnbull, S. (2010), 'Crime as entertainment: The case of the TV crime drama', *Continuum: Journal of Media and Cultural Studies*, 24: 6, pp. 819–827.

—— (2014a), *The TV Crime Drama*, Edinburgh: Edinburgh University Press.

—— (2014b), 'A suitable job for a woman': Women, work and the television crime drama', *Continuum: Journal of Media and Cultural Studies*, 28: 2, pp. 226–234.

Vered, K. O. and Humphries, S. (2014), 'Postfeminist inflections in television studies', *Continuum: Journal of Media and Cultural Studies*, 28: 2, pp. 155–163.

Ward, R. (1958), *The Australian Legend*, London: Oxford University Press.

Williams, M. (2012), 'The gender politics of underbelly razor', *Southerly*, 72: 2, pp. 9–24.

Writer, L. (2009), *Razor*, Sydney: Pan Macmillan Australia.

Notes

1 The *Underbelly* voice-over is consistent throughout the series and is voiced by Caroline Craig, who played policewoman Jacqui James in the first season of *Underbelly*.

2 'Ocker' refers to an uncultured Australian who speaks with a broad accent.
3 Australian drama *Satisfaction* focused on the lives of a group of workers in an upmarket brothel. It ran for three seasons, but was only available on pay TV.
4 Anne Summers' 1975 book *Damned Whores and God's Police* 'analysed woman's position in Australian society as a colonized sex' (Schaffer 1988: 8).

Contributors

Kim Akass is a Senior Lecturer in Film and TV in the School of Creative Arts, University of Hertfordshire. She has, with Janet McCabe, co-edited and contributed to a number of edited collections in the 'Reading Contemporary TV' series for I.B. Tauris including *Quality TV: Contemporary American TV and Beyond* (2007) and *TV's Betty Goes Global: From Telenovela to International Brand* (2012). She is currently writing about the representation of motherhood in the media and is one of the founding editors of the journal *Critical Studies in Television* (Sage) and managing editor of CSTonline.

Vicky Ball is Senior Lecturer in Cinema and Television Histories, De Montfort University. She has published articles on gender and British television drama and is currently writing a book about the British female ensemble drama (2017). She is co-investigator on the AHRC funded project 'Women's Work, Working Women: A Longitudinal Study of Women Working in the Film and Television Industries (1933–1989)' and a member of the Committee of the Women's Film and Television Histories Network: UK/Ireland.

Milly Buonanno is *Professor Benemerita* at La Sapienza University of Roma. She is currently the co-director of the research programme GEMMA (GEnder and Media MAtters) at the Department of Communication and Social Research and the director of the Observatory of Italian TV Drama. Her scholarship encompasses television theory and history, TV drama, feminist media studies, journalism. She is the author, editor or co-editor of more than fifty books, including the *Sage Handbook of Television Studies* (2014), the monographs *Italian TV Drama and Beyond* (2012) and *The Age of Television* (2008) and is the editor-elect of *Intersections*, a forthcoming international journal of gender and communication.

Elisa Giomi is Associate Professor in Sociology of Communication and Gender and Media at Roma Tre University. Her research interests focus on gender identity, gender violence and media representations. She sits in the editorial board of *AG-About Gender. International Journal of Gender Studies*. Her latest publications include *Moral Panic: The Issue of Women and Crime in Italian Evening News* (2013), *Gender e Media* (2015), and the forthcoming co-authored book *Relazioni brutali. Media, genere, violenza* (2017).

Joke Hermes is Professor of practice based research in Media, Culture and Citizenship at Inholland University and teaches television at the University of Amsterdam. Her work focuses on gender, media, popular culture and audience research on which she has published widely. She is founding co-editor of the *European Journal of Cultural Studies*.

Samantha Joyce is Assistant Professor of Global Communication at Saint Mary's College of California. Her research interests include *telenovelas*, media representation, gender and television theory and history. She is the author of *Brazilian Telenovelas and the Myth of Racial Democracy* (2012). Her work has appeared in *International Journal of Communication*, *Brazilian Journalism Review*, *Lumina* and elsewhere.

Jorie Lagerwey is Lecturer in Television Studies at University College Dublin. Her research interests include gender, religion and celebrity on television and other digital media. She is the author of *Postfeminist Celebrity and Motherhood: Brand Mom* (2016). Her work has also appeared in *Cinema Journal*, *Studies in Popular Culture*, *Spectator*, Flowtv.org and elsewhere.

Antonio La Pastina is an Associate Professor at Texas A&M University in College Station. His research interests include media reception, audience ethnography, media representations of non-mainstream groups and diasporic cultures. His work has appeared in several edited books and journals including *Critical Studies in Media Communication*, *Journal of Broadcasting and Electronic Media*, *Global Media and Communication*, *Gazette* and *Communication Research*.

Amanda D. Lotz is Professor in the Departments of Communication Studies and Screen Arts and Cultures at the University of Michigan. She is the author of *The Television Will Be Revolutionized* (2007; rev. 2nd ed. 2014), *Cable Guys: Television and American Masculinities in the 21st Century* (2014) and *Redesigning Women: Television After the Network Era* (2006), and co-author, with Timothy Havens, of *Understanding Media Industries* (2011; 2nd ed. 2016) and, with Jonathan Gray, of *Television Studies* (2011).

Janet McCabe is Senior Lecturer in Film and Television at Birkbeck, University of London. She is the managing editor of *Critical Studies in Television* and writes widely on feminism, representation and contemporary television. She is author of *The West Wing* (2012) and co-editor of several collections (with Kim Akass), including *Quality TV: Contemporary American TV and Beyond* (2007), *Reading Sex and the City* (2004) and *TV's Betty Goes Global: From Telenovela to International Brand* (2013).

Diane Negra is Professor of Film Studies and Screen Culture and Head of Film Studies at University College Dublin. A member of the Royal Irish Academy, she is the author, editor or co-editor of ten books including the forthcoming *The Aesthetics and Affects of Cuteness* (2016).

Contributors

Andrea Press is the William R. Kenan Jr Professor of Media Studies and Sociology at the University of Virginia. Her most recent book is *The New Media Environment* (with Bruce Williams, 2010). She is also author of *Women Watching Television* (1991), *Speaking Of Abortion* (1999) and co-editor of the forthcoming *Handbook of Contemporary Feminism, Media and Class* and *The Communication Review*. Her forthcoming book is *FemiNEXTing*. She has written on online misogyny for *Slate* and the *Chronicle of Higher Education*.

Leigh Redhead is a postgraduate student at the University of Wollongong, Australia, where she is completing a Ph.D. on Australian noir fiction and writing a noir novel set in an alternative community. She is also the author of four crime novels, *Peepshow* (2004), *Rubdown* (2005), *Cherry Pie* (2007) and *Thrill City* (2010), featuring stripper/private investigator Simone Kirsch.

Yeidy M. Rivero is Professor in the Departments of Screen Arts and Cultures and American Culture at the University of Michigan. Her research centers on television history, media and globalization. She is the author of *Tuning Out Blackness: Race and Nation in the History of Puerto Rican Television* (2005), *Broadcasting Modernity: Cuban Commercial Television, 1950–1960* (2015) and co-editor (with Arlene Dávila) of *Contemporary Latino Media: Production, Circulation, Politics* (2015).

Sue Turnbull is Professor of Communication and Media Studies at the University of Wollongong and Director of the Research Centre for Texts, Culture and Creative Industries. Her publications include *The Television Crime Drama* published by Edinburgh University Press (2014) and *The Media and Communications in Australia* (2014) co-edited with Distinguished Professor Stuart Cunningham. She is a frequent media commentator on television and radio in Australia who writes on crime fiction for the Fairfax Press.

Barbara Villez is Professor of Legal Language and Culture at University Paris 8. She is the director of the research center JILC (Justices, Images, Languages, Cultures) and is associate researcher at the Institut des Hautes Etudes sur la Justice in Paris and the Laboratoire de communication et politique (CNRS), where she directs a network of television series scholars. She has widely written on representations of justice and legal professions in television; recent publications are *Séries télé:vision de la justice* (2005), *Television and the Legal System* (2010), *Law and Order. La justice en prime time* (2014).

Suzanna Danuta Walters is Professor of Sociology and Director of the Women's, Gender, and Sexuality Studies Program at Northeastern University. She is the author of numerous books, including *Material Girls: Making Sense of Feminist Cultural Theory* (1995), *All the Rage: the story of gay visibility in America* (2001) and, most recently, *The Tolerance Trap: How God, Genes, and Good Intentions are Sabotaging Gay Equality* (2014). She currently serves as the Editor-in-Chief of *Signs: Journal of Women in Culture and Society*.

Bruce Williams is the Ambassador Henry J. Taylor Professor and Chair of Media Studies at the University of Virginia. His most recent books are *After Broadcast News: Media Regimes, Democracy, and the New Information Environment* (with Michael X. Delli Carpini, 2012) and *The New Media Environment* (with Andrea L. Press, 2010). He co-edits the *Communication Review*, and has held visiting appointments at Hebrew University and London's Stanhope Center for Communications Policy Research. His new book engages media representation of war.

Index

A
Accorsi, Stefano, 58
Adams, Sam, 10
Adele, 257
Akass, Kim, xi, 8, 17, 30, 68, 69, 78, 192, 267
Albrecht, Michael, 7
Algemeen Dagblad (newspaper), 96, 97
Alias el mexicano (RCN, 2013–2014), 156n4
Aliens (Cameron, 1986), 112
Alvetti, Celina, 230–231
Amazon, 139n2
American Horror Story. Asylum (FX, 2012–2013), 9
The Americans (FX, 2013–), 8, 9
Anderson, Christopher, 67
Anderson, Elijah, 247
Ang, Ien, 92–93
Angela, Sharon, 74
Angela (Torre, 2002), 29
antiheroine television
   advent of, 3–4, 7–11
   criticism of, 13–14
   curious feminism and, 4–5
   feminist reading of, 10–13, 42–43, 87
   male antiheroes and, 5–8
   role and significance of, 14–16
   See also mafia women; motherhood; women-in-prison (WIP) drama; *specific shows*
Arlen, Harold, 63n4
Armstrong, Jennifer, 10
Arnold, Sara, 3
Arquette, Patricia, ix
Arthurs, Jane, 166, 172
The Australian Legend (Ward), 262
Autostraddle (website), 193
Avatar (Cameron, 2009), 223–224

B
Baantjer (RTL, 1995–2006), 93, 95
The Bachelor (ABC, 2002–), 260
Bad Girls (ITV, 1999–2006)
   character types in, 173–175
   context of, 166–167
   heroines in, 177
   lesbianism in, 163, 164–166, 175–176
   motherhood in, 177
   queer feminist reading of, 167–170, 175–176
   scholarship on, 164
   success of, 163–164
Bad Girls: The Inside Story (Reynolds and McCallum), 174–175
Baehr, Caroline, 52
Bakhtin, Mikhail, 174
Ball, Vicky, x, 18, 42, 166, 167
Ballantyne, Elspeth, 190
Band of Gold II (ITV, 1996), 166
Barreca, Regina, 67
Barthes, Roland, 92, 93
Batchelor, John, 263
Battersby, Roy, 172
Beauvoir, Simone de, 68, 99–100
Beck, Bernard, 108

Beck, Richard, 5
Beck, Ulrik, 14
Beerekamp, Hans, 89, 91
Benavides, Hugo, 144, 148, 150
Benjamin, Jan, 93
Bennett, Laura, 6
Bentham, Jeremy, 169
Bernard, April, 205
Bernardi, Paloma, 227
The Big C (Showtime, 2010–2013), 115
The Bill (ITV, 1984–2010), 171
Bises, Stefano, 46n2
Bittencourt, Vagne, 221
Blay, Zeba, 10
Block B: Unter Arrest (RTL, 2015–), 192
Boardwalk Empire (HBO, 2010–2014), 77–79, 259, 265
Bobbitt, Betty, 186
Bogle, Donald, 245
Bolívar, Gustavo, 156n5
Bombert, Victor, 12, 16
Borino-Quinn, Denise, 76
Born in Flames (Borden, 1983), 209
Bourdieu, Pierre, 10–11, 34
Bourgois, Philippe, 247
Bourke, Terry, 184, 185–186, 187–189
'The Boys Light Up' (song), 268
Brabon, Benjamin, 15
Bradshaw, Lara, 108, 115
Braham, Sophie, 268
Brandão, Maria Cristina, 226, 230, 231
Brandt, Carlo, 57
Breaking Bad (AMC, 2008–2013)
    antihero in, 6, 130, 138, 183, 201, 265
    Penoza and, 92
    realism in, 259
    La reina del sur and, 156n3
    women in, 11
The Bridge (FX, 2013–2014), 139n1
Bridget Jones' Diary (Maguire, 2001), 260
Britton, Dana, 239
Bron/Broen (SVT1, DR1, 2011), 183
Brooks, Peter, 31

Broom, Maria, 253n6
Broussard, Philippe, 43
Brown, Effie, ix, xiiin1
Brown, Jeffrey A., 114
Brown, Shamyl, 245, 247
Bruner, Jerome, 14
Brunsdon, Charlotte, 4, 30, 31, 166, 172, 183, 267
Bryant, Judy, 186–187
The Buddha of Suburbia (BBC, 1993), 166, 167
Budgeon, Shelley, 15
Buonanno, Milly, xi, 16, 30, 87, 165
Buried (Channel 4, 2003), 171
Burns, Carol, 189
Burns, Ed, 240
Burt, Daniel, 259, 271
Buscemi, Steve, 77
But I'm a Cheerleader (Babbit, 1999), 207
Butler, Judith, 55
Butsch, Richard, ix
Buzzanell, Patrice M., 113
Byerly, Caroline, 14

C

cable television, 130–131. *See also specific cable channels*
Café con aroma de mujer (RCN, 1994–1995), 146–147
Caged (Cromwell, 1950), 184
Caged Heat (Demme, 1974), 184, 204
Calzone, Maria Pia, 29, 42
Camorra, 29, 40–41. *See also Gomorra. La serie* (Sky Atlantic, 2014–)
Campbell, Jack, 264
Canale 5 (Italian network), 31. *See also Squadra antimafia* (Canale 5, 2009–)
Cannold, Leslie, 273
Il capo dei capi (Canale 5, 2007), 31
The Carnival of Images (Mattelart and Mattelart), 225
Carey, Kevin, 240
Carter, Cynthia, 235n2

Castro, Natalia, 229, 231
Casualty (BBC, 1986–), 166
Cavallari, Simona, 31
Celblok H (SBS 6, 2014–), 192
Chaddha, Anmol, 239
Channel 5 (British network), 192
Channel Nine (Australian network), 257, 274
Channel Ten (Australian network), 184, 185, 187, 192–193
Charlie's Angels (ABC, 1976–1981), 185
Charlton, Tope Fadiran, 204
Chianese, Dominic, 73
The Children's Hour (Wyler, 1961), 207
O Clone (Rede Globo, 2001–2002), 225
The Closer (TNT, 2005–2012), 139n1
Clover, Carol, 107, 111, 121
Collet, Nicole, 63n1
Collins, Andrew, 39
'Contrabando y traición' (song), 156n4
Cook, Pam, 168–169
Cormack, Danielle, 190–191, 261
Coronation Street (ITV, 1960–), 169, 173
Corsica. See *Mafiosa* (Canal Plus, 2006–2014)
Corsica Libera (political party), 52
Corticchiato, Philippe, 63n2
Corton, Eric, 92, 93
Costa, Flávio, 227
Costa, Nanda, 225–226
Coulthard, Lisa, 11
The Count of Monte Cristo (Dumas), 149
Cox, Laverne, 195, 208, 215n2
Craig, Caroline, 276n1
Cranston, Brian, xi
Creeber, Glen, 30, 166
Creed, Barbara, 270
crime series, 171–172. See also *specific shows*
Crossroads (ITV, 1964–1988), 173, 185
Cunningham, Stuart, 188
curious feminism, 4–5

D
Da Silva, Nicole, 190–191, 193
D'Acci, Julie, 8, 30, 42

Dahl, Tove Stang, 170–171
Dallas (CBS, 1978–1991), 92–93, 138
Damages (FX, 2007–2010; DirecTV, 2011–2012), 8, 129
Damned Whores and God's Police (Summers), 277n4
Damon, Matt, ix
Danes, Claire, x, 129
'Danny Boy' (song), 269
daughter archetype, 111–112
Davidson, Darren, 191
Days of Our Lives (NBC, 1965–), 173
de Matteo, Drea, 73
De Pablos, Emiliano, 157n8
Deadwood (HBO, 2004–2006), 138, 268
Deggans, Eric, 138
Dekker, Jeroen, 99
DeLaria, Lea, 203, 207
D'Enbeau, Suzy, 113
Destroy the Joint (website), 196
Devine, Tilly, 257–258. See also *Underbelly: Razor* (Nine Network, 2011)
Dexter (Showtime, 2006–2013), 6, 183, 229
Dias, Laryssa, 227
Dieckman, Adriana, 227
Difficult Men (Martin), 5, 8–9
Distretto di polizia (Canale 5, 2000–2012), 31
Doane, Mary Anne, 169, 223
Docker, John, 171, 174
double entanglement, 14, 260, 266, 272
Douglas, Susan, 127
Doyle, John, 8, 10
dual hermeneutics, 34, 43
Dueños del paraíso (Telemundo, 2015), 153, 157n8
Dumas, Alexander, 149
Dunham, Lena, x
Duval, Daniel, 51
Dynasty (ABC, 1981–1989), 138

E
Early, Frances, 11, 107
Elba, Idris, 246, 248

Elementary (CBS, 2012–), 9
Elle (magazine), x
Ellen (ABC, 1994–1998), 164
emotional realism, 92–93
Empire (FOX, 2015–), 10
Engrenages (Canal Plus, 2005–), 53
Enlightened (HBO, 2011–2013), 9
Enloe, Cynthia, 3, 4
Enos, Mireille, 129
Erignac, Claude, 61
excusatio, 111–112, 113
Explode Coração (Rede Globo, 1995–1996), 225
Express (magazine), 53

F
Facebook, 88, 201
Falco, Edie, 67
Fantástico (Rede Globo, 1973–), 227
Faria, Maria Cristina Brandão de, 226, 229, 231
The Farmer Wants a Wife (Nine Network, 2007–), 260–261
feminism
 antiheroine television and, 10–13, 42–43, 87
 curious feminism, 4–5
 motherhood and, 99–100, 127
 See also liberal feminism; post-feminism; queer feminism; second-wave feminism
Feminist Culturalist Television Criticism, 108
Feminist Film Theory, 108
Ferlin, Danielly, 222
Fernandes, Guilherme Moreira, 224, 229, 231
Fiandaca, Giovanni, 29
Fillières, Hélène, 51, 55
Fine, Kerry, 14, 43, 133
Firestone, Shulamith, 100
Five Women (drama-documentary), 172
Five Women (Parker), 172
Flores, González, 157n6
Forbrydelsen (DR1, 2007–2012), 183

Forster, Douglas, 108, 114
Foucault, Michel, 72, 169, 222–223, 227–228, 232–233
Fox-Genovese, Elizabeth, 99
Foxtel (Australian network), 191–192
Franco, Jorge, 156n4
Franich, Darren, 6
Fraser, Nancy, 69, 71–72, 73
Fraticelli, Eric, 54
FremantleMedia, 191
Friedan, Betty, 100
From Media to Mediations (Martín-Barbero), 222–223

G
Gabrielle, 193–194
Galantuomini (Winspeare 2008), 29
Game of Thrones (HBO, 2011–), 138
Gandolfini, James, xi, 5–6, 8, 29, 68
Gannascoli, Joseph R., 73
Garber, Jenny, 186
Garrone, Matteo, 39
Gaspar de Alba, Alicia, 144
De Gelderlander (newspaper), 94, 96
gender pay gap, ix
gentle sexism, 266–267
Gentry, Caron E., 11, 13
Genz, Stephanie, 15
Geraghty, Christine, 3, 173, 177
Gill, Fiona, 263
Gill, Rosalind, 14, 108, 119, 268
Gillard, Julia, 261, 272–273
Gillard, Lawrence Jr, 248
Gillota, David, 108
Giomi, Elisa, xi, 17, 111
Girls (HBO, 2012–), 201
Gjelsvik, Anne, 107
Gledhill, Christine, 31
Globo Network, 221–222, 224–225
The Godfather trilogy (Coppola 1972, 1974, 1990), 32, 33, 35, 70, 112
Goede Tijden, Slechte Tijden (RTL4, 1990–), 93

Goffman, Erving, 55, 247
Gomes, Mayra Rodrigues, 223–224
Gomorra (Garrone 2008), 39
Gomorra. La serie (Sky Atlantic, 2014–), 29–30, 39–43
Gomorra (Saviano), 39
González Flores, Francisca, 157n6
The Good Men Project (Marcotte), 7
GoodFellas (Scorsese, 1990), 112
The Governor (ITV, 1995–1996), 171
Graziani, Frédéric, 54, 63n4
Gregg, Melissa, 258
Gribaudi, Gabriella, 29
Grimaldi, Dan, 74–75
Groenier, Rivka, 94, 96
Grundy, Reg, 185
Gunn, Anna, 11
Guthrie, Gillian, 272
Gutiérrez-Albilla, Julián Daniel, 222, 223, 232

H
Haerter, Leandro, 229, 232
Hall, Stuart, 186
Hamburger, Esther, 224
Hamm, John, xi
Hannam, David, 183
Harburg, Edgar Yipsel, 63n4
Hardie, Giles, 191
Harris, Geraldine, 42
Harrison, Laura, 108, 114, 128–129
Hartley, John, 87
Harvey, Peter, 268
Hauck, Emmanuelle, 57
HBO (US cable network), 131. *See also specific shows*
Heffernan, Bill, 272
Heidensohn, Frances, 170–171
Elshtain, Jean Bethke, 170
Hendrickx, Monic, 87, 89–91, 93, 96, 101
Henegan, Jean, 10
Hennessey, Stewart, 168
Herald Sun (newspaper), 196
Herman, Alison, 8

Herman, Didi, 151, 164, 165–166, 167, 175–176
Hermes, Joke, xi, 17, 95, 99
heroine television, 4
heteronormativity, 164–165, 170–171
heterotopia, 222–224, 227–228, 232–233
Hilder, Jo, 259
Hill, John, 172
Himberg, Julie, 192
Hollows, Joanne, 15
Holmes, Ian, 185
Holmlund, Chris, 260
Homeland (Showtime, 2011–), 8, 129
Hopewell, John, 147
Hornery, Andrew, 192
House of Cards (Netflix, 2013–), 8, 9
How to Get Away with Murder (ABC, 2014–), 10
Howard, Douglas, 6
human trafficking, 117, 222, 226–227, 230
Hummell, Rosita Cordeiro de Loyola, 230–231
Humphreys, Sal, 260, 268
Hyatt, Michael, 245

I
I Love Lucy (CBS, 1951–1957), 163
Idato, Michael, 194
Images of Incarceration (Wilson and O'Sullivan), 171–172, 174, 176
Imperioli, Michael, 74
In Praise of Antiheroes (Bombert), 12
Ingrascì, Ombretta, 29
Inness, Sherrie A., 11, 30, 43, 107, 119
International Labor Organization (ILO), 230
Isto é (newsmagazine), 227
Ivey, Dana, 77

J
Jacka, Elizabeth, 188
Janowitz, Will, 72
Jaramillo, Deborah, 108, 156n3
Jefferson, Tony, 186

Jermyn, Deborah, 30, 183
Jewkes, Yvonne, 54
Johnson, Hassan, 245–246
Johnson, Lisa, 67
Johnston, Deirdre D., 99
Jolie, Angelina, 266–267
Jones, Marcus, 6
Judd, Ashley, 266–267
Justice (ITV, 1971–1974), 171
Justified (FX, 2010–2015), 8, 9, 127–128, 129–130, 131–133, 137–138

K
Kalem, Toni, 73
Kaling, Mindy, x
Kaplan, E. Ann, 13, 37, 39, 128, 250
Kateb, Reda, 58
Keeping up with the Kardashians (E! 2007–), 260
Kelly, Joe, 272
Kelly, Lisa, 9
Kelly, Ned, 257, 263
Kennedy, Kathleen, 11, 107
Kennedy, Liam, 252
Kerman, Piper, 201, 203–204
Kill Bill vol. 1 (Tarantino, 2003), 111
Kill Bill vol. 2 (Tarantino, 2004), 111
The Killing (AMC, 2011–2014), 9, 129
The Killing of Sister George (Aldrich, 1968), 207
Killoran, Ellen, 5
King, John, 222
King, Michelle, x
King, Neil, 30, 107
Kirkpatrick, Maggie, 187–188
Knox, David, 193
Kohan, Jenji, x, 107, 201, 206
Korthuis, Pieter Bart, 95–96, 97
KRO (Dutch public broadcaster), 88
Kroenert, Tim, 259

L
The L Word (Showtime, 2004–2009), 192, 202
La Pastina, Antonio, x, xi, 19, 224–225,

LaPlace, Maria, 32
Larabee, Ann, 262
Larke-Walsh, George, 30
Larner, Wendy, 75
Larsson, Stig, 111
Lawrence, Jennifer, ix
Leadbelly: Inside Australia's Underworld (Sylvester and Rule), 258
Leap, Jorja, 247
Leccia, Pierre, 56
Lehman, Val, 190, 257
Leigh, Kate, 257–258. *See also Underbelly: Razor* (Nine Network, 2011)
lesbianism
   in *Bad Girls*, 163, 164–166, 175–176
   heteronormativity and, 164–165
   in *The L Word*, 192, 202
   in *Orange is the New Black*, 205–211
   in *Prisoner*, 186, 189–190
   in *La reina del sur*, 149–153
   in *Wentworth*, 186, 189–191, 192–194, 195
   in *The Wire*, 243–244, 249
Levine, Elana, 7
Levita, Alain de, 92, 93–94
Levy, Ariel, 268
Lewis, Lincoln, 270
Leyda, Julia, x
liberal feminism
   Boardwalk Empire and, 77–79
   The Sopranos and, 67–77, 78–79
Limburg, Dirk, 90
De Limburger (newspaper), 101
liminality, xi, 11–12, 109
Lippman, Laura, 245
'Little Boxes' (song), 114
Littleton, Cynthia, 147
Logie Award, 194
Lombardi, Rodrigo, 226
Lombroso, Cesare, 117
Lotz, Amanda, xi, 3, 7, 11, 17, 30, 130, 192
Love, Heather, 203–204
Lovejoy, Dierdre, 242
Luther (BBC, 2000–2010), 171

Lyonne, Natasha, 207
Lyons, Margaret, ix, 6

M
Maas, Ruud, 87, 96, 101
Macdonald, Kelly, 77
Maciak, Phillip, 5
Mad Dogs (Sky, 2011–), 171
Mad Max, 257
Mad Men (AMC, 2007–2015), 139n1, 201
Maddison, Stephen, 169
Mafia, 29–31, 34–35. *See also Mafiosa* (Canal Plus, 2006–2014); *The Sopranos* (HBO, 1999–2007); *Squadra antimafia* (Canale 5, 2009–)
mafia women
   in *Boardwalk Empire*, 77–79
   Camorra and, 29, 40–41
   Express on, 53
   in *Gomorra. La serie*, 29–30, 39–43
   Mafia and, 29–31, 34–35
   in *Mafiosa*, 51–61
   in *The Sopranos*, 29, 39, 67–77
   in *Squadra antimafia*, 29–30, 31–38, 42–43
Mafiosa (Canal Plus, 2006–2014)
   Sandra as contradictory character in, 57–61
   Sandra as leader in, 51–57
   Sandra as metaphor for Corsica in, 51–53, 61–62
Maiden, Samantha, 272
Mainhold, Gunther, 144, 156n3
Mainhold, Rosa María Sauter de, 144, 156n3
Maliepaard, Emiel, 150
Maltese Falcon (Huston, 1941), 241–242
Mäntymäki, Tiina, 43
Marchand, Nancy, 70, 128, 134
Marcotte, Amanda, 7
Marinucci, Mimi, 167
Marmo, Marcella, 29
Marshall, C. W., 239
Martín-Barbero, Jesús, 155n1, 222–223, 232–233
Martin, Brett, 4–5, 8–9, 253n7

Martindale, Margo, 127
Martínez, María Paula, 146
Masters of Sex (Showtime, 2013–), 9
Mattei, Bruno, 112
Mattelart, Armand, 225
Mattelart, Michèle, 225
Matos, Patrícia, 228
Mayne, Judith, 169
McCabe, Janet, XI, 8, 17, 30, 68, 69, 78, 192, 267
McCallum, Jamie, 174–175
McCaughey, Martha, 30, 107,
McCormack, Patty, 74
McCree, Sandi, 245
McCullum, Julito, 245–246
McGahan, Anna, 267
McHugh, Kathleen, 270
McIlveen, Hannah, 208–209
McKee, Alan, 183, 184, 186
McLaughlin, Lisa, 235n2
McLennan, Rebecca, 210–211
McManus, Ann, 174
McNamara, Mary, 9–10
McQuade, Kris, 191, 195
McRobbie, Angela, 14–15, 42, 186, 260, 266, 272
McTighe, Peter, 183, 188, 190
Meerman, Grieteke, 101
Megavision (Chilean network), 150
Meireles, Totia, 226, 230
Mellencamp, Patricia, 169
melodrama
   in soap operas, 93
   Sons of Anarchy and, 138
   Squadra antimafia and, 31–32, 37–38
   in *telenovelas*, 221, 222–224, 232–233
   Wentworth and, 196–197
Mepham, John, 87
Mercille, Julien, 108
Messenger, Chris, 32
Michaels, Meredith, 127
Michelini, Giulia, 29, 42
Midgley, 163, 174,
MILF stereotype, 115, 119, 270

Millbank, Jenni, 163, 164–166, 167
Millennium Trilogy (Larsson), 111
Miller, Laura, 240
Milos, Sofia, 29
mirror, 223–224
Mittell, Jason, 7, 11, 14, 32, 239, 245, 250
Mizejewski, Linda, 11, 30, 260, 266–267
Modleski, Tania, ix, 173
Mondaca Cota, Anajilda, 144, 146
Moreira, Guilherme, 226, 230, 231
Morris-Marr, Lucie, 196
Moseley, Rachel, 15, 166
motherhood
   in *Bad Girls*, 177
   career and, 129
   as *excusatio*, 112
   feminism and, 99–100, 127
   in *Gomorra. La serie*, 29–30, 40
   in *Justified*, 127–128, 129–130, 132–133, 137–138
   in *Penoza*, 87–90, 95–98, 100–101
   Showtime and, 115, 129
   in *Sons of Anarchy*, 127–128, 130, 133–138
   in *The Sopranos*, 71–72, 128, 253n7
   in *Squadra antimafia*, 29–30, 36–38, 114
   in *Underbelly: Razor*, 263, 264, 270
   in *Weeds*, 107, 108–109, 112, 113–114, 115, 117–118, 128–129
   in *The Wire*, 245–247, 248–249
A Mother's Eye (Roiphe), 99
Moynihan, Daniel Patrick, 253n2
Moynihan Report, 241
myth, 93

N
Nair, Yasmin, 205, 208
narco telenovelas, 143, 156n4. *See also La reina del sur* (Telemundo, 2011)
narcocorridos, 156n3–4
Nashville (ABC, 2012–), 9
National Organisation of Women (NOW), 188
Nauta, Hans, 89, 96
Negra, Diane, 15, 68, 115, 259, 260,

Neighbours (Seven Network, 1985; Network Ten, 1986–2010; Eleven, 2011–), 183, 188, 192
Nelson, Robin, 42
neo-liberal capitalism
   Boardwalk Empire and, 77–79
   Penoza and, 87–88
   The Sopranos and, 67–77, 78–79
Neroni, Hilary, 11, 32, 34, 107, 112, 118
Netflix, 139n2. *See also specific shows*
The Netherlands
   crime drama in, 93–95
   women and motherhood in, 98–99
   See also Penoza (NPO 3, 2010–2015)
Network Ten. *See* Channel Ten (Australian network)
Neuvic, Thierry, 52
New York Review of Books (magazine), 205
Newman, Michael, 7
Nicholls-King, Melanie, 243
Nijenkamp, Johan, 89
Nikita (Besson, 1990), 111
Nikolas, Akash, 8
Nine Network (Australian network), 257, 274
'The Nips are Getting Bigger' (song), 264
Nogueira Joyce, Samantha, x, xi, 19, 150
Notes on a Scandal (Eyre, 2006), 207
Number 96 (Network Ten, 1972–1976), 184, 185
Nurse Jackie (Showtime, 2009–2015), 8, 115, 129, 137
Nussbaum, Emily, 8–9, 67

O
Obama, Barack, 240
O'Brien, Michaeley, 266
O'Donnell, Hugh, 94
Of Woman Born (Rich), 99
Olmstead, Kathleen, 240
Onkenhout, Paul, 92, 94, 96
Onoyan, Phareelle, 52
Opzij (magazine), 96
Orange is the New Black (Netflix, 2013–)
   Prisoner and, 183

race, sex and class in, 204–211
reception and popularity of, 9, 201–203
Wentworth and, 193–194, 195
Oranges are Not the Only Fruit (BBC, 1990), 166
O'Rawe, Catherine, 29, 30
Orphan Black (BBC America, 2013–2016), 9
#OscarsSoWhite, ix
O'Sullivan, Sean, 171–172, 174, 176
Otto, Socratis, 195
Out of the Past (Tourneur, 1947), 241–242
Owen, Susan, 107
Oz (HBO, 1997–2003), 179n2, 205

P

Pablo Escobar, el patrón del mal (Caracol, 2012), 156n4
Padovani, Marcelle, 53
Paes, Dira, 226
Páez Varela, Alejandro, 156n2
Pagen, Hugues, 63n1
Palmer, Patricia, 186
Panopticon, 169
Paoli, Filippo Antonio Pasquale, 52
La parábola de Pablo (Salazar), 156n4
Parker, Mary-Louise, 107, 129
Parker, Tony, 172
Parks, Shelley, 176
Paskin, Willa, 5, 10, 257
Pasquale, Artie, 74–75
Pastore, Vincent, 73
Patel, Dhaval, 224–225
Payán, Tony, 156n2
Pennicott, Josephine, 259
Penoza (NPO 3, 2010–2015)
  budget and production of, 93–95
  motherhood in, 87–90, 95–98, 100–101
  as 'polder' crime drama, 90–93
Perez, Glória, 221–222, 224–225, 226–227, 229, 232
Perez, Hiram, 223
Pérez Reverte, Arturo, 143, 144, 146, 150, 156n4
Perkins, Miki, 196

Pickering, Karen, 258, 271
Pinkett-Smith, Jada, ix
Piñón, Juan, 146, 147, 156n3
Playing the Field (BBC One, 1998–2002), 166
Policewoman (NBC, 1974–1978), 185
Porto, Mauro, 224
Portrait of a Marriage (BBC, 1990), 166
post-feminism
  Australian society and, 271–273
  Bad Girls and, 177
  double entanglement and, 14, 260, 266, 272
  overview of, 260–261
  Underbelly: Razor and, 258, 259, 261–271
Potter, Tiffany, 239
Press, Andrea, x, 19, 240
Preston Crayford, Chelsie, 261
prison drama, 171–173. *See also* women-in-prison (WIP) drama
Prisoner: Cell Block H (Network Ten, 1979–1986)
  Bad Girls and, 163, 172–173
  British television and, 179n2
  context and development of, 183–186
  reception and popularity of, 186–189, 257–258
  Within These Walls and, 172–173
  Wentworth and, 192–193, 194–195, 196
  See also Wentworth (Foxtel SoHo, 2013–)
Project Greenlight (HBO, 2001–2005, 2015), ix

Q

Queer as Folk (CH4, 1999–2000), 166, 167
queer feminism, 167–170, 175–176

R

Rabelais and his World (Bakhtin), 174
Racy, Sonia, 227
Radulovich, Lara, 183
The Rag Trade (BBC, 1961–1963), 163
RAI (Italian public service broadcasting), 30–31
Raney, Arthur, 245
rape-revenge motive, 111

Ray Donovan (Showtime, 2013–), 6, 265
The Razor Wars (Writer), 257, 264, 265
Read, Chopper, 258
Readhead, Leigh, xii, 19
Reading Sex and the City (Akass and McCabe), 8
Real Women (BBC One, 1998), 166
Red Widow (ABC, 2013), 95
Reddick, Lance, 242, 244
Reeves, Jimmie, 191
La reina del sur (Pérez Reverte), 143, 144, 146, 150, 156n4
La reina del sur (Telemundo, 2011)
   gendered spaces in, 147–153
   normalization strategies in, 119, 120
   rape-revenge motive in, 111
   as revolutionary, 153–154
   scholarship on, 144
   sexuality in, 143–144, 149–153
   women's relationships in, 143–147, 149–153
Resistance Through Rituals (Hall and Jefferson), 186
Revenge (ABC, 2011–2015), 138
The Revolution Was Televised (Sepinwall), 5
Rey, German, 154n1
Reynolds, Jodi, 174–175
Reynolds, Malvina, 114
Rhimes, Shonda, x
Ribeiro, Isadora, 225
Rich, Adrienne, 29, 99, 157n6
Rincón, Omar, 146, 155n1
Rivero, Yeidy, x, 18
Roberts, Robin, 107
Robinson, Jocelyn, 184–185
Robson, Ruthann, 165
Roderiguez, Amanda, 193
Rodríguez Gacha, José Gonzalo, 156n5
Roiphe, Anne, 99
'Rolling in the Deep' (song), 257
Romano, Emilio, 147
Romanzo criminale (Sky, 2008–2010), 31
Rongione, Fabrizio, 58

Ronsini, Veneza, 228–229, 232
Rosario Tijeras (RCN, 2010), 146–147, 156n4
Rosenberg, Alyssa, 6, 8, 10
Rosniak, Justin, 266
Rottenberg, Charlotte, 67, 68, 78
Roush, Matt, 240
Rowles, Dustin, 8
Rubio, Carlos, 150
Rule, Andrew, 258
Ryan, Amy, 242
Ryan, Maureen, 10, 11

S
Sá Santos, Leonardo, 230
Sacks, Arthur, 70
Salazar, Alonso, 156n5
Salve Jorge (Rede Globo, 2012–2013), 221–222, 223–224, 225–232
San Filippo, Maria, 150, 152
Sarikakis, Katharine, 4
Satisfaction (Showcase, 2007–2010), 277n3
Savage, Angela, 259
Saviano, Roberto, 39
Saving Grace (TNT, 2007–2010), 139n1
Scandal (ABC, 2012–), 8, 9
Schaffer, Kay, 263, 268, 271, 277n4
Shafter, Daniel, 245
Schama, Simon, 99
Schatz, Tomas, 70
Schechner, Richard, 59
Scherer Garcia, Julio, 144
Schiavo, Marcio, 224–225
Schirripa, Steve, 76
Schubart, Rikke, 107, 111, 119
Screen Australia, 191
Scum (BBC, 1977), 171, 172
The Second Stage (Friedan), 100
second-wave feminism, 260, 267–268
Segal, Katey, 127
Señora Isabel (Canal A, 1993–1994), 146–147
Sepinwall, Alan, 5
Sex and the City (HBO, 1998–2004), 8–9, 131, 260

Shafter, Daniel, 245
Shannon, Michael, 77
Shapiro, Stephen, 240
Shed Productions, 163
Sheridan, Sue, 43
The Shield (FX, 2002–2008), 130
Showtime (US cable network), 115, 129, 131, 192. *See also specific shows*
Sifuentes, Lírian, 228–229, 232
Sigler, Jamie-Lynn, 72
The Silence of the Lambs (Demme, 1991), 111
Simon, David, 240
Simons, Margaret, 99, 100
Sin tetas no hay paraíso (Bolívar), 156n4
Sin tetas no hay paraíso (Caracol network, 2006–2010), 143, 156n4
Singer, Ben, 32
Sirico, Tony, 73
Sjoberg, Laura, 11, 13
Skirrow, Gillian, 42, 171
Sky (Italian digital satellite television platform), 31. *See also Gomorra. La serie* (Sky Atlantic, 2014–)
Smart, Barry, 172
Smart, Carol, 172
Snare, Annika, 170–171
Snitow, Ann, 100
Snyder, Katie, 108, 116, 177
soap operas
   emotional realism in, 92–93
   love triangle in, 89
   in The Netherlands, 93–94
   See also specific soap operas
social merchandizing, 224–225
Sohn, Sonja, 242
Some Women (BBC One, 1969), 172
Sons of Anarchy (FX, 2008–2014), 9, 127–128, 130, 133–138
The Sopranos (HBO, 1999–2007)
   antihero in, 5–6, 9
   Carmela Soprano in, 67–77, 78–79, 112
   Gandolfini's death and, 5–6, 8
   motherhood in, 71–72, 128, 253n7
   Penoza and, 90–92
   Prisoner and, 257–258
   Sons of Anarchy and, 134, 138
   success of, 131
   women in, 29, 39, 112
Spain, Daphne, 148
Spigel, Lynn, ix
Split Enz, 264
Squadra antimafia (Canale 5, 2009–), 29–30, 31–38, 42–43, 114
Stanley, Eric, 202–203
Starr, Joey, 58
Stein, Sara H., 107
Steiner, Linda, 235n2
Stella Dallas (Vidor 1937), 38
Stevens, Izzy, 270
Stevenson, Ana, 272
Stewart, Sara, ix
structure of feeling, 15–16
Summers, Anne, 277n4
The Sunday Telegraph (newspaper), 268
super series, 157n8
surveillance, 169
Sutter, Kurt, 134
Swanson, Debra H., 99
The Sweeney (ITV, 1975–1978), 171
Sydney Morning Herald (newspaper), 196, 259, 271
Sylvester, John, 258

T
'Tainted Love' (song), 257
Taking Lives (Caruso, 2004), 266–267
Takken, Wilfred, 89, 92
Tasker, Yvonne, 11, 15, 30, 68, 107, 111, 112, 260
Tavira, Alberto, 150
Taylor, Ella, 95
Taylor, Jeremy Lindsay, 261
Telemundo, 147
telenovelas
   complexity of, 222–224

female identity in, 227–233
forceful women in, 146–147
melodrama in, 221, 222–224, 232–233
narco telenovelas, 143
social merchandizing and, 224–225
See also specific telenovelas
Televisa (Mexican network), 150
Telles, Lucas, 224
Terminator 2 (Mattei, 1990), 112
Thames Television, 163
This Life (BBC2, 1996–1997), 166
Thomas, Claire, 186
Thomas, June, 6
Thornham, Sue, 30, 38
Time (magazine), 195
Tipping the Velvet (BBC One, 2002), 166
Top of the Lake (Sundance TV, 2013), 9
Toppano, Peta, 185–186, 189
Torre, Roberta, 29
Torres, Izabelle, 227
Traister, Rebecca, 240
Trial and Retribution (ITV, 1997–2009), 171
Truitt, Jos, 3
Turnbull, Sue, xi, 18, 186, 258–259, 266, 268
Turturro, Aida, 76
TVN (Chilean network), 153
Twisted (Kaufman, 2004), 266–267
Twitter, 88, 193, 201

U
Ulabi, Neda, 253n4
Underbelly (Nine Network, 2008), 258–259
Underbelly: Razor (Nine Network, 2011)
context of, 257–258, 271–273
lack of realism in, 259, 264
motherhood in, 263, 264, 270
post-feminist reading of, 258, 259, 261–271
United Nations Office on Drugs and Crime Survey (UNODC), 230
United States of Tara (Showtime, 2009–2011), 8, 115, 129
UnREAL (Lifetime, 2015–), 10

V
Vaage, Margrethe Bruun, 11–12
van der Jagt, Marijn, 91, 94
van der Kooi, Walter, 90–91
van Engen, Marloes, 98–99
van Gelder, Henk, 89, 95
van Nimwegen, Nico, 98
van Rhee, Annemart, 96, 97
van Rooijen, Diederik, 89, 91, 94–95
van Wiggen, Femke, 96
Van Zandt, Maureen, 75
Van Zandt, Steven, 73
Vande Berg, Leah, 107
VanDerWerff, Todd, 6
Variety (magazine), 188
Venkatesh, Sudhir A., 239, 247
Vered, Karen, 260, 268
Veronica Mars (UPN 2004–2006; The CW, 2006–2007), 111
Villez, Barbara, xi, 17
Viviani, Christian, 37
De Volkskrant (newspaper), 96

W
Wallander (BBC, 2008–2010), 166
Walsman, Leeanna, 191
Walters, Suzanna Danuta, x, xi, 18, 108, 114, 128–129
Ward, Russel, 262
Warshow, Robert, 68, 69, 70, 71
Watson, Reg, 183, 185
Weeds (Showtime 2005–2012)
deviation from gender norms in, 107–108, 113–114, 118–120, 201
excusatio in, 111–112, 113
Justified and, 137
Kohan and, 107, 201
motherhood in, 107, 108–109, 112, 113–114, 115, 117–118, 128–129
Nikolas on, 8
normalization strategies in, 114–118
La reina del sur and, 156n3
sexuality in, 107–108, 116–118, 119

Sons of Anarchy and, 137
  women as criminals in, 108–111
Wentworth (Foxtel SoHo, 2013–), 183–184, 186, 189–197, 257, 274
West, Dominic, 253n1
White, Rosie, 11, 30
Widows (BBC One, 1983), 171
Wigmore, Lucy, 267
Will and Grace (NBC, 1998–2006), 164
Williams, Bruce, x, 19, 250
Williams, Linda, 30, 32, 37, 169
Williams, Marise, 262, 266
Williams, Raymond, 15–16
Williamson, Felix, 261
Willmore, Allison, 3, 9–10
Willson, Sandra, 185–186
Wilson, David, 171–172, 174, 176
Wilson, Jason, 258
Wilson, William Julius, 239
Winspeare, Edoardo, 29
The Wire (HBO, 2002–2008)
  female characters in, 239–240, 241, 242–251
  male characters in, 240–242
  realism in, 239, 240, 259

Wisdom, Robert, 246
Within These Walls (ITV, 1974–1978), 163, 171, 172–173, 185
The Wizard of Oz (Fleming 1939), 63n4
women-in-prison (WIP) drama
  characters and tropes in, 12, 184–185, 203–204
  exploitation cycle of, 168–169, 204
  as problematic, 172–173
  La reina del sur as, 149–151
  See also specific shows
Women's Prison (Seiler, 1955), 184
Writer, Larry, 257, 264, 265

X
Xavier, Nilson, 225

Y
Yaquinto, Marilyn, 112

Z
Z Cars (BBC, 171 1962–1978), 171
Zaccaria, Anna Maria, 39
Zalcock, Beverley, 163, 184–185
Zemon Davis, Natalie, 14, 173–174

www.ingramcontent.com/pod-product-compliance
Lightning Source LLC
LaVergne TN
LVHW080328140426
836100LV00006B/19